PREFACE

THE five Letters which follow deal with the conquest and subjugation of Mexico between the years 1519 and 1526. I have translated them from the edition originally published by Rivadeneyra and now by Hernando Sucesores.

A word as to the spelling of proper and place names: they will be found to differ in certain instances from accepted usage. I have adopted the shorter Mexican form wherever possible, in preference to the longer and honorific one. The place-names are mostly as Cortés wrote them. I have forborne to substitute their modern equivalent. It is worth remarking that there can be no absolute standard of accuracy in spelling, since the Conquistadores had to translate the native sounds (which they probably heard imperfectly) into terms of Castilian vowels and consonants. Sixteenth-century Castilian, moreover, differed in pronunciation from that of today. It resembled far more Spanish as it is now spoken in South America. The *z* and *c* (before *e* and *i*) were not yet lisped: the sound of *x* approximated to that of *ch* in modern French. Thus *z* and *s* were (in proper names) almost interchangeable, also *f* and *h*.

I have adopted the modern rule of accentuation throughout—*i.e.*, words ending in a consonant (other than *n* or *s*) are accented on the final syllable; words ending in a vowel (or *n* or *s*) are accented on the penultimate syllable. Any accent departing from this rule is marked accordingly. Passages which have been abridged (either as lacking interest or being

PREFACE

incidental to the main account) are set in italic. The rest of the matter is in Cortés's own words.

In writing the Introduction I consulted principally the following works:

> Gomara, *Historia de la Conquista de Méjico (Segunda Parte de la Historia de las Indias)*.
> Bernal Diaz del Castillo, *Verdadera Historia de la Conquista de Ultra Mar*.
> Fray Bartolomé de Las Casas, *Breve Historia de la Destrucción de las Indias* and *Historia de las Indias*.
> *Relación hecha por el Señor Andrés de Tapia*.
> Various *documentos inéditos* containing other letters of Cortés, his will, etc.

The notes I have purposely kept as scanty as possible, since I am of the opinion that the best translation of this kind should need almost none.

For the frontispiece I am indebted to the kindness of F. A. Macnutt, Esq., and Messrs. G. P. Putnam's Sons. The reproduction originally appeared in Mr. Macnutt's very complete edition of the Letters.

For the map showing Cortés's route to Honduras my thanks are due to A. P. Maudsley, Esq. (and the Hakluyt Society) for permission to combine two maps which appeared in his edition.

J. B. M.

BRYANSTON SCHOOL,
DORSET,
1928.

INTRODUCTION

§ 1. HIS LIFE

HERNANDO CORTÉS was born in 1485 at Medellín, a small town on the southern bank of the Guadiana in what is now the province of Badajoz. His parents were poor but gentle. His father, Martin Cortés, had been in command of a small company of light infantry in the army. His mother, connected with the Pizarro family, was also of noble birth. Like many another future leader he was a weak and sickly child.

As a boy of fourteen he was sent to the University of Salamanca, some hundred and fifty miles to the north. There he lived in the house of an aunt, amused himself in the sleepy friar-ridden town as best he could, learnt something of law, and still more of life. But the lad was not cut out for a scholar. Two years were enough to convince him of it, though not his parents; and at sixteen he was back without their consent in Medellín, "rowdy, overbearing, restless, and in love with the profession of arms." To one of such a temper, and there were many like him in Renaissance Spain, two roads lay open,—the one leading east, the other west. In Italy Gonsalvo de Córdoba, the great Captain, was establishing a Spanish Kingdom in Naples. From the Indies tales of strange lands and peoples, of fabulous monsters and animals, above all, of gold, came back in the mouths of mariners to Cadiz and Lisbon, and were immediately carried through the country.

Cortés decided upon the second. An opportunity offered itself. Nicolás de Ovando, Governor of Hayti (or as it was then called, the Isla Española), was preparing to sail from Seville, and Cortés set out for that town. Ovando knew his family and was pleased to grant him passage in one of his boats.

An untoward incident which might have had fatal consequences intervened. His earliest chronicler records it thus: " Cortés was to have accompanied this commander with many other noble Spaniards; but in the meantime clambering one night over some roofs close by his lodgings on his way to a young woman with whom he had relations, he fell from a wall in ill-repair which broke under his weight. Whereupon, as he lay half-buried on the ground, he narrowly escaped being run through by a neighbour with his sword, and would have been so had not an old woman darted out of her house, on whose very porch he had noisily crashed, and held back her son-in-law, who had also rushed out at the noise, entreating him not to strike until he should have found out who the man was."

The severe bruises resulting from this fall brought on a fever which greatly undermined his health, and it was not until he was nineteen years of age that he realized his ambition and set sail from Spain for the West Indies in 1504. Meanwhile he had made an abortive attempt to go to Italy, but had got no further than Valencia, where he spent nearly a year in dissipation and poverty.

The ship in which he sailed, one of a party of five, met with bad weather, and was the last to arrive in the Port of San Domingo, her crew having suffered considerable hardships. Cortés immediately applied to the Governor, Don Nicolás de Ovando, who was absent from the island, but was very hospitably received by his secretary Medina, in his place. To suggestions of settling quietly in the country Cortés replied with some bluntness that he had come for gold. A small rising among the Indians under a native

Queen Anacoana was put down soon after with undue severity. Cortés under the command of a certain Diego Velázquez had the opportunity of displaying natural military gifts above the ordinary and was rewarded by the Governor with lands and a certain number of Indian serfs (a *repartimiento*) to work them. The next few years were uneventful. He spent them as a gentleman colonist, raising crops, breeding sheep and horses. He was popular, affable with his neighbours, ready to join in gambling of various kinds, " not seeming to mind greatly whether he lost or won."

Women had always a great attraction for him and brought him at this time more than once into irregular brawls, sudden affairs of the knife and dagger. In all he came off safely. A white scar under the lower lip alone told of a narrow escape. At the same time that he was farming, gaming and making love, he was making money.

In 1511, when Diego Velázquez was entrusted with the command of a force to subjugate the neighbouring island of Cuba, it was natural that he should turn to this energetic and promising junior and request his help on the expedition. He himself " was ill-suited for fighting on account of his portly build," and consequently allowed Cortés a freer hand. The latter " seemed to be everywhere at once, carrying out manœuvres, marches, never taking the credit due to another, but never permitting another to come before him either in council or execution; rather himself coming before many; by which means he got himself very much liked by the soldiers and highly esteemed by his chief." In any case the natives were extremely primitive, almost unarmed, and timid, so that the task of conquest was an easy one. Cortés received fresh grants of land and Indians on its conclusion and settled at Santiago in the extreme south of the island, in company with a certain Juan Xuárez, a native of Granada.

Once again his attentions to a woman involved him in a dispute which had its ludicrous as well as its dangerous side. Briefly, Xuárez had brought over his four sisters, with his mother as chaperone from Spain. They were poor, buxom, of good birth but indiscreet, and eager to make successful marriages with the colonists of the New World. Cortés was attracted to the fourth and the most handsome, but after relations had proceeded some way, drew back and refused to marry her. A storm was raised. The Governor (himself, it was whispered, not indifferent to the charms of the second daughter) listened favourably to the claim made by several friends of the family that Cortés should marry the young lady, and was perhaps still more influenced by the allegations of disloyalty made against him at the same time. Thereupon he ordered Cortés officially to fulfil his word to the lady and on his refusal imprisoned him. Subsequent events read rather like a romance. Cortés broke bolt and padlock and escaped, making straight for sanctuary in the parish church. There, after some days, incautiously leaving the porch for a moment, he was recaptured by the Governor's guards and placed in irons on board ship in the harbour. Again he escaped, letting himself down into a small rowing boat. Finally in rough weather he took to the water, his clothes and secret documents tied in a bundle on his head, and thus reached land, when for a second time he sought sanctuary in the church.

Somehow or another the quarrel was patched up; the Governor was reconciled with a man he could ill afford to lose; and Cortés married the lady. There seems little doubt that there was more gravity in the charges of disloyalty to his chief than Gomara, his official biographer, describes, or than Cortés himself would have cared to admit.

He seems to have entirely regained his position

in Velázquez's favour and in the years that followed became *alcalde* of Santiago, a post corresponding in many ways to that of an English mayor but holding in addition the supreme judicial power throughout his district.

As is reported in the First Letter (see pp. 1-2) both Francisco Hernández de Córdoba in 1517 and Juan de Grijalba in 1518 explored the coast of the newly discovered land, Yucatán, and made one or two landings. Albarado was sent back with a single ship and no very considerable quantity of treasure to report to the Governor. The news of land to the south, and hence opportunities of getting gold and slaves, both of which commodities were running short in the Islands, spurred Velázquez to action.

He proceeded to fit out another fleet, solicit the necessary licences from Spain and Hayti, with a view to obtaining the lion's share of whatever treasure was to be found. Cortés was cast for the part of jackal. He was obviously far too big a man for the part: and suspecting this, Velázquez did not allow his candidature and appointment to pass through as smoothly as the First Letter would give one to suppose. Grijalba actually returned to Santiago three days before the new expedition set out, so that an opportunity was thus given the Governor of revising his plans and perhaps changing his commander. Whether he actually did so must remain uncertain. Accounts vary greatly. Las Casas, who knew Cortés in Mexico and discussed the matter with him, described him as hurriedly stowing provisions on board and bidding a hasty farewell to the Governor at dead of night. Afterwards, he says, when Cortés put in at various ports in Hayti and the Islands, he received repeated orders from Velázquez to return, all of which he disobeyed. Diaz del Castillo, however, a hardy fighting man, who was actually a member of the expedition, denies this roundly, and declares that Cortés took his departure from Santiago with all due ceremony, and at any rate an outward show of good relations between the Governor and himself. These accounts represent the two extremes. Neither is wholly true. Both Velázquez and Cortés were men of their century. They were both ambitious, and while it is barely credible that the Governor should have had no fears as to Cortés's subsequent conduct before he left Cuba, it is also extremely likely that Cortés with his genius for handling men would manage to avoid any open breach of the peace.

He was thirty-four; and the ambition which he had nourished fifteen years before seemed now about to be realized. Without bearing Velázquez any definite grudge he had no intention of playing second fiddle to him indefinitely. On landing in Yucatán, he perceived suddenly the horizon open out before him. What had been designed as an insignificant trading expedition changed swiftly to a well-formed plan of conquest. Throwing off his allegiance to Velázquez, Cortés resolved to treat direct with the Emperor.

The doings of Cortés in the years that followed, 1518–1526, are described adequately enough in the Letters. They were years of toil such as would suffice many men for a lifetime. By 1524, Mexico City had been won, lost and reconquered, and the various provinces were steadily coming under the Spanish rule. Cortés's two years' journey (1524–1526) overland to Honduras represented a continuous and heroic struggle against enormous natural odds, but could add little to the glory which he had already achieved.

Meanwhile there had been trouble in Mexico (see p. 360). The imperial revenue officers who had arrived in 1524 wrote bitter letters of accusation against Cortés to the King. He had in addition private enemies only too eager to secure power and gold for themselves during his absence. Finally, as he describes in his Fifth Letter, Ponce de León came out from Spain as High Commissioner with full powers to enquire into all matters affecting New Spain. León's unfortunate death led to the office being assumed by Estrada, his bitterest enemy. For nearly two years he was harassed by legal suits and accusations. Chafing at the restraints put upon him, and on the advice of his friends, he determined at last to set sail for Spain and put his case before the Emperor in person.

Cortés landed near the little town of Palos (about 100 miles north of Cádiz) probably in May 1528. His train was magnificent: native princes followed him, vaulters, jugglers, dwarfs; there were wild birds and animals, tigers, lions, pelicans, " a great store of cloaks of feathers and skins, shields, featherwork, mirrors of polished stone, and many other things of like nature, including treasure in gold and jewels to the value of some 300,000 *pesos*."

It was a great homecoming for the lad who had left Medellín to seek his fortune. The Emperor received him graciously. He was made Marqués del Valle. He received wide lands, knightly orders: but there were shadows over the picture. At his brightest and most triumphant moment a few stray clouds seemed intent on dimming his full glory, and they were steadily to darken and overspread the sky during the remaining years of his life. Gonzalvo de Sandoval, his comrade, fellow-townsman and greatest friend, fell sick and died but a few days after his landing. The news of his father's death had already met him in New Spain. He was still in mourning for his wife. For nine days he turned aside from festivities to visit the shrine of Our Lady of Guadalupe. But the dead must bury their dead. He is forty-three. Life still calls him. Soon his marriage with Doña Juana de Xúñiga, niece of the powerful Duque de Becquar, is an accomplished fact. He will return to New Spain (the official document appointing him Captain-General is dated July 6th 1592): he binds himself to send out ships to explore the Southern seas, tries long and earnestly to obtain in addition the post of Governor, but fails; and so sets sail a successful, disappointed man for Mexico.

His second stay lasted for ten years until 1540. It was a difficult period. For a year business proceeded peacefully enough between the Captain-General and the government officials, but after February 1531 complaints became frequent. "He had too much influence over the natives. He attempted to revenge himself on private enemies," and the like.

Cortés had retired to Cuernabaca, built a palace and a church there, and devoted himself to farming and improving the land. But such occupations could not hold his restless and ambitious spirit for long. On his side he complained of systematic attempts to reduce his revenue and powers. Above all, the expeditions which he had promised to make to the South proved as expensive as they were fruitless. Two had failed through mutiny, shipwreck and hostile natives, when in 1536 he determined to set out himself. He sailed north-west up the Gulf of California, suffered two years of incredible hardships, being tossed hither and thither by tempests, and was away so long that his wife sent out another expedition to search for him. This was the manner of man whose sole employment in life seemed destined to be that of gentleman farming.

In 1540, disillusioned and with a mass of litigation on his shoulders, he returned with his family to Spain, where he was received coolly though respectfully by the Council of the Indies. Charles V was away in Flanders. Nothing could be done without obtaining his private ear: that gained, all things were possible. Cortés thus joined the Emperor's suite, and accompanied his master in the expedition against Algiers (1541). It was a disastrous affair. The heights above the city were taken, but a storm blew up, in which almost the whole of the royal fleet was dashed on shore and destroyed. Cortés himself and his two sons narrowly escaped drowning, and he lost the very valuable jewels which he habitually carried on his person. More grievous still, he was not called to the council of war which decided on retreat, and declared bitterly that "with God's good help and the soldiers who were in the camp he would have taken Algiers."

There is sadness in the twilight of a brilliant and momentous life. The tale that Cortés ever besieged the door of the Emperor's coach, answering the haughty query of the monarch, "Who is this man?" with the words: "One who gave your Majesty more provinces than he possessed cities"—is in all probability an idle one. But they were grey years which followed his return to Spain. Constantly in money difficulties, forced to request where once he would have commanded, Cortés saw with bitterness other stars rising in the New World,—Balboa, Pizarro,—and the treasures of Peru already rivalling those of Mexico. The old servant was no longer needed. His past services seemed forgotten.

His last letter to the Emperor was dated February 3rd 1544, from Valladolid.

"I thought," he writes, "that having toiled in my youth it should profit me to find rest in my old age: and so for forty years I have laboured, going sleepless, eating poorly and at times not at all, bearing armour on my back, risking my life in dangers, freely spending my means and years, and all in the service of God, bringing sheep into His fold in a hemisphere far removed from ours, as yet unknown and unwritten of in the scriptures, increasing and spreading the fame and dominions of my King, bringing under his yoke and royal sceptre many and great realms and kingdoms of barbarous men and peoples, conquered by my own person and at my own expense, owing no help to any man, but rather hindered greatly by many envious and ambitious men who like leeches have grown fat upon my blood. . . . I begged your Majesty in Madrid to be pleased to make plain his royal will to repay me for my services. . . . Your Majesty informed me that orders should be given to the Council of the Indies to dispatch the business quickly, for your Majesty was willing that I should not have to fight a case against the Exchequer: but when I approached the Council they told me that I must defend myself against the Exchequer's suit, and obey the ruling of the courts. . . .

"I am old, poor and in debt in this realm to the tune of over twenty thousand ducats, without counting a hundred thousand more that I brought with me . . . for I have not left the court a moment, and have had three sons with me there, to say nothing of lawyers, solicitors, and so on. . . .

"Again and again I have begged your Majesty to be pleased to join together the judges of the Council of the Indies with judges of the other royal councils, that they may give judgment on the deed by which your Majesty was pleased to grant to his vassal a small part of all that he had won for your Majesty . . . and this without delay: for should the matter drag on much longer, I must lose all and return to my own house. I am no longer of an age to spend my time travelling from inn to inn, but must rather settle down and make up my account with God. It is a long one, and I have but short time to balance it, but it will be better to lose my fortune than my soul. . . .

"*El Marqués del Valle.*"

INTRODUCTION

Officialdom, however, was untouched: the lawsuits in Spain and the Indies dragged on: Cortés was ignored. On the back of the letter, which may still be seen, an unknown hand scribbled *Nay que responder* (" There is no need for reply ").

In 1547 negotiations were on hand for the marriage of his daughter. She was to return to Spain and meet her prospective bridegroom, the Marqués de Astorga. But the full amount of dowry was not forthcoming. The contract broke down. Cortés obtained permission to go back to Mexico. He set out for Seville but was taken ill: feeling his end was near he retired to the little town of Castelleja de la Cuesta, where he died on the 2nd of December, 1547.

§ 2. THE MAN

" Hernando Cortés was of good stature, broad-shouldered, deep-chested; pale in colour, the hair and beard somewhat thin: . . . as a boy headstrong, so on coming to manhood, sober." Thus writes Gomara, his official biographer, in Spain. Bernal Díaz had perhaps occasion during the years of fighting in Mexico to observe him more critically. " His complexion was rather ashen," he says, " and his look serious. Had his face been bigger it would have looked better. . . . He was deep-chested, well-made, not stout (or only a little), strong, muscular, somewhat bow-legged; a good rider, skilled in the use of all weapons, and above all a great heart and spirit, which is what is most to the point !"

He was a man on whom greatness when it came sat easily. " In all he did, in his presence, bearing, conversation, manner of eating and of dressing, he gave signs of being a great lord." His dress was plain but rich: no silk or satin: no jewels "save a slender and very valuable golden chain bearing an image of Our Lady. . . ." Servants, however, he had in large numbers, and his household plate as befitted a great nobleman, great store of gold and silver vessels and the like. "He insisted on being treated like a noble lord", says Gomara, "but with such gravity and courtesy that it neither offended nor appeared strange to anyone." Withal, a companionable man among his equals or those whom he chose for the time to make so: "very affable," says Díaz, "with all his officers and comrades, especially with those of us who originally sailed with him from Cuba." He would listen to their counsel though he always followed his own, being "obstinate, especially in matters of war."

He was "much given to women, and without restraint": so that "being so free in other men's houses he was jealous in his own." "A great hand at games of cards and dice, he was very pleasant in his play, delighting in such jokes as gamesters are wont to use."

This was the outward husk of Cortés as he appeared to his comrades. To posterity he stands out above everything else as a warrior and a leader of men. In his Reports to the Emperor Cortés is far from exaggerating his own deeds. He bore himself habitually as "a very valiant captain," says Díaz. At Otumba, when the little Spanish force in retreat was surrounded by a body of Indians at least twenty times as large, "the battle went on" reports Cortés (see p. 124) "until it pleased God that one of the enemy should be killed who must have been so important a chief that on his death all fighting straightway ceased." He does not say that it was he himself who spied the Mexican Eagle flying above a palanquin in the very midst of the enemy throng, and who, charging forward with one or two comrades, succeeded in cutting down the chieftains guarding it and capturing the banner, at which reverse the Indians fled from the field.

As a leader Cortés knew better than any how to treat his subordinates. "He sometimes swore ' On my conscience !' and if annoyed with one of his officers whom he knew well would exclaim: ' *Mal pese a vos !*' (*Confound you !*), but he never spoke bitter or wounding words to any captain or soldier: and in this," adds Díaz, " he was very long-suffering, for there were certain unruly soldiers under him who at times were insulting in the extreme, but he replied always with moderation; the most that he would say, being ' Silence! and in future be more careful as to what you say, or it will cost you dearly.' "

His qualities as a tactician and a general reveal themselves plainly during the narrative of his various campaigns in Mexico. True, he was fighting against a primitive people, but they were warlike and vastly superior in numbers. He was careful about details. " Often at night he would make the round of the sentries and visit the huts of the men, and any whom he found without his arms to hand or going unshod he would reprimand severely, telling him, " it's a worthless sheep that can't carry its own wool."

Discipline was enforced at once with tact and severity. Certain stringent rules for active service are set out on p. xxxv.

But the disciplinarian was also a born leader of men. Cortés had the power of making great decisions himself and of persuading others to make them. " The courage never to submit or yield," was what distinguished him from his subordinates in many a moment of crisis,—in Tlascala, when every voice was loud in urging further retreat to the north and safety; in Honduras, when food had run out and both retreat and further advance seemed alike impossible.

With this Napoleonic quality of determination went a certain ruthlessness. Cortés himself reports the massacring of thousands of Indians at Cholula, the burning of four hundred chieftains after the insurrection in Pánuco, the cutting off of the hands of fifty more.

Yet this man is found in his letters and proclamations expressing sentiments of Christian piety. Was it not the merest hypocrisy for a man such as Cortés to pretend to be religious? The question misjudges both Cortés and the century in which he lived.

In a sense it would be true to say that all men born in the fifteenth century were religious: not that they were any whit less commercially-minded and self-seeking than to-day; certainly less sensitive and far less humane. But they inherited certain beliefs which they were schooled to hold without a question. Blasphemy was still one of the cardinal sins. Heaven, hell, purgatory, redemption and damnation were certainties, not vague philosophical speculations which might or might not come off.

The whole formed in their minds a seemingly rigid framework by which human actions could be measured and to which they must conform. In practice the religious framework proved singularly easy to distort, with the result that there were no actions so brutal or so mercenary for which an apparently divine sanction could not be found.

A compromise between treasure-hunting, empire-building, and the spreading of the gospel was therefore easily effected; and the paradox of preaching an evangel of peace by means of the sword and musket was never perceived.

That the religion of Cortés should have been on

such a plane is not in itself surprising. Among his contemporaries it was only the man of philosophic temper who could rise above it: and Cortés was essentially a man of action.

On first entering Mexico he had been desirous of pacifying Muteczuma and proceeding cautiously in the stamping out of idolatry. But in the actual temples of the Mexicans, the walls reeking and thick with blood, all moderation left him. " I shall take no small pleasure in fighting for my God against your gods which are none," he shouted to the priests; and before the Spaniards whom he had sent for could arrive, he took up an iron bar which happened to be there and began to attack the great stone idols. " On my word as a gentleman," said Andrés de Tapia, one of his companions, " even now I seem to see him looming hugely above us as he leapt forward and balanced for a moment, holding the bar by its middle, before bringing it down with a crash on the topmost eye of the idol, tearing the whole gilded mask from its face."

It is easy to perceive in this scene a crowd of half-formed emotions. Above all there was perhaps a sense of outraged decency. The Castilian rather than the Christian was revolted. But a profounder, more truly religious sense may well have been operative.

It is clear, however, that the character of Cortés was far from being one of mere ruthless severity. There is abundant evidence both in the Letters and elsewhere to show that once the actual fighting was over Cortés was only too ready to concern himself with the treatment of the native population. He had seen the evil effects of slavery in the Islands. The Spanish conquerors of Cuba were rewarded by gifts of land and Indian slaves (*repartimientos*) either captured in Cuba or, later, transported thither from Yucatán. These slaves were then employed in gold-mining, pearl-fishing and tilling the ground. The sexes were segregated. The conditions of their life reached an extreme of misery and degradation. Las Casas estimates that out of a hundred slaves so acquired at the beginning of a year only thirty would be left alive at the end of it.

We find Cortés consequently eager to prevent a recurrence of such conditions in New Spain. In 1524 he writes to the Emperor:

" I have lived twenty years in the Islands and have experience of the evils wrought there and the causes of them, on which account I have taken great care to avoid their manner (of dealing with the natives) and to order matters after a very different way."

He limits so far as he is able the powers of the settlers over the native Indians; and bitterly complains (in the Third Letter) that he has been forced against his will to make certain *repartimientos* of native serfs, because he has nothing else to give his men.

In Honduras, however (see p. 366), he prevents the carrying off of slaves to Hayti, and forces the Governor to order the return of many such who had been enslaved.

Years later, when drawing up his will, he writes: XXXIX: *Item*: " Since there have been many doubts and opinions as to whether natives of New Spain (either captured in war or bought) can rightly be held as slaves, and since up to the present this matter has not been decided, I direct my son and heir, Don Martín, and those who shall afterwards succeed him in my estate to use all diligence in verifying this matter to the peace of my conscience and their own."

Both the vices and virtues of Cortés lie near the surface. Ambition, cruelty to gain his ends, unscrupulousness: these are offset by fearlessness, invincible courage, and humanity when his ends have been attained.

He ſtands therefore not as the laſt of the Crusaders (as some have wished to present him) but as one of the earlieſt and greateſt of the Elizabethans.

§ 3. COMRADES AND CONTEMPORARIES

It is useless to look through a single man's eyes at his contemporaries if one would see them truly.

Cortés, great man though he was, is no exception to the rule. He disliked certain men—not so much because they had betrayed or injured him but as usually happens because he had deceived and damaged them—and accordingly belittled and maligned them to the Emperor. It was essential for his own success that he should do so. Of these Diego de Velázquez was one. He muſt not be judged solely on the evidence of Cortés's Letters. He himself, writing to the Licenciado Figueroa, the imperial judge and representative in the Weſt Indies—has a very different tale to tell; not that it is truer.

"As you will have heard," he says, "I sent a fleet over eight months ago to the lands and islands newly discovered by me in the name of your Highness, in which in addition to all things necessary, I despatched six hundred men, under the command of one Hernán Cortés, as seeming to me a prudent man, and one who had long been in my employ both as a friend and servant; as such I had always treated him with great consideration, honouring him with my own person and goods, . . . and on this account and for the great experience which he very properly had from having seen my ways of dealing with Spaniards and natives in these parts as also for the confidence I had in him, it seemed to me that your Highness would be better served by him in the new lands than by another, notwithstanding that among the six hundred men I sent there were many gentlemen of much better birth than he. . . ."

Andrés de Tapia arrived at Santiago in Cuba some few days after Cortés had set out.

" I don't know what Cortés's intentions are towards me," the Governor told him, " but I think evil. For he spent everything he had on the expedition and is actually in debt, and received officials into his service with an air as if he had been a nobleman in Spain. However," added Velázquez, " I shall be delighted for you to join his company."

At this time, as has been said, Velázquez was a man well past his prime. He was born at Cuéllar in Spain, somewhere about 1460 and had seen seventeen years' military service before coming west to the New World. By the time he came to deal with Cortés most of his energy was gone. He hoped to gain gold through him, though indifferently sure of his allegiance. It was only when he saw the gold slipping past him into the hands of the Emperor that he began violently to stir up trouble, both at home in Spain—where the Bishop of Burgos and the Council of the Indies were warned of the doings of the renegade adventurer—and by direct action in Mexico itself.

The whirligig of time was simply bringing in his revenges. He had acted in almost exactly similar fashion himself in 1511, though he was not candid enough to own it. As the " richest and most respected man in Santo Domingo, one who had held important offices, and had even been employed by Don Bartolomé Colón (uncle of Columbus)," relates Las Casas, he had naturally been chosen by the new Governor, Don Diego Colón (himself a son of Columbus), to lead the expedition to conquer Cuba. " Withal," con-

INTRODUCTION

tinues Las Casas, " he was a very pleasant, companionable man, rather given to loose joking in conversation (after the fashion of youths that have not
been too well brought up), but knowing how to maintain his authority when he liked. . . . He was
prudent; thought to be a little thick-headed, but those
who thought so usually found themselves deceived."

Arrived in Cuba he had quickly subjugated the
natives, using not less cruelty than others. He fell
out with the Admiral from whom he held his deputy
governorship; succeeded by underhand means in
securing the same appointment direct from the King,
so that he could not be dismissed; " and thus " (as
Gomara and others of Cortés's partisans would have
it) " had served the admiral just as Cortés afterwards
served him."

Yet with a little good fortune, or less able management on the part of Cortés, Velázquez would have
succeeded in retaining a vicarious suzerainty over New
Spain.

Pánfilo de Narváez, whom he sent to depose Cortés
from his position of Captain-General, capture him (and
it was understood, kill him), had already served under
him in Cuba; and had the reputation of being " a
man of honour, steadfast, but not over prudent, very
bold in fighting against the Indians, and perhaps
against others as well, but with this grave fault, that
he was careless about details."

Considering its importance Cortés says remarkably
little about the *affaire* Narváez.

His arrival with eighteen ships at Vera Cruz, where
one of the King's officials was illegally arrested, and
the advance to Cempoal with the fruitless negotiations
which ensued, are described at some length, but the
final *coup* on which Cortés's whole future depended is
passed over very rapidly (see pp. 99–107). Luckily
that long-memoried and long-winded officer, Bernal

INTRODUCTION

Díaz del Castillo, writing some thirty years later, gives a very full account of it. For the night attack on Cempoal against a Spanish force four times as large was in many ways an astonishing business.

"Cortés made us a magnificent oration," says Bernal Díaz, "after which the companies were told off for their respective positions.

"I was under a certain Captain, Pizarro (not he of Peru)," he continues, "our orders being to take the artillery, which was the most dangerous part of the attack. . . . But as I was a great friend of the Captain Sandoval, he begged me if I were still alive to join up with him and follow him once we had taken the guns; the which I promised to do."

It was raining: they had nothing to eat, and spent the hours thinking of what was ahead of them. Finally the pipes and drums started up and they marched off. On approaching the little town Cortés passed back the word for silence. Two sentries we surprised, and one escaped yelling "To arms! to arms! Cortés is coming!" After that it seemed but a moment while they were charging forward across the sodden ground to the guns. The match-holes had been closed up with wax to keep the rain out. The defenders fumbled and lost their nerve. Only one shot was fired, but it killed three men. (Cortés says that no one was hurt.) Díaz himself seeing Sandoval ahead caught up with him and rushed up the steps leading to the gate of the courtyard. They were armed with pikes and fought there a good long time. Suddenly Narváez's voice was heard: "Santa Maria, help! They've killed me! I've lost an eye!" Even then it was some time before he was captured, since he had taken refuge at the top of the highest tower. Finally "a certain Martín López, very long in the body, set fire to the thatched roof, upon which they all came rolling down upon us."

Narváez was immediately put into irons. "Cortés coming up, ignorant of this, what with the heat and the burden of his armour while he rushed from place to place giving orders to our men, was so out of breath that he tried twice to ask Sandoval, without being able to get the words out. 'What's happened to Narváez? What's happened to Narváez?'

"'Here he is!' Sandoval answered: 'Here he is! And under very good guard!' on which Cortés still very breathless replied: 'Take care, Sandoval, my lad, that you and your men don't leave him for a minute!' and was off again, ordering proclamation to be made that all of Narváez's men should drop their arms and forthwith range themselves under the banner of your Majesty, in the royal name of Hernando Cortés, his Captain-General and Chief Justiciar."

Narváez made no attempt to continue the contest. His men all deserted to Cortés, and his ships and stores were seized. Exactly when he was allowed to leave Mexico seems uncertain. Later he must have returned to Spain, for in 1527 he is starting out from San Lucas de Barrameda, just north of Cádiz, in command of an expedition bound for Florida.

Accident made Bernal Díaz del Castillo a historian. Francisco López de Gomara, who became Cortés's secretary on his return to Spain in 1540, published his *Historia General de las Indias* in 1552. Its Second Part, the *Conquista de Méjico*, served a double purpose: it provided both a narrative of events and an apologia for its central figure—Cortés. Out in Mexico, living on the estate he had won in Guatemala (and *regidor* of the neighbouring town of Santiago de los Caballeros), Bernal Díaz read, and forthwith flew to his pen in protest. His own *Verdadera Historia* was the result.

He had been among the very first who discovered Yucatán in 1517, had visited it no less than twice before Cortés so much as set foot there, accompanied him in all his campaigns and fought in one hundred and nineteen battles and armed encounters. " Yet," he complains, " the first time that Cortés wrote to the Emperor all the honour and glory of our conquests he took to himself, and made no mention of the names of his captains and valiant soldiers nor recalled their deeds, but simply: ' This I did, that I ordered one of my officers to do . . .' and the like."

In his long work (it contains over 300,000 words) Díaz has not refrained from giving whatever details about his comrades an extraordinarily tenacious memory could recollect.

It is a real service. Men whose names but appear for a moment in Cortés's official account put on a new solidity of flesh and blood.

There were three of his Captains, Diaz allows, whom Cortés did praise to the Emperor " as worthy to be held in as high esteem as the most famous warriors in all the world."

Gonzalvo de Sandoval, High Constable of New Spain and joint Governor with Estrada for some eleven months (*hijo* Sandoval, as Cortés often called him), was the Conqueror's fellow townsman and nearest friend. " He was well-proportioned," says Díaz, " and muscular; very valiant; the face rather full, the hair and beard somewhat curly and chestnut-coloured. His voice was not very clear, rather strange and hoarse, and he lisped a little. He knew no letters save they were writ very big and bold, and had no love of gold or fine clothes, only desiring to do his duty as became a valiant leader. . . ."

His early death at Palos, but a few days after landing in Spain, was surrounded by circumstances of sordid tragedy sadly out of keeping with the exploits of his life. The ingots which he brought with him from the New World were stolen under his very eyes while he lay helpless by a rascally innkeeper in whose care he had been left by his comrades.

Cortés, returning, came only in time to find his friend sinking faſt and to see the laſt sacraments adminiſtered.

Pedro de Albarado was of a very different ſtamp. An older man than Sandoval, he had accompanied Grijalba's expedition to Yucatán in 1518. "He had a merry, smiling face," said Díaz, "and a very amorous glance. The Indians nicknamed him *Tonatio*, that is, the Sun, he was such a brilliant figure. He was lissom, a good rider, and above all of frank and open conversation. His clothes were always well-groomed and coſtly; round his neck he wore a golden chain, and a diamond ring on his finger. . . ."

From Cortés's narrative it is plain that Albarado's headſtrongness more than once put the whole party in danger. He arrived two days before his commander in Cozumel and immediately carried off certain gold ornaments from the temples and some forty head of hens from the houses which the terrified natives had abandoned. Cortés on his arrival clapped his pilot in irons, and "rebuked Albarado severely, telling him that the new lands were not to be pacified in that manner."

Then there was the crowning inſtance of headſtrong folly on Albarado's part when left in charge of the garrison in the capital, which all but loſt Mexico to the Spaniards. A judicial enquiry was held into the affair some time afterwards, but no definite conclusion was arrived at. It is certain that Cortés spoke his mind freely at the time, although he could not afford to dispense with the services of his unruly subordinate.

Later, Albarado as Governor of Guatemala ſteadily extended the Spanish power in the South Eaſt, and finally met his death in 1537 when rescuing an officer of his, one Criſtóbal de Oñate, from a tight corner. It was a ſtrange end.

INTRODUCTION

One of the Spaniard's horses was wounded, and its rider dismounted. Maddened, the horse bore down upon the Governor and before it could be stopped had attacked him and crushed him severely. His injuries were so severe that on being moved from camp in a litter (which, says Díaz, was the direct cause of his death) he fainted, and died a few hours later.

The third of Cortés's most trusted captains, Cristóbal de Olid, proved treacherous to him, when sent on the expedition to Honduras, and the melancholy end of his career, which was the executioner's block, is recounted in the Fifth Letter.

But it is not only these three Captains and their kind that Díaz describes so minutely. There are few so humble as to escape his memory or his pen.

"Let not any be surprised," says Díaz, "that I should still remember their names, their ages, conditions, faces . . . for we were five hundred and fifty companions who ever held converse together, standing side by side in watches as in attacks, in battles and skirmishes, and passing among us the names of those who were killed or who were taken alive by the enemy to be sacrificed."

He was eighty at least when he finished his book. For many years now they have been with him, those old companions, day and night—the aged warrior still slept in his clothes, his arms ready to hand—and he has but to summon them up, one by one,—

"There came also with us another very valiant soldier, one Juan Ruano,—he died at the bridges; there came also Bernardino Vázquez de Tapia, a man of great importance and very rich, he died in his bed . . ., likewise a good soldier came with us, short of one hand, which had been cut off by the Justices in Castille,—he died in the power of the Indians: there was another soldier named Tuvilla, lame in one foot, who claimed to have got his wound under the Great Captain at Garellano. . . ."

And so the long line goes on:—obscure soldiers of fortune, very ordinary men of their hands, whose names have been thus recorded by one of their comrades, as those without whom Cortés could never have conquered the kingdom of New Spain.

"God pardon him his sins," concludes the old warrior, "and to me too, and grant me a good end, which is of greater importance than all the conquests and victories we had over the Indians."

§ 4. ETHICS OF CONQUEST

"Conquest" has always been held an ugly word: so much so that even conquerors themselves have been chary of it. The Norman William crossed the channel, as he announced, to assume a kingdom which was his by right of a rival's oath. Alaric the Goth led his barbarian mercenaries southward to the sack of Rome with the proclaimed intent of securing arrears of pay long overdue.

In like fashion the *conquistadores* of the New World might invent a hundred plausible reasons by which the white man was entitled to oust the native from the soil. They were bringing the benefits of a higher civilization: they were instituting orderly forms of government and administration of justice: above all they were spreading the true faith and guiding an erring flock into the fold. Such arguments have their weight, as they must always have: but they cannot obscure the main issue. The *conquistadores* were engaged primarily on the business of conquering.

INTRODUCTION

The war which Cortés waged in Mexico was essentially a war of conquest.

Between the Spaniards who conquered the New World and the buccaneering Englishmen of Elizabeth's reign who successfully robbed them of a large portion of its spoils there was indeed little to choose. The methods of Cortés in Mexico differed little from those adopted by the English in North America, in India and in New Zealand during the succeeding centuries. Moreover it would be untrue to suppose that sixteenth century Spain was entirely without its prophets to cry out upon the means taken to effect a conquest, which must appear to the more civilized minds of our day as iniquitous.

No voice was louder in denunciation than that of a Dominican Friar, Bartolomé de Las Casas. He had accompanied Ovando to Hayti in 1502, and spent the greater part of his life in the Islands and New Spain, refusing finally the wealthy archbishopric of Chiapa for the humble see of Cuzco where he died. His *Short Account of the Destruction of the Indies* was published at Seville in 1552. There is no hesitancy about the attack of this bishop militant.

" From that year of 1518," he says, " until today, which is now in the year 1542, has swelled up and come to a head all the wickedness, injustice, violence and tyranny which the Christians have done in the Indies. . . . I affirm it as very certain and approved that during these forty years (1502–1542) owing to the aforesaid tyrannies and infernal works of the Christians more than twelve million souls, men, women and children, have perished unjustly and tyrannically; and in truth I believe I should not be overstepping the mark in saying fifteen millions. . . ."

" Two ways," he continues, " have in general been used by those who come to the Indies calling themselves Christians to extirpate and root out these wretched people utterly from the land.   One, by unjuſt, cruel, bloody and tyrannical wars: the other, after they have killed off all those who could long or sigh for liberty, that is to say, all chiefs and warriors, they oppress those that remain, being commonly only children and women, with the moſt horrible and relentless and pitiless slavery to which ever men or beaſts were put."

Las Casas is at no pains to find a motive:

"The cause of the Chriſtians having killed and deſtroyed such an infinite number of souls has been simply that their whole end was the acquiring of gold and riches in the shorteſt time so that they might rise to lofty positions out of all proportion to their worth: in a word the cause of such ills has been their insatiable ambition and covetousness. . . ."

This is a "railing accusation" indeed.   There are two further passages which should be compared directly with the accounts given by Cortés.   The firſt deals with the *requerimiento*.

"That pernicious blindness," says our Friar in a fine burſt of fury, "which has always possessed those in charge of the government of the Indies, with regard to ordering the conversion and salvation of the natives, which in very truth has ever been poſtponed in the effect, has reached such a pitch that a method has been devised and put into practice by which a *requerimiento* is to be pronounced to the Indians bidding them come to the true faith and do homage to the Kings of Caſtile: which if they fail to do, war shall be made on them with fire and sword, and they shall be killed and enslaved."

To these orders, "ſtupid, absurd, worthy of vituperation, eternal shame and damnation," as Las Casas remarks, the local governor succeeded in putting the crowning touch of the inane.   For ſtarting out one night during a time of peace to loot a native town "which it was reported contained much gold," he solemnly ordered the *requerimiento* to be read in

Spanish under shelter of the trees some distance from the town: " Chiefs and Indians of this land of such and such a town, know by these presents that there is a God, and a Pope and a King of Castile, who is lord of these lands, and come to do him homage . . ." etc., and then proceeded with the greatest complacency to murder men, women and children in their beds.

It must be doubted whether the reading of the *requerimiento* described by Cortés on p. 43 was appreciably more effective.

The second passage deals with the massacre of Cholula (*cf.* p. 57). Las Casas describes it as follows:

" In this place when the chief men among the natives, both priests and nobles, had come out to receive them, the Christians determined to make there such slaughter as would (in their words) teach the natives and spread fear of their prowess to every corner of the land. For such was ever the determination of the Spaniards in whatever land they entered. . . .

"The Spaniards had asked for some five or six thousand Indians to act as bearers, upon which these came together in the courtyard of their dwelling. Having got them all into the courtyard certain armed Spaniards placed themselves at the gate to prevent their escape, and all the others put hands to their swords and began cutting them down with both swords and lances so that not a single one escaped but was thus butchered where he stood."

He adds a gruesome detail.

" Two or three days later certain Indians still alive pushed their way out covered with blood from the mass of dead bodies and appeared weeping before the Spaniards begging them for pity's sake to spare them, on whom however the Spaniards had no compassion but cut them to pieces almost as soon as they appeared."

It is plain that Las Casas is a far from trustworthy

witness here. He says nothing of the supposed plot, gives no extenuating circumstances, fails to mention that there were several thousand Tlascalan allies who could not be stayed from butchering freely in the city, or finally that (as Cortés says) " two days later all the city was as full of people, including both women and children, all going about in safety, as if nothing had occurred."

In questions of numbers, places, motives even, Las Casas often errs. But there can be no doubt as to the truth of many of the atrocities perpetrated in the Islands, and on the Mainland. They form an indictment against the Conquistadores as a whole which cannot be denied.

It would be easy to assume from this that the army by which the Conquest of Mexico was effected was an undisciplined array of freebooters in which every man was playing for his own hand: but it would be wrong. Cruelties and brutalities to natives on the part of individuals there might be: but the discipline was strict. Witness a few of the rules which Cortés had proclaimed to his men before setting out from Tlascala on the reconquest of Mexico (see p. 138).

First : Inasmuch as experience has shown us and we see each day with what solicitude the natives of these parts venerate their idols by which Our Lord God is highly displeased and the Devil greatly served; and whereas by removing them from such error and idolatry and bringing them to a knowledge of the true catholic faith, we shall not only be laying up eternal glory to our souls but also ensuring the aid of God in things temporal; therefore, I, Hernán Cortés, Captain-General and Chief Justiciar in New Spain, exhort and command all Spaniards in my company to hold as their principal end that of rooting out the aforesaid idolatries from the natives and bringing them to a knowledge of God and the true Catholic Faith. . . .

INTRODUCTION

Item : Since by false swearing and blasphemies God is greatly displeased, . . . I order that no person of whatever condition shall dare to say " I don't believe in God," or " Damn it " (*Pese !*) or " God has no power ": and the same to be understood of Our Lady and all the saints; under pain of the ordinary penalties and 15 *pesos* of gold.

Item : Since by gaming, blasphemies and many other indecencies are encouraged, I order that from now on no person play at cards or other games of chance, under penalty of losing all he has gained and twenty *pesos* of gold.

This rule to be relaxed on active service.

Item : No man to dare put hand to sword or dagger to strike another Spaniard, under penalty, for a gentleman of 100 *pesos*, and for a common soldier, 100 lashes.

Item : No captain to lodge in any other place than that assigned to him by the officer in command.

Item : No booty to be taken until the enemy is completely defeated.

Item : All booty to be brought immediately to me at the common store, under penalty of death and loss of all his goods.

It is plain that this was no rabble army, whose rank and file could not be kept in hand, and whose atrocities were therefore those of the nameless and irresponsible common soldiery. The atrocities were real enough and they were in general ordered by the leaders. But the impulse behind them was not so much one of terrorism (as Las Casas suggests): it was one of fear.

Fear, as it is probably the most primitive of all emotions, so it is the most potent to reduce men to the level of beasts.

The Aztec natives whom Cortés's men had to contend against in New Spain were of very different stock from those whom they had hunted with greyhounds in Cuba. These " gentle sheep " (as Las Casas was pleased to call them) indulged in cannibalism and human sacrifices. Thousands upon thousands of native victims had thus met their deaths on the altars of Mexico and Yucatán: later, during the siege of the capital the Christians themselves were to see the naked bodies of their comrades, white amid the dusky hordes which surrounded them, being borne up for sacrifice to the high idol towers. That Spanish brutalities were dictated in large measure by fear becomes plain in many passages of the Letters.

The massacre of Cholula was obviously the work of men who were badly scared, and had good reason to be so. Albarado left in the capital while Cortés rides to oppose the further advance of Narváez (see p. 107) acts not only as the coward but the bully. Very various reasons were given at the court-martial both by himself and those who were with him: " the priests in disobedience to Cortés's strict orders were preparing to make human sacrifices again." " Some of the natives had shouted that it would be the turn of the white men next." " An insurrection was being plotted," and so on. Through all his defence there shows plainly the figure of a man naturally headstrong and brutal whose nerves were very badly on edge.

Whatever deeds Cortés himself must finally be judged guilty of there is no doubt that he was habitually both more resolute and more cool-headed than any of his subordinates. A crowning example of this is given in an account of the spasmodic fighting with neighbouring tribes which followed the retreat from Mexico to Tlascala.

Since this is a passage which has been omitted from the end of the Second Letter we will quote it in some detail.

" The city of Huaquechula," relates Cortés, " had sent in chiefs with messages of submission. Moreover they brought the request that a small Spanish force should be sent there to assist them in capturing and putting to death a body of Mexican chieftains who had established themselves within the city and who were in communication with some thirty thousand of the enemy without." Cortés accordingly despatched some troops. " But the Spaniards," continues Cortés, " heard in a neighbouring town that the natives of Huaquechula were banded together with the Mexicans to entice them upon that pretext into the aforesaid city and there set upon them and kill them all. And as they were not wholly recovered from the fear that the natives of the capital had inspired in them, this news spread panic among them, and the Captain whom I had sent in command made such investigations as he thought proper, and placed under arrest all those chieftains from Huaquechula who were accompanying them: and so returned with them to Cholula, which is but four leagues from here, whence he sent them all back to me under a strong guard, together with the proofs which he had obtained. He wrote me, moreover, to say that his men were terror-stricken, and regarded the enterprise as one of extraordinary difficulty. I questioned the prisoners by means of the interpreters I had with me: and having used all diligence to discover the truth, it seemed to me that the Captain had not understood them aright. Thereupon, I ordered them to be freed, and satisfied them as to my trust in them as loyal vassals of your majesty."

Cortés accordingly set out and successfully concluded the expedition in person; " desiring," as he says, " to show no weakness nor fear before the natives, whether friends or enemies." Such were the actual difficulties of the Conqueror.

It is easy to see that had Cortés been anything less than himself, such blots on the history of the Conquest as the massacre of Cholula and the torturing and final execution of Guatimucin, might well have been normal occurrences rather than isolated instances.

§ 5. THE LETTERS

Cortés's letters to the Emperor from Mexico are termed in Spanish *cartas-relaciones*—half letters, half despatches. They are not literary masterpieces. The vocabulary is very small. The same expressions, of time, place, action, are continually used, as in most documents of the official kind. Yet with a small vocabulary, his style is wordy and often involved. The one artistic effect of which he is a master is that of under-statement: and it is a device which he employs unconsciously.

On the whole his prose is solid, never pedantic, controlled and forceful. Through it one perceives a man who of the two tools preferred the sword; yet on occasion could wield the pen in a fashion that was at least eminently workmanlike.

These five letters were all written from various cities in New Spain between the years 1519 and 1526. They vary greatly in length, the second, third and fourth being the longest, each containing in the original some 40,000 words, while the first and fourth run to 10,000 and 20,000 words respectively.

First Letter.

Cortés's first letter to the Emperor written in June or July 1519 has never been recovered. There is, however, little doubt about its contents. The Rica Villa of Vera Cruz had just been founded; and its

INTRODUCTION

Justiciary and Council lost no time in despatching a letter to Spain, to give, as they said, "a certain and true account of all that had been discovered in the two preceding years." The writer of this letter, it is clear, saw and perhaps copied in large part what Cortés himself was writing. It was this letter from Vera Cruz which was discovered in the Imperial Archives of Vienna during the last century.

The search revealed in addition what is now the Fifth Letter, which had previously been unknown.

In this First Letter the earliest discoveries of the mainland from 1517 onwards are sketched in a somewhat lengthy passage which has been abridged.

Diego de Velázquez, a year later (as will be seen from the letter, p. 2), was obviously dissatisfied with what had been accomplished. He now set to work to fit out another expedition which should prove more advantageous to himself. It was for this expedition that he chose Cortés as leader.

The new Captain of men obviously showed a very different front to fortune than Grijalba, whose chances of success had been as rosy as his own. It is the man who makes the occasion.

At the end of the letter, the worthy Justiciary and Council of Vera Cruz endeavour at some length to justify their illegal proceeding in founding a settlement. It is not difficult to perceive the hand of Cortés here.

It will be noted that to commend further their action the citizens decided with Cortés to send the whole of the treasure (not merely the royal fifth) to the Emperor.

Second Letter.

"The first letter is the weakest, the second the most interesting; the third, the most dramatic," writes a French critic—M. Désiré Charnay. Actually the

xlii

word "dramatic" may just as properly be applied to the second. There are passages of wonder and horror in this letter which might well belong to the Arabian Nights. The drama opens with the breaking-up of the boats; there follow the cautious but perilous advance into the heart of a hostile country, and the audacious capture of its monarch: the sky seems to have cleared, but suddenly the natives who have hitherto accepted the strangers as immortals to whom they owe allegiance, are violently disturbed by the arrival of rival " gods " in the shape of Pánfilo de Narváez with reinforcements from Velázquez. Open resistance succeeds and the climax is reached with the frenzied scenes of the *noche triste*, " the sorrowful night "— and the days of retreat that follow. Finally the remnants of the army arrive in Tlascala, and to their keen relief are well received by the natives.

The indomitable Cortés waits hardly till his wounds are healed before he is again in the field attacking neighbouring tribes who have been stirred up to rebel by the victorious Culuans. Despite all the fears of his men he is determined on reconquest: and already he embarks upon the task.

The Reconquest proper belongs to the Third Letter, and the account of certain preliminary operations which occurs at the end of the Second Letter has consequently been omitted.

Third Letter.

This letter may be split up into three portions: (*a*) the advance of Cortés into Culua and the capture and destruction of the various towns surrounding the great lakes; (*b*) the assault on the capital itself and its final submission: (*c*) various enterprises undertaken by the Conqueror to extend his power throughout Mexico, and the arrival of Cristóbal de Tapia from

Spain, as agent of the Crown to examine the details of conquest.

The second portion describing the taking of Tenochtitlan is given in its entirety. The two other portions have been somewhat abridged.

Both this and the second letter were made public very soon after their arrival in Spain. A little German printer in Seville published the second on November 8th 1522 and the third on March 30 of the following year. They were almost immediately translated into Latin and Italian and sold in Germany and Italy.

Fourth Letter.

This letter is mainly concerned with affairs of organization. The visit of Garay, causing rebellion in Pánuco, and concluding with the Frenchman's death, is the most important incident. Elsewhere certain abbreviations have been made, particularly at the beginning where Cortés reports the progress of various expeditions.

Sandoval was sent east and succeeded in reaching the river Guasacualco and there founding the town of Espíritu Santo four miles from its mouth. Meanwhile messengers arrived from the ruler of Michoacan with presents and an offer to become a vassal of the great white Emperor. An officer proceeded to the province, and thence without orders further west to Coliman, where in spite of his forty horsemen and some hundred Spanish foot he suffered a defeat from the natives.

Albarado was sent south-east to Tututepec, where he succeeded in subduing the natives, holding the ruler of the province and his son captive. The inhabitants of Segura de la Frontera were ordered to proceed thither and found a new town of the same name. Albarado then returned to the capital. In his absence

INTRODUCTION

the town revolted and new *alcaldes* were set up. Cortés immediately despatched an officer, who returned with the ringleaders in chains.

The letter was published in Spain both at Toledo and Zaragoza in the year 1526.

Fifth Letter.

The expedition to Honduras started out with a long train of servants, butler, majordomo, treasurer, the keeper of the gold and silver plate, surgeon, numerous pages, falconers, even jugglers and tumblers, relates Bernardo Díaz del Castillo. A huge herd of swine accompanied the triumphant procession to provide fresh meat for the travellers.

But it was soon apparent that the journey was to be no picnic. At times the marshy ground rendered any advance at all impossible. Detours had to be made; bridges built; horses supported by bundles of rushes. Cortés was perhaps physically not quite the man that he had been. " I saw that he was much stouter," says Díaz de Castillo, " when we returned from the Higueras." Moreover, he relates, " he now formed a habit (which he had not had in Mexico) of always taking a short nap after the midday meal (failing which his food disagreed with him), and so no matter whether it rained or shone he would lie down under a tree . . . and would always sleep a little before recontinuing the march."

But the old spirit is there. He passes through the various river-villages and towns, most of whose inhabitants have fled, endures the bitterest extremes of hunger and toil, climbs the *sierras* on the eastern side, and finally arrives at Naco. There he finds remnants of treachery and desertion such as were but too common among the early settlers. The wretched survivors are rescued. Cortés conducts that singularly daring expedition up the river to obtain maize for his starving companions. He then proceeds further east and founds a successful settlement on the northern coast of Honduras.

Meanwhile he was being given out for dead in Mexico. He says little in the Letter of what happened in his absence. Two accounts were sent to the Emperor and the Council of the Indies respectively. The truth may be culled from both.

Cortés had left Alonso de Estrada (*tesorero*) and Rodrigo de Albórnoz (*contador*) in charge of the government. Hearing rumours of insurrection and misdemeanour he sent back two other officials from Tabasco with extensive powers. These were Gonzalo de Salazar (*factor*) and Per Almíndez Chirinos (*veedor*). They proved far more successful in securing obedience and were no less dishonest. Months passed and no news came from Cortés. Salazar and Chirinos, who now had the government in their own hands, proclaimed the Governor dead, and proceeded to raid his house and property. Rodrigo de Paz, whom Cortés had left as his steward and Chief Sheriff in New Spain, was arrested, accused of hoarding gold for his master which rightly belonged to the Emperor, twice put to the torture, and finally hanged after a trial farcical in its injustice. All Cortés's possessions, including slaves and cattle, were seized, and the two despots proceeded to govern Mexico unrestrained. The procurators of the various towns and country districts were required to subscribe to a document, drawn up of course by Salazar and Chirinos, begging the Emperor to confirm them in their offices.

Despotism, however, was not allowed to remain a monopoly of the two rulers. Ill-treatment of the native population grew rife, and Indian risings took place in all parts. On January 29th 1527 a courier at last arrived in Mexico with letters from the Governor.

At the news that he was still alive adherents hastened to rally to his cause. Estrada and Albórnoz were encouraged to make a stand. Within a few days Salazar was taken prisoner after an hour's fighting, and Chirinos was skulking in sanctuary.

Cortés returned at the beginning of June in 1526 to find the country more or less at peace. His triumphant route from Vera Cruz to the capital was lined with eager throngs of natives: they cried out " Malinche, Malinche ": tears of joy streamed from their eyes. There could have been no more eloquent testimony to the misgovernment of the country during his long absence.

Letters of Hernando Cortés

THE FIRST LETTER

First Letter sent to the Queen, Doña Juana and the Emperor, Charles V, her son, by the Justiciary and Council of the Rica Villa of Vera Cruz on the 10th of July, 1519.

Most High, Mighty and Excellent Princes, Great and Catholic Sovereign Lords:

We have good reason to believe that your Majesties have been informed by the letters of Diego Velázquez, Admiral's Deputy in the Island of Cuba, of the new land that was discovered some two or more years ago in these parts, which was first called Cozumel and afterwards Yucatán[1], without being either the one or the other as your Majesties shall see from our account. For the reports so far given to your Majesties of this land, its size, riches, the manner in which it was discovered and many other details, were not and could not be exact, since no-one had then ascertained the particulars which we are now sending you in this letter. We shall therefore deal with this land from its first discovery up to its present state, that your Majesties may know what land it is, the people which possess it, their manner of living, rites and ceremonies, religious beliefs, and what fruit your Majesties may hope to receive from it and have already received, so that in everything your Majesties may order matters as shall be most profitable to them. And the true and certain account is after this fashion.

(*In* 1517, *three gentlemen of means left Cuba for the south. The leader was one Francisco Hernando de Córdoba, and they were assisted financially by a certain Diego Velázquez, Admiral's Deputy in the Island. They touched land at Campoche, found the natives fairly friendly but averse to their landing, and dropped down coast to another little native port, named Machocobón. There some fighting took place : twenty-seven Spaniards were killed, and all the rest wounded. Upon this, Hernando de Córdoba, himself seriously wounded, set sail for Cuba, and returned to acquaint Velázquez with the strange land they had found and the all-important fact that it was rich in gold.*

Velázquez immediately sent off to the Jeronymite Fathers in Hayti, who had been empowered by the late regent, Cardinal Ximénez, to grant licenses for exploration in the Indies. He sent at the same time to the royal court in Spain, claiming to have discovered the new land at his own cost. The necessary licenses were obtained, and a relative of his, Juan de Grijalba, was despatched with three ships and some seventy men to explore the coast and treat with the natives. The little island of Cozumel was discovered lying to the east of Yucatán, and the captain landed for fresh water, but did not penetrate inland. Further south, Ascension Bay was discovered on the eastern coast, and named. The ships then retraced their path northward along the coast, turned the point of Yucatán and sailed west. Grijalba made one or two cautious landings but obtained little gold, and had more than one brush with the natives. He finally arrived at the mouth of a large river which he named after himself, Rio de Grijalba, and sailed up a certain distance ; but he soon returned to the sea and pursued his way further west to the Bay of San Juan, from which place he sent back one of the ships to Velázquez with all the gold that he had so far been able to obtain. It was no considerable quantity. The letter then proceeds :)

Diego Velázquez being thus put out at the small amount of gold which had been brought back and eagerly desirous of more, determined without so much as a word to the fathers of San Jerónimo to equip a little fleet of fast sailing vessels to go in search of his relative Grijalba; and in order to do it less at his own cost he suggested to Hernando Cortés, *alcalde*[2] of the neighbouring town of Santiago, that they between them should fit out eight or ten ships, for at that time Hernando Cortés owned better ships than any other man in the island and it was thought that more people would be eager to go with him than with any other. Cortés being thus approached and desirous of serving your Majesties forthwith proposed to spend his whole fortune in equipping the fleet, nearly two-thirds of it entirely at his own cost, supplying both the ships themselves and the necessary provisions and in addition bestowing money on persons who wished to sail with the fleet but were unable to provide themselves with the necessities for the voyage.

The fleet thus equipped, Diego Velázquez appointed Hernando Cortés to be Captain for the purpose of visiting the new land, bartering with the natives, and effecting what Grijalba had failed to do. The entire disposition of the fleet was in the hands of Diego Velázquez although he supplied but a third part of it at his own expense, as your Majesties may see from the instructions and powers which H. Cortés received from Velázquez in the name of your Majesties, and which we now send by the hand of our messengers. And your Majesties should know that the greater part of the said third which Velázquez contributed was spent on wine, clothes and other things of little value, to be sold to us later at a much higher price than he gave for them, so that we can truly declare that among the Spanish subjects of your Majesties in the West Indies Diego Velázquez has made good deals and put his money out at very profitable rates of interest.

H. Cortés accordingly left Cuba and began his voyage with ten ships and four hundred fighting men, among whom were many knights and gentlemen, seventeen being mounted. The first land they touched was the Island of Cozumel, now called Santa Cruz, as we mentioned, and on landing at the part of San Juan de Portalatina the town was found entirely deserted, as if it had never been inhabited. Cortés wishing to know the cause of such a flight ordered the men to disembark and took up his abode in the town. It was not long before he learnt from three Indians captured in a canoe as they were making for the mainland of Yucatán that the chiefs of the Island at the sight of the Spanish ships approaching had left the town and retired with all the Indians to the woods and hills, being very afraid of the Spaniards as not knowing what their intentions might be. Cortés, replying by means of the native interpreter whom he had with him, informed them he was going to do them no harm but admonish them and bring them to the knowledge of our Holy Catholic Faith, that they might become vassals of your Majesty and serve and obey him, as had all the Indians and peoples of those parts which are already peopled with Spanish subjects of your Majesties. On the Captain reassuring them in this manner they lost much of their former fear, and replied that they would willingly inform their chieftains who had taken refuge in the hills. The Captain thereupon gave them a letter by which the chiefs might approach in safety and they departed with it promising to return within the space of five days. After waiting for the reply some three or four days longer than the allotted time and seeing that they had not reappeared Cortés decided to search out the coast on either side of him, in order that the Island should not remain entirely deserted, and accordingly sent out two captains each with a hundred men, ordering them to proceed to either extremity of the Island and to hold conversations with any Indians they might meet, telling them that he was awaiting them in the port of San Juan de

Portalatina in order to speak with them on behalf of your Majesty; such Indians they were to beg and urge as best they could to come to the said port but were to be careful not to do any harm to them, in their persons, their houses or their goods, lest the natives should be rendered more timid and deceitful than they were already. The two captains departed as they were commanded and returning within four days reported that all the towns which they had come across were desolate. They brought with them, however, ten or a dozen people whom they had managed to persuade, among whom was an Indian chieftain to whom Cortés spoke by means of his interpreter bidding him go and inform the chiefs that he would in no wise depart from the Island without seeing and speaking to them. The chieftain agreeing left with the second letter for the chiefs and two days later returned with the head chief to inform Cortés that he was the ruler of the Island and was come to see what he wanted. The Captain informed him that he wished them no harm, but that they should come to the knowledge of the true faith, and should know that we acknowledged as lords the greatest princes of the earth and that these in their turn obeyed a greater prince than he, wherefore what he desired of them was not otherwise than that the chiefs and Indians of that Island should likewise obey your Majesties, and that doing so they would be favoured, no-one being able to do them harm. The chief replied that he was content so to do and sent for all the other chieftains of the Island, who coming rejoiced greatly at all that the Captain Hernando Cortés had spoken to their chief, and were reassured in such manner that within a very few days the towns were as full of people as before, and the Indians went about among us with as little fear as if they had already had dealings with us for many years.

It was at this time that the Captain learned that certain Spaniards had been held captive for the last seven years by some native chiefs in Yucatán: their vessel bound from the mainland had foundered somewhere south of Jamaica and they had escaped in the rowing boat to this land where ever since they had been held prisoner by the Indians. Cortés had had certain instructions to look out for these Spaniards before leaving Cuba and now on hearing news of them and the land where they were it seemed to him he would be doing no small service to God and to your Majesty in rescuing them from the prison and captivity in which they lay; and forthwith he would have set out in person with the whole fleet to rescue them, had not the pilots dissuaded him saying that he could in no wise do this since the fleet and all his men would surely be lost by reason of the excessive roughness of the coast and the absence of any harbour or place where he could land from his ships. Cortés accordingly abandoned this project and immediately dispatched certain Indians, who informed him they knew the chieftain in whose power the Spaniards were; he gave them a letter in which he explained to his countrymen that the only reason for his not coming in person with his fleet to rescue them was that the landing on the rough and rocky coast was impossible, but he urged them to make every effort to escape by canoe and he would meanwhile await them in the Island of Santa Cruz.

Three days after the departure of the Indians, Cortés, deeming the arrangement not wholly satisfactory and thinking that the Indians would be unable to effect all he desired, decided to send two brigs and a smaller vessel with forty of his own men to the mainland in order to take the Spaniards on board if they arrived there, and sent in addition three more Indians bearing another letter with instructions to land and make search for the Spaniards. On arriving at the coast the three Indians landed and disappeared on their search as Cortés had commanded; six days the ships awaited off the coast with no little difficulty, for more than once they nearly slipped anchor and ran aground, the sea being exceedingly rough as the pilots had reported. Finally, seeing no signs either of the Spanish prisoners or of the Indians who had gone to seek them, they decided to return to where Cortés was waiting for them off the Island of Santa Cruz; Cortés was deeply grieved to hear of their failure on their return and the next day gave orders to embark, fully intending to land on Yucatán even though the whole fleet should be lost and also to verify whether the report which Juan de Grijalba sent to Cuba were true, in which he declared that it was mere idle talk that anyone had ever landed on that coast or that certain Spaniards had been taken captive and imprisoned there.

With this firm intent Cortés had embarked all his men save only some twenty who still remained with him on the shore; the weather was very fine and particularly favourable for leaving port, when suddenly a contrary wind got up and showers of rain fell on them from the quarter whither they were going to sail, in such fashion that the pilots urged him strongly not to embark seeing that the weather was now so unsuited for leaving harbour. Accordingly Cortés gave a general order to disembark and next day at noon a canoe was seen in sail proceeding towards the island. On its arrival at the place where we were we discovered in it one Spaniard who had been taken prisoner, whose name was Gerónimo de Aguilar, who told us the manner of his capture and of the length of his captivity, which was as we above related to your Majesty; and that change in the weather which suddenly came about was held by us and truly as a great mystery and miracle of God, by which it is thought that nothing can be undertaken in your Majesty's service which will not turn out well. This Gerónimo de Aguilar informed us that the other Spaniards who were lost with him were scattered far in the interior of the country which he assured us was very large, and that it would be impossible to rescue them without landing and spending much time in that land.

Accordingly, as the Captain Hernando Cortés saw that stores were already beginning to run short and that the men would suffer much from hunger should he delay there any longer, and the true object of his voyage rest unattained, he decided, his men agreeing, to depart; and so hoisting sail they left that Island of Cozumel, now Santa Cruz, very peaceably inclined, so much so that if it were proposed to found a colony there the natives would be ready without coercion to serve their Spanish masters. The chiefs in particular were left very contented and at ease with what the Captain had told them on behalf of your Majesties and with the numerous articles of finery which he had given them for their own persons. I think there can be no doubt that all Spaniards who may happen to come to this Island in the future will be as well received as if they were arriving in a land which had been long time colonized. The Island of Cozumel is small, without so much as a single river or stream; all the water that the Indians drink is from wells. The soil is composed solely of rocks and stones, a certain portion of it being woody. The Indians' only produce is that obtained from bee-keeping, and our procurators are sending to your Majesties samples both of the land and of the honey for your Majesties' inspection.

Your Majesties must know that when the Captain told the chiefs in his first interview with them that they must live no longer in the pagan faith which they held they begged him to acquaint them with the law under which they were henceforth to live. The Captain accordingly informed them to the best of his ability in the Catholic Faith, leaving them a cross of wood which was fixed on a high building and an image of Our Lady the Virgin Mary, and gave them to understand very fully what they must do to be good Christians, all of which they manifestly received with very good will, and so we left them very happy and contented.

On leaving the Island we set our course for Yucatán and ran along the North coast until we arrived at the great river, said to be the River Grijalba, which is, as we have already related to your Majesties, the point to which the Captain Grijalba, a relative of Diego Velázquez, had beforehand penetrated. The entrance to that river is so shallow that not one of the large ships could sail up it. However the Captain, Hernando Cortés, in his devotion to the service of your Majesties and being desirous of sending a true report of all there is to know in the new land, decided to proceed no further along the coast until he had discovered the secret of the river and of the towns which are on its banks, for they are rumoured to be fabulously rich in gold. Accordingly he transferred all the men that he had with him in the fleet into the brigs and smaller boats, and we advanced up the river with the intent of spying out the land and examining the towns.

On arriving at the first town we found the Indians in boats drawn up on the shore near the water. The Captain proceeded to speak to them both by means of the native interpreter whom we carried with us and of Gerónimo de Aguilar who spoke and understood perfectly the language of the country, telling them that he came to do no harm but only to speak to them on behalf of your Majesties, and accordingly requested them that they would see fit to allow us to land, since we had no place to sleep that night save on the brigs

9

and smaller boats in the middle of the river and in these there was not even room enough for us to ſtand; as for returning to our ships it was too late, since they had been left outside in the open sea. The Indians on hearing this, replied that from where he was he might parley with them as he would, but that neither he nor his men were to land on their shore and that they would repel any attempt to do so. Immediately after this their bowmen began to draw up in line so as to be prepared to shoot at us, at the same time threatening us and bidding us depart. The day being much advanced (for the sun was on the point of setting) the Captain decided to retire to the sandy beach which lay in front of the town on the other side of the river, and there we landed and slept that night. Early next morning a few Indians approached us in a canoe bringing several chickens and enough maize to make a meal for a few men and bidding us accept these and depart from their land. The Captain however spoke to them through the interpreters giving them to underſtand that in no wise would he depart from that land before he had found out the secret of it in order to be able to send your Majeſties a true account, and again begged them not to be offended at his projeˆt nor to deny him entrance for they also were ſubjeˆts of your Majeſties. However they ſtill forbade us to make a landing and urged us to depart. On their return to the town the Captain decided to move, and ordered one of his captains to go with two hundred men by a path which had been discovered during the preceding night to lead to the village. He himself embarked with some eighty men on the brigs and boats and took up his position in front of the town ready to land if they would permit him to do so: even as he approached he found the Indians in war paint and armed with bows and arrows, lances and small round shields, yelling that if we would not leave their

10

land and wanted war it should begin at once, for they were men to defend their own homes. Cortés attempted to speak with them four times (your Majesties' notary who accompanied him witnessed to the same to the effect that he did not desire war) but seeing that it was the determined will of the Indians to resist his landing and that they were beginning to shoot their arrows against us, ordered the guns which we carried to be fired and an attack to be made. Immediately after the discharge of our guns and in the landing which followed a few of our men were wounded, but finally the fury of our onslaught and the sudden attack of our comrades who had come up in the rear of the enemy forced them to fly and abandon the village, which we accordingly took and settled ourselves in what appeared to be the strongest part of it. In the evening of the following day two Indians arrived from their chiefs bringing a few very inferior gold ornaments of small value and told the Captain that they offered him these in order that in exchange he might leave the land as it was before and do them no hurt. Cortés replied saying that as to doing them no hurt it pleased him well, but as to leaving the land they should know that from henceforward they must acknowledge as lords the greatest princes of the earth and must be their subjects and serve them; by doing which they would obtain many favours from your Majesties who would help them and defend them from their enemies. On this they replied that they were content to do this, but nevertheless still begged him to leave their land, and so we arrived at friendly terms.

Having patched up this friendship the Captain pointed out that the Spanish troops who were with him in the village had nothing to eat and had brought nothing from their ships. He therefore asked them to bring us sufficient food so long as we remained on land, which they promised to do on the following day, and so departed. But the next day and another passed without any food arriving so that we were faced with extreme shortness of provisions, and on the third day a few Spanish soldiers asked leave of the Captain to visit some of the near-lying farms and see if they could obtain some food. The Captain, seeing that the Indians were not coming as had been agreed, sent out four officers with more than two hundred men to search the neighbourhood for any provisions, and on their way they fell in with large numbers of Indians who shot at them with arrows so furiously that more than twenty Spaniards were wounded; and had not Cortés been quickly apprised of their danger and rescued them, as he succeeded in doing, there is little doubt that more than half the Spaniards would have been killed. In such wise we regained our camp, those that were wounded were attended to, and those weary with fighting were refreshed. Cortés perceiving the wrong the Indians had done him in pursuing the war instead of bringing provisions as they had promised, ordered ten horses and mules to be landed from among those which had been brought in the ships and everyone to keep a sharp look out, since he suspected that the Indians heartened by the success of the day before would advance to attack our camp with intent to do us harm. Everyone was thus on the alert and on the following day he sent other officers with three hundred men to where the battle had taken place to see if the Indians were still there or what had become of them: and very shortly afterwards he sent forward two more officers with the rearguard of a hundred men, he himself taking his way privily on horseback with ten mounted men to one side of the main path. Proceeding in this order the vanguard came upon a large body of Indians who were advancing to attack our camp, so that had we not gone out to meet them that day it is very

possible we should have been hard put to it. And
again the captain of artillery made certain represen-
tations (as your notary can bear witness) to the Indians
whom he met in full war paint, crying to them by means
of the native heralds and interpreters that we wanted
not war but peace with them: their only answer was
given not in words but in arrows which began to fall
very thickly. The leading party was thus already
engaged with the Indians when the two officers in
command of the rearguard came up, and it was not
until two hours later that Cortés arrived in a part
of the wood where the Indians were beginning to
encircle the Spaniards in the rear, and there he continued fighting against the Indians for about an hour;
moreover such was their number that neither those
among the Spaniards who were fighting on foot perceived those on horseback nor knew in what part of
the field they were, nor could those on horseback so
much as perceive one another as they surged hither
and thither among the Indians. However, as soon
as the Spaniards perceived the horsemen they attacked
still more briskly and almost immediately the Indians
were put to flight, the pursuit lasting half a league;
whereupon Cortés seeing that the Indians were
routed and that there was no more to be done (his
men moreover being very wearied) gave orders that
all should gather together in some farmhouses nearby,
and on assembling there it was found that twenty
men were wounded not one of whom, however, died
nor of those wounded on the previous day. And
so having attended to the wounded and laid them
upon stretchers, we regained our camp taking with us
two Indians who were captured there. These Cortés
ordered to be loosed, and sent them with letters to the
chieftains telling them that if they were willing to
come to where he was he would pardon them the evil
they had done and would be their friend. Accord-

ingly the very same evening two Indians who purported to be chieftains arrived, declaring that they were very grieved at what had occurred and that the chieftains as a body begged him to pardon them and not punish them further for what was passed nor kill any more of their people, for over two hundred and twenty Indians had fallen; the paſt was paſt and henceforward they were willing to be subjeċts of that prince of whom he had spoken, and such they already held themselves to be, and bound themselves to do him service whenever anything in your Majeſties' name should be desired of them.

In this wise they sat down and peace was made. The Captain then enquired of them by the interpreter what people it was who had fought in that battle, and they replied that tribes from eight provinces had joined together in that place and that according to the reckoning and liſts which they possessed they would be about forty thousand men, for they could well reckon up to such a number. Thus your Majeſties may truly believe that this battle was won rather by the will of God than by our own ſtrength, for of what avail are four hundred (and we were no more) againſt forty thousand warriors?

Having thus entered upon very friendly terms, they gave us during the four or five days that we were there about one hundred and fifty *pesos*[3] of gold all told, but comprised of ornaments so poor in themselves, yet held by them in such eſteem, that it was plain that their country is almoſt entirely lacking in gold, for there is small doubt that the little that they had had come to them from other parts by means of barter.

The soil is excellent and very fertile, both in maize and fruits, and the rivers abound in fish and the other produce which they use for food. The village is situated on the bank of the river we have already described from which we entered upon a plain con-

14

taining many farms and cultivated lands which belong to them and which they till. We admonished them of the wrong they did in adoring the gods and idols which they possess and gave them to understand that they must come into the knowledge of our own blessed faith, leaving behind us on parting a great wooden cross which was placed high up, and with which they were much pleased, declaring that they would hold it in the greatest veneration. So we left the Indians in this manner as our friends and the loyal subjects of your Majesties.

Cortés accordingly set sail to pursue his voyage and came to the harbour and bay of San Juan which is the place where Captain Juan de Grijalba had certain dealings with the natives as we have described at length to your Majesties above. As soon as we arrived there the natives of the land came to discover what ships they might be which approached, but since the day was already very advanced (night having almost fallen) the Captain gave orders that we were to remain in the ships and that no one was to attempt to land. The next morning Cortés and a large number of his men put on shore and found there two headmen among the Indians to whom he gave certain personal ornaments and spoke to them by the means of interpreters giving them to understand that he had come to these parts by order of your Majesties to acquaint them with those things that they must do in his service, and to this end he requested that they should go straightway into the town and bring their chief or chiefs out to speak with him; and that they might more surely come he gave them as a present to the chiefs a pair of shirts and doublets, one of satin the other of velvet, and for each a bonnet of fine red cloth and a couple of belts such as are used for hawking; so they departed bearing these gifts to the chieftains. Accordingly a little before noon on the following day a chief returned with them from the town with whom Cortés had speech, informing him by his interpreter that he had come to do them no harm but rather to declare to them that from henceforth they were to be subjects of your Majesties and must serve and give him whatever their country produced as do all those who are his subjects: to which the chief replied that he was very content to become your Majesties' subject and that it pleased him well to serve and have as his lord such mighty princes as the Captain had declared your Majesties to be. Upon this the Captain told them that since he showed such good will towards his king and lord, he should soon see for himself the rewards which your Majesties would henceforward bestow upon him: and saying this he caused him to be arrayed in a shirt of holland cloth, a flowing velvet jacket and a girdle of gold with which the chief was highly delighted and satisfied, and declared that we should wait there while he returned to his own land when on the morrow he would bring us that by which we should know more truly the desire he had to serve your Majesties, and so bidding farewell departed. On the following day he returned as he had promised bearing a white cloth which he ordered to be spread out before the Captain, and thereupon made him a gift of certain precious trinkets of gold which he placed upon the cloth, and of which among others which we received later we give a detailed account to your Majesties in a list which our procurators bear with them. Having bidden farewell to us the chief finally departed to his own dwelling in great content.

Now as many of us who ventured in this fleet were persons of rank, knights and gentlemen, eager to serve our Lord and your Majesties, and desirous alike of extending the power of their royal crown and increasing their dominions and revenue, we joined ourselves together at this time and conferred with the

Captain Hernando Cortés, pointing out that this land
was fruitful, rich in gold, so far as could be judged
from the samples which the chief had brought us, and
that the chief and all the natives seemed to bear us
very good will; on which account it seemed to us
profitable to the service of your Majesties that the
instructions given by Diego Velázquez to the Captain
Hernando Cortés should not be carried out in that
land, to wit that as much gold as possible should be
obtained by barter from the natives, and once obtained
an immediate return made to Cuba, by which the said
Diego Velázquez and our Captain would alone reap
the fruits of the expedition: but to all of us it seemed
better that a town should be founded there in the name
of your Majesties with a justiciary and council, so
that in this land your Majesties might possess over-
lordship as in their other kingdoms and domains;
for, the land once settled with Spaniards, in addition
to the royal dominions and revenues being increased,
your Majesties might be graciously pleased to grant
favours both to us and to settlers who should come
from further lands.

And thus agreed we joined ourselves together, no
man being dissentient, but with one mind and purpose we made a demand of the said Captain in which
we declared: That since he must perceive how agreeable it was both to the service of God and your Majesties
that this land should be settled, giving him the reasons
which have been set forth above to your Majesties,
we therefore required him to cease forthwith from such
barter with the natives as he had come to do, since by
such means the land would be truly destroyed and your
Majesties done no small disservice: likewise we asked
and required him to appoint *alcaldes* and *regidores*[4] for
the town which was to be founded by us, all this with
certain protestations if so be he should not carry out
what we demanded. On our presenting this request

the Captain replied that he would give his answer on the following day, and considering how agreeable our request was to the service of your Majesties, he accordingly replied, saying that he was desirous above all things of doing some service to your Majesties, and hence unmindful of the profit which would accrue to him should he continue bartering as had been his intention (by which he might reimburse himself for the great expenses incurred with the aforesaid Diego Velázquez in the fitting out of the fleet) but rather putting all this aside, he was well pleased and content to do what we demanded, since it was agreeable to the service of your Majesties. And upon this he began immediately with great diligence to settle and found a town to which he gave the name of the Rica Villa of Vera Cruz, and appointed those whose names appear at the foot of this letter as *alcaldes* and *regidores* of the town, duly receiving from us the solemn oath as is wont and customary on such occasions.

This done, on the following day we entered into our office and charges, and being thus met together we sent to the Captain Hernando Cortés asking him in the name of your Majesties to show us the powers and instructions which the aforementioned Diego Velázquez had given to him on coming to these parts. He lost no time in sending for them, and having seen, read and carefully examined them we found that to the best of our understanding the Captain no longer held any authority according to the documents before mentioned, and such authority having expired he could no longer execute justice or act as Captain. But it appeared to us well, most excellent Princes, that for the sake of peace, quietness and good government amongst us, there should be one person elected in your Majesties' name to act in this town and district in the service of your Majesties as Chief Justice and Captain General of the forces, to whom we should all

18

pay respect until such time as your Majesties having received our report should provide other means by which your Majesties might best be served. Now there was no person better fitted for such a charge than Hernando Cortés, for in addition to being just such a man as is fitting for an office of this kind, he is very greatly desirous of serving your Majesties, and not only has he wide experience of the islands and mainland of these parts, by reason of which he has always given a good account of himself, but he spent freely what he had in order to accompany this fleet in the service of your Majesties, and moreover held of small account (as we have already related) all that he might gain should he continue bartering with the natives as was his first intent, and accordingly we appointed him in your Majesties' name Chief Justice and *alcalde mayor*, and received from him the oath which is necessary in such case. This done, as was agreeable to the royal service of your Majesties, we received him in his official capacity in our public assembly as Chief Justice and Captain of your Majesties' royal armies, and thus he will remain until such time as your Majesties may provide what is more agreeable to their royal service. We desire to give an account of all this to your Majesties so that they may know what has been done here and the state and manner in which we now remain.

This matter concluded, being united in public assembly we agreed to write to your Majesties sending them all the gold, silver and jewels which we have obtained in this country over and above the fifth part which belonged to them by right, and it was agreed that by giving the whole of the first fruits, not keeping so much as a single thing for ourselves, we should be doing some service to your Majesties and show plainly the very great zeal that we have in their service, as we have already displayed in adventuring our lives and fortunes. This being agreed upon, we elected as our messengers Alonso Fernández Portocarrero and Francisco de Montejo, whom we send to your Majesties with all the aforementioned treasure, that they may on our behalf kiss their royal hands and in our name and the name of this town and council beg your Majesties to favour us with certain things necessary to the service of God and your Majesties and the common weal of this town, as is more minutely set out in the special instructions which we have given them. Which requests with all due respect we humbly beg your Majesties to grant, and to concede all those privileges which in the name of this council and of ourselves they may beg, for in addition to your Majesties doing great service to our Lord in this matter, they will be conferring a very signal favour on this town and council such as we daily hope may be the pleasure of your Majesties.

In a former paragraph of this letter we said that we are sending an account of this land that your Majesties may be better informed of its peculiarities, its riches, the people who possess it and the beliefs, rites and ceremonies which they hold. The land which in the name of your Majesties we now occupy stretches for some fifty leagues on either side of this town; the coast is entirely flat and on the sea shore there are sandy beaches stretching sometimes for two miles and more. Inland, behind the sand dunes, the land is also flat, comprising very fine meadow lands and river banks, such as cannot be bettered in all Spain, as pleasing to the eye moreover as they are fertile in producing all manner of crops, and very well looked after and of easy access, all kinds of herds being found there both grazing and for use as beasts of burden.

All kinds of hunting is to be met with in this land and both birds and beasts similar to those we have in Spain, such as deer, both red and fallow, wolves, foxes, partridges, pigeons, turtle doves of several kinds, quails, hares and rabbits: so that in the matter of birds and beasts there is no great difference between this land and Spain, but there are in addition lions and tigers about five miles inland, of which more are to be found in some districts than in others. There is a great range of very fine mountains, some very high and one in particular overtopping all the rest, from which one can discern a great expanse of the sea and land; indeed it is so high that if the day be not very clear its summit cannot be seen at all since the top half of it is entirely covered with clouds, and on other occasions when the weather is very fine one can see its summit rising above the clouds so white that we judge it to be snow: this the natives also confirm, but since we have not seen it very clearly although approaching quite near to it, and considering that this region is exceptionally hot we cannot affirm it to be so for certain. We shall endeavour to find out by personal observation about this and other matters of which we have heard reports in order to send your Majesties a true account of it, as well as of the riches of the country in gold, silver and precious stones, of all of which your Majesties may form some idea from the samples which we are sending them. To our mind it is probable that this land contains as many riches as that from which Solomon is said to have obtained the gold for the temple: but so little time has passed since our landing that we have been unable to explore the country further than some five leagues inland and some ten or a dozen leagues along the coast on either side of the place where we first landed; from the sea much more may be seen and more we certainly saw while skirting the coast in our ships.

The natives who inhabit the island of Cozumel and the land of Yucatán from its northern point to where we are now settled, are of middle height, and well-proportioned, except that in our district they disfigure their faces in various ways, some piercing the ears and introducing large and extremely ugly ornaments, others the lower part of the nose and upper lip in which they insert large circular stones having the appearance of mirrors, others still piercing the thick underlip right through to the teeth and hanging therefrom round stones or pieces of gold so heavy that they drag the lip down, giving an extraordinarily repulsive appearance. They wear as clothes a kind of highly coloured shawl, the men wear breech clouts, and on the top half of the body cloaks finely worked and painted after the fashion of Moorish draperies. The common women wear highly coloured robes reaching from the waist to the feet and others which cover only the breast, all the rest of the body being uncovered; but the women of high rank wear bodices of fine cotton, very loose fitting, cut and embroidered after the fashion of the vestment worn by our bishops and abbots. Their food is composed of maize and such cereals as are to be found on the other Islands, *potuoyuca*[5] almost exactly similar to that eaten in Cuba, except that they roast it instead of making it into bread; in addition they have whatever they can obtain by fishing or hunting; and they also breed large numbers of hens similar to those of the mainland which are as big as peacocks. There are a few large towns very passably laid out. The houses in those parts which can obtain stone are of rough masonry and mortar, the rooms being low and small, very much after the Moorish fashion. Where no stone can be got they build their houses of baked bricks, covering them over with plaster and the roofs with a rough kind of thatch. Certain houses belonging to chiefs are quite airy and have a considerable number of rooms; we have seen as many as five inner corridors or *patios* in a single house and its rooms very well laid out around them, each person of importance having his own private servants to wait upon him. The wells and tanks of water are also contained inside, together with rooms for the servants and underservants of which there are many. Each one of the chief men has in front of the entrance of his house a large patio, and some as many as two, three or four, sometimes raised a considerable way off the ground with steps leading up to them, and very well built. In addition they have their mosques, temples and walks, all of very fair size, and in them are the idols which they worship whether of stone, clay or wood, the which they honour and obey in such a manner and with such ceremonies that many sheets of paper would not suffice to give your Majesties a minute and true account of them. These private mosques where they exist are the largest, finest and most elaborately built buildings of any that there are in the town, and as such they keep them very much bedecked with strings of feathers, gaily painted cloths and all manner of finery. And always on the day before they are to begin some important enterprise they burn incense in these temples, and sometimes even sacrifice their own persons, some cutting out their tongues, others their ears, still others slicing their bodies with knives in order to offer to their idols the blood which flows from their wounds; sometimes sprinkling the whole of the temple with blood and throwing it up in the air, and many other fashions of sacrifice they use, so that no important task is undertaken without previous sacrifice having been made. One very horrible and abominable custom they have which should certainly be punished and which we have seen in no other part, and that is that whenever they wish to beg anything of their idols, in order that their petition may find more acceptance, they take large numbers of boys and girls and even of grown men and women and tear out their heart and bowels while still alive, burning them in the presence of those idols, and offering the smoke of such burning as a pleasant sacrifice. Some of us have actually seen this done and they say that it is the most terrible and frightful thing that they have ever seen. Yet the Indians perform this ceremony so frequently that, as we are informed and have in part seen from our own scanty experience since we have been in this land, there is no year passes in which they do not thus kill and sacrifice fifty souls in every such temple, and the practice is general from the island of Cozumel to the region in which we have now settled. Your Majesties can therefore be certain that since the land is large and they seem to have a large number of temples there can be no year (so far as we have been able up to the present to ascertain) in which they have not sacrificed in this manner some three or four thousand souls. Your Majesties may therefore perceive whether it is not their duty to prevent such loss and evil, and certainly it will be pleasing to God if by means of and under the protection of your royal Majesties these peoples are introduced into and instructed in the holy Catholic Faith, and the devotion, trust and hope which they now have in their idols turned so as to repose in the divine power of the true God; for it is certain that if they should serve God with that same faith, fervour and diligence they would work many miracles. And we believe that not without cause has God been pleased to allow this land to be discovered in the name of your royal Majesties, that your Majesties may reap great merit and reward from Him in sending the Gospel to these barbarian people who thus by your Majesties' hands will be received into the true faith; for from what we know of them we believe that by the aid of interpreters who should plainly declare to them the truths of the Holy Faith and the error in which they are, many, perhaps all of them, would very quickly depart from their evil ways and would come to true knowledge, for they live more equably and reasonably than any other of the tribes which we have hitherto come across.

To give your Majesties full and detailed account of this land and people would probably be only to include many errors, for there are many particulars which we have not seen for ourselves but only heard from the natives, and consequently we are only venturing to report those things which can definitely be vouched for as truth. Your Majesties may well command full investigation to be made, and that done, if it so please your Majesties, a true account may be made to our holy Father, that all diligence and good order may be applied to the work of converting these people, since from such conversion so much good fruit may be expected: his Holiness may thus see fit to permit evil and rebellious people having first been warned to be proceeded against and punished as enemies to our holy Catholic Faith, such punishment serving as a further occasion of warning and dread to those who still rebel, and thus bringing them to a knowledge of the truth, and rescuing them from such great evils as are those which they work in the service of the devil: for in addition to those which we have already reported to your Majesties, in which children and men and women are killed and offered in sacrifice, we know and have been informed without room for doubt that all practice the abominable sin of sodomy. In all of which we beg your Majesties to provide as may seem to them most fitting to the service of God and of your royal Majesties and that we who remain here in your service may constantly enjoy your Majesties' favour and protection.

Among other matters which our messengers are instructed to convey to your Majesties there is one in particular which on our behalf they will beg your Majesties, to wit, that no kind of authority, governorship nor judicial powers in these parts be given or granted to Diego Velázquez, Admiral's Deputy in Cuba, and should any such charges have already been given that they should be revoked, since it is not in the interests of the crown that Diego Velázquez or any other person should hold any dominion or privileges whatsoever except it were by the express will of your Majesties in this new land, seeing that it abounds in riches, according to what we have already obtained and what we hope to obtain in the future. Moreover, besides being against your Majesties' interest to bestow any office upon the said Diego Velázquez we know that should he receive such an office, we, your Majesties' subjects who have settled and are living in this land, would be extremely ill-treated by him, for we have good reason to think that what we have already done in your Majesties' service in despatching such gold and silver and precious stones as we have been able to obtain in this land, would be far from well-pleasing to him, as was plainly to be seen in the conduct of four of his servants who happened to be in our town and who, perceiving our intention to send all the treasure to your Majesties, which was done, proclaimed loudly that it were better to send it to Diego Velázquez and other things by which they endeavoured to stir up the people against sending it to your Majesties: for which actions we arrested them and they are still in prison awaiting sentence, of the result of which we will inform your Majesties in due course. Accordingly, from what we have seen of the doings of Diego Velázquez and from our own experience of him we are greatly afraid that if he were to come to this land armed with some authority he would treat us badly, as he has done in Haiti since he had charge of the government, doing justice to no man save according to his own humour, and punishing those whom he chose in passion and anger, not in reason and equity. In such fashion has he destroyed many good men, bringing them to the lowest degree of poverty, refusing them Indian slaves, taking all for himself and likewise all the gold that they have collected without giving them any part in it; and this he could do having bands of ruffians and other aids ready to hand; and indeed since he is the Governor and assessor of taxes no one dares do otherwise than as he desires knowing and dreading that he can utterly destroy him. But of these things your Majesties have no cognizance nor has any report of them ever reached their ears since the representatives who come to your court from the said Island are his servants and fashioned after his pattern, being kept very well content by frequent gifts of Indian slaves from their lord: likewise representatives who come to him from the village communities to discuss matters concerning the country people find it easy to do what he bids them, for he freely gives them Indian slaves to content them; and when these procurators return to their villages and give an account of what they have done, the people's one reply is that poor persons should not be sent as representatives since by giving them a single Indian chieftain Diego Velázquez can get them to do anything he wants. Moreover since the *regidores* and *alcaldes* who possess Indian servants are afraid of Diego Velázquez taking them away from them, they dare not reprimand the representatives who have betrayed their trust by giving way to Diego Velázquez, and in these as in many other ways he carries on in a fine manner. By which your Majesties may see that all those good reports coming from the Island concerning Diego Velázquez and the rewards asked on his behalf simply represent so many Indian slaves which he has given to the various procurators and not that the village councils are contented or desire any such rewards for him, for they would prefer to see the procurators punished.

Since the above complaints were notorious to all

those residing or dwelling in the Rica-Villa of Vera Cruz, they joined with the procurator of this council and begged and required us by a signed declaration that in their name we should entreat your Majesties not to confide such offices nor any of them to the said Diego Velázquez, but rather that he should be required to furnish an account of his government and should be removed from the office which he now holds in Cuba, for if such account were made the truth of this matter would be plain and evident. We therefore beg your Majesties to appoint an examining judge that the whole matter which we have related to your Majesties may be examined by him as concerns the island of Cuba as also other parts, for it is our intention to sift the matter that your Majesties may see whether it is just or right that he should hold royal offices in these parts or in those other parts where he resides at present.

The procurator, citizens and inhabitants of this town have also begged us in their name to entreat your Majesties to appoint Hernando Cortés Captain and Chief Justice of your Majesties and to give him their royal seal and licence, that he may continue justice and good government amongst us until this land is conquered and subject, or such time as may please your Majesties, knowing him to be a person well fitted for such a post. The which request and entreaty we send by the hands of our representatives to your Majesties humbly begging them both this and all other favours which may be asked by the said representatives, and that they may hold us as their very loyal subjects as we have been in the past and shall ever be.

Finally the gold, silver, jewels, bucklers and clothes which we send your Majesties by the hands of our representatives, over and above the fifth which belongs to your Majesties by right, are offered as a token of loyalty by the Captain Hernando Cortés and the members of this council, all of which things are attested in the enclosed list by the said representatives as your Majesties may see.[6]

From the Rica-Villa of Vera Cruz the 10th of July 1519.

THE SECOND LETTER

*The Second Despatch of Hernando Cortés to the Emperor :
sent from Segura de la Frontera on the 30th of
October, 1520.*

Most High Mighty and Catholic Prince, Invincible
Emperor, and our Sovereign Liege:

By the boat which left New Spain on the
16th of July 1519 I sent your Majesty a long and
particular account of all that had occurred up to that
time in the new land from the time of my first arrival
here. Which account Alonso Hernández Puerto-
carrero and Francisco de Montejo brought to you,
as representatives of the city of Vera Cruz, which town
I founded in your Majesty's name. And from that
time not having had the opportunity (as also lacking
vessels and being occupied in the conquest and pacification of the land and hearing moreover nothing of the
said ship and envoys), I have omitted to send a further
account to your Majesty of what has since been
done: for which omission God knows how grieved I
have been. For I am desirous that your Majesty
should know of matters concerning this land, which
is so great and marvellous that, as I wrote in my
former letter, your Majesty may well call himself
Emperor of it with no less reason and title than
he now does of Germany, which by the grace of
God your Majesty possesses. And since to attempt
to describe in detail even those things alone which
are worthy of description in these new lands and
dominions of your Majesty were an endless task, I
must beg your Majesty to pardon me if I fail to give
as lengthy an account as I ought; for neither my own
forces nor the amount of time which I can at the
moment command would suffice me for the task. In

short I will endeavour to tell your Majesty the truth with as little falsehood as I can and particularly that which it is necessary your Majesty should know at the present moment. And I must also beg your Majesty to pardon me if I do not always specify time and place with any great certainty, or omit the names of certain cities and towns as also of their lords, who have offered their services to your Majesty and acknowledged themselves as his subjects and vassals. For a late misfortune, of which as I proceed your Majesty shall have full details, caused me to lose all the writings and deeds which I have made with the natives of these lands and many other belongings.

In my former letter, most excellent Prince, I informed your Majesty of all the towns and villages which up to that time had offered their services and which I held as subject and conquered. And I also mentioned that I had had news of a great ruler named Muteczuma who according to the reckoning of the natives lived from ninety to a hundred leagues from the coast and port where I had landed. And that, moreover, confiding in the power of the Almighty and with the royal name of your Majesty behind me, I intended to advance and see him wherever he might be found: and I even call to mind offering, so far as this lord was concerned, what was far beyond my unaided powers, for I promised your Majesty that I would bring him either dead or in chains if he would not submit himself subject to your Majesty's crown.

With this avowed intention and aim I left the city of Cempoal, which I named Sevilla, on the sixteenth of August with fifteen horsemen and three hundred foot as well accoutred for war as my resources and the short space of time would permit. In the town of Vera Cruz itself I left one hundred and fifty men with a dozen horse busied in building the fortress which is now nearly finished; and the whole province of Cempoal with the neighbouring mountains I left under the charge of the same town; the province includes as many as fifty thousand warriors and fifty villages and strongholds, all very secure and of peaceable disposition, and as certain and loyal subjects of your Majesty at the present moment as they have ever been: for they became subjects of that same Muteczuma as I have been informed but little time past and that by force; but on hearing from me of your Majesty and of his great and royal state they declared themselves willing to be the subjects of your Majesty and my friends, begging me to defend them from that lord who ruled them by force and tyranny, taking their children to kill and sacrifice them to his idols and giving them other grievous causes for complaint of which they informed me. But since that time they have been ever sure and loyal servants to your Majesty and I think they will ever remain so having been delivered from the tyranny of Muteczuma and always being treated with kindness and consideration by myself. Moreover for the greater security of those who remain in the city I brought with me several of their chief men together with other persons who were of no small service to me on the way.

Now, as I believe I wrote to your Majesty, certain of those in my company who were friends and servants of Diego Velázquez were vexed at what I did in your Majesty's service, and indeed certain of them were desirous of leaving me and quitting the land, in particular four Spaniards, by name, Juán Escudero, Diego Cermeño, Gonzalo de Ungría, pilots, and Alonso Peñate. These men, as they afterwards confessed, had decided to seize a brig which was in the port together with a certain amount of provisions in the way of bread and salt pork, kill the captain and set sail for Cuba to inform Diego Velázquez of the vessel which I was sending to your Majesty, what it contained and the route which it was to take, so that

Velázquez might send out ships to intercept it, which indeed on getting to hear by other means of its departure he did: for, as I have been informed, he dispatched a light caravel after my vessel which would have captured it had it not already passed the ſtrait of the Bahamas. These men confessed moreover that there were others who had the same design of informing Diego Velázquez of the treasure ship's departure. In view of their confessions I punished them according to the law and (as it seemed to me) the exigencies of the moment and the furtherance of your Majeſty's intereſts. Further, in addition to those who desired to quit the land because they were friends or servants of Diego Velázquez there were others who seeing the great extent of the land, its natives, their manners and numbers, so large in comparison with so few Spaniards, were of the same mind. Accordingly, thinking that if I left the ships there they would make off with them and leave me praćtically alone, by which had been prevented the great service which has been done to God and to your Majeſty in this land, I found a means under the pretence that the ships were no longer navigable to pile them up on the shore. On this all abandoned any hope of leaving the land and I set out relieved from the suspicion that once my back was turned I should be deserted by the men whom I had left behind in the town.

Eight or ten days after having broken up the ships on the coaſt and having already left Vera Cruz for Cempoal, which is four leagues diſtant, to pursue my march inland, news came to me from the town that four vessels were scouring the coaſt; the captain whom I had left in Vera Cruz went out to them, and they informed him that they belonged to Francisco de Garay, Lieutenant and Governor of the Island of Jamaica, and were on a voyage of discovery. My captain thereupon told them that I had settled this land in the name of your Majesty and had founded a town but a mile away from where their ships were riding, that he could accompany them thither and inform me of their coming, and would provide them with anything that they might need, himself offering to guide their ships into the harbour which he pointed out to them. They replied that they had already taken note of the harbour, for they had passed in front of it, and would do as he advised. The captain thereupon returned in his boat, but the ships did not follow him nor venture into the harbour, but were still sailing along the coast, no man knowing what they intended to do. On receiving this news from the captain I immediately returned to the town of Vera Cruz, where I was informed the ships were anchored some three miles down the coast and that no one had as yet landed. From there, accompanied by a few men, I went towards the coast to have speech with the strangers, and was hardly arrived within a league of them when I met three men coming from the ship, among whom was one who told me he was a notary and had brought the other two to act as witnesses to a certain document which the captain had ordered him to present to me: the document set forth for my information that he had discovered land and desired to settle it; he therefore bade me come to an agreement with him as to boundaries since he wished to make his settlement some five miles down the coast past Nauthla, a city some twelve leagues from Vera Cruz and now known as Almería. I bade these men tell their captain to come to the harbour of Vera Cruz where we would confer together so that I might know on what venture he was come. And if his ships or crew had need of anything I would help them to it as best I could; for since he said he was come on your Majesty's service they were to tell him that I desired nothing better than the occasion of doing some service to your Majesty and that in helping him I deemed that

I should be doing such. They replied that neither the captain nor any of his men would in any wise visit me on land: and thinking they must have done some evil deed on the land that they should be thus chary of meeting me, I ordered my men to hide very secretly (for night had already fallen) near to the coast and immediately opposite the point where their ships lay at anchor, and there remain until noon of the following day, for I thought that the captain or pilot would be sure to land and intended to find out from them what they had done or in what part they had been, and if they had done any harmful deed on the land to send them prisoners to your Majesty, but not a soul left the ship. Accordingly, seeing that they made no attempt to land I stripped off the clothes of those who had come to me with the demand and dressed three of my Spaniards in them, ordering them to go down to the beach and call to the ship. As soon as they were seen a boat put off for the shore containing as many as ten or a dozen men with crossbows and muskets, upon which the Spaniards withdrew a little from the beach to a grove hard by as if seeking its shelter. Four of the party leapt out, two with crossbows and two with muskets, who were immediately surrounded by the men whom I had placed in ambush on the beach and were forthwith captured. One of them, who was the captain of one of the ships, put a match to his flintlock and would have killed the captain (whom I had left in Vera Cruz) but owing to the mercy of God the match missed taking fire. Those who remained in the rowing boat put off to sea and before it had reached the big ships they were already hoisting sail without knowing or caring to know what became of the rest of their party. From those who were taken prisoners I learnt that they had reached a river some thirty leagues down the coast from Almería and had there been favourably received by the natives, had obtained

36

food from them in exchange for wares and had seen them wearing a certain amount of gold but very little. They had however been successful in obtaining nearly three thousand *castellanos*[7] of the metal. They had not landed but had seen certain towns so near to the river bank that they could be easily perceived from the ships. None of the houses was of stone but made entirely of straw, except that the floor was built up smooth by hand. All this later I had more certainly from the great lord Muteczuma and certain natives from that country at his court.

I proceeded, most powerful lord, through the land of Cempoal for three days, in which land I was everywhere received by the natives with great friendliness and hospitality. On the fourth day I entered a province by the name of Sienchimalen, in which there is one town in particular of great strength and built in a position immensely strong by nature, for it stands on the one side of a rocky hill, and to enter it there is but a narrow defile cut in steps, which can only be traversed by men on foot and even they would find it hard enough if the natives should decide to defend the pass. In the plain there are a number of villages and scattered farms with anything from two to three or even five hundred labourers working in them, so that in all there are some five or six thousand warriors; and all this is under the lordship of Muteczuma. Here they received me well and gave me very ample provisions for my journey, saying that they knew well that I was going to see Muteczuma, their lord, and that it was certain that he was my friend since he had sent to tell them that they would please him by welcoming me in every way. I repaid their courtesy, saying that your Majesty had knowledge of their lord, and had ordered me to visit him, which was now my sole intention. Thus I proceeded over a pass which lies at the further end of this province and which we named

Nombre de Dios pass, it being the first we had crossed
in this land. The pass moreover is so rocky and at
such an altitude that there is not one in Spain more
difficult to pass. We crossed, however, in safety and
without any mishap. On the other side of the pass
there are more farms scattered round a fortified town,
Ceycoccnacan, which also belongs to Muteczuma.
We were received here no less well than by the folk
of Sienchimalen and were informed anew of the desires
of their lord which did not differ from what we had been
told before. I likewise left them well contented.

From there I proceeded three days' march through
a desert land uninhabitable on account of its barrenness,
lack of water, and great cold; in which place God
knows what hardships of thirst and hunger were
suffered by my men, and in particular we were assailed
by a whirlwind of hailstones and rain in which I thought
many were like to die of cold: and certain Indians from
Cuba who were scantily clothed did indeed thus perish.
At the end of these three days we crossed another pass
less rocky than the first at the top of which was a
small tower almost like a roadside chapel, in which
certain idols were kept and around which more than a
thousand cartloads of logs neatly cut had been piled,
for which reason we called it the Pass of Wood. Descending from the pass between two very steep ranges
we came down into a valley, well populated though
with folk, as it appeared, who were very poor. Having
proceeded some two leagues through the land without
learning its name we arrived at a flatter part where the
chief of that region seemed to have his dwelling; for the
houses there were the best and finest that we had yet
seen since descending from the mountains, being built
all of stone and very new, and containing many very
fine large living-rooms and finely-built rooms for
sleeping: the valley and town, we learnt from its lord
and people, who received us very hospitably, both bore

the name of Caltanmi. And after speaking with the chief on behalf of your Majesty, telling him the reason of my adventuring into these parts, I enquired whether he were a vassal of Muteczuma or of another persuasion. He, marvelling that I should ask him, replied by demanding who was not a vassal of Muteczuma? meaning by that that he was the lord of all the world. Upon this I hastened to contradict him, setting forth the great power and dominions of your Majesty and informing him that many other and greater lords than Muteczuma were vassals of your Majesty esteeming it no slight honour, and such Muteczuma and all the natives of these lands must also be: therefore I demanded that he should also submit himself as a vassal, for as such he would be honoured and favoured, but on the contrary if he should be unwilling to obey he would be punished. And that he should show himself willing in your royal service I requested him to give me some gold which I would send to your Majesty. To this he replied that he had gold but that he would not give it to me without Muteczuma's orders; on receiving such orders, however, he would give up his gold, his person, and whatsoever he had. To avoid any unpleasantness or mishap in my intent or road I spoke him as fairly as I could telling him that very soon Muteczuma would send to him bidding him give up the gold and what more he had.

Two other chieftains came to see me here who owned farms in that district, one four leagues down the valley the other two leagues further up: they brought me a few golden collars of little weight or value and seven or eight slaves. Having been lodged by the ruler some four or five days I now left him very contented and passed on to the township of the other chieftain, standing as I said two leagues up the valley, and which is called Ixtacamaxtitlan. This township must extend for some three or four leagues along the bank of the

39

little·river which runs through the middle of the valley, the houses being built in a more or less rough line. Perched on an exceptionally lofty ridge is the chieftain's house with as stout fortifications as you may find in the whole of one half of Spain and surrounded in addition with a wall, barbican and ditch: on this ridge there are as many as five or six thousand inhabitants, living in well-built houses and somewhat better off than the people lower down in the valley. I remained three days in this township, both to recover from the hardships which my men suffered in the desert and to await the return of four messengers, natives of Cempoal, who had come with me and whom I had sent from Caltanmi to a great province known as Tlascala which was said to be near us, as indeed it was: they had told me, moreover, that the people of Tlascala were friends of theirs but very deadly enemies of Muteczuma, and they were eager that I should ally myself with the Tlascalans since they were a strong, fierce tribe, their land was surrounded on two sides by that of Muteczuma with whom they had continuous wars, and they would in all probability be delighted to assist me if Muteczuma should decide to oppose me in any way. The aforesaid messengers however did not return during all the time that I was in the valley which was eight days in all; and on asking the principal guides whom I had brought with me from Cempoal the cause of their delay, they replied that they must have gone a long way and could not return so promptly. Upon this, finding that they did not come and being assured by the Cempoal guides in such unequivocal terms of the friendliness and trustworthiness of the people of that province, I departed thence.

At the exit of the valley I found a great wall of rough stone about one and a half times the height of a man, crossing the whole valley from one ridge to the other, about twenty foot broad and with a parapet about a foot and a half broad running its entire length, from which one could fight. The entrance, moreover, was ten paces wide and ran for about thirty yards in the form of a double arc like a ravelin, in such fashion that the entrance turned on itself instead of proceeding straightforwardly. On enquiring the object of this wall I was told that it was built as a frontier between themselves and the province of Tlascala who were enemies of Muteczuma and always at war with him. The inhabitants of the valley begged me, since I was going to visit Muteczuma, their natural lord, not to pass through the land of his enemies, for it might be that they would be evilly disposed and would do me some harm; they themselves would conduct me through territories all acknowledging Muteczuma's sovereignty and in them I should be well received. Those of Cempoal, however, warned me not to do this but to accompany them, for my hosts were only desirous of losing me the friendship of the Tlascalans; Muteczuma's subjects were all evil men and traitors and they would inveigle me into a position from which I could not escape. Since I put more trust in the Cempoallans than in my hosts I took their advice, which was to follow the road to Tlascala proceeding with my men as cautiously as I could. I myself with as many as seven horsemen rode on in front a good half league or more with no presentiment of what afterwards befell us, but in order to spy out the land, so that if anything untoward occurred I should know of it and be in a position to warn and give orders to my men.

Having thus proceeded four leagues over the brow of the hill, two horsemen who had gone on in front of me perceived several Indians wearing the feathers which they are accustomed to wear in time of war, together with swords and shields, who on seeing them immediately set off in flight. As soon as I rode up

I ordered our guide to call to them that they should approach us without fear, and myself rode towards them. There would be about fifteen of them. On this they closed and began to throw javelins, calling out to the rest of their number who were in the valley, and finally attacking us with such fury that they killed two of our horses, wounded three others and likewise two horsemen. At this moment the rest of their company appeared to the number of some four or five thousand Indians. Eight horsemen had now joined me, not counting those who had dismounted when their horses were killed, and we held them, making several charges until the main body of Spaniards should come up, one of the horsemen having been sent back to tell them to do so: in these charges we did them some damage killing between fifty and sixty of them, without receiving any casualties ourselves, since they fought with tremendous fury and recklessness: but as we were all mounted we could charge forwards and backwards through their ranks without danger. On seeing our men draw near, they retired for they were but few[8] and left us the field. Upon this, certain messengers came up claiming to be from the rulers of the province and with them two of the messengers whom I had sent, who declared that their lords had no hand in what had been done, that they were a confederation of townships and that it had been done without their permission; for the which they were deeply grieved and would requite me for the horses which had been killed, for they desired to be my friends, and that I was come in a good hour and would be well received by them. I replied thanking them and telling them that I would hold them as friends and would go as they said. That night I was forced to sleep in a dried-up river bed but a mile beyond where this took place, it being late and my men very tired. I observed the best precautions I could, posting guards and sentinels both on horse and on foot throughout the whole night until day was come, when I took road again, keeping the vanguard and main body well in touch with one another and the swiftest riders in front. On arriving at a small village soon after sunrise the other two messengers came up with us weeping, and informed us that they had been bound and would have been killed had they not escaped during that night. At that moment not two stones' throw away a large number of Indians in full war-dress appeared with a tremendous shout and began to attack us, shooting innumerable arrows and other missiles.

I began to deliver my *requerimiento* in due form by means of the interpreters with me and in the presence of a notary: but the more I endeavoured to admonish them and treat them with peaceable words, the more fiercely they attacked us. Seeing then that demands and protestations were alike useless we began to defend ourselves as we could, and thus they continued attacking us until we were surrounded on all sides by more than a hundred thousand men, with whom we contended throughout the day until an hour before sunset when they retired. In this battle, with the half dozen cannon which I had, five or six muskets and the thirteen horsemen who remained, I did them great damage, without suffering anything worse than the toil and weariness of long hours of fighting without food.

And in this it was plainly manifest that God was fighting on our side, that among so great a multitude of people of such fury and skill in war and with such various arms with which to attack us, we came off so free. That night we made ourselves secure in a small tower containing their idols which stood on a slight eminence and then at very early dawn I sallied out leaving two hundred men in the camp and all the guns, and since I was now attacking I took with me the horsemen and a hundred Spaniards on foot together with four hundred Indians from among those whom I brought from Cempoal and three hundred from Ixtacamaxtitlan. And before they had time to gather together I burnt some five or six little villages, each of about a hundred inhabitants, took about four hundred prisoners both men and women, and regained the camp fighting with them but without receiving any casualties. Next day at daybreak more than a hundred and thirty-nine thousand men advanced upon our camp, so many that they seemed to cover the whole plain, and with such determination that several of them succeeded in forcing an entrance and came to handgrips with my men: we marched out against them and by the good will of our Lord helping us in four hours we had cleared a space so that they could not attack the camp directly although they still made a few charges in other parts of the field. And so we were fighting until darkness came and they retired.

Next day I again sallied out in a different direction before daybreak without being perceived by them and with my horsemen, a hundred foot and my faithful Indians, burnt more than ten townships, in some of which there were over three thousand houses, and the inhabitants there fought against me, for no other Indians came up. And as we bore the banner of the cross and were fighting for our faith and in the service of your Majesty, God gave us such victory in your Majesty's cause that we killed many Indians without ourselves receiving any hurt: and shortly after noon, by which time the forces of the Indians had gathered together from all sides, we were back again in camp with the victory already won.

On the following day messengers came to me from the chieftains saying that they desired to be vassals of your Majesty and my friends, and begging me to forgive their past evil doing. They brought food and certain feather ornaments which they wear and value highly. I told them in reply that they had done very wrong but that it pleased me to be their friend and pardon them what they had done. On the morrow nearly fifty Indians came up who, it appeared, were men of some importance among them, saying that they were bringing us provisions, but paying close attention to the exits and entrances of the camp and certain huts in which we were living. The Cempoallan Indians came to me and bade me be warned that these men were evilly disposed, and had come to spy and find out how they could defeat us and (as it seemed very certain to them) for no other reason. I took one of them carefully aside without the others perceiving it and closeting him with myself and one or two interpreters threatened him that I might get the truth from him: upon which he confessed that Sicutengal who is the captain of this province was stationed with a large force beyond the range of hills which fronts the camp in order to fall upon us that night, for, said they, they had already attempted an attack by day and had nothing by it, and they would now try by night when their men would not fear the horses nor the cannon shot and swords. He confessed further that they had been sent to spy out our camp and those places in which it could be entered and in what way our straw huts might be set alight and burnt. Forthwith I took another of the Indians and questioned him in like manner, upon which he confessed almost in the same words, and I proceeded thus to threaten five or six, and they all confirmed these words. Seeing this I ordered the whole fifty to be arrested and their hands cut off, which done I sent them back to tell their lord that night and day whenever and however many times he should come against us he should see what manner of men we are.

With this I fortified the camp as strongly as I could, placed my men at such posts as seemed best and remained thus on guard until sunset: and as night was falling the Indians began to descend the valleys on either side of us, thinking that their advance to surround us and thus be nearer to execute their plan was unperceived. But as I was forewarned I saw them, and it occurred to me that to allow them to approach the camp would be extremely dangerous, for in the night being unable to see my preparations they would approach without fear, and moreover, the Spaniards being unable to see them might in certain instances lack their usual courage in fighting; above all I was afraid lest they should set fire to any part of the camp: for any such accident would have been so damaging to us that not one of us would have escaped: accordingly I determined to go out against them with all my horse either to await them or put them to rout in such wise that they should not reach the camp. And thus it fell out that when they learnt that we were advancing on horseback to attack them, without a moment's delay or so much as a cry they took to the cornfields which covered the whole country and lightened themselves somewhat of the provisions they were carrying for feasting and triumphing over us if they should succeed in obtaining a complete victory: thus they retreated that night and left us unharmed. For several days after this I did not leave camp save to visit the immediate neighbourhood in order to prevent the advance of certain Indians who engaged in shouting and some slight skirmishing.

Having thus rested somewhat I rode out one night, after going the rounds of the first guard, with a hundred foot, the Indians and my own horsemen as before, and a league from the camp no less than five of the horses and mares fell and could in no wise proceed further, upon which I had to send them back to camp: and although all my companions urged me to turn back on account of the evil omen yet I held on my course, considering that God is more powerful than nature. Before dawn I lighted upon two towns in which I killed many people, but abstained from burning houses, since the flames would have betrayed my presence to other towns which were hard by: and just as dawn was breaking I fell upon another town so great that, as I afterwards found by a later examination, it contained more than twenty thousand houses. I attacked it so suddenly that all rushed out unarmed, the women and children naked, into the streets, and I was beginning to do them no small hurt. Upon this, seeing that they could make no resistance certain chieftains of the town came running up to me begging me to do them no more harm, for they were willing to be vassals of your Majesty and my friends, and saw plainly that they were to blame in having refused to believe me; but from that time onward I should see that they would always do what I should bid them in your Majesty's name, and they would be your Majesty's very loyal subjects. More than four thousand of them now came up to me desiring peace, and drew me aside to an excellent dish of food: and thus I left them pacified, and returning to the camp found all the men that I had left in it greatly terrified thinking that some peril had overtaken me, when they saw the horses return the night before: but on hearing of the victory which God had been pleased to give us and how I had left those people in peace they were right glad: for I can bear witness to your Majesty that there was not one amongst us who was not heartily afraid at finding himself so far in the interior of the country among so many and such warlike people and so destitute of help from any part. So much so that with my own ears I have heard groups of men saying almost publicly that it was Pedro Carbonero[9] who had put them in a hole from which there was no getting out. Nay, more: I overheard some fellows in a hut saying (they did not see I was

47

there) that I was mad to get myself into a position from which I could not escape, but that they were not going to stay in it, for they were going to make their way back to the coast, and if I liked to come back with them, well and good, and if not, they would abandon me. Many times indeed they begged me to go back, but I heartened them saying that they should remember that they were the subjects of your Majesty and that we had the opportunity of gaining for your Majesty the greatest kingdoms and dominions in the world. And in addition to doing that, as Christians we were obliged to fight against the enemies of our Faith, and were gaining treasure for ourselves in the other world by doing so, and winning the greatest honour and glory that any men had ever won up to our own times. Let them consider that God was on our side, and to Him nothing is impossible, which they might plainly see by the victories we had already won, in which so many of our enemies had fallen, but not a single one of ourselves. And other things I said to them of this nature, heartened by which and your Majesty's royal favour they recovered their spirits, and I brought them to my opinion and to doing what I was set upon, which was to complete the discovery which I had begun.

On the following day at ten o'clock Sicutengal, the captain general of this province came to me, with as many as fifty of the principal citizens and begged me on his part and on that of Magiscatzin, the ruler of the whole province of Tlascala, and many other chieftains, that I would be pleased to admit them to the royal service of your Majesty and to my friendship, and would pardon them their past wrong-doing, for they knew not whom we were, and had now made trial of all their forces both by day and night attacks in order to avoid being the subjects of any man: for at no time had this province ever been subject, nor had they ever acknowledged a lord, but had always lived free and exempt from time immemorial; and had ever defended themselves against the great power of Muteczuma, his father and grandfathers, who held all the land in subjection, but them they had never succeeded in subduing, although surrounding their territory on every side so that no one could go out of it in any place: for which reason they ate no salt since there was none in their land and they could not venture abroad to buy it in other parts, nor did they wear any clothes of cotton since on account of the cold cotton did not grow in their land, and many other things they lacked on account of their being thus shut in, but the same they suffered cheerfully in return for being subject to no man. They had therefore wished to hold out against me in like manner, and to such end, as they had said, had exhausted all their forces, but they now saw clearly that neither those nor any traps which they had been able to devise would any longer suffice them; and hence they would rather become subjects of your Majesty than die and see their houses, their women and children all destroyed. I spoke them peaceably, telling them they should know that they had themselves to blame for the damage they had suffered, and that I had come to their land thinking that I was coming among friends, for so the Cempoallans had assured me they were and desired to be. I had therefore sent on my messengers ahead to let them know that I was coming and that I desired their friendship: but without replying to me they had attacked me as I came all unsuspectingly along the road and had killed three of my horses and wounded others: on top of this, having first fought with me they then sent messengers saying that what had been done was without their license and consent, certain tribes having taken the offensive unbeknown to them: but they themselves had punished them and desired my friendship.   I, thinking it true, had told them that it pleased me well, and would visit them the next day safely in their houses as in the houses of my friends, but they again had waylaid me and fought against me throughout the day until nightfall, notwithstanding that I had saluted them peaceably; and I brought to their memory all the ills that they had done against me, and many other things which I omit from fear of fatiguing your Majesty.   Finally they offered themselves as subjects and vassals of your Majesty in his royal service, and offered likewise their persons and fortunes, and this service they did and have done up to the present, and I think they will ever do so, from what I have to relate to your Majesty hereafter.

I remained in camp, not stirring from it for the next six or seven days for I dared not yet trust them, although they asked me to come to the great city in which all the chief men of the province resided: on the chiefs thus coming to beg me to enter the city, saying that I should be better entertained and provided there with all necessary things, for they were ashamed to see me so ill lodged seeing that they held me as their friend and we were both vassals of your Majesty, I at last yielded to their entreaties and came into the town which is about six leagues from my camp. The city is indeed so great and marvellous that though I abstain from describing many things about it, yet the little that I shall recount is, I think, almost incredible.   It is much larger than Granada and much better fortified.   Its houses are as fine and its inhabitants far more numerous than those of Granada when that city was captured.   Its provisions and food are likewise very superior—including such things as bread, fowl, game, fish and other excellent vegetables and produce which they eat.   There is a market in this city in which more than thirty thousand people daily are occupied in buying and selling, and this in addition to other similar shops which there are in all parts of the city. Nothing is lacking in this market of what they are wont to use, whether utensils, garments, footwear or the like. There are gold, silver and precious stones, and jewellers' shops selling other ornaments made of feathers, as well arranged as in any market in the world. There is earthenware of many kinds and excellent quality, as fine as any in Spain. Wood, charcoal, medicinal and sweet smelling herbs are sold in large quantities. There are booths for washing your hair and barbers to shave you: there are also public baths. Finally, good order and an efficient police system are maintained among them, and they behave as people of sense and reason: the foremost city of Africa cannot rival them.

The province contains many wide-spreading fertile valleys all tilled and sown, no part of it being left wild, and measures some ninety leagues in circumference. The order of government so far observed among the people resembles very much the republics of Venice, Genoa and Pisa for there is no supreme overlord. There are many chieftains all of whom reside in the capital city, the common people being tillers of the land and vassals of these chieftains, each of whom possesses certain land of his own. It is to be supposed that they have some system of justice for punishing wrongdoers, for a native of this province stole some gold from a Spaniard, and on my informing Magiscatzin, who is the foremost chieftain, a search was made and the thief was pursued to the city of Cholula which is near by, the gold was recovered and the man handed over to me for punishment. I thanked them for the diligence they had shown in the matter, but told them that since I was in their land I should prefer them to punish the thief according to their custom, since it was an affair with which I did not wish to meddle. They thanked me, took the thief, and after a public announcement of his crime led him through the great market and there placed him at the foot of a sort of stage which is in the middle of it: the crier ascended the stage and in a loud voice again rehearsed his crime, which being perceived by all they struck him a few blows with great clubs on the head and so killed him. Moreover we have seen many other criminals in prisons for theft and other evil doing. According to a rough census which I had made, there are in this province some hundred and fifty thousand people, who together with another smaller adjoining province known as Guajocingo live all after this fashion without a supreme overlord: those of Guajocingo are no less vassals of your Majesty than the Tlascalans.

At the time, most catholic Lord, that I was encamped outside the city and while still at war with the natives, six of Muteczuma's chief vassals came to me with some two hundred men in their service, to tell me that he would be very willing to be a vassal of your Majesty and my friend, and that I should bethink me what would be fitting for him to give your Majesty every year as tribute, whether in gold, silver and jewels, or slaves, stuffs and other such things as he had, for he would give all these on condition that I did not enter his land, the which he was unwilling I should do on account of its great sterility and lack of food, by reason of which I and all those who accompanied me would suffer hardship: with these chieftains he sent me a thousand *pesos* of gold and the same number of cotton garments such as they wear. The chiefs remained with me until the fighting was over and had good opportunity of seeing what my men could do, and later both the conditions of peace that were laid down for the province and the desire of all both high and low to enlist themselves as subjects of your Majesty. All this, as they showed, pleased them but little, and they tried in many ways to embroil me with the natives, saying that they did not speak the truth when they avowed friendship, and were only making such assertions in order to plan some treachery in safety. The natives of the province on the other hand were always advising me not to trust Muteczuma's vassals, whom, they said, were traitors and always dealt treacherously, for by no other means had they subjected all the land. This, said they, was their advice which they gave as true friends and persons who had had long experience of Muteczuma's men. I was not a little pleased to see such discord between the two, since it seemed highly propitious to my plan, and I should thus in all probability discover a means to subject them more swiftly: as a common proverb runs—*De monte, etc.*[10]: I even recalled to mind the passage of the Evangelist which says: "Every kingdom divided against itself is brought to desolation." Accordingly I continued to treat with both one and the other, thanking each in secret for the advice he gave me, and professing to regard each with greater friendship than the other.

After having stayed more than twenty days in the city, Muteczuma's messengers, who were still with me, asked me to go to a town about six leagues off from Tlascala and called Cholula, whose inhabitants were friends of Muteczuma, their lord. There we should learn the will of Muteczuma whether I should visit his land or not, and some of them would return to speak with him and tell him what I had declared to them and would bring back a reply to me. The head men of the Tlascalans, however, on hearing of what was proposed and that I had agreed to go to the aforesaid city came to me in great grief begging me in no wise to go, for certain treachery was being prepared in that city by which both I and all my companions would be killed: to that end Muteczuma had sent fifty thousand men from his own country which borders the city on one side and now held them in garrison but two leagues off: the royal road, moreover, which was the one usually used had been barred and a new one made with many pits containing sharp stakes set up on end and then covered over in such fashion that the horses would fall therein and be maimed: many of the streets in the city, they added, had been walled up, and great quantities of stones piled up on the flat roofs, so that having once entered the city they could take us and overcome us at their pleasure: and as proof of what they said I was to consider that the rulers of that town had never come to have speech with me, though they were close at hand, and nearer than those of Guajocingo who nevertheless had come: let me but send to speak with them and I should see that they would refuse to come. I thanked them for their advice and asked them to give me messengers who would speak with them on my behalf. This they did, and I sent to the rulers asking them to come to see me, for I wished to speak with them on behalf of your Majesty and tell them of the cause of my visit to this land. The messengers departed and gave my message to the rulers of the city, upon which two or three persons of slight authority returned with them saying that they came on behalf of their lords who were prevented from coming by sickness. The Tlascalans assured me that this was a trick, that the messengers were men of no importance and that I should not on any account set out until the chief men of the city had visited me. I spoke to the representatives and told them that it was not fitting for the ambassador of so mighty a prince as your Majesty to deliver his message to such persons as themselves and that even their masters little merited to hear it; so that if within three days they had not appeared before me to render obedience to your Majesty and offer themselves as his vassals, I should march against them and destroy them, and deal with them as with rebels who were unwilling to submit to your Majesty's dominion. And to this end I sent them an official order signed by myself and a notary, setting forth a full account of your Majesty's royal person and of my arrival, declaring that all these parts and other greater lands and kingdoms belong to your Majesty, and that those who were willing to be his vassals would be honoured and rewarded, whilst on the other hand those who were rebellious would be punished according to the law.

On the morrow some if not all of the chief men of the aforesaid city came to me saying that the reason for their not coming before was that the Tlascalans were their enemies and they dared not enter their land. They were persuaded, moreover, that I had heard evil things spoken of them which I was not to believe since it was from the lips of their enemies that I had heard it, and that if I would come to their city I should recognise the falseness of what I had been told and the truth of what they now declared. Moreover, from that time forth they gave and offered themselves as vassals to your Majesty which they would ever be, serving your Majesty and giving as tribute whatsoever he might command. All these things a notary took down by means of the interpreter whom I had with me. Finally I determined to go with them, both to avoid any show of weakness and because I thought from that place to carry on negotiations with Muteczuma, since as I have said his land bordered the city, and travellers passed freely along the road from one state to the other without any search being insisted upon.

The Tlascalans were grieved at my decision and warned me repeatedly that I was making a mistake, but seeing that they had become vassals of your Majesty and my friends they were willing to accompany me and help me in whatever adventure might offer itself: so that in spite of my forbidding it and begging them to desist, for there was no need of them, yet nearly a hundred thousand well-armed men followed me to within two leagues of the city: and there after a great deal of persuasion on my part they left me, except for some five or six thousand. That night I camped in a dry river bed in order that my late hosts might return without causing scandal in Cholula and since it was now growing late I did not wish to enter the city at so advanced an hour. Early next morning they came out of the city to receive me on the road with great noise of trumpets and drums, and many of their so-called priests dressed in the vestments they wear in the temples and singing in the same fashion: with much ceremony they brought us to the entrance of the city and lodged us in fine buildings where all the men of my company were much at their ease. Thither they brought us food though in no very great quantity. On the way we came across many signs of that which the Tlascalans had warned us against; for we found the royal road closed and another made, a few pits though not many, some of the streets blocked and large quantities of stones on all the flat roofs of the houses. This put us more on our guard and determined us to act with greater caution.

I found there certain messengers of Muteczuma who were come to speak with the Cholulans. To me they said nothing more than that they were come to learn from our hosts what had been decided upon between us in order that they might report the same to their lord: they thus departed after having spoken with them, including one who had been with me in Tlascala and was the chief among them. During the three days I was there they provided us with very indifferent food which grew worse each day, and the nobles and chief men of the city hardly ever came to speak with me. And being somewhat perplexed by this I learnt through the agency of my interpreter, a native Indian girl[11] who came with me from Putunchan (a great river of which I informed your Majesty in my first letter), that a girl of the city had told her that a large force of Muteczuma's men had assembled nearby, and that the citizens themselves, having removed their wives, children and clothes, intended to attack us suddenly and leave not one of us alive. The native girl had added that if she wanted to escape she had better go with her, and she would look after her. On hearing this I took one of the natives of the city secretly aside without anyone perceiving it and interrogated him: whereupon he confirmed all that the native girl and the Tlascalans had told me. On the strength of such evidence and the signs of preparation that I perceived, I determined to surprise rather than be surprised, and sending for some nobles of the city I told them that I wished to speak with them and assembled them all in a certain room; and meantime I ordered that our men should be on the alert and that at the sound of a musket shot they should fall upon a large number of Indians who were either close to or actually inside our quarters. So it was done; for having got the nobles into the room I left them, leapt on my horse and ordered the musket to be fired, upon which we fell upon the Indians in such fashion that within two hours more than three thousand of them lay dead. And that your Majesty may see how prepared they were, suffice to say that before I left our quarters the Indians had all the streets posted and their men ready armed, although as we took them by surprise it was no difficult matter to rout them, especially without their leaders whom I had already taken prisoner; I also set fire to several towers and fortified houses in which they defended themselves and continued to do us damage. In this manner I carried the fight through the city, leaving our quarters which were very strong under a stout guard for nearly five hours, until I had driven the natives out of the greater part of the city, in which task I was helped by some five thousand of the Tlascalan Indians and three hundred from Cempoal. Upon this, returning to our quarters I demanded from the nobles whom I had captured for what cause they desired to kill me thus treacherously. They replied that they were not to blame, for the Indians of Culua who are the vassals of Muteczuma had urged them to it, and Muteczuma himself had fifty thousand men ready armed at a place which as it afterwards appeared was not above a league and a half away to accomplish the project. But now that they saw how they had been deceived, if I would permit (said they) one or two of them to leave the city they would recall the people, including women and children, and household belongings which they had removed outside and if I would but pardon them their fault they swore that henceforward no one should thus deceive them and they would ever be sure and loyal vassals of your Majesty and my good friend. Upon this having sternly reprehended their evil doing I released two of them and by the morrow the city was full of women and children, all going about in perfect safety, as if the past events had never occurred. I then set free all the other nobles whom I had imprisoned and they promised to serve your Majesty very loyally. By the end of fifteen to twenty days the city was become again so peaceful and so populous that the absence of any of its citizens seemed to pass unnoticed, markets and business generally being carried on through the city as before. Finally I persuaded the people of this city, Cholula, and the Tlascalans to become friends, for they had been so before, and it was but little time since Muteczuma had enticed the Cholulans by gifts into friendship with him and made them enemies of the Tlascalans.

This city of Cholula is situated in a plain, with

about twenty thousand houses within its walls and as many in the suburbs outside. It is self-governing and has definite boundaries. The people are on the whole better clothed than those of Tlascala for the higher class of citizens all wear a kind of Moorish cloak over their other clothes, in shape, cloth and trimming, very similar to those seen in Africa, but with this difference that they have slits through which the hands can be thrust. All have been very loyal subjects of your Majesty since the revolt and very obedient to what I have had occasion to command them in your Majesty's name; and I think they will continue to be so. The city is very fertile, with many small holdings, for there is an abundance of land which is for the most part well irrigated, and indeed its exterior is as fine as any in Spain, for while built on the flat it has many towers. I can myself vouch to your Majesty to having counted more than four hundred of them from the height of a little mosque, and they were all turrets of mosques. The city is better fitted for Spaniards to live in than any other I have seen on our journey from the coast, for it possesses certain common lands and streams for pasturing cattle such as we have seen nowhere else; the number of people in these parts is usually so great that there is not a palm's breadth of land which is not tilled: even so, many suffer from lack of bread, and there are many poor who beg from the rich in streets, houses and market places just as they do in Spain and other civilized countries.

I spoke to the messengers of Muteczuma who were with me of the treachery which was planned against me in that city, telling them that the rulers insisted that it had been done by Muteczuma's advice, but that I could not think that such a powerful prince would send me such honoured messengers to declare his friendship and at the same time covertly attempt to injure me by another's hand, so that if things did not turn out as he had thought he might escape the blame. For if such were the case and he did not keep his word with me I should change my intent, so that instead of coming to his land, as now, desirous of seeing and speaking with him as a friend, holding conference together in all peace and reasonableness, I should enter his territory at war, doing him all the damage that I could as to an enemy; the which would grieve me not a little, for I should always prefer to have him as a friend and take his advice on all things which should require to be done in this land. His men replied that they had been with me many days and knew no more of what had been planned than those within the city until after it had actually happened; but they could not believe that it had been done by the advice or consent of Muteczuma, and begged me before deciding to abandon his friendship and make war upon him, that I would inform myself well of the matter, giving permission to one of them to go and speak with Muteczuma on condition that he would return very quickly. This city is about twenty leagues away from Muteczuma's palace. I accordingly gave permission for one of them to go and within six days he returned together with the first one who had gone, bringing me ten plates of gold, fifteen hundred different garments, and great store of chickens and *panicap*[12], a kind of liquor which they drink. They reported that Muteczuma was much grieved to hear of the rising attempted in Cholula and especially that I should think that it had been by his consent or advice; for he assured me that it was not so, that the soldiers in garrison there were certainly his, but that they had been induced to revolt by the Cholulans themselves. In time to come I should see by his actions whether what he had sent to tell me was true or not, but still he begged that I would not trouble myself to visit his land, for it was sterile and we should suffer much privation: finally, wherever I might be I was to send to him for what I required and he would dispatch it to me in good measure. I replied that my visit to his land could not be put off, for I was bound to send an account of it to your Majesty, but that I believed what he said; so that since it was essential that I should visit him he should make the best of it and not oppose my coming in any way, for to do so would be to bring great danger upon himself and great regret to me for anything that might subsequently happen. Seeing that I was determined to visit him and his land he replied by messenger saying that I was welcome and that he would await my coming in the great city in which he lived and sent me a large number of his troops since I was already entering upon his territory. These men intended to lead me by a certain road on which they had prepared some kind of ambush, as was afterwards apparent, for many Spaniards whom I sent forwards to examine the land saw signs of it, and the road itself was intercepted by so many bridges and difficult places that had we gone by it the plan might very easily have been carried out. But as it has pleased God always to lead the affairs of your Majesty since your Majesty's childhood, and I and my companions were venturing upon your royal service, another way was made manifest to us which although somewhat rough was less dangerous than that by which they wished us to travel, and it fell out in this wise:

Eight leagues from this city of Cholula there are two marvellously high mountains whose summits still at the end of August are covered with snow so that nothing else can be seen of them. From the higher of the two[13] both by day and night a great volume of smoke often comes forth and rises up into the clouds as straight as a staff, with such force that although a very violent wind continuously blows over the mountain range yet it cannot change the direction of the column. Since I have ever been desirous of sending your Majesty a very particular account of everything that I met with in this land, I was eager to know the secret of this which seemed to me not a little marvellous, and accordingly sent ten men such as were well fitted for the expedition with certain natives to guide them to find out the secret of the smoke, where and how it arose. These men set out and made every effort to climb to the summit but without success on account of the thickness of the snow, the repeated wind storms in which ashes from the volcano were blown in their faces and also the great severity of the temperature, but they reached very near the top, so near in fact that being there when the smoke began to rush out, they reported that it did so with such noise and violence that the whole mountain seemed like to fall down: thereupon they descended, bringing a quantity of snow and icicles for us to see, which seemed a novelty indeed, it being so hot everywhere in these parts according to the opinion of explorers up to now: especially since this land is said to be in the twentieth degree of altitude where great heat is always found. On their way to this mountain, as it happened, they came across a road, and on asking the natives whither it led they replied to Culua and that it was a good road, whereas the other by which the Culuans wished to take us was not. My men proceeded along it until they came to the two mountains between which it runs, and from the pass they looked down upon the plains of Culua, the great city of Tenochtitlan and the lakes which surround it, which I shall describe later to your Majesty, and returned very joyful at having discovered such a good road; at which God knows how relieved I was. Upon this I told the messengers of Muteczuma who were to guide me to his country, that I wished to go by that road since it was shorter

than the one they spoke of. They replied that I
was perfectly right, it was shorter and a better road,
but that they did not use it because going by it one
day's march would lie through the land of the Guajocingo who were their enemies and that thus we
should lack those necessary provisions which would
be supplied to us in Muteczuma's territory, but that
since I was set on it they would arrange for provisions
to be sent out from the city to us on the road. And
in such manner we set out still fearing that they would
attempt to practise some deceit upon us, but as we
had already publicly declared our road to lie thither
I thought it well not to abandon it or retrace our
steps lest they should think that we lacked spirit to
attempt it.

Two days after leaving Cholula we climbed the pass
between the two mountains which I have already
described, from which we could discern the province
of Chalco belonging to Muteczuma, and on descending it, two leagues before arriving at any town, I
came upon some fine newly erected buildings, large
enough to lodge both me and all my men very comfortably for the night, although I was accompanied by
over four thousand Indians from Tlascala, Guajocingo, Cholula and Cempoal; moreover there was
abundance of food, great fires and plenteous supply
of wood in all the lodging houses, for the weather was
very cold by reason of the nearness of the two mountains and the snow with which they were covered.

There came to speak with me here certain persons
who appeared to be chiefs, among whom was one said
to be the brother of Muteczuma. They brought me
some three thousand *pesos* of gold, and on behalf of
him who had sent them begged me to return and not
to put myself out to visit his city, for, they said, his
land was lacking in provisions, the road was extremely
bad, and all was under water so that one could only

enter it by canoes, together with many other hindrances which they put in the way of my going. They had orders to find out all that I lacked, for Muteczuma, their lord, would willingly give it to me: and they themselves would join to give to me each year a certain amount, which they would bring to me at the coast or wherever else I desired. I received them well and gave them several gifts from Spain such as they prize highly, especially to him whom they declared to be the brother of Muteczuma, and as to their embassy I replied that if it were in my hand to return I would do it to please Muteczuma, but that I was come to this land on the command of your Majesty and that what your Majesty had chiefly desired me to give him an account of was this same Muteczuma and his great city, of both of which your Majesty had long had knowledge. They should therefore tell him from my part that he should be reconciled to my visit, for neither to his person nor to his realm would any evil result but rather good, and if after seeing me his wishes were still that I should leave the land I would do so; finally that we should better arrive at the part which he was to play in your Majesty's service by conversation with one another than by means of third persons however trustworthy they might be. With this reply they returned. In this lodging, from certain signs and preparations that we saw in it, the Indians thought that they would be able to attack us one night, upon which I observed such precautions that they changed their plans and that night secretly retired a large body of troops whom they had placed near to the buildings on the mountain ridges, the movement being seen by many of our guards and outposts.

Early the next day I struck camp for a town two leagues farther on called Amecameca, capital of the province of Chalco, which must number more than twenty thousand people, including the villages for some two miles round it. In this town we lodged in some excellent dwellings belonging to the chief ruler of the place. Many people of seeming importance came to speak with me there, saying that Muteczuma their lord had sent them to await my coming, and that they were bidden to provide me with all I needed. The ruler of the province gave me as many as thirty slaves and three thousand *castellanos*, and during the two days that we were there provided us very liberally with all our food. The next day, accompanied by the chiefs who had come from Muteczuma, I advanced four leagues to a little town lying on the shores of a great lake, half of it being indeed in the water, and the land half protected by a steep and rocky ridge, where we camped very comfortably. But here again they were desirous of trying their strength against us, though, as it seemed, without fear of danger to themselves, for they intended to attack us at night when we were unprepared. But as I was proceeding extremely cautiously they found me forewarned: and that night I posted such a strong guard that the spies who came across the water in canoes as also those who climbed down the mountain slope to see if it were safe to attack were taken and killed by our men to the number of some fifteen or twenty before dawn came: in such wise that few indeed returned to report what they had seen, and seeing us thus ever on the watch they decided to abandon their plan and let us alone. Next morning as I was about to depart from the town some ten to a dozen chiefs came up, among whom was a great lord, a youth of some five and twenty years to whom they all showed great respect (so much so that on his descending from the chair in which he was carried all the rest proceeded in front of him clearing away the sticks and stones from his path) and informed me that they came at Muteczuma's bidding to accompany me, and begged

me to pardon their lord for not coming in person to
see and receive me on account of his being sick; his
city, however, was close at hand and since I was
determined to go there we would journey together,
and I should learn from his own lips the zeal he had
in your Majesty's service; nevertheless, he requested
me that if it were possible I should abstain from going
there, for I should suffer much hardship and want
and he himself would be ashamed to be unable to provide for me as he would like, and on this last point
the chiefs insisted at great length; indeed, they were
almost come to the point of saying that they would
hold the road against me if I continued my advance.
I pacified them and satisfied them as best I could,
giving them to understand that no evil could result
from my visit but rather great good.   So they departed
after I had given them a few trinkets such as I carried
with me.

I followed them, accompanied by many persons
who seemed of great importance as indeed they afterwards turned out to be, continuing along the road
which led by the shore of the vast lake, in which course
I had not gone above a mile when I saw within the
lake about two stones' throw away a little town of
perhaps one or two thousand inhabitants, completely
fortified and surrounded by water so that there was no
entrance by land whatsoever, and with an infinite number of turrets as it seemed from the shore.   A league
further on we entered upon a narrow causeway but
some ten feet wide which led across the lake for two
thirds of a league arriving finally at a city, which though
small was the most beautiful that we had yet seen,
both for its finely built houses and towers and the
excellent arrangement of its foundations which were
built entirely in the water.   In this city, which would
contain about two thousand persons, they received us
very cordially and supplied us liberally with food.

There the ruler and chief men came to me requesting that we should stay the night, but those of Muteczuma's men who were accompanying me urged me not to stay there but to pass on to another city but three leagues distant called Iztapalapa which is ruled by a brother of Muteczuma, and this we did. The exit from this city where we fed and whose name escapes me for the moment is by another causeway rather over a league in length which leads to dry ground. On approaching Iztapalapa its ruler came forth to meet me as did the ruler of Culuacan, another large city some three leagues distant, and many other chief men, who presented me with four thousand *castellanos*, some slaves and garments, and made me very welcome,

This city of Iztapalapa must contain from twelve to fifteen thousand inhabitants, and is situated on the shore of a large salt lake half in and half out of the water. Its ruler possesses certain new houses not yet finished which are as fine as the best in Spain, I mean in size and workmanship as regards stonework, carpentry, floors, and fittings for every kind of household service, but excepting sculptures and other luxuries which are known in Spain but unknown here. There are many lofty rooms and sunk gardens with flowering trees and shrubs; likewise there are pools of fresh water very beautifully hollowed out with steps in them leading down to the bottom. This chief has a fine garden adjoining his house, with an observatory containing magnificent corridors and rooms commanding it, and within the garden a very fine lake of fresh water in the form of a square, the sides very delicately chiselled out, and round it a goodly path of well beaten earth broad enough for four people to pass abreast and extending four hundred paces along each side or sixteen hundred in all. Behind the path and between it and the outer wall of the garden the space is filled with a profusion of bamboos and reeds, behind which there are trees and flowering shrubs, and within the lake there are innumerable fish and birds, such as wild duck, widgeon, and other waterfowl, and in such number that often they almost cover the surface of the water.

On the following day I set out again and after half a mile entered upon a causeway which crosses the middle of the lake arriving finally at the great city of Tenochtitlan which is situated at its centre. This causeway was as broad as two lances and very stoutly made such that eight horsemen could ride along it abreast, and in these two leagues either on the one hand or the other we met with three cities all containing very fine buildings and towers, especially the houses of the chief men and the mosques and little temples in which they keep their idols. In these towns there is quite a brisk trade in salt which they make from the water of the lake and what is cast up on the land that borders it; this they cook in a certain manner and make the salt into cakes which they sell to the inhabitants and neighbouring tribes. I accordingly proceeded along this causeway and half a league from the city of Tenochtitlan itself, at the point where another causeway from the mainland joins it, I came upon an extremely powerful fort with two towers, surrounded by a six foot wall with a battlement running round the whole of the side abutting on the two causeways, and having two gates and no more for going in and out. Here nearly a thousand of the chief citizens came out to greet me, all dressed alike and, as their custom is, very richly; on coming to speak with me each performed a ceremony very common among them, to wit, placing his hand on the ground and then kissing it, so that for nearly an hour I stood while they performed this ceremony. Now quite close to the city there is a wooden bridge some ten paces broad, which cuts the causeway and under which the water can flow freely, for its level in the two parts of the lake is constantly changing: moreover it serves as a fortification to the city, for they can remove certain very long and heavy beams which form the bridge whenever they so desire; and there are many such bridges throughout the city as your Majesty will see from that which I shall presently relate.

When we had passed this bridge Muteczuma himself came out to meet us with some two hundred nobles, all barefoot and dressed in some kind of uniform also very rich, in fact more so than the others. They came forward in two long lines keeping close to the walls of the street, which is very broad and fine and so straight that one can see from one end of it to the other, though it is some two-thirds of a league in length and lined on both sides with very beautiful, large houses, both private dwellings and temples. Muteczuma himself was borne along in the middle of the street with two lords one on his right hand and one on his left, being respectively the chief whom I described as coming out to meet me in a litter and the other, Muteczuma's brother, ruler of Iztapalapa, from which only that day we had set out. All three were dressed in similar fashion except that Muteczuma wore shoes whereas the others were barefoot. The two lords bore him along each by an arm, and as he drew near I dismounted and advanced alone to embrace, but the two lords prevented me from touching him, and they themselves made me the same obeisance as did their comrades, kissing the earth: which done, he commanded his brother who accompanied him to stay with me and take me by the arm, while he with the other lord went on a little way in front. After he had spoken to me all the other lords who were in the two long lines came up likewise in order one after the other, and then re-formed in line again. And while speaking to Muteczuma I took off a necklace of pearls and crystals which I was wearing and threw it round his neck; whereupon having proceeded some little way up the street a servant of his came back to me with two necklaces wrapped up in a napkin, made from the shells of sea snails, which are much prized by them; and from each necklace hung eight prawns fashioned very beautifully in gold some six inches in length. The messenger who brought them put them round my neck and we then continued up the street in the manner described until we came to a large and very handsome house which Muteczuma had prepared for our lodging. There he took me by the hand and led me to a large room opposite the patio by which we had entered, and seating me on a daïs very richly worked, for it was intended for royal use, he bade me await him there, and took his departure. After a short time, when all my company had found lodging, he returned with many various ornaments of gold, silver and featherwork, and some five or six thousand cotton clothes, richly dyed and embroidered in various ways, and having made me a present of them he seated himself on another low bench which was placed next to mine, and addressed me in this manner:

"Long time have we been informed by the writings of our ancestors that neither myself nor any of those who inhabit this land are natives of it, but rather strangers who have come to it from foreign parts. We likewise know that from those parts our nation was led by a certain lord (to whom all were subject), and who then went back to his native land, where he remained so long delaying his return that at his coming those whom he had left had married the women of the land and had many children by them and had built themselves cities in which they lived, so that they would in no wise return to their own land nor acknowledge him as lord; upon which he left them. And we have always believed that among his descendants one

would surely come to subject this land and us as rightful vassals. Now seeing the regions from which you
say you come, which is from where the sun rises,
and the news you tell of this great king and ruler who
sent you hither, we believe and hold it certain that he
is our natural lord: especially in that you say he has
long had knowledge of us. Wherefore be certain
that we will obey you and hold you as lord in place
of that great lord of whom you speak, in which service
there shall be neither slackness nor deceit: and throughout all the land, that is to say all that I rule, you may
command anything you desire, and it shall be obeyed
and done, and all that we have is at your will and
pleasure. And since you are in your own land and
house, rejoice and take your leisure from the fatigues
of your journey and the battles you have fought;
for I am well informed of all those that you have been
forced to engage in on your way here from Potonchan,
as also that the natives of Cempoal and Tlascala have
told you many evil things of me; but believe no more
than what you see with your own eyes, and especially
not words from the lips of those who are my enemies,
who were formerly my vassals and on your coming
rebelled against me and said these things in order to
find favour with you: I am aware, moreover, that they
have told you that the walls of my houses were of gold
as was the matting on my floors and other household
articles, even that I was a god and claimed to be so,
and other like matters. As for the houses, you see
that they are of wood, stones and earth." Upon this
he lifted his clothes showing me his body, and said:
" and you see that I am of flesh and blood like yourself and everyone else, mortal and tangible."

Grasping with his hands his arms and other parts
of his body, he continued: " You see plainly how they
have lied. True I have a few articles of gold which
have remained to me from my forefathers, and all that

I have is yours at any time that you may desire it. I am now going to my palace where I live. Here you will be provided with all things necessary for you and your men, and let nothing be done amiss seeing that you are in your own house and land."

I replied to all that he said, satisfying him in those things which seemed expedient, especially in having him believe that your Majesty was he whom they had long expected, and with that he bade farewell. On his departure we were very well regaled with great store of chickens, bread, fruit, and other necessities, particularly household ones. And in this wise I continued six days very well provided with all that was necessary and visited by many of the principal men of the city.

I have already related, most catholic Lord, how at the time when I departed from the town of Vera Cruz in search of this ruler Muteczuma, I left in it a hundred and fifty men to finish the fortress which I had already begun: likewise how that I had left many neighbouring towns and strongholds under the dominion of your royal Majesty, and the natives very peaceably disposed and loyal subjects of your Majesty. Being in the city of Cholula I received letters from the officer whom I left in Vera Cruz, by which I learnt that Qualpopoca, the native ruler of Almería, had sent in messengers to say that he desired to become a vassal of your Majesty, the reason for his delay being that enemy country lay between him and Vera Cruz and he had been chary of passing through it, but that if four Spaniards would return to his land, the enemies through whose country they would have to pass would refrain from molesting them and he would come forthwith to make his submission. The officer, thinking the message to have been sent in good faith, for many others had done the same, sent four Spaniards as requested. But Qualpopoca having once received them into his house ordered them to be killed in such fashion that it should appear that he had no hand in it, and two of them thus died, but the other two escaped wounded through the woods. Upon this the officer went against the city of Almería with fifty Spaniards on foot and two on horse, and two field guns, together with eight or ten thousand Indian allies, fought with the natives of the city and killed many of them, and expelled the remainder from the town, which they burnt and utterly destroyed; for the Indians whom they took in their company being enemies of Almería went about this business with much diligence. Qualpopoca with certain other chiefs who had come to aid him escaped by flight, but from certain prisoners taken in the city they found out who were assisting in its defence and the reason for their having put the Spaniards to death. They declared that it was Muteczuma who had ordered Qualpopoca and the other chieftains as his vassals to fall upon those who had offered themselves as subjects in your Majesty's service so soon as I should leave Vera Cruz, and to take every opportunity of killing the Spaniards whom I had left there, that they might not aid them in any way: this, they said, was the reason for their having acted in this manner.

Having passed six days, then, in the great city of Tenochtitlan, invincible Prince, and having seen something of its marvels, though little in comparison with what there was to be seen and examined, I considered it essential both from my observation of the city and the rest of the land that its ruler should be in my power and no longer entirely free; to the end that he might in nowise change his will and intent to serve your Majesty, more especially as we Spaniards are somewhat intolerant and stiff-necked, and should he get across with us he would be powerful enough to do us great damage, even to blot out all memory of us in the land; and in the second place, could I once

73

get him in my power all the other provinces subject to him would come more promptly to the knowledge and service of your Majesty, as indeed afterwards happened. I decided to capture him and place him in the lodging where I was, which was extremely strong: and that there might be no scandal or public disturbance over his imprisonment I bethought me among all the means by which this might be effected of what the officer had written to me from Vera Cruz, and how he had found out that all had been done according to Muteczuma's orders. Accordingly, posting a strong guard at all the crossways of the streets I went to Muteczuma's palace as I had oftentimes done before, and after having conversed with him light-heartedly with many jokes and his having given me certain golden trinkets and a daughter of his together with other daughters of noble birth to some of my companions, I told him that I knew of what had occurred in the city of Nauthla or Almería and of the Spaniards who had met their death there; that Qualpopoca excused himself by declaring that all that he had done was by Muteczuma's orders and that as his vassal he had been unable to do aught else; but since I believed that it was not as Qualpopoca had said but that rather he was attempting to excuse himself of the crime, it seemed to me that he and the other chiefs who had taken part in the murder of the Spaniards should be sent for, so that the truth might be known and they might be punished, above all that your Majesty might have clear proof of his (Muteczuma's) loyalty, so that these evil tidings might not provoke your Majesty to wrath against him in place of the goodwill your Majesty bore him, since, I said, I was very well persuaded that the contrary of what these men declared was the truth.

Forthwith he sent for certain of his men to whom he gave a small figure carved in stone after the fashion of

a seal, which he wore tied round his arm, and commanded them to go to Almería, which is some sixty
or seventy leagues from the capital, and bring back
Qualpopoca together with such others as they should
find were responsible for the death of the Spaniards,
and if not willingly then in chains: and should they
attempt to resist arrest they should enjoin certain
neighbouring tribes, whom he detailed, to take up arms
against them and capture them, so that in no wise
should they return without them. The messengers
forthwith set out: and on their departure I thanked
Muteczuma for the zeal he displayed in the capture
of those who had killed the Spaniards, of which affair
I should have to give a particular account to your
Majesty. It but remained for him to come to my
lodging until such time as the truth of the matter
should be more manifest and he be shown free of blame;
and I earnestly begged him to be in no way grieved
at this, for he should not be there as a prisoner but in
all liberty; I would place no impediment in the ordering
and command of his dominions, and he should choose
whatever room he liked in the palace where I was
lodged and be there entirely at his ease: for it was
certain that he should receive no annoyance or grief,
but that in addition to his domestics those of my
company would serve him in whatever he should
require. On this matter we conversed long rehearsing
many things which would take too long to recount
to your Majesty and indeed do not bear directly on the
case: so that I will say no more than that he finally
agreed to accompany me; and forthwith gave orders
for rooms to be prepared, which was done in very
elaborate and complete fashion. Upon this many
nobles presented themselves and removing their
clothes which they placed under their arms they
brought in barefoot a litter somewhat roughly decorated: weeping, they conveyed him in complete silence

to the palace where I was lodged and without any actual disturbances in the city although there were signs of some agitation. But on this being known to Muteczuma he gave orders that it should cease; and thus there was complete calm as there had been before, and as, indeed, continued during the whole time that I kept Muteczuma prisoner; for he was much at his ease, and waited upon with such service as was observed in his own palace which was of extraordinary magnificence as I shall afterwards describe. Moreover I and those of my company cheered him in every way we could.

Some fifteen to twenty days after his imprisonment those who had been sent for Qualpopoca returned bringing with them Qualpopoca himself, a son, and fifteen persons whom they declared had taken a principal part in the murder. They brought Qualpopoca in a litter quite in the manner of a great ruler, as indeed he was. The prisoners were handed over to me and I saw to it that they were well guarded. After they had confessed that they had murdered the Spaniards, I questioned them whether they were vassals of Muteczuma. On this Qualpopoca replied asking me, ' Of what other lord could he be vassal ?' as much as to say that there was none other and that consequently he was his vassal. Likewise I asked them whether what had been done there was by his command, and they replied, " No," although later when the sentence of burning was put into execution all declared with one voice that Muteczuma had sent them such a command and by his command it had been done. They were consequently burnt in a public square without any disturbance being made, and on the day of their execution seeing the confession they had made I ordered Muteczuma to be put in chains which terrified him not a little. After having held speech with him, however, that same day they were taken off at which he was greatly pleased and thereafter I conftantly endeavoured to cheer and content him as much as I could; especially in that I always published and declared to the natives, both chiefs and such as came to see him, that your Majefty was well pleased that Muteczuma should retain his dominion, recognizing that which your Majefty held over him, and that they would be serving your Majefty in obeying him and considering him as their lord as they had done before I came to their land. And such was the good treatment which he received and his content that more than once or twice I offered him his liberty begging him to go to his own palace, and he told me whenever I suggefted it that he was much at his ease there and had no wish to depart, since he lacked nothing of what he required, juft as if he were in his own house; and it might be that returning to his former palace the nobles who were his vassals would importune him or persuade him to do something contrary to the services of your Majefty, whereas his wish was to serve your Majefty in everything that he could: but that now when they asked anything of him he could reply that such was not within his power and so excuse himself from doing it. Many times he asked leave of me to go and amuse himself in certain pleasure houses which he had both within and without the city, and on no occasion did I refuse him. Often he went out on pleasure bent with five or six Spaniards a league or two beyond the city, and always returned very cheerfully and contentedly to the palace in which I kept him. Always on such occasion he made many presents of jewels and clothes both to the Spaniards who went with him and to his own people, by whom he was always accompanied in such numbers as never fell below three thousand, the majority of whom were nobles and chiefs; always, too, he regaled them with numerous banquets and entertainments of which those who accompanied him were never tired of repeating.

When I recognized the very real desire that he had to serve your Majesty, I requested him, that I might give your Majesty a more minute account of this land, to show me the mines from which he drew his gold, the which he declared himself very ready and willing to do. Upon this he sent for certain of his servants and divided them two by two for each of the four provinces from which gold was obtained; and he made me choose Spaniards to go with them and see how the metal was mined; I accordingly appointed two Spaniards to accompany each pair of guides. One party went to a province known as Cuzula eighty leagues from the capital, whose natives are subject to Muteczuma, and there they were shown three rivers from all of which they brought me samples of gold of good quality, although obtained by very primitive apparatus similar to that used by other Indian tribes; on the way my men informed me they passed through three provinces, very fertile, with many towns, cities and other smaller centres, and with so many fine buildings that, so they said, there are not finer in all Spain. In particular they reported that they had seen a fortified garrison which is larger, stronger and better built than the castle of Burgos. The people, moreover, of one of these provinces, called Tamazulapa, were more fully clothed than in others we have seen and as it appeared to them very intelligent.

(The others had like success, bringing samples of gold, and reporting particularly favourably on the province of Malinaltepec, lying to the south close to the sea.)

And since according to the Spaniards who went there, there is everything needful for the settlement of small farms and the washing of gold, I made the request to Muteczuma that seeing that the province of Malinaltepec was most suited for it he should settle a small farm there for your Majesty, and he carried out the suggestion with such zeal that in two months' time already about a hundred and ten acres of maize and ten of beans had been sown, and two thousand square feet of cacao, a fruit resembling our almonds which they sell crushed, and of which they have such stores that they are used as money throughout the land to buy all necessities in the public markets and elsewhere. Moreover he built several very fine dwellings in one of which in addition to ordinary rooms he constructed a large tank of water, and placed some five hundred ducks there, of which they have a great quantity, using their feathers which they pluck from them each year for making clothes; he added also as many as fifteen hundred head of chicken, together with much very useful furniture · and equipment, which were reckoned by my men who examined them more than once to be worth something near twenty thousand golden *pesos*.

(Cortés here gives particulars of an attempt to find a really good harbour on the northern coast and of the expedition of ten of his men, accompanied by an Indian guide, to what was probably Guasacualco, where they met a very friendly native chief and established the beginning of a settlement at the mouth of the river there with his full consent and assistance.)

I have already described, most powerful lord, how on approaching the great city of Tenochtitlan an important chief came out to meet me on behalf of Muteczuma, who I afterwards discovered was a near relation of the king and ruled a province near by, called Culuacan. Its capital is a very fine city which is close to the salt lake and six leagues from Tenochtitlan by water though ten by land. This city is known as Tezcuco and must contain some thirty thousand inhabitants. Very fine houses and mosques are to be found in it as also large and beautifully decorated temples. There are also large market-places. Besides this city he owns two more, the one three leagues from Tezcuco called Oculma, the other six leagues away, Otumba. Each one has some three or four thousand inhabitants. The province of Culuacan has many other villages and scattered farms, with a quantity of very fertile land under tillage. It is bounded on one side by the province of Tlascala of which I have already spoken to your Majesty. Now this chief, whose name is Cacamazín, after the imprisonment of Muteczuma rebelled both against the dominion of your Majesty, which he had accepted, and against Muteczuma. And notwithstanding that many times he was ordered to obey your Majesty's royal commands he stubbornly refused, although in addition to my request Muteczuma himself also sent word to him: but he replied that if we required anything from him we should go to his land and should there see what he was worth and what manner of service he was under obligation to render. Accordingly, since neither threat nor request would move him I asked Muteczuma his opinion as to how best we might deal with him that his rebellion might not go unpunished; upon which he replied that to attempt to take him in open warfare would be to run great risk, for he was a powerful lord and had great stores of arms and men, and would not be taken without the loss of many lives; but that he himself had secretly in his employ a number of chief men who lived in the land of Cacamazín and were in his pay, and he would instruct these persons to win over some of Cacamazín's men to our side so that they could thus capture him in safety. Muteczuma accordingly laid his plans in such a manner that these hirelings persuaded Cacamazín to meet them in Tezcuco in order to confer with them as important persons upon such things as it was fitting should be done to maintain his position, for, said they, it grieved them to see him doing things which would bring about his ruin.

They met together in a very pleasant house belonging to Cacamazín situated on the border of the lake and built in such a manner that canoes can be paddled under it and so reach the lake: there they had canoes secretly in readiness with a strong body of men in case Cacamazín should resist capture. In the middle of the conference he was arrested by the chief men before Cacamazín's followers perceived anything, was lowered into the waiting canoes and conducted across the lake to the capital which as I said is about six leagues distance. On his arrival he was placed in a litter, as his position demanded or as was their custom, and brought before me: I immediately had him put in chains under a strong guard. Later, on Muteczuma's advice, I placed his son Cucuzcazín in command of the province in your Majesty's name, and saw to it that all the smaller towns and nobles of the province recognized him as lord, which they did without dispute, and he himself has been very obedient to any commands which I have given him on the part of your Majesty.

Some few days after the imprisonment of Cacamazín, Muteczuma proclaimed an assembly of all the chiefs of the neighbouring towns and districts; and on their coming together he sent for me to mount to the platform where he already was and proceeded to address them in this manner: " Brothers and friends, you know well that for many years you, your fathers and your grandfathers have been subjects and vassals to me and to my forefathers, and have ever been well treated and held in due esteem both by them and me, as likewise you yourselves have done what it behoves good and loyal vassals to do for their lords; moreover I believe you will recollect hearing from your ancestors that we are not natives of this land, but that they came to it from another land far off, being led hither by a powerful lord whose vassals they all were; after many years he returned to find our forefathers already settled in the land married to native wives and with many children by them in such wise that they never wished to go back with him nor acknowledge him as lord of the land, and upon this he returned saying that he would come again himself or send another with such power as to force them to re-enter his service. And you know well that we have always looked to this and from what the captain has told us of the king and lord who sent him hither, and the direction from which he came I hold it certain as ye also must hold it, that he is the lord whom we have looked to, especially in that he declares he already had knowledge of us in his own land. Therefore while our ancestors did not that which was due to their lord, let us not so offend now, but rather give praise to the gods that in our times that which was long expected is come to pass. And I earnestly beg of you, since all that I have said is notorious to everyone of you, that as you have up till now obeyed and held me as your sovereign lord, so from henceforth you will obey and hold this great king as your natural lord, for such he is, and in particular this captain in his place: and all those tributes and services which up to this time you have paid to me, do you now pay to him, for I also hold myself bound to do him service in all that he shall require me: and over and above doing that which is right and necessary you will be doing me great pleasure."

All this he spoke to them weeping, with such sighs and tears as no man ever wept more, and likewise all those chieftains who heard him wept so that for a long space of time they could make no reply. And I can

assure your Majesty that there was not one among the
Spaniards who on hearing this speech was not filled
with compassion. After some time when their tears
were somewhat dried they replied that they held him as
their lord and had promised to do whatever he should
bid them, and hence that for that reason and the one
he had given them they were content to do what he
said, and from that time offered themselves as vassals
to your royal Majesty, promising severally and collec-
tively to carry out whatever should be required of them
in your Majesty's royal name as loyal and obedient
vassals, and duly to render him all such tributes and
services as were formerly rendered to Muteczuma,
with all other things whatsoever that may be commanded them in your Majesty's name. All this took
place in the presence of the public notary and was duly
drawn up by him in legal form and witnessed in the
presence of many Spaniards.

Some days after this formal acknowledgment of
service to your Majesty I was speaking to Muteczuma
and told him that your Majesty was in need of gold for
certain works which he had in hand; I asked him to
send some of his own men, to whom I would add an
equal number of Spaniards, to the estates and houses
of those nobles who had publicly offered themselves
as vassals of your Majesty, asking them to do your
Majesty some service with what riches they might
possess; for over and above your Majesty's need of
gold, it would be made manifest that they were beginning to serve him, and your Majesty would perceive
more surely the zeal they had in his service: moreover
I requested that he himself might give me some portion
of his treasure that I might send it to Spain as I had
already sent gold and other articles to your Majesty
with my previous messengers. He thereupon asked
me to send him the Spaniards whom I had chosen and
immediately divided them two by two and five by five

between the several cities and provinces, whose names (since they were numerous and my manuscripts have been lost) I cannot recollect, save that some of them were as much as eighty and a hundred leagues from the capital. With my men he sent his own, ordering them to visit the rulers of those cities and to require of each one of them in my name a certain measure of gold. And so it came about that each one of those lords to whom he sent gave very freely when he was asked, whether jewels, small bars and plates of gold and silver, or other valuables which he possessed; of all this treasure gathered together the fifth due to your Majesty amounted to over two thousand four hundred *pesos* of gold, exclusive of all the ornaments in gold, silver and featherwork, the precious stones and other costly articles which I set aside for your Majesty, which would be worth some hundred thousand ducats and more; and which apart from their value were so marvellous on account of their novelty and strangeness as to be almost without price, for it is doubtful whether any of all the known princes of the world possesses such treasures and in such quantity. And let this not appear fabulous to your Majesty, for in truth there was not a living thing on land or sea of which Muteczuma could have knowledge which was not so cunningly represented in gold, silver, precious stones or featherwork as almost to seem the thing itself: of all of which Muteczuma gave me great store for your Majesty, not to mention others of which I gave him examples to copy, and he had them reproduced in gold, such as images, crucifixes, medallions, carved jewels and necklaces, and many other ornaments belonging to us which I persuaded him to have copied. There fell likewise to your Majesty as a fifth part of the silver which was obtained over a hundred marks, which I bid the natives work up into dishes large and small, porringers, cups and spoons, the which they did as perfectly as we were able to give them instructions. In addition to this Muteczuma gave me many garments belonging to himself which, considering that they were woven of cotton without any admixture of silk, could not, I think, be matched in all the world: among them were both men's and women's clothes and bedspreads such as could not be bettered had they been of silk: there were also hangings resembling tapestry work which could be used in large rooms and churches, together with counterpanes and other coverings for the bed both of feathers and of cotton, variously coloured and likewise exquisitely made, and many other things so numerous and so ingenious that I cannot describe them to your Majesty. He also gave me a dozen blowpipes with which he used to shoot arrows, the workmanship of which I am again as little able to describe to your Majesty, for they were decorated all over with excellent little paintings in natural colours of birds, animals, trees, flowers, and other objects, and the mouthpieces and tips of gold extending some six inches as also a band in the middle of the same metal elaborately worked. He also gave me a gilded pouch of netting for pellets (such as they shoot with) which he told me he would also provide me with in gold, moulds of gold for making the same, and many other things too numerous to mention. For to give your Majesty a full account of all the strange and marvellous things to be found in this great city of Tenochtitlan would demand much time and many and skilled writers, and I shall be able to describe but a hundredth part of all the many things which are worthy of description.

But before beginning to relate the wonders of this city and people, their rights and government, I should perhaps for a better understanding say something of the state of Mexico itself which contains this city and the others of which I have spoken, and is the principal seat of Muteczuma. The province is roughly circular in shape and entirely surrounded by very lofty and rocky mountains, the level part in the middle being some seventy leagues[14] in circumference and containing two lakes which occupy it almost entirely, for canoes travel over fifty leagues in making a circuit of them. One of the lakes is of fresh water, the other and larger one of salt. A narrow but very lofty range of mountains cuts across the valley and divides the lakes almost completely save for the western end where they are joined by a narrow strait no wider than a sling's throw which runs between the mountains. Commerce is carried on between the two lakes and the cities on their banks by means of canoes, so that land traffic is avoided. Moreover, since the salt lake rises and falls with the tide sea water pours from it at high tide into the fresh water lake with the rapidity of a mountain torrent, and likewise at low tide flows back from the fresh to the salt.

The great city of Tenochtitlan is built in the midst of this salt lake, and it is two leagues from the heart of the city to any point on the mainland. Four causeways lead to it, all made by hand and some twelve feet wide. The city itself is as large as Seville or Córdova. The principal streets are very broad and straight, the majority of them being of beaten earth, but a few and at least half the smaller thoroughfares are waterways along which they pass in their canoes. Moreover, even the principal streets have openings at regular distances so that the water can freely pass from one to another, and these openings which are very broad are spanned by great bridges of huge beams, very stoutly put together, so firm indeed that over many of them ten horsemen can ride at once. Seeing that if the natives intended any treachery against us they would have every opportunity from the way in which the city is built, for by removing the bridges from the entrances and exits they could leave us to die of hunger with no possibility of getting to the mainland, I immediately set to work as soon as we entered the city on the building of four brigs, and in a short space of time had them finished, so that we could ship three hundred men and the horses to the mainland whenever we so desired.

The city has many open squares in which markets are continuously held and the general business of buying and selling proceeds. One square in particular is twice as big as that of Salamanca and completely surrounded by arcades where there are daily more than sixty thousand folk buying and selling. Every kind of merchandise such as may be met with in every land is for sale there, whether of food and victuals, or ornaments of gold and silver, or lead, brass, copper, tin, precious stones, bones, shells, snails and feathers; limestone for building is likewise sold there, stone both rough and polished, bricks burnt and unburnt, wood of all kinds and in all stages of preparation. There is a street of game where they sell all manner of birds that are to be found in their country, including hens, partridges, quails, wild duck, fly-ca chers, widgeon, turtle doves, pigeons, little birds in round nests made of grass, parrots, owls, eagles, vulcans, sparrow-hawks and kestrels; and of some of these birds of prey they sell the skins complete with feathers, head, bill and claws. They also sell rabbits, hares, deer and small dogs which they breed especially for eating. There is a street of herb-sellers where there are all manner of roots and medicinal plants that are found in the land. There are houses as it were of apothecaries where they sell medicines made from these herbs, both for drinking and for use as ointments and salves. There are barbers' shops where you may have your hair washed and cut. There are other shops where you may obtain food and drink. There are street porters

such as we have in Spain to carry packages. There
is a great quantity of wood, charcoal, braziers made
of clay and mats of all sorts, some for beds and others
more finely woven for seats, still others for furnishing
halls and private apartments. All kinds of vegetables
may be found there, in particular onions, leeks, garlic,
cresses, watercress, borage, sorrel, artichokes, and
golden thistles. There are many different sorts of
fruits including cherries and plums very similar to
those found in Spain. They sell honey obtained
from bees, as also the honeycomb and that obtained
from maize plants which are as sweet as sugar canes;
they also obtain honey from plants which are known
both here and in other parts as *maguey*[15], which is
preferable to grape juice; from *maguey* in addition
they make both sugar and a kind of wine, which are
sold in their markets. All kinds of cotton thread
in various colours may be bought in skeins, very
much in the same way as in the great silk exchange
of Granada, except that the quantities are far less.
They have colours for painting of as good quality
as any in Spain, and of as pure shades as may be
found anywhere. There are leathers of deer both
skinned and in their natural state, and either bleached
or dyed in various colours. A great deal of chinaware
is sold of very good quality and including earthen
jars of all sizes for holding liquids, pitchers, pots,
tiles and an infinite variety of earthenware all made
of very special clay and almost all decorated and
painted in some way. Maize is sold both as grain
and in the form of bread and is vastly superior both
in the size of the ear and in taste to that of all the
other islands or the mainland. Pasties made from
game and fish pies may be seen on sale, and there are
large quantities of fresh and salt water fish both in
their natural state and cooked ready for eating. Eggs
from fowls, geese and all the other birds I have

described may be had, and likewise omelettes ready made. There is nothing to be found in all the land which is not sold in these markets, for over and above what I have mentioned there are so many and such various other things that on account of their very number and the fact that I do not know their names, I cannot now detail them. Each kind of merchandise is sold in its own particular street and no other kind may be sold there: this rule is very well enforced. All is sold by number and measure, but up till now no weighing by balance has been observed. A very fine building in the great square serves as a kind of audience chamber where ten or a dozen persons are always seated, as judges, who deliberate on all cases arising in the market and pass sentence on evildoers. In the square itself there are officials who continually walk amongst the people inspecting goods exposed for sale and the measures by which they are sold, and on certain occasions I have seen them destroy measures which were false.

There are a very large number of mosques or dwelling places for their idols throughout the various districts of this great city, all fine buildings, in the chief of which their priests live continuously, so that in addition to the actual temples containing idols there are sumptuous lodgings. These pagan priests are all dressed in black and go habitually with their hair uncut; they do not even comb it from the day they enter the order to that on which they leave. Chief men's sons, both nobles and distinguished citizens, enter these orders at the age of six or seven and only leave when they are of an age to marry, and this occurs more frequently to the first-born who will inherit their father's estates than to others. They are denied all access to women, and no woman is ever allowed to enter one of the religious houses. Certain foods they abstain from and more so at certain periods of the year than at others. Among these temples there is one chief one in particular whose size and magnificence no human tongue could describe. For it is so big that within the lofty wall which entirely circles it one could set a town of fifteen thousand inhabitants.

Immediately inside this wall and throughout its entire length are some admirable buildings containing large halls and corridors where the priests who live in this temple are housed. There are forty towers at the least, all of stout construction and very lofty, the largest of which has fifty steps leading up to its base: this chief one is indeed higher than the great church of Seville. The workmanship both in wood and stone could not be bettered anywhere, for all the stonework within the actual temples where they keep their idols is cut into ornamental borders of flowers, birds, fishes and the like, or trellis-work, and the woodwork is likewise all in relief highly decorated with monsters of very various device. The towers all serve as burying places for their nobles, and the little temples which they contain are all dedicated to a different idol to whom they pay their devotions.

There are three large halls in the great mosque where the principal idols are to be found, all of immense size and height and richly decorated with sculptured figures both in wood and stone, and within these halls are other smaller temples branching off from them and entered by doors so small that no daylight ever reaches them. Certain of the priests but not all are permitted to enter, and within are the great heads and figures of idols, although as I have said there are also many outside. The greatest of these idols and those in which they placed most faith and trust I ordered to be dragged from their places and flung down the stairs, which done I had the temples which they occupy cleansed for they were full of the blood of human victims who had been sacrificed, and placed in them the image of Our Lady and other saints, all of which made no small impression upon Muteczuma and the inhabitants. They at first remonſtrated with me, for should it be known, they said, by the people of the country they would rise againſt me, believing as they did that to these idols were due all temporal goods, and that should they allow them to be ill used they would be wroth againſt them and would give them nothing, denying them the fruits of the earth, and thus the people would die of ſtarvation. I inſtructed them by my interpreters how miſtaken they were in putting their truſt in idols made by their own hands from unclean things, and that they muſt know that there was but one God, Lord of all, Who created the sky, the earth and all things, Who made both them and ourselves, Who was without beginning and immortal, Whom alone they had to adore and to believe in, and not in any created thing whatsoever: I told them moreover all things else that I knew of touching this matter in order to lead them from their idolatry and bring them to the knowledge of Our Lord: and all, especially Muteczuma, replied that they had already told me that they were not natives of this land but had come to it long time since, and that therefore they were well prepared to believe that they had erred somewhat from the true faith during the long time since they had left their native land, and I as more lately come would know more surely the things that it was right for them to hold and believe than they themselves: and that hence if I would inſtruct them they would do whatever I declared to be beſt. Upon this Muteczuma and many of the chief men of the city went with me to remove the idols, cleanse the chapels, and place images of the saints therein, and all with cheerful faces. I forbade them moreover to make human sacrifice to the idols as was their wont, because besides being an abomination in the sight of God it is prohibited by your Majesty's laws which declare that he who kills shall be killed. From this time henceforth they departed from it, and during the whole time that I was in the city not a single living soul was known to be killed and sacrificed.

The images of the idols in which these people believed are many times greater than the body of a large man. They are made from pulp of all the cereals and greenstuffs which they eat, mixed and pounded together. This mass they moisten with blood from the hearts of human beings which they tear from their breasts while still alive, and thus make sufficient quantity of the pulp to mould into their huge statues: and after the idols have been set up still they offer them more living hearts which they sacrifice in like manner and anoint their faces with the blood. Each department of human affairs has its particular idol after the manner of the ancients who thus honoured their gods: so that there is one idol from whom they beg success in war, another for crops, and so on for all their needs.

The city contains many large and fine houses, and for this reason. All the nobles of the land owing allegiance to Muteczuma have their houses in the city and reside there for a certain portion of the year; and in addition there are a large number of rich citizens who likewise have very fine houses. All possess in addition to large and elegant apartments very delightful flower gardens of every kind, both on the ground level as on the upper storeys.

Along one of the causeways connecting this great city with the mainland two pipes are constructed of masonry, each two paces broad and about as high as a man, one of which conveys a stream of water very clear and fresh and about the thickness of a man's body right to the centre of the city, which all can use for drinking and other purposes. The other pipe which is empty is used when it is desired to clean the former. Moreover, on coming to the breaks in the causeway spanned by bridges under which the salt water flows through, the fresh water flows into a kind of trough as thick as an ox which occupies the whole width of the bridge, and thus the whole city is served. The water is sold from canoes in all the streets, the manner of their taking it from the pipes being in this wise: the canoes place themselves under the bridges where the troughs are to be found, and from above the canoes are filled by men who are especially paid for this work.

At all the entrances to the city and at those parts where canoes are unloaded, which is where the greatest amount of provisions enters the city, certain huts have been built, where there are official guards to exact so much on everything that enters. I know not whether this goes to the lord or to the city itself, and have not yet been able to ascertain, but I think that it is to the ruler, since in the markets of several other towns we have seen such a tax exacted on behalf of the ruler. Every day in all the markets and public places of the city there are a number of workmen and masters of all manner of crafts waiting to be hired by the day. The people of this city are nicer in their dress and manners than those of any other city or province, for since Muteczuma always holds his residence here and his vassals visit the city for lengthy periods, greater culture and politeness of manners in all things has been encouraged.

Finally, to avoid prolixity in telling all the wonders of this city, I will simply say that the manner of living among the people is very similar to that in Spain, and considering that this is a barbarous nation shut off from a knowledge of the true God or communication with enlightened nations, one may well marvel at the orderliness and good government which is everywhere maintained.

The actual service of Muteczuma and those things which call for admiration by their greatness and state would take so long to describe that I assure your Majesty I do not know where to begin with any hope of ending. For as I have already said, what could there be more astonishing than that a barbarous monarch such as he should have reproductions made in gold, silver, precious stones, and feathers of all things to be found in his land, and so perfectly reproduced that there is no goldsmith or silversmith in the world who could better them, nor can one understand what instrument could have been used for fashioning the jewels; as for the featherwork its like is not to be seen in either wax or embroidery, it is so marvellously delicate.

I was unable to find out exactly the extent of Muteczuma's kingdom, for in no part where he sent his messengers (even as much as two hundred leagues in either direction from this city) were his orders disobeyed; although it is true there were certain provinces in the middle of this region with whom he was at war. But so far as I could understand his kingdom was almost as large as Spain. Most of the lords of these various provinces resided, as I have said, for the greater part of the year in the capital, and the majority of them had their eldest sons in Muteczuma's service. The king had fortresses in all these provinces armed with his own men, and also overseers and tax-collectors to see to the services and rent which each province owed him, and which was inscribed in written characters and pictures on a kind of paper they have, by which they can make themselves understood. The manner of service rendered differed for each province according to the quality of its land, in such manner that every kind of produce

94

that grew in the various parts of the country came to
the royal hand. He was feared by all both present
and distant more than was any other monarch in the
world. He possessed many houses of recreation both
within and without the city, each with its own special
pastime, built in the most ingenious manner as was
fitting for such a mighty prince: of which I will say
no more than that there is not their like in all Spain.
Another palace of his (not quite so fine as the one we
were lodged in) had a magnificent garden with balconies
overhanging it, the pillars and flagstones of which were
all jasper beautifully worked. In this palace there was
room to lodge two powerful princes with all their
retinue. There were also ten pools of water in
which were kept every kind of waterfowl known in
these parts, fresh water being provided for the river
birds, salt for those of the sea, and the water itself
being frequently changed to keep it pure: every
species of bird, moreover, was provided with its own
natural food, whether fish, worms, maize or the
smaller cereals. And I can vouch for it to your
Majesty that those birds who ate fish alone and nothing
else received some two hundred and fifty pounds of it
every day, which was caught in the salt lake. It
was the whole task of three hundred men to look
after these birds. Others likewise were employed in
ministering to those who were ill. Each pool was
overhung by balconies cunningly arranged, from which
Muteczuma would delight to watch the birds. In
one room of this palace he kept men, women and
children, who had been white since their birth, face,
body, hair, eyebrows and eyelashes. He had also
another very beautiful house in which there was a
large courtyard, paved very prettily with flagstones
in the manner of a chessboard. In this palace there
were cages some nine feet high and six yards round:
each of these was half covered with tiles and the other

half by a wooden trellis skilfully made. They contained birds of prey, and there was an example of every one that is known in Spain, from keſtrel to eagle, and many others which were new to us. Of each species there were many examples. In the covered part of every cage there was a ſtake on which the bird could perch and another under the wooden grating, so that the birds could go inside at nighttime and when it was raining and in the daytime come out into the sun and air. They were fed daily on chickens as their sole fare. Other large rooms on the ground floor were full of cages made of ſtout wood very firmly put together and containing large numbers of lions, tigers, wolves, foxes and wild cats of various kinds; these also were given as many chickens as they wanted. There were likewise another three hundred men to look after these animals and birds. In another palace he had men and women monſters, among them dwarfs, hunchbacks and others deformed in various ways, each manner of monſter being kept in a separate apartment, and likewise with guards charged with looking after them.

His personal service was equally magnificent. Every morning at dawn there were over six hundred nobles and chief men present in his palace, some of whom were seated, others walking about the rooms and corridors, others amusing themselves in talk and other diversions, but none entering the actual apartment where he lay. The servants of these nobles filled two or three large courtyards and overflowed into the ſtreet, which was very large. They remained there all day, not quitting the palace until nightfall: at the time when the king took his meals food was served to them with equal profusion and rations were likewise dispensed to their servants and followers. His larders and wine cellars were open daily to all who wished to eat and drink. The meal was served

by some three or four hundred youths. The dishes
were innumerable since on every occasion that the
king ate or drank every manner of dish was served to
him, whether it were meat, fish, fruit, or herbs of
whatever kind was found in the land. Since the
climate is cold every plate and dish had under it a
little brazier filled with lighted coals that it might not
get cold. All the dishes were placed in a large hall
in which he took his meals. It was almoſt entirely filled
but kept ever fresh and clean, the King himself being
seated on a small delicately fashioned leather cushion.
While he ate some five or six ancient nobles ſtood
a little way off to whom he gave morsels from his own
dish. One of the youthful servitors remained on
foot to place the dishes before him and remove them,
and he requeſted from others who were further off
anything which was lacking. Both at the beginning
and end of the meal he was always given water with
which to wash his hands, and the towel on which he
dried his hands was never used again, nor likewise
were the plates and dishes on which the food was
brought ever used twice and the same with the little
braziers which were also new for every meal. Every
day he changed his garments four times, always putting
on new clothes which were never worn more than
once. The nobles always entered his palace barefoot,
and those who were bidden to present themselves
before him did so with bowed head and eyes fixed on
the ground, their whole bearing expressing reverence;
nor would they when speaking to him lift their eyes
to his face, all of which was done to show their pro-
found humiliation and respeƈt. That such was the
motive I am certain because certain of the nobles
rebuked the Spanish soldiers for speaking to me
without due shame in that they looked me full in the
face, which seemed to them the height of disrespeƈt.
When Muteczuma went abroad, which was seldom,

all who were with him or whom he met in the street turned away their faces and avoided looking at him, some of them prostrating themselves on the ground until he had passed. One of the nobles always preceded him bearing three long thin rods, for the purpose, as I think, of intimating the royal presence. For on his descending from the litter he bore one in his hand and carried it with him wherever he went. In short the various ceremonies which this ruler observed were so many and curious that there is not space here to recount them, and I think that not even the sultans themselves or other eastern potentates were surrounded by such pomp and display.

In this great city I was now busied in providing such things as seemed profitable to your Majesty's service, pacifying and subduing many provinces containing great numbers of large cities, towns and fortresses, discovering mines, and finding out and enquiring many secrets of these lands under the rule of Muteczuma, as also of others bordering on them of which he knew, which are so extensive and marvellous that their existence is almost incredible: all this with the goodwill and pleasure of Muteczuma and all the natives of these lands as if they had recognized from the beginning your Majesty as their natural lord and governor, and now did with no less goodwill all these things which they were bidden in your Majesty's royal name.

In such business and in other matters no less important I spent the months from November 1519 until the beginning of May of this year, when being in all peace and quietness in this city with many of my men abroad in various parts occupied in pacifying and settling the land, one day certain native messengers arrived from the coast somewhat below the port of San Juan to tell me of the arrival of eight or ten ships, and on their heels came a message from a Spaniard whom I kept on the coast to send me news of any ship arriving, saying that " on that day he had just sighted a single ship off the harbour of San Juan but had seen no others, and believed it was the vessel which I had sent your Majesty which was now due back."

I immediately dispatched two Spaniards to the port to find out how many ships had arrived and return with the news as quickly as possible: likewise two to the town of Vera Cruz, and another to the captain whom I had sent with one hundred and fifty men to settle the province and harbour of Guasacualco, telling him wherever he was when the messenger arrived to proceed no further until receiving further orders from me.

A whole fortnight followed in which I heard no more news nor had any reply to my messages, which disturbed me not a little. Then I heard from some Indians that the ships had anchored in the harbour of San Juan and carried in them eighty horses, some eight hundred men, ten or a dozen guns, all of which was set down in pictures on a piece of native paper to be shown to Muteczuma. Further, they said, the Spaniards whom I had placed on the coast together with the messengers whom I had sent were with the strangers and the captain had instructed them to tell me that he would not let them go. Upon this I decided to send a friar who was of my company with a letter signed by myself and the *alcaldes* and *regidores* of the city of Vera Cruz who were with me in the capital, addressed to the captain and his men who had come to the port, which set out in great detail all that had happened to me in this land, that I had conquered and pacified many cities and fortresses, holding them subject to your royal Majesty, and had imprisoned the native monarch in the city in which I now was: I desired to know who they were, whether they were subjects of your Majesty with royal license to settle or not; moreover, if they were in any want I would do my best to provide them with what they lacked, and this whether they were your Majesty's subjects or not. But in the latter case I requested them on behalf of your Majesty to depart immediately from these lands, warning them if they did not that I should proceed against them with all the forces I could command both of Spaniards and natives and would capture or take them prisoner as strangers who were bent on trespassing on the land and dominions of my king and master. Five days later twenty Spaniards arrived from Vera Cruz bringing with them a priest and two citizens whom they had captured in the town. From these I learnt that the fleet and men came on the orders of Diego Velázquez under the command of a captain, by name Pánfilo Narváez, a citizen of Cuba. Among his eight hundred men, they said, he had eighty musketeers and twenty crossbowmen, and he was come calling himself captain general and Governor's deputy over all these parts for the aforesaid Diego Velázquez, for which title he bore due license from your Majesty. He had, they added, learnt from my messengers whom he was keeping imprisoned both where I was and all that I had succeeded in doing in this kingdom. They themselves had been sent by Narváez to Vera Cruz to see if they could bring the inhabitants over to his side and persuade them to rebel against me; and with them they brought me more than a hundred letters promising the citizens that if they would do as they were bidden they should receive great favours from Diego Velázquez and if not they should be treated with all harshness, together with many other threats and promises. Almost at the same time one of the Spaniards who had been sent to Guasacualco arrived with letters from his captain Juan Velázquez de León who sent me the same news and told me in addition that he had received a letter from Narváez urging him as a kinsman of Diego Velázquez to throw in his lot with him. Not only, however, had he refused to do so, but more faithful to your Majesty's service he turned immediately to retrace his steps and rejoin me with all the men he had with him. From the captured priest and messengers I learnt further that Diego Velázquez had been moved to dispatch this force against me by reason of my having sent my report and the treasures of this land direct to your Majesty, and was now determined to kill both myself and many of my company whose names had already been decided upon. Moreover, so I discovered, Figueroa, the presiding judge in the island of Haiti together with others of your Majesty's officials, had sent one Lucas Vázquez de Ayllón with power to stop the aforesaid Diego Velázquez from sending the fleet, but had been unable to stop him, and was even now in the port of San Juan, hoping to prevent the harm which must result from the arrival of the fleet, for its evil designs and intents were known to all.

Accordingly I sent a letter to Narváez saying that I had learnt who was in command of the forces which had arrived and was delighted that it should be he, because I had feared something very different when my messengers did not return: but that nevertheless I was surprised that he did not give me news of his arrival knowing as he did that I was in this land on the service of your Majesty, and seeing that he had long since been my friend and was as I had reason to believe come equally on your Majesty's service; and still more so that he should have sent letters in an endeavour to suborn people who were already of my company to rise against me and join forces with him, just as if we were on the one side infidels and on the other Christians, or one of us vassals of your Majesty and the other his enemies: which behaviour I begged he would no longer continue. Moreover, as I had heard, he had publicly proclaimed himself captain general and Governor's deputy on behalf of Diego Velázquez, and had appointed *alcaldes* and *regidores* and administered justice, all which things were of great disservice to your Majesty and against the law, for this land now belonging to your Majesty and being peopled by your Majesty's subjects, such things could only be done by one bearing the special license of your Majesty, which, if he bore, I requested him to present it before me and the council of Vera Cruz, and it should be obeyed by me as the command of my king and master and carried out in so far as should be fitting to your Majesty's royal service. I likewise gave the priest a letter to the *licenciado* Ayllón whom, as I afterwards learnt, Narváez had already taken prisoner together with his two ships.

The day that this priest left, a messenger arrived from Vera Cruz to inform me that all the natives in those parts, especially the Cempoallans, had risen in favour of Narváez, and on account of the forces which he had would not assist in holding the city for me, for they had had news that Narváez intended to camp in that city and was already very near it. Moreover, knowing what his designs were against all of us, if he should march against them, they intended to abandon Vera Cruz and take to the mountains until receiving further instructions from me. Upon this, seeing the great danger which was imminent and thinking that the Indians would not dare to rebel in my presence, I decided to advance to where he was.

I accordingly quitted the capital that same day leaving the Spanish quarters very well provided with maize and water and garrisoned with five hundred men and several guns. I myself had about seventy Spaniards and certain of the chief nobles of the city. I spoke to Muteczuma himself before setting out, reminding him that he was a vassal of your Majesty, and that he was now to receive the reward of his services; I was leaving in the charge of my men all the gold and jewels which he had given me to send to your Majesty, and was going out against people whom I believed to be evil despots and not your Majesty's vassals. He promised me to provide my men with all things necessary, to guard what I had left there for your Majesty, and that his men would take me by a road which led entirely through his dominions and would provide for me on the way. Moreover, if they were evil people as I thought, he begged me to acquaint him and he would go out with great numbers of his warriors to fight them and drive them from the land. For this I thanked him, assured him that your Majesty would grant him great favours, and gave many trinkets and clothes both to him, his son and many nobles who were with him. At Cholula I met Juan Velázquez who as I have said was returning with his men from Guasacualco, and fifty leagues further on Father Olmedo whom I had sent to the port. He brought me various news about Narváez, some of which I have already related; and in addition, that certain gold ornaments had been given him on the part of Muteczuma, and he had given certain things in return bidding the messengers tell Muteczuma that he would set him free and would take me and all my company prisoner and would then depart from the land. Finally I learnt that he was resolved to possess the land under his own authority, and that should we refuse to accept him as captain general in the name of Diego Velázquez he intended to attack us, for which reason he had treated with the natives of the land, especially with Muteczuma, by means of his messengers. Seeing then the great disservice that would follow to your Majesty, and although he bore orders from Diego Velázquez to take and hang certain of my company (myself included) if he should capture us, I continued steadily to advance until we were some fifteen leagues from his headquarters at Cempoal. There two priests together with Andrés de Duero met me, declaring on behalf of Narváez in answer to my letter that I was to acknowledge him as captain general and surrender the land to him; on which condition he was willing to hand over to me such ships and provisions as I needed and let me go free together with such men and treasure as I was able to take. I repeated that I had seen no license from your Majesty authorizing this request and if he possessed such it should be duly presented before me and the council of Vera Cruz according to Spanish law; but until that was done nothing should tempt me to do what he suggested: but rather I and my men would die in defence of the land which we had conquered and maintained in peace and order on behalf of your Majesty, not being traitors and disloyal subjects to our king. After much vain argument of a like nature we agreed that Narváez and ten persons should meet myself and ten others under a flag of truce, and he should there show me his license if such he had. I on my part sent him a signed declaration of truce and received one from him in exchange. I had good reason to believe, however, that he did not mean to observe this: indeed, two of the ten were instructed to kill me while the rest held off my men, for they deemed that with my death their object was achieved, as indeed it would have been, if God had not brought such plans to naught by certain news which came to my ears. Knowing this I wrote to Narváez telling him that I could not meet him in such circumstances and warning him that if he and his men would not appear before me to learn what their duty was towards your Majesty I should proceed against them as traitors and rebellious vassals and would take them prisoner according to the law.

SECOND LETTER

The only reply which Narváez made to this was to take prisoner my messenger and certain other Indians whom I had sent, and after making great display of his troops before them, to threaten them with what would befall them if they would not consent to surrender the land. Seeing then that in no way could I prevent this evil, and that the natives were daily being led to rebel further, I put aside all fears of possible danger, thinking myself happy to die in the service of my king and defending his lands from usurpation; and therefore putting my trust in God I gave Gonzalvo de Sandoval, *alguacil mayor*, orders to go with eight men and arrest Narváez and those who called themselves *alcaldes* and *regidores* in his name: I myself with one hundred and seventy men, all on foot and without any guns, followed close behind him, to support him if Narváez and his men should attempt to resist.

Narváez heard from the natives of our approach on Cempoal where he was stationed and sallied out on to the plain with eight horse and some five hundred foot, not counting those that he left behind in his camp, which was the largest temple in the city. Not perceiving us, however, he thought that the Indians had been tricking him and retired, keeping his men on the watch and posting two sentinels almost a league out from the city. Desiring to avoid all scandal I thought that our purpose would best be attained by proceeding by night, without being perceived if that were possible, straight to Narváez's lodging, which I and all my men knew well, and there arresting him. Accordingly on the night of Whit Sunday a little after midnight I advanced upon his camp and immediately came across the two sentinels, one of whom was captured, from whom I learnt how Narváez's men were positioned, but the other escaped. I consequently pushed on as fast as I could to prevent his giving them news of our advance, but he succeeded in arriving some half an hour before us. When finally I came up to where Narváez was, all his men were already armed and mounted, with two hundred soldiers ready posted to guard each building. We arrived so quietly, however, that when they at last perceived us and gave the call to arms I was already entering the courtyard of his lodging in which all his men were gathered. Three or four towers which rose at the corners and all the other strong buildings were also in their possession. In one of these towers where Narváez had his own rooms there were no less than nineteen guns placed in position, but we made such a rush to mount the steps that they only had time to fire one of them which by the mercy of God did not go off and so hurt no one. In this manner Sandoval and his men fought their way right up to Narváez's bedroom where he and some fifty others were opposing them, and notwithstanding that many times they ordered him to give himself up to your Majesty he obstinately refused until the tower was fired and he surrendered. In the meantime, while Sandoval was arresting Narváez I with the rest of my men was defending the entrance to the tower against those who were coming to their master's help, and training the guns on them which we had captured I thus fortified myself: in such wise, that without any fatalities (barring two men who were killed by a cannon-ball) in the space of one hour all those who were to be arrested were in chains and the rest disarmed; the latter now very readily promised obedience to your Majesty, saying that they had been misled by their commander: and all now recognizing the evil intent of the aforesaid Diego Velázquez and Narváez were very joyful in that God had thus remedied it. For I can assure your Majesty that had not God mysteriously worked in this matter and victory had fallen to Narváez, it would have been the greatest hurt done for many years in this land among Spaniards one to another.

Two days after Narváez's arrest I sent one officer back to Guasacualco and another north to that river, which Francisco de Garay's ships reported they had seen. I remained with the rest of my men and sent a messenger to Tenochtitlan to tell the Spaniards there what had occurred.

He was back in twelve days bringing me letters from the *alcalde* from which I learnt that the Indians had attacked the garrison on all sides, fired many parts and made several mines: my men were in great difficulty and danger and would surely die, unless Muteczuma would order the attack to cease, for they were still completely surrounded and although not actually fighting could not venture so much as two steps outside the garrison. A large part of the stores I left them had been captured and the three brigs burnt. They were in great need and begged me for the love of God to come to their relief as soon as I could. Seeing their necessity and that if they were not rescued, besides their being killed by the Indians, and all the gold and jewels belonging to your Majesty and ourselves being captured, we should also lose the greatest and noblest city of all that have been discovered in the new world, which lost all else would follow, I immediately recalled the officers whom I had sent out, telling them to assemble by the shortest way in the province of Tlascala where I was with all my men. We accordingly joined forces again and I found myself at the head of seventy horses, five hundred foot and a fair number of guns. I immediately gave the order to advance as quickly as possible on the city, and the whole way not a single servant of Muteczuma's came out to meet me as was usual, and the whole land seemed disturbed and practically deserted. I was not a little suspicious at this, thinking that the Spaniards whom I had left in the town were now all killed, and that the whole forces of the nation were gathered together waiting to ambush me in some defile where they would be able to take me at a disadvantage. I therefore advanced as cautiously as I could until reaching Tezcuco, which as I have mentioned to your Majesty is on the shore of the great lake. There I enquired of the inhabitants about the Spaniards in the capital and was informed that they were still alive. On this I told them to bring me a canoe and I would send one of my men to find out, adding that in the meantime while he was gone one of their chiefs was to stay with me under custody. At the moment that he was embarking another canoe arrived from across the lake containing a Spaniard from whom I learnt that they were all alive except four or five whom the Indians had killed, but that the natives had surrounded the garrison, would not let them pass beyond, and would only provide necessary food at exorbitant rates of exchange, but that since they had heard of my approach, they had behaved somewhat better; Muteczuma himself, they said, had declared that they were only waiting for my return to allow us to go freely about the city as formerly. In the same canoe there was a native bearing a message from Muteczuma in which he said that he could well imagine that I should be vexed at what had taken place in the city and should come with intent to do him harm, but begged me to put aside my wrath for it had grieved him as much as myself: nothing, he said, had been done with his will and consent, and many other things he added by which he hoped to placate my wrath: finally he begged me to lodge in the city as before, when my commands would be obeyed with no less promptitude than in the past. I sent back word saying that I was in no wise angry with him for I knew well his good will towards me, and that I would do as he said.

Next day (being the eve of Saint John the Baptist) I set out and camped for the night on the road but three leagues from the capital. On the day of Saint John after having heard mass I entered the city about midday, seeing few people about, and certain doors at the crossroads and turnings taken down, which appeared to be a bad sign, although I considered that it was done out of fright for what had already occurred and that my entrance would serve to calm them. I went straight to the fortress and the great temple next to it in which my men had taken up their quarters, and where they received us with such joy as if we had given them back their lives which they counted already lost: and so we remained there very much at ease throughout the rest of that day and night, thinking that all disturbance had settled down. Next day after hearing mass I despatched a messenger to Vera Cruz giving them the good news that I had entered the city to find the Christians alive and the city now quiet. But in half an hour he returned all covered with bruises and wounds, crying that the whole populace of the city was advancing in war dress and all the bridges were raised. And immediately behind him came a multitude of people from all parts so that the streets and house-roofs were black with natives; all of whom came on with the most frightful yells and shouts it is possible to imagine.

The stones from their slings came down on us within the fortress as if they were raining from the sky; the arrows and darts fell so thickly that the walls and courtyards were full of them and one could hardly move without treading on them. I made sallies in one or two parts and they fought against us with tremendous fury; one of my officers led two hundred men out by another door and before he could retire they had killed four of them and wounded both him and many others. I myself and many of my men were also wounded. We killed but few of them for they were waiting for us on the other side of the bridges, and did us much damage from the flat house-tops with ſtones: some of these flat roofs we gained possession of and burnt the houses. But there were so many and so ſtrongly fortified, being held by such numbers of natives and all so well provided with ſtones and other missiles, that we were not numerous enough to take all of them nor to hold what we had taken, for they could attack us at their pleasure.

The fight went on so fiercely in the fortress itself that they succeeded in setting fire to it in many parts, and actually burnt a large portion, without our being able to ſtop the flames until laſt we broke down a ſtretch of wall and thus prevented it from spreading further. Indeed, had it not been for the ſtrong guard I placed there of musketeers, crossbowmen and guns they would have entered under our eyes without our being able to ſtop them. We continued thus fighting all day until night was well come, though even then the yelling and commotion did not cease. During the night I ordered the doorways which had suffered by the fire to be repaired and all other places of the fortress which seemed to me weak. I decided upon the squads that were to defend the various parts of the fortress on the morrow and also the one that was to sally out with me to attack the Indians outside: I also ordered the wounded to be looked to, who numbered more than eighty.

As soon as it was day the enemy began to attack us with greater fury even than the day before: they came on in such numbers that the gunners had no need to take aim but simply poured their shot into the mass. Yet in spite of the damage done by the guns, for there were three arquebuses without counting muskets and crossbows, they made so little impression that their effect could hardly be perceived, for wherever a shot carried away ten or a dozen men, the gap closed up with others so that it seemed as if no damage had been done. Upon this, leaving such suitable guard as I could in the fortress I sallied out and got possession of a few houses, killing many of those who were defending them: but their numbers were so great that although we had done still greater damage it would have had but slight effect. Moreover, whereas we had to continue fighting all the day they could fight for several hours and then give way to others, for their forces were amply sufficient. They again wounded as many as fifty to seventy Spaniards that day, although no one was killed, and so we fought on till nightfall when we had to retire worn out to the fortress.

Seeing then the great damage that our enemies did us, and that they could wound and kill us almost unhurt themselves, we spent the whole of that night and next day in making three wooden engines, each one of which would protect twenty men when they had got inside it: the engines were covered with boards to protect the men from the stones which were thrown from the housetops; and those chosen to go inside were crossbowmen and musketeers together with others provided with pickaxes, hoes and iron bars to burrow under the houses and tear down the barricades which they had erected in the streets. All the while these wooden affairs were being made fighting did notc ease for a moment, in such wise that as we prepared to make a sally out of the fortress they attempted to force an entrance, and it was as much as we could do to resist them. Muteczuma, who was still a prisoner together with his son and many other nobles who had been taken on our first entering the city, requested to be taken out on to the flat roof of the fortress, where he would speak to the leaders of the people and make them ſtop fighting. I ordered him to be brought forth and as he mounted a breaſt-work that extended beyond the fortress, wishing to speak to the people who were fighting there, a ſtone from one of their slings ſtruck him on the head so severely that he died three days later: when this happened I ordered two of the other Indian prisoners to take out his dead body on their shields to the people, and I know not what became of it; save only this that the fighting did not cease but rather increased in intensity every day.

The day that Muteczuma was wounded they called out to me from the place where he had been ſtruck down saying that some of the native captains wished to speak to me; and thither I went and spent much time talking with them, begging them to cease fighting againſt me, for they had no reason to do so, and should consider that I had always treated them very well. They replied that I should depart and abandon their land when they would immediately ſtop fighting; but otherwise they were of a mind to kill us, or die themselves to a man. This they said, as it appeared, in order to persuade me to leave the fortress, when they would fall upon us at their pleasure between the bridges as we left the city. I replied that they were not to think that I besought them for peace because I feared them in any way, but because I was grieved at the damage I was doing them and should have to do them, and in order not to deſtroy so fine a city: to which they ſtill replied that they would not cease fighting until I should leave the city.

The wooden conſtructions having been finished I sallied out next day to capture certain roofs and bridges. The wooden affairs went firſt, and behind them four guns and numerous crossbowmen and soldiers bearing shields, with more than three thousand

SECOND LETTER

Tlascalan Indians who had come with me and acted as servants to the Spaniards. Coming to a bridge we placed the engines close against the walls of the house and put up the ladders which we carried with us to mount on to the roof. The enemy, however, were so numerous defending the bridges and roofs, and the stones which they cast down on us so many and large that they put the wooden erection out of action, killed one Spaniard and wounded many more, without our being able to gain so much as a foot of ground, although we fought stubbornly for it from early morning until noon, upon which we returned sad at heart to the fortress.

This check roused their spirits to such an extent that they forced their way almost to the inner towers and succeeded in taking the temple, the chief tower of which was quickly filled with as many as five hundred Indians, all seemingly of high rank. Forthwith they proceeded to carry up large stores of bread, water and other food, together with plentiful supplies of stones. Most of them, moreover, were armed with long lances with heads of flint broader but no whit less sharp than our own; and from their position they did great damage to my men within the fortress for they were very close. The Spaniards two or three times attacked this tower and attempted to mount it, but as it was very tall and steep, having more than a hundred steps, and those above were well provided with stones and arms and moreover protected to a certain extent since we had been unable to take the neighbouring roofs, they were forced to descend every time they attempted, and suffered many casualties; whereupon the natives in other parts of the city were so encouraged as to rush on the fortress without any signs of fear. Seeing that if our enemies were allowed to hold the tower they would not only do us much damage but would encourage the rest, I sallied out from the fortress, though disabled in the left hand from a wound received in the first day's fighting. Tying my shield on to my arm, however, I made for the tower followed by certain others and we surrounded it entirely at its base; this was done with no great difficulty, although not without danger, since my men had to deal with the enemy who were rushing up on all sides to support their comrades. I myself with a few behind me began to mount the staircase of the tower. And although they defended themselves very furiously, so much so that three or four Spaniards were knocked spinning downstairs, nevertheless with the help of God and our Gracious Mother, to whose honour the building had been dedicated and crowned with her statue, we finally got up the tower, and fought with them on top so fiercely that they were forced to leap down on to certain flat roofs, between which and the tower there was a gap of about a yard. There were about three or four of these all about eighteen feet below the top of the tower. Some fell right to the ground and were either broken by the fall or dispatched by the Spaniards who were below. Those who escaped on to the flat roofs continued to fight with extreme bravery so that it was more than three hours before we finished with them, and then there was not a man left alive. And your Majesty may well believe that had not God broken their ranks twenty of them might have stopped a thousand men from mounting the tower. Nevertheless those who died fought very valiantly. When it was all over I set fire to this tower and the other towers of the temple, having already abandoned them and removed all the images of the saints which we had placed there.

They lost somewhat of their pride on our taking this stronghold from them; so much so that on all sides their attack slackened, on which I returned to the housetop and spoke to the captains with whom I had already held speech and who were somewhat dismayed by what they had seen. On their approach I bade them note that they could not help themselves, that each day we should do them great hurt and kill many of them; already we were burning and destroying their city and would have to continue so to do until nothing of it or of them remained. To which they replied that they plainly perceived this but were determined to die to a man, if need be, to finish with us. And they bade me observe that the streets, squares and rooftops were all packed full of people, and that they had reckoned that if twenty-five thousand of them were to die for every one of us yet we should perish sooner, for we were few and they were many; and they gave me to know that all the bridges in the streets had been removed, as was indeed the case excepting a single one. We had therefore no way of escape except by water. Moreover, they knew well that we had but slight store of food and drinking water so that we could not hold out long without dying of hunger, even if they should not kill us themselves. And in truth they were perfectly right: for had we no other foes than hunger and general shortness of provisions, we were like to die in a short time. Many other arguments were put forward each supporting his own position.

After nightfall I went out with a few Spaniards and taking them off their guard succeeded in capturing a whole street in which we burnt more than three hundred houses. So soon as the natives had rushed there I returned by another street where I likewise set fire to many houses, especially to certain ones with low flat roofs lying close to the fortress from which they had inflicted great damage upon us. What was done that night inspired them with great terror, and the same night I turned my engineers on to repairing the wooden structures which had been put out of action the previous day.

In order to follow up the victory which God had given us I sallied out as soon as dawn broke along the street where they had repulsed us the day before and which we found no less strongly defended than on the former occasion. However, our lives and honour were at stake, for the road joined up with the causeway leading to the mainland; though there were eight broad, deep gaps to be crossed where the bridges had been, and the whole street was lined with many flat-roofed houses and high towers: nevertheless we pushed forward with such determination and spirit that God helping us we gained four of the bridges from the enemy during the day and burnt all the towers and houses right up to the last one of them: notwithstanding that during the previous night they had built up strong barricades of clay and earth so that our guns and crossbows were rendered ineffective. The bridges or rather where the bridges had been were filled up with clay and earth from the barricades and a great quantity of wood and stones from the houses we had destroyed. All this was not done without grave danger and the wounding of many of my men, but that night I placed a strong guard at the bridges to make certain that they should not be recaptured. Early next morning I again advanced; and God granting us equal good fortune and success, in spite of the innumerable natives who were defending the huge barricades in front of the gaps they had made during the night, we won them all and blocked them up: in such wise that certain of my men on horseback followed up the victory by charging along the causeway right to the mainland. In the meantime while I was busied in the work of repairing and blocking up the bridges they came to call me in great haste saying that the Indians were advancing on the fortress and asking for peace, certain of their chieftains being come there to speak with me. Immediately, leaving all my men there and a few guns I went back with only two horsemen to see what they wished. The chieftains told me that if I would give my word that they should not be punished for what had already been done, they would raise the blockade, restore the bridges and roads, and serve your Majesty as heretofore. They begged me to send for one of their priests whom I had captured who was in some way the chief priest of their religion. He was sent for, spoke to them and made an agreement between them and myself. Then, it seemed, they sent messengers, or so they said, to the captains and people who were in the town to tell them to cease attacking the fortress and all other fighting. With this we bade farewell to each other and I went inside to eat. But while I was still at my meal they came running to tell me that the Indians had attacked the bridges which we had won from them during the day and had killed several Spaniards: which news, God knows, came to me as a sore blow, for I thought we should have no more difficulty having once cleared our way of retreat. I leapt to my horse and galloped as fast as I could along the causeway followed by a few others on horseback. Without stopping I charged straight at the Indians and succeeded in winning back the bridges, pursuing them right to the mainland. The infantry was tired, wounded and dismayed, and not one of them followed me: in a moment I saw the great danger I was in, and thinking to return across the bridges I found them taken again and already partially unblocked. The causeway was lined with people on either side both on land and in canoes on the water, who attacked us with spears and stones so fiercely that had it not been the will of God mysteriously to save us, it would have been impossible for us to escape, and already it was being published among those who remained in the fortress that I was dead. On coming to the laſt bridge before the city, I found all those who had accompanied me on horseback already fallen into the gap and one horse swimming about without a rider. It was therefore impossible for me to pass, and I was forced to turn and face my enemies single-handed, keeping them at bay for some time so that the horses could get across. The bridge itself was almoſt deſtroyed and I finally passed over with some difficulty, there being one place where my horse had to leap across a gap some six feet wide. Both my horse and myself, however, were well armed and were consequently not wounded, suffering only bruises. We thus remained victorious that night with the four bridges in our possession. I left a ſtrong guard over those newly won and went back to the fortress, where I ordered a wooden bridge to be built capable of allowing forty men to pass at once. Seeing then the great danger we were in and the damage that the Indians did us each day, and fearing that they might entirely break up the causeway as they had done the others, in which case there was nothing but death for all of us, being moreover repeatedly requeſted by all my men to leave the city, moſt of them now being so badly wounded that they could hardly fight, I decided to make the attempt that very night. Accordingly I got together all the gold and jewels belonging to your Majeſty that I could and placed them in a separate room, where I had them made up into various bundles, and handed them over to certain officials of your Majeſty whom I specially appointed in your Majeſty's royal name. I likewise besought the *alcaldes* and *regidores* together with all others present to assiſt me in carrying the treasure to a place of safety, for which purpose I gave one of my own mares which was loaded with as much as it could carry: I appointed certain Spaniards, both my servants and those of others, to accompany the mare with the gold, and the remaining amount was divided between all the men by the aforesaid royal officials, the *alcaldes* and *regidores* and myself. Upon this, abandoning the fortress we sallied out as secretly as we could with great treasure both of your Majesty and of my soldiers and myself, taking with us a son and two daughters of Muteczuma, Cacamacin, ruler of Culhuacan, and his brother whom I had put in his place, together with other rulers of cities and provinces whom I held prisoners. On coming to the first of the gaps in the causeway from which the Indians had removed the bridges the wooden bridge which I had ordered to be made was thrown across without much difficulty, for there was no one to offer any resistance save a few sentinels. These however gave the alarm so effectively that before we had arrived at the second an innumerable mass of the enemy were upon us, attacking us on all sides both from the water and the land. I myself hurried forward with five horsemen and a hundred foot, swimming across the gaps in the causeway, and thus reached the mainland. Leaving that body as a vanguard, I turned back to the rear where I found them fighting very desperately, and receiving infinitely more damage than they had yet done, both the Spaniards and the Tlascalan Indians who were helping us. Frightful execution was done on these, as also on the natives by the Spaniards. Many Spaniards and horses had been killed, all the gold, jewels, clothing and other things we were carrying were lost, and in addition all the guns. Rallying those who were still alive I urged them forward, and myself with three or four horsemen and as many as twenty foot who were brave enough to stay with me kept in the rear, beating off the Indians until we arrived at the city of Tacuba which is at the other end of the causeway, in which fighting God knows the peril and toil I suffered. Every time that I charged the enemy I returned covered with arrows and darts and beaten with stones: for since there was water on both sides they could strike at us unharmed and without fear of those who were on the land. Then on our charging them they would leap into the water, in such wise that they received very little hurt, though there were some who in the press stumbled one against the other and thus fell and were killed. With such difficulty and fatigue I got all my men to Tacuba without losing any further Spaniard or Indian save one horseman who was with me in the rearguard, and not for a moment did the enemy stop fighting both in front and on either flank but principally in the rear where all the people came pouring out upon us from the city.

On arriving at Tacuba I found all my men gathered together in a square not knowing where to go. I immediately ordered them to hasten to the outskirts of the city before more troops should come in and capture the flat rooftops, from which the natives would do us much hurt. Those of the vanguard said they did not know in which direction to go, on which I ordered them to remain in the rear, and myself led the vanguard out of the city and waited there in some ploughed fields. When the rearguard came up I found that they had had several casualties, both Spaniards and Indians having been killed, and much gold had been dropped on the way which the natives were busy in picking up. There I remained until all my forces had passed, holding off the Indians and thus giving the foot soldiers time to take possession of a strong tower and buildings situated on a hill which they took without further casualties. For I did not leave the place nor allow any of the enemy to pass until they had succeeded in taking it, and God knows what fatigue and toil we suffered there, for there was not a horse out of the twenty-four remaining to us which could run, nor a horseman who could raise his arm, nor a foot soldier unwounded or fit to fight. Coming up finally to the buildings we fortified ourselves in them, and there the enemy surrounded us and kept us surrounded until nightfall without giving us a moment's rest. In this retreat it was found later on calling the lists that one hundred and fifty Spaniards lost their lives, forty-five horses and more than two thousand of the Tlascalan Indians who had come to serve the Spaniards; among those killed were also the son and daughter of Muteczuma and all the other chiefs whom I held prisoner.

That night at midnight thinking not to be seen we abandoned the tower and outbuildings very cautiously, leaving many fires lighted inside, but ignorant of the road or in what direction to go, having only one of the Tlascalan Indians as a guide who said he would bring us to his country providing they did not stop us on the way. Their sentinels, however, perceived us very soon and immediately gave the alarm to a number of townships close by from which crowds of natives sallied out and followed close on our heels until morning. Just as dawn was breaking five of our horse going on in front as an advance guard came upon some squadrons of the enemy drawn up in the road, and succeeded in killing some of them and scattering the rest who thought there were more horse and foot in the rear. Seeing that the enemy was increasing on all sides I gathered my men together and those who were fit to strike a blow I split up into squadrons, placing them in the van, in the rear and on both sides, with the wounded in the middle, and dividing up the horsemen in the same manner. So we continued all that day beating off the enemy on all sides in such wise that from the time we set out in the middle of the previous night we did not go above three leagues. However it was God's will as night was coming on that we should see a tower and buildings perched on a hill where we fortified ourselves as we had done before. That night they left us in peace, although a little before dawn there was another alarm caused by nothing more than the fear which we all possessed of the multitudes of the enemy who were continuing in pursuit.

The next day I again set out in the same order, keeping an eye upon both van and rearguard. The enemy still kept up with us on one side and another, yelling and giving the alarm to the whole district which is thickly populated. Those of us who were on horseback though few in number charged them several times, but did little damage, for as the ground was somewhat broken they retreated before us to the hills. We continued thus throughout that day marching along the shore of the lakes until we came to a fair-sized town where we expected to meet with some opposition from the inhabitants. But as we came up they abandoned it and fled to other townships near by. Accordingly we camped there both that day and the next, for the men whether wounded or whole were weary and worn out with hunger and thirst, and the horses were no less exhausted: there, fortunately, we found some maize which we ate and cooked to take with us on the march. Next day we again set off still harassed by the enemy who attacked us in the van and rear, yelling and making charges from time to time. We pursued the road as directed by our Indian guide and suffered much toil and hardship by it for we were many times forced to go out of our way. It was already late when we came to a collection of huts grouped together in a plain where we camped that night. We were now running very short of provisions. Early next day we began our march but

were not yet on the road when the enemy had already
come up with the rearguard and had begun skirmishing with them. After proceeding two leagues we
came to a large town at the right of which there
were a few Indians gathered together on a little hill.
Thinking to capture them, for they were very near
the road, and also to discover whether any more of
the enemy could be seen from the hilltop, I left the
main body accompanied by five horsemen and ten or
a dozen foot and rode round the hill. Behind it
there was a large town filled with people with whom
we engaged so fiercely, that the ground being rocky
and covered with stones and their numbers far exceeding ours, we were at last forced to retreat to the village
occupied by our main body. I myself came off badly,
being wounded in the head from two stones. Having
had my wounds bound up I gave orders to leave the
village for it seemed to me too insecure as a camping
place. In this wise we continued our march, the
Indians still following us in large numbers and attacking us so fiercely that four or five Spaniards and as
many horses were wounded and one horse killed.
God knows what a loss it was to us and our grief at
its death, for our whole safety lay (after God) in the
horses; however, its flesh somewhat consoled us and we
ate every bit of it, leaving neither skin nor anything
else, such was our hunger. For since leaving the
large town by the lake we had eaten nothing except
maize cakes (and there were not enough of those
to go round) and greenstuff which we had gathered
from the fields.

Seeing then that the enemy increased each day in
numbers and in fury while we were growing weaker
I gave orders that night for the wounded and sick
whom we had hitherto carried on the haunches of
the horses and our own backs to make themselves
some kind of crutches and other contrivances by

which they could manage to get along so that the horses and fit men might be free to fight. It seemed as if the Holy Spirit himself inspired me in this matter according to what befell us on the following day: for in the morning having advanced on our road about a league and a half from where we had been encamped, a great number of Indians sallied out to meet us, so many that in front, rear and on all sides the whole plain as far as one could see was black with them. They attacked us so fiercely on every side that we could hardly recognize each other so closely were the enemy mingled with us. And in truth we thought our laſt day had come, the ſtrength of the Indians being overpowering and our own powers of resiſtance almoſt at an end, seeing that we were worn out and almoſt all wounded and faint with hunger. Nevertheless Our Lord deigned to show His great power and mercy towards us; so that in spite of all our weakness we broke down their pride and obſtinacy, killing many of them, including many chieftains and leaders; for their numbers were so great that they got in each other's way and could neither fight nor fly. Struggling thus we continued a great part of the day until by God's will one of their chieftains was killed who muſt have been so important that with his death the battle entirely ceased. So we continued our way somewhat relieved although ſtill consumed with hunger until we arrived at a little house set in the midſt of the plain where we camped that night and in the open fields. Already a few hills in the province of Tlascala could be descried, at which our hearts were filled with not a little thankfulness. For we knew the land now and the road by which we should have to travel. Nevertheless we were not very certain in our minds of finding the natives of that province ſtill subječt to your Majeſty and friendly to us; for on seeing us returning in such plight they might decide, we thought, to put an end to our lives and thus recover the liberty which they once enjoyed. This thought and anxiety made our hearts as heavy as they had been when we were engaged in battle with the Culuans.

The following day was clear and we set out on a broad road leading straight to the province of Tlascala, for few of the enemy were now following us although there were numerous large townships close by; far in the rear, however, from the top of several small hills they still uttered yells of defiance. And so that day which was Sunday, the 8th of July, we left the whole land of Culua and came to the province of Tlascala to a town called Gualipán of some two or three thousand inhabitants, where we were very well received by the natives, and our hunger and fatigue somewhat appeased. Most of the provisions which they gave us, however, had to be paid for in money, and they even refused to take anything but gold which in our great need we were forced to give them. We remained in this town three days. Magiscatzin and Sicutengal both came to see me, together with all the lesser chieftains of Tlascala and some of Guasu-cingo. They all showed much grief for what had befallen us and endeavoured to console me, saying that they had warned me many times that the Culuans were traitors and that I should beware of them, but I had never been willing to believe it. Still seeing that I had escaped with my life I must be of good heart, for they would aid me to the death in revenging myself on the Culuans for the hurt they had done me. For besides being obliged to do so as being vassals of your Majesty they themselves mourned many sons and brothers who had met their death in my company and many other injuries which in the past they had received; so that I could hold it very certain that they would be my loyal and faithful friends to the death.

Moreover seeing that I was wounded and all my men worn out they bade us go to the city four leagues away and take our rest there, and they would help us to recover from our fatigue and labours. I thanked them and agreed to their suggestion, giving them sundry little trinkets which I had preserved and with which they were very pleased, and we set off with them for the city where we were also very well received. Magiscatzin himself brought me a finely made bed of wood with certain coverings such as they use on which to sleep, for we had nothing with us, and likewise he helped all in so far as he was able.

I had left in this city a few sick men when I was returning to Tenochtitlan and certain of my servants with plate, clothes and other household furniture and light provisions which I had with me, in order to travel seeing that anything might happen to us on the way. Likewise all my diaries and the treaties I had made with the natives of these parts were left together with the beds and clothes of all the men who accompanied me and who carried with them nothing more than what they stood up in. I now learnt that another of my servants had arrived from Vera Cruz in my absence bringing food and other things for me and accompanied by five horsemen and five and forty foot. He had set out with those I had left in the city and all my plate and belongings as well as that of my companions—including seven thousand *pesos* of gold melted down which I had left in two large chests together with other ornaments loose, more than thirteen thousand *pesos* of gold in pieces brought back by the captain who had been sent to settle the province of Guasacualco, and many other things totalling rather more than thirty thousand *pesos*— and all had been murdered on the way by the Culuan Indians who captured all the treasure that they were carrying. Many other Spaniards, I learnt, had been

killed by the Culuans on the road leading to Tenochtitlan, thinking that I was peacefully settled in the
capital and that the roads were safe as they had been
before.

At this news, I assure your Majesty we were as
sad as we could well be, for in addition to the actual
loss of men and goods, it brought to our memory all
those whom we had lost at the hands of the enemy at
the bridges in the capital and on the road. More
especially I was put in great anxiety lest the natives
should also have risen against the townsfolk in Vera
Cruz, and that those whom we took to be our friends
might not have rebelled on hearing of our repulse.
I immediately sent out messengers to find out the truth
accompanied by Indian guides, who were to make
their way to Vera Cruz across country, and let me
know as quickly as possible what had occurred there.
God be praised, they found the Spaniards there in
good health and the natives very peaceful. Which
news requited us for our past loss and sadness; although
for them it was bad news enough to hear of the ill
fortune of our expedition and our final retreat. I
remained in this province of Tlascala twenty days
recovering from the wounds I had received, for what
with the long journey and lack of attention they had
become much worse. I attended likewise to the
healing of those of my company who were wounded.
Some died either from their wounds or the fatigue of
the march, others remained maimed and lame, for
their wounds were very severe and there was very
little in the way of effective treatment. I myself lost
the use of two fingers of my left hand.

Seeing that many were killed, and that those who
had escaped were weak, wounded, and demoralized
by the perils and toils which they had passed through,
and fearing those dangers which were still to come
(and in truth it seemed they might be upon us at

any minute) my men more than once begged me to return to Vera Cruz and there fortify ourselves, before the natives of the land, who for the moment seemed friendly but might soon realize our weakness and unpreparedness, should join with our enemies and seize the passes that lay between us and Vera Cruz; they could then attack us and the inhabitants of that city separately, whereas if we once joined forces at Vera Cruz with the boats there as well, we should be infinitely ſtronger, and could defend ourselves in case of attack until help should arrive from the Islands. But I considered that to show signs of weakness to the natives, especially to our friends, would result in their abandoning us and going over to our enemies all the sooner; so calling to mind that fortune always favours the brave, that we were Chriſtians, and confiding in the infinite goodness and mercy of God who would not permit us all to perish, or that such a noble land which was already on the point of being subjected should be loſt to your Majeſty, I determined that nothing should prevail upon me to cross the passes between us and the sea: but rather, putting aside all thought of toils and dangers that might beset us, I told them that in no wise would I abandon this land for I considered that to do so would not only be shameful to my person and full of danger for us all, but also disloyal in the higheſt degree to your Majeſty. I was therefore determined to turn upon the enemy wherever I could, and attack him by whatever means were possible.

Having been in this province twenty days, although I was not yet recovered from my wounds and my men were ſtill very weak, I left it for Tepeaca, the natives of whom were allies of the Culuans, and had, I was informed, killed a dozen or so Spaniards on the road from Vera Cruz. Immediately on my entering the province large numbers of the natives came out to oppose us and stop our advance as best they could, taking up their positions in strongholds built on the top of steep hills. There is not space to give your Majesty all the particulars of this war, so I will simply say that although the province is very large in about three weeks I had pacified most of the towns and villages in it; and the chieftains had duly come in to offer themselves as vassals of your Majesty. I have moreover banished from this province all those Culuans who had come hither to persuade the natives to make war on us and prevent them whether they were willing or not from being our friends. In such wise that up to this moment I have been busied in carrying on the war, which is still not quite finished, a few towns and villages still remaining to be subjected: the which with God's help will soon be accomplished and they will remain like the others subject to your Majesty. In a certain part of this province, namely where the ten Spaniards were killed, since the natives were always very rebellious and warlike, I made slaves of those who were captured in arms, of whom a fifth were handed over to your Majesty's officials. For in addition to having murdered the Spaniards and rebelled against your Majesty's service they eat human flesh, a fact so notorious that I send your Majesty no further proof of it. I was also moved to enslave them in order to frighten the Culuans, and because moreover the natives are so numerous that if a signal and severe warning is not given them, they will never mend their ways. In this war we had the aid of the Indians from Tlascala, Cholula and Guasucingo, by which our friendship with them has been much strengthened and we are confident that they will continue to serve your Majesty as his loyal vassals. When the province had been thus pacified I held many conversations with your Majesty's officials as to the order which should be observed in its future government. Seeing that the natives had rebelled before, that the Culuans were their neighbours and might persuade them to revolt again, and above all that the coast road to Vera Cruz has only two bad passes very rocky and steep, both of which are on the borders of this province and could be easily defended by the natives, we finally decided that a town should be established in the most suitable part of this province of Tepeaca, and that the necessary officials should be appointed. Whereupon I christened the town Segura de la Frontera in your Majesty's name and appointed *alcaldes*, *regidores* and other officials according to the law. And for the greater security of the townsfolk, in the place decided upon, they have already begun to bring materials for a fortress, for there is plenty of suitable stone in these parts and they will make haste to finish building it as quickly as possible.

(Cortés proceeded straightway with the reconquest of the central provinces of Mexico, which on hearing of the Christians' retreat from Tenochtitlan had thrown off their allegiance to the Spaniards. Thirteen horse and two hundred foot with thirty thousand Tlascalan Indians were sent off to the city of Guacahula to aid the ruler against the Culuans. The Spaniards feared treachery from the city and finally Cortés went thither himself. Great slaughter was done on the enemy and both Guacahula and Izzucan, four leagues off, surrendered to Cortés. Other rulers began to come in from the cities and provinces round about and were accepted again as vassals. Cortés then continues):

In such wise your Majesty may rest assured that in a very short space of time all that was lost or at any rate the greater part of it will have been regained, for daily messengers arrive from many provinces and cities which were formerly subject to Muteczuma, seeing that those who do so are well received and well treated by me, whereas those who oppose me are daily destroyed.

From those who were taken prisoner in Guacahula, in particular from one badly wounded Indian, I learnt in some detail what had happened in Tenochtitlan. On the death of Muteczuma a brother of his, Guatimucin, ruler of Iztapalapa, had succeeded him, for Muteczuma's two sons were killed in crossing the bridges; and of his two remaining sons one was reputed to be mad and the other paralyzed. They were fortifying the capital as also all other cities within their territory; and were making many enclosures, pits and ditches, and many kinds of weapons. In particular I learnt that they were making lances as big as pikes to use against the horses, some of which we have already seen in this province of Tepeaca.

I am sending four ships to Hayti to bring back horses and men to reinforce us; and also sending to purchase another four to be loaded at Santo Domingo with horses, arms, crossbows, and powder, which is what is most lacking in these parts. For foot soldiers with shields are of little use by themselves, the enemy being so numerous and defending themselves in such great cities and fortresses. When these reinforcements arrive I intend to return to attack the capital and the surrounding country, and I believe, as I have already told your Majesty, that in a very short space of time it will return to the state in which it was before, and the past losses will be restored. Meanwhile I am building twelve brigs to use on the lake which surrounds the capital. The decking and other parts of them are already being made so that they can be carried overland and then put together close to the lake so as to save time. Nails are also being made for them, pitch and oakum prepared, and also sails and oars, and all other things necessary. And I can assure your Majesty that until I have succeeded in this end I think to take no rest nor spare any possible effort or means, taking no account of whatsoever toil, peril or cost in which it may involve me.

I have already said that Guatimucin was preparing for war, and I have just heard that he has sent messengers through all the provinces once subject to Muteczuma granting his vassals exemption from all taxes for a year on condition that they wage relentless war in every way they can on all Christians so as to kill them and banish them from the land, and likewise on such tribes as allied themselves to us as our friends. And although I trust God that his intentions will be frustrated, yet I find myself at great difficulty to aid and reinforce our Indian allies, who come daily from villages all over the land to beg for aid against the Culuans, their enemies and ours, who are waging war upon them with all their strength, on account of the friendship they have shown us: and I am unable to succour them as I should like. However I am confident, as I said, that it will please God to supplement our feeble resources and send help swiftly, both His own and that which I am sending for from Hayti.

From what I have seen and noted as to the similarity which the whole of this country bears to Spain, in fertility, size and the cold, as well as in many other things in which they resemble one another, it seemed to me that the most suitable name for this land would be New Spain, and so it was duly christened in the name of your royal Majesty. I humbly beg your Majesty to approve this and order that it be so named.

I have now written to your Majesty though in uncouth speech the true account of all that has happened in these parts which it is most necessary for your Majesty to know. In another letter which accompanies this one I entreat your Majesty to send out a trustworthy person to make enquiry and examination of everything and inform your Majesty of it; I venture humbly to make this request a second time and shall esteem it a signal favour as a means of giving entire credit to all that I have written.

Most high and excellent prince, may Our Lord God long preserve the life and royal person of your sacred Majesty and increase his powerful state for many years to come, with addition of many greater kingdoms and dominions, as your royal heart desires.

From the town of Segura de la Frontera in New Spain on the 30th of October in the year 1520.

From your Sacred Majesty's very humble slave and vassal who kisses the royal hands and feet of your Highness.

HERNÁN CORTÉS.

THE THIRD LETTER

Sent by Don Hernando Cortés, Captain-General and Chief Justice of Yucatán to the Emperor Don Carlos.

Most High and Mighty Prince, very Catholic and Invincible Emperor, and our Sovereign Lord:

By the hand of one Alonso de Mendoza, a citizen of Medellín, I sent to your Majesty from this New Spain on the 5th of March of last year, 1521, a second account of all that had happened here; this I had already completed on the 30th of October 1520, but bad weather and the consequent loss of three ships prevented my sending it to your Majesty earlier. I informed your Majesty that after being forced to quit Tenochtitlan, I had subsequently attacked the province of Tepeaca which had rebelled, and reduced them to the service of your Majesty. It was my firm resolution to return and avenge ourselves on the inhabitants of the capital who were the prime movers in these rebellions; and to that end I was beginning to make thirteen boats to engage the enemy on the water if those of the city persisted in their evil designs. Meanwhile I sent to Hayti for reinforcements of men, horses, guns and arms, and sent money to your Majesty's officials there to cover all necessary expenses. And I can assure your Majesty that until such time as we should be victorious over our enemies I gave no thought to rest, nor ceased to strain every nerve to that end, putting aside as of no account whatever danger, toil or cost it might involve me in and hurrying forward preparations to leave the province of Tepeaca with the fixed resolve to return and combat against the inhabitants of the capital.

Accordingly, most powerful Prince, in the middle

135

of the month of December of the said year, 1520, I marched out from the town of Segura de la Frontera, leaving at the earnest request of the natives a Captain and some seventy men behind, and sent all the foot ahead to Tlascala, some nine or ten leagues off, where the brigs were being built; I myself with some twenty horse went to sleep that night at Cholula. The natives had asked me to go there, since many of their chief men had died of the smallpox which rages in these lands as it does in the Islands, and they wished me with their approval and consent to appoint other rulers in their place. We were very well received upon our arrival, and having satisfactorily concluded the business which called me there, I explained that my road lay toward the provinces of Mexico on whom I was going to make war, and begged them, since they were vassals of your Majesty and therefore sworn friends with us to the death, to assist us with troops in the war and give those Spaniards who might pass through their lands such treatment as is due between friends. They promised me this, and after two or three days more in the city I left for Tlascala which is some six leagues distant, where I was received with much pleasure by both Spaniards and the natives of the city. On the following day all the chieftains of the city and province came to me saying that Magiscatzin, the principal ruler of them all, had died of the smallpox, but left a son about thirteen years old, who thus inherited his father's territories: they begged me to invest him with them, which I did in your Majesty's name, and all were very well contented.

On arriving in the city I found that the master carpenters and shipwrights were working hard at the timbers and decking of the boats and had made good progress with them. I immediately sent to Vera Cruz for all the iron and nails that they had, together with sails, rigging and other necessary gear.

Moreover, since there was no pitch, I got certain Spaniards to manufacture it on a nearby hill. In such wise everything needful for the boats was being prepared so that when, God willing, we should have advanced into the central provinces of Mexico, I should be able to send for them thence, which would be some ten or a dozen leagues from Tlascala. Accordingly, during the fifteen days that I was there my only cares were to hurry on the work of the carpenters and see that every man's arms were ready for our march.

On Boxing Day I held a review of all troops in Tlascala: they were 40 horse, 550 foot, including 80 crossbowmen and musketeers, and eight or nine field guns but very little powder. I split the horsemen up into four squadrons, ten in each, and the foot into nine companies of up to seventy in each. Having thus arranged them I addressed them all in these terms: "You are aware that in order to do service to his Majesty the Emperor we came to settle in this land, the inhabitants of which declared themselves vassals of his Majesty, and so remained for some time receiving good works from us, as we from them. But without cause the people of Culua, who are those dwelling in the great city of Tenochtitlan and all other provinces subject to them, not only rebelled against his Majesty but also slew many of our company, our kinsmen and our friends, and drove us forcibly from their land. Remember what trials and toils we have passed through, and consider how fitting it is to the service of God and his Catholic Majesty to turn and recover that which is lost, for which we have on our side just cause and reason; first, we are fighting to spread the faith against a barbarous people, second, we are serving his Majesty, third, we have to secure our very existence, fourth, many of the natives are joining us as our allies, all of which are potent causes to cheer our spirits. I beg you then, be cheerful and of a good courage."

I had drawn up certain orders in the name of your Majesty touching discipline and other details of active service, and now ordered these to be publicly read, requesting that they should be duly observed and kept, from which great profit would accrue to God and to your Majesty. All promised to do so, and said that they would either die with a good will for our faith and in the service of God and your Majesty, or they would succeed in recovering what had been lost, and avenging the treachery of the inhabitants of Tenochtitlan and their allies. I thanked them in the name of your Majesty; and so highly contented we returned to our lodgings.

On the following day, that of Saint John the Baptist, I called all the rulers of Tlascala together, and told them, as they knew already, that I was going to take the road against our enemies on the morrow; they could see for themselves that Tenochtitlan could only be taken by means of the brigs which were being built there; and I begged them to provide the Spaniards whom I left there in charge with whatever they needed and continue the fair treatment we had ever received from them, so that the boats might be ready when I should send for them from Tezcuco (if God should give us the victory). They promised to do as I asked and wished to send certain warriors with me on my way. Moreover they would themselves come with the boats with every fit man in the land, and were willing to die with me or avenge themselves on the Culuans, their deadly enemies. Next day, on the 28th of December, the Day of the Holy Innocents, I left with all my men in marching order, and we slept that night at Tezmoluca, a township some six leagues off, in the province of Guajucingo, the natives of which have ever maintained with us the same friendship and alliance as those of Tlascala.

THIRD LETTER

I was aware, most Catholic Lord, that the natives of Mexico were preparing armies and making numerous pits, barricades and stockades throughout their land in order to prevent our entering it, which they now knew that I was determined to do. Knowing this, and moreover how cunning and fierce they are in warfare, I had many times considered where best we could take them unawares. They knew that we had knowledge of three roads, and I therefore decided to take the Tezmoluca road (between the volcano and the mountain land) because the pass through which it led was the stiffest and roughest of the three; I thought that they would therefore guard it less strongly. On the following day, accordingly, having heard mass and commended ourselves to God we set out for Tezmoluca. I myself led the van with ten horse and some seventy light-armed foot, all picked men. We proceeded thus by the pass in as orderly fashion as we could, and halted four leagues from the town, at the top of the pass which was the boundary of Culuan land. And although it was tremendously cold, yet with the large quantities of wood we carried we managed pretty well. Next day, which was Sunday, we continued our way through the pass now on the level, and I sent four foot soldiers to reconnoitre the land. We now began to descend the pass: I ordered the horse to go first, then the crossbowmen and musketeers, and finally the rest of the men in due order; for however much we might take them off their guard we felt certain that they would dispute our passage or surprise us by some sudden ambush or charge. The four horsemen and foot soldiers going on in front found the road blocked with trees and branches, huge pine-trees and cypresses having been thrown across the road looking as if they had been but freshly cut: they proceeded further thinking to come to the end of them, but found the road still worse blocked. The whole pass was indeed so thick with trees and shrubs and the path so stopped up that they could only advance with great difficulty. They were forced to dismount from their horses and grew more fearful the more they advanced. They had gone some way when one of the four cried out: "Brothers, let us go no further, if so it seem good to you, and return to inform the Captain of the obstruction we have found, and the great danger we are running in not being able to use our horses: but if you think otherwise we will go on, for I am ready to give my life as soon as anyone in order to put an end to this business." The others replied that they thought his counsel good, but did not think it would look well to return until they had sighted some of the enemy or knew how long the road was. So they went on, but seeing the road still stretching out before them they sent one of the foot soldiers back to report what they had found. I continued to advance with the vanguard, commending ourselves to God, and sent back word to the rear to press on as fast as they could and not be afraid, for they would soon find themselves in the open. We overtook the four horsemen in front and after another half a league's difficult journey it pleased God to bring us out on the plain where I waited for the rest of my men, and on their arrival bade them all give thanks to God in that he had brought us safely out of that pass to the open ground, where we now saw stretching in front of us the provinces of Mexico and Tenochtitlan spread out round the great lakes. And although we rejoiced greatly to see them, yet recollecting the past hurt we had received there we felt a certain sadness and resolved every man to return from them victorious or leave our bones there: with which resolution we marched forward as cheerily as if we had been going upon a picnicking expedition. The enemy had by this time perceived us and immediately began to send up great smoke columns all over the plain. I turned back and encouraged my men bidding them bear themselves as they had ever done and as was expected of their persons, and repeating that not one should step aside from the path but should march forward in strict order. Already some of the Indians on the farms and villages nearby were beginning to shout to the rest of their compatriots to join them and attack us at certain bridges and difficult places which lay before us. We marched forward so rapidly, however, that before they could come together, we were already on level land. A few bands of Indians placed themselves in our way, and I ordered fifteen horsemen to charge them: this they did, spearing and killing several of them without receiving any hurt. We then continued our way towards Tezcuco, one of the largest and finest cities in these parts. The foot, however, were tired out, so that night we slept at Coatepec, a township subject to Tezcuco and some three leagues this side of it, which we found deserted. It occurred to us that night that in the city and its province of Aculuacan there might very well be at that time over a hundred and fifty thousand men ready to fall upon us: accordingly, I myself with ten horsemen went the round of the first watch, and saw to it that our men kept very much on the look-out.

Next day, which was Monday, December 31st, we again set out in our usual order, and a quarter of a league from Coatepec, as we rode along, anxious and arguing among ourselves as to whether the citizens of Tezcuco were going to meet us with peace or with war (and deciding that the latter was more probable), we were met on the way by four Indian chiefs bearing a golden banner on a staff, weighing four marks in gold, by which they gave us to understand that they were coming in peace: the which God knows how eagerly we desired and had need of, being so few and cut off from all help in the very midst of our foes. I knew one of the four Indians, and therefore commanding my men to halt approached them. Having saluted me they said that they came on behalf of one Guanacacin, ruler of that city and province, to request me to do no harm to his land, since those who had done us wrong were the inhabitants of Tenochtitlan and not they themselves, who were indeed willing to be vassals of your Majesty and our good friends; finally, he said, if we would visit their city we should see by their works the truth of their words. I replied through my interpreters that they were welcome, and I rejoiced to receive their friendship; but while they denied having fought against us in Tenochtitlan they must remember that but five or six leagues from Tezcuco and in certain towns subject to them five of my horsemen and some forty-five foot had been killed, together with more than three hundred Tlascalan Indians who were acting as bearers, and at the same time a great quantity of gold and cloths and other things had been stolen, so that since they could not clear themselves of this crime they were bound as punishment to restore all that belonged to us: on which condition notwithstanding that they were all worthy of death I was willing to make peace with them since they had requested it; but if they would not agree to this I should have to proceed against them with great severity. They replied that they had handed over all that they had stolen to the ruler and chiefs of Tenochtitlan, but would seek out all that they could and restore it to me. They then asked me whether I would prefer to lodge that night in one of two townships which are as it were suburbs of Tezcuco or proceed straight to the city some league and a half further on. It appeared afterwards that they desired me to do the first. I replied, however, that I intended to make no stop until I had reached the city, and they agreed to this, saying that they would go on in advance and prepare lodgings for us. They accordingly went on. On arriving at the townships certain chieftains came out from them bringing us food, and at midday we entered the main body of the city, and came to our lodgings which were in a large house formerly belonging to the father of Guanacacin, the ruler of the city. Before retiring for the night I gave strict orders to all my men that no one without my permission was to leave the buildings, which were indeed so large that had we been double our number we could still have lodged there very comfortably. I did this that the natives of the city might be reassured and remain in their houses; for it seemed to me that not more than a tenth part of the usual population was to be seen, and in particular no women or children, which was a sign of very little confidence on the part of the natives.

That night, which was New Year's Eve, we arranged where the various companies were to sleep, still rather anxious at seeing so few people about and those that we saw very unsettled, but finally concluded that they were afraid to show themselves about the city, and at this conclusion were somewhat relieved. It was already late when a few Spaniards went up to some high flat roofs overlooking the whole city, and discovered that all the natives were abandoning it, some with their belongings embarking on the lake in canoes, others going off up the hillside. I immediately forbade their departure, but as it was late and night came on they were too quick for us and orders were useless. In this way the ruler of the city (whom I was eager to have in my power) made off with all the chief men to Tenochtitlan, six leagues away over the lake, taking most of their belongings with them. It was for this reason that the messengers had come out to meet us so as to delay me and prevent my entering the city and doing any damage.

We remained three days within the city, seeing no Indians, for they neither dared attack us, nor did we make any attempt to sally out and seek them, my fixed intention being to make peace with them whenever they should come and ask for it. During this time the chieftains of the three large townships, Coatinchan, Guaxuta, and Autengo, which are as I have said joined to the city, came to me, weeping and begging me to forgive them for abandoning their land; for the rest, they said that they had not fought against me, at any rate not willingly, and they promised henceforward to do everything that I might command them in the name of your Majesty. I replied through my interpreter that they were well aware how kindly I had always treated them, and that for abandoning their homes and the other matters they must be held to blame; since they promised me their friendship let them return with their wives and children; and as they should give me proof of their words so would I treat them: on this they went away not very contented as it seemed to us.

At this news the ruler of Tenochtitlan and the other chieftains of Culua (by which name must be understood all the provinces subject to the capital) sent messengers to Coatinchan and Guaxuta to remonstrate with them, telling them that they would soon kill all of us and bidding them come into the city and take up their residence there. The messengers, however, were immediately seized, bound and brought to me, whereupon they said that the real object of their visit was to propose terms of peace between myself and those of the capital. This the chieftains of Guaxuta and Coatinchan strongly denied. While not believing them I was nevertheless eager to make peace with the inhabitants of the capital, since on that depended peace or war with all the other provinces which had rebelled, and I accordingly ordered the messengers to be unbound and not to be afraid for I intended to send them back with a message to their lords. I desired no war with them, I said, although I had good reason for it, but rather to be friends as we had been before; and in order to bring them more easily to the service of your Majesty I added that the chiefs who had made war on me were now dead; the past, I said, should be considered past, provided they did not give me cause to destroy their lands and cities, which would grieve me much. With this I let the messengers go forth and they promised to bring me a reply. The rulers of Coatinchan and Guaxuta after this business became on better terms with me, and in your Majesty's name I pardoned their past faults, so that they remained very contented.

Having been in Tezcuco something over a week without any encounter, spending the time in fortifying our camp and making all preparations either for attack or advance, but finding that they did not appear, I left the town with some hundred and fifty foot, eighteen horse, thirty musketeers, and three to four thousand Indian allies, and advanced along the shore of the lake to the town of Iztapalapa, two leagues from the capital by water and six from Tezcuco. The city must contain as many as ten thousand souls and has at least two parts built on the water. Its ruler had been the brother of Muteczuma, to whose position he had succeeded on that king's death, and it was he who had been the prime mover in attacking us and driving us from the capital. For this reason I determined to advance against them. We were seen by the inhabitants at least two leagues off, upon which a few warriors came out on the plain and others in canoes on the lake. Consequently, we advanced the last two leagues fighting both with those on land and those who landed from the water, until we reached the city. Nearly two-thirds of a league behind us they were breaking down the causeway, which acted as a dyke between the fresh and the salt lakes, as your Majesty may see from the map I sent him of the city of Tenochtitlan. The water immediately began to run across with great violence from the salt lake to the fresh, although the lakes are here quite half a league apart. We, mindless of this trick, what with our eagerness for victory rushed on into the city still hotly engaged with the enemy. But they being warned had abandoned all the houses on the mainland and had moved people and chattels alike to the houses built in the lake, where those who were fleeing rallied and fought with us very stubbornly. Yet God gave his own such strength that we forced them back into the water, some standing breast high, others swimming off, and captured many of the houses built in the water, so that on that day over six thousand of them, men, women and children, perished; for our Indian allies, seeing the victory God gave us, would not stay their hands from slaying on right and left. Night came down and I gathered my men and set fire to some of the houses we had captured. As the flames shot up it seemed that Our Lord himself inspired me to recall to mind the broken causeway or dyke which we had seen as we came along, and revealed to me the great danger that we were in. Immediately I turned with all my men and as quickly as possible we made our way out of the city, the night being now very dark. On coming to the stream—it would be now about nine o'clock— we found it flowing so furiously that we passed it leaping from boulder to boulder, and even then lost a few of our Indian allies and all of the booty we had taken in the city: and I can assure your Majesty that had we not passed the stream that night or even had waited but three hours more not one of us would have escaped; we should have found ourselves cut off by the water without any means of crossing. For when dawn came we saw that the level of the water in the two lakes was now the same and no more water flowing across the gap, but the whole of the surface of the salt lake was full of canoes with armed men in them, thinking they would take us there. That day I returned to Tezcuco fighting once or twice with Indians who had landed from the lake, although we did them little damage since they rushed back to their canoes whenever we faced them. I found my men quite safe, having had no encounter with the enemy, and very joyful at our coming and the news of our victory. One of those who was with me died the next day as the result of his wounds: he is the first man the Indians have killed in fight up till now.

(During the following days various cities sent in messengers to make their peace with Cortés: among these was Otumba. Sandoval was sent to convoy messengers on their way back to Tlascala and then to proceed to the province of Chalco, which was reputed to be friendly. He successfully beat off enemy attacks and returned with Chalco chieftains and two sons of the late king. They both agreed to become vassals of the Spanish Empire and give proofs of their loyalty. Cortés received them gladly. The conquering expedition was cut off from direct connection with Tlascala by enemy country. A youth, however, who had been left behind with the Spanish garrison disobeyed orders and made a dangerous cross-country journey by night to bring the news to Cortés in Tezcuco that a ship with reinforcements had arrived at Vera Cruz. The messengers returned from Chalco saying that on account of their allegiance to Cortés they were being attacked and

begged for help. Cortés advised them to seek the assistance of the Tlascalans as allies : fortunately at that moment messengers from Guajucingo and Guacachula arrived, reporting that they had kept a look-out from the summits of the hills surrounding the plain of Mexico, and seeing many smoke columns were anxious as to the fate of Cortés : they were ready at any time to assist him with men and arms. Cortés took the opportunity of uniting these tribes with those of Chalco against the Culuans, their common enemy. Cortés then continues :)

Hearing that the brigs were now finished I sent Sandoval with fifteen horse and two hundred foot to bring them to us, giving them orders to attack and lay waste the large town (subject to Tezcuco on the Tlascalan border) whose inhabitants had been responsible for the death of five horsemen and some forty-five foot soldiers on their way from Vera Cruz to Tenochtitlan at the time when we were besieged there, and all unprepared for such treachery. On entering Tezcuco this time we had found the skins, hoofs and horseshoes nailed up on the walls of some of their temples and placed there very carefully as a sign of victory, together with many clothes and other belongings of the Spaniards, which they had offered to their idols. The very blood of our companions and brothers was strewn and sacrificed all over their idol towers, which was so piteous a sight that it renewed in our minds all our past troubles. The traitors living in that town, and in certain others near by, had received the Christians very well when they arrived, so as to reassure them, and then perpetrated the greatest act of cruelty that was ever done, for while they were descending a steep hill all on foot and leading their horses so that they could not avail themselves of the animals, the enemy ambushed on either side of the road suddenly leapt out on them, killed some and took others alive to Tezcuco in order to sacrifice them and tear the hearts out of their bodies in front of their idols. This is what must have occurred, for when Sandoval passed that way, certain of his men entered a house in a small township between Tezcuco and the actual town where the treachery was committed, and found the following words written in charcoal on the whitewashed wall: " Here lay captive the hapless Juan Yuste." He was one of the five gentlemen on horseback, and in truth the sight was enough to break the hearts of all that saw it. On Sandoval's approach to the town, the inhabitants, recognizing the greatness of their crime, began to fly. Our men and the Indians pursued them and killed many, taking also captive large numbers of women and children who were sold as slaves. Moved by compassion, however, Sandoval was unwilling to destroy them utterly, and before he left even persuaded the natives to return to the town, so that it remains populated to this day, having repented for what was done there in the past.

Sandoval then proceeded some five or six leagues to the Tlascalan town which lies nearest to the Culuan frontier, and there found Spaniards and natives carrying the brigs. The next day they continued their way, the decking and timbers being borne by some eight thousand men, a marvellous sight to see, as also it seems to me it is to hear of, that thirteen brigs should be carried eighteen leagues overland: I can assure your Majesty that from front to rear of the column was a matter of two leagues. Eight horsemen and a hundred Spanish foot went in the van, and on either flank two Indian chiefs with over ten thousand warriors apiece: in the rear were another hundred or so Spanish foot and eight horsemen, together with the Indian chief Chichimecatecle, with ten thousand more Indian warriors all ſtrongly armed. This chief on leaving Tlascala had led the van in charge of the decking, the timbers being in charge of the other two Captains in the rear: but on entering Culua the maſter shipwrights gave orders for the timbers to be carried in the van and the decking to come behind, it being heavier and more difficult to manage in case of attack. Chichimecatecle, having always been with his warriors in the van took this as an affront, and it was the moſt difficult matter to get him to go to the rear, for he wished to occupy the position of danger if any such should arise: even when this firſt point was gained he was unwilling that any of the Spaniards should remain in the rear, for he is a man of great spirit and wished to have the honour to himself. Two thousand Indian bearers accompanied them carrying viĉtuals. In this order they proceeded on their way, and on the fourth day arrived in this city of Tezcuco with much rejoicing and beating of drums. I went out to meet them, and so long was the column, as I have said before, that more than six hours elapsed after the firſt files had entered the city until the laſt were in. Having thanked the chiefs for their good works I saw to it that they were lodged and provided for as well as I could. They told me that they were desirous of pitting themselves againſt the Culuans, and that I should look to it, for they and their volunteers had come with the fixed intention of avenging themselves upon their enemies or dying with us. I thanked them and begged them to take their reſt for soon I would give them their hands full of fighting.

When all these warriors from Tlascala had reposed themselves three or four days, and certainly for Indians they were a very fine body of men, I ordered twenty-five horsemen, three hundred foot, fifty musketeers and bowmen, carrying with them six small field guns, to be ready to march and without a word to anyone

left the city at nine o'clock in the morning, the
Indian chiefs accompanying me with thirty thousand
men all marching in their respective companies in
good order. Four leagues from the city, when it
was already late afternoon, we fell in with an enemy
squadron which our horsemen charged and put to
rout. The Tlascalans, who are very fleet of foot,
followed them up and slew many of them. That night
we slept in the open, having posted a very good guard.
Next day we continued our march. I had not yet
announced what was my objective, being distrustful
of certain of the Tezcuco Indians who were with us,
thinking that they might warn the Mexicans, for as
yet we could not be sure of them. Going forward
we came to a township known as Xaltocan, situated
in the middle of a lake with many large canals cutting
off approach from the mainland. The inhabitants
had fortified it very strongly round about so that the
horsemen could not enter it, and now uttered loud
cries, assailing us with a hail of darts and arrows: our
foot soldiers, however, succeeded in forcing an entrance though with difficulty, expelled the inhabitants
and burnt a large part of the town. That night we
went forward and camped a league further on, and on
taking our way again in the morning found the enemy
still before us yelling from afar off (as they are wont
to do in war) which is certainly a frightening thing to
hear. We followed them and doing so came to a
large and beautiful city named Guatithlan which we
found uninhabited and slept there that night.

*(Next day a little force advanced as far as Tacuba
which it attacked and took possession of.)*

During the seven days that we remained in Tacuba
not one passed in which we did not have certain
meetings or skirmishes with the natives. The Tlascalan chieftains and men delivered many challenges

to the inhabitants of the capital, and there were many gallant encounters. Large numbers of the enemy were killed at this time without any of our men being in danger, for many times we advanced along the causeways and bridges leading to the city, although meeting with stout resistance from their numerous defences. They often pretended to allow us to enter, saying: "Come in, come in and enjoy yourselves." At other times they would say: "Do you think that there is a Muteczuma reigning over us now, so that you can do whatever you like?" Once when such talk was being held I approached a gap in the causeway from which the bridge had been removed and signed to our men to remain quiet. Seeing that I wanted to speak, they also bade their men be silent, and I asked them, "Why are you so mad as to wish to destroy yourselves? If there is a chief among you let him come here for I wish to speak to him." They replied that all the numerous warriors whom I saw there were chiefs, so that I could say what I wished. As I replied nothing they began to revile me: and one of my men, I know not whom, told them that they would die of hunger, for we would not let them go out of that place to seek for food. They answered that they were in no want and when they should be they would eat both us and the Tlascalans. On this one of them brought out a cake of maize flour and threw it towards us saying, "Take and eat this if you are hungry; for we are not," and they straightway began to utter yells and fight against us. Accordingly, since the main object of my visit to Tacuba had been to hold speech with the inhabitants of the capital and find out their disposition, and as it was now apparent that my stay there could effect nothing, I determined at the end of six days to return to Tezcuco and make all haste with the fitting out of the brigs so that we could attack them by both land and water. On the second day of our retreat, thinking that we were afraid, a large number of the enemy gathered together and followed us. Seeing this I ordered the foot to go on ahead with all speed, five horsemen accompanying them as a rearguard. I myself with twenty horse remained behind, arranging ourselves in four small parties in ambush, so that the enemy would pass by thinking that all had gone on, and then on my giving the signal of "*Santiago*" we would fall on them in the rear. When the moment came we charged out and struck many of them with our lances, pursuing them for more than two leagues over country as flat as the palm of one's hand. In this way many fell at the hands both of ourselves and of our Indian allies and they abstained from following us any further. At noon of the next day we regained Tezcuco and were received by Sandoval whom I had left in command of all the men; they rejoiced much at our arrival, having had no news of us since the day of our departure and being very anxious as to our success. On the morrow the chiefs and leaders of the Tlascalans asked my leave and departed to their own land very contented and bearing certain spoil which they had taken from the enemy.

(*Two days later the Chalco Indians again appealed for help against the Culuans. Sandoval was sent with twenty horse and three hundred foot to help them. The Spaniards were victorious and took Huastepec and also the very strongly fortified town of Ayacapisthla where the fighting was so fierce that the river surrounding the town ran with blood. Imprudent Culuan chiefs were taken prisoner. Reinforcements of powder, muskets and crossbows came from Vera Cruz, the road being now quite open, and also news of three ships which had arrived with many men and horses on board,* "which in our great need God miraculously sent us for our succour." *Cortés emphasizes that he was seeking every means to conclude some kind of peaceful treaty with the inhabitants of the capital, and now sent the recently captured chiefs with messages to them, but all was of no avail.*)

On Friday, the 5th of April of 1521, I again quitted the city of Tezcuco with thirty horse and three hundred foot, leaving behind twenty horse and some further three hundred foot under the command of Gonzalo de Sandoval, *alguacil mayor*[16]. Over twenty thousand of the Tezcuco Indians accompanied me, and in this order we went to sleep that night at Tlalmanalco, a town in the province of Chalco where we were very well received and lodged. On the morrow we arrived at Chalco itself where I stayed only long enough to speak with its rulers and tell them my intention which was to make a circuit of the lakes, which done I trusted to find the thirteen brigs completed and ready for launching, a matter of great importance. Accordingly after speaking with them we left at dusk and came to a neighbouring town where some forty thousand Indian warriors joined us, and there we spent the night. The natives informed us that the Culuans were awaiting us in the field and I therefore ordered all my men to be awake and on the alert at dawn. We then heard mass and took the road, myself riding in the van with twenty horse, leaving ten others in the rear; and in this manner we passed between some very steep and rocky hills. At two o'clock in the afternoon we came to a very lofty rugged peak on the top of which were a great multitude of women and children and the sides of it full of armed warriors. They began immediately to utter piercing shouts, and sent up large numbers of smoke columns, using slings and other weapons to beset us with stones, darts, and arrows, in such wise that on approaching nearer we suffered no small hurt. Although perceiving by this that they dared not await us in the open field, and notwithstanding that our road lay rather to one side, yet I deemed it would be cowardly to pass by without giving them some cause for regret. And so in order that our allies should not think that we abstained from motives of fear I began to reconnoitre round the peak which was almost a league in circuit and certainly so strong that it seemed madness to attempt to capture it, while to surround them and force them to surrender out of sheer hunger would take too long for my purpose. Accordingly, being in this perplexity I determined to scale the crag on three sides, of which I had already taken note, and gave orders to Cristóbal Corral, an officer in charge of seventy foot whom I always kept in my company, to attempt the stiffest climb with his men, sending off a number of bowmen and slingers to follow him. Two other officers, Juan Rodríguez de Villafuerte and Francisco Verdugo, with other men and some bowmen were to attempt a second side; and Pedro Dircio and Andrés de Monjaraz the third. On hearing a musket shot they were all to charge forward and either win the summit or die. When the signal was given they succeeded in taking two of the positions but not the third, for there was neither hold for hand nor foot, such was the stiffness and difficulty of the ascent. Moreover the enemy rolled and threw down so many stones from above that even the small pieces which broke apart in their fall were the source of infinite danger: the resistance of the enemy was indeed so fierce that two Spaniards were killed and more than twenty wounded, so that on that side they could in no wise go forward. Seeing this, and that reinforcements were arriving for the enemy in such numbers that they covered the plain,

I ordered the officers to retreat, and attacking those who were below we drove them entirely from the plain, killing many with our lances and pursuing them for over an hour and a half. Their numbers were so great that the horsemen dispersed to this side and that, and on gathering together again I learnt that a league or so off some of them had discovered another peak also occupied with natives, but not so strongly defended and with a township nearby out on the plain; water moreover was to be found there which was said to be lacking where we were at the moment. Sad enough at having failed to gain the victory we departed and slept that night near the second peak, which time we passed in no small toil and want, there being no water to be found there after all, and neither we nor our horses had drunk any water during the whole day: and so right through the night we heard a great noise from the enemy of drums, trumpets and cries.

At daybreak some of my officers accompanied me to examine the peak which was apparently almost as strongly fortified as the other; but two neighbouring hills, taller yet less steep, rose above it and were occupied by numerous warriors to defend them against attack. My officers and certain other gentlemen accompanying took their shields, as I did also myself, and advanced to the foot of it, the horses having been led off to the water about a league away. Our only object was to examine the strength of the peak and where it could best be attacked: but my men seeing our movements though they had had no commands from me followed us, and as we arrived at the foot the natives of the neighbouring hills thought that I intended to make a frontal attack, upon which they abandoned their position and rushed down to help their friends. Seeing the disorder in which they were and that by taking the hills we could inflict great damage on those who were holding the main position, I ordered the officer to advance quietly with his men and take the higher of the two hills which they had abandoned; so it was done. I with the rest of the men began to climb the other hill where the greater number of defenders were to be found; and by the mercy of God we gained the first ridge of it and reached a height about equal to that on which the enemy was fighting (which had indeed seemed a position well nigh impossible to gain at the least without infinite danger). Already one of my officers had placed his flag on the highest point of the peak and from there had begun to direct the fire of the muskets and crossbows on the enemy. Seeing the hurt they received and considering what might yet befall them, they made signals to surrender and laid down their arms. My design is ever to give these people to understand that we desire to do them no harm especially if they are willing to become vassals of your Majesty, and I ordered that no further hurt should be done them. On their coming up to speak with me I received them well: and on this, seeing how well they were treated they reported it to their comrades on the other peak, who notwith-standing that they had been victorious determined to become vassals of your Majesty and come to crave pardon for what had been done. I remained in the neighbouring township two days, from which place I sent the wounded back to Tezcuco and then returned to Huastepec.

(*During the next five days Yautepec, Xilotepec and Yactepec were taken, with a certain amount of fighting. The band moved steadily onward.*)

At nine o'clock next morning I came in sight of a very strongly fortified town called Cuernabaca, held by large bodies of native troops, and surrounded by ridges and gorges some of which were as much as sixty foot deep. The only entrance for horsemen was by two gates, the exact position of which we did not know and which we only finally discovered after riding for a league and a half round the town. There were also wooden bridges, but these had been removed and the inhabitants were now so fortified and secure that had our numbers been ten times as great they would have availed us nothing. On our approaching them they hurled darts, arrows and stones at us at their pleasure, but being thus occupied they failed to notice one of the Tlascalan Indians who succeeded in getting across at a very difficult place. Suddenly perceiving him, however, the enemy thought that the Spaniards were entering there and immediately they began to fly panic-stricken, the Indian pursuing them: three or four youths of my company and two more of another, seeing the Indian get across, followed him and reached the further side. I with the horsemen rode on round towards the hills and found an entrance to the town, the enemy still being occupied in hurling darts at us, since there was nothing more between us than a ravine about as broad as a wine cellar. They were still intent on pouring in their missiles on us and had not yet so much as seen the five Spaniards when these took them in the rear and began to use their knives: and such was the suddenness of their attack, the enemy knowing nothing of their comrades' flight, that they were too amazed to fight and the Spaniards cut them down. As soon as they saw what had happened they began to fly. Our foot soldiers were by now inside the town and had begun to burn it; the natives abandoned it and fled to the hills although many of them were killed by the pursuing cavalry. At midday we found the way in for the horses and took up our quarters in houses surrounding a garden, practically all the rest being burned. Late that day, seeing that even their strong fortifications had been unable to defend them and fearful that we should kill them out on the hillside, a ruler and chief man came in to offer themselves as vassals of your Majesty. I received them as such and they promised me to remain in future our faithful friends, saying that they had only come so late to request our friendship since they thought that by first allowing us to do them such great damage their faults would be wiped out and we should be less angered with them.

We slept that night in the town, and in the morning continued our march through the region covered with pines but, like the pass which succeeded it, desert and arid. We proceeded with great toil and without any water, so much so that many of the Indians who went with us perished of thirst, and so six leagues further on we stayed for the night in some farm buildings. At dawn we were again on the road and sighted a great city, Suchimilco, built on the·fresh water lake, whose inhabitants being apprised of our advance had raised many blockades and dykes and had removed all the bridges giving entrance to the city, which is actually some three or four leagues from the capital. It was now full of picked warriors determined to defend themselves and ask no quarter. On arriving before the city and having gathered all my men together in very good order I dismounted and went forward with certain foot soldiers towards the first barricade behind which there seemed an infinite number of warriors. We forthwith began to assault it, the bowmen and musketeers did them great damage, and they finally abandoned it, the Spaniards leaping into the water and swimming across to dry ground. In half an hour we had gained the greater part of the city; the enemy had retreated to the waterways and fought both on the banks and in their canoes, till nightfall. Some made proposals of peace, other still fought on, and so often did they advance these proposals without putting them into effect that we fell to the ruse which they were employing for two ends, the one, to gain time to remove their belongings, the other, to delay until the Mexicans and inhabitants of the capital should have time to come to their relief. Two Spaniards were killed that day, on account of their having left their comrades in search of booty, and got themselves into such a desperate position that they could not be rescued. Late in the day the enemy made an attempt to surround us in such fashion that we could not escape from the city with our lives. Gathering together in large numbers they decided to advance at that point where we had ourselves forced an entrance. We were amazed to see with what fury and dash they suddenly came on. Six horsemen and myself who were nearer than the others charged forward into the midst of them. They, frightened of the horses, began to fly, and so we spurred out of the city after them, killing many, although in grave danger ourselves: for they were of such spirit that many of them were hardy enough to await the charge of our horses with sword and shield. While we were engaged with them very fiercely, the horse which I rode sank down exhausted. Some of the enemy seeing me on foot turned on me and I had to defend myself with my lance. One of the Tlascalans perceived, however, that I was in danger and came to my aid. He and another youth succeeded in raising the horse: and at this moment the other Spaniards came up and the enemy fled from the field. The horsemen who had arrived and myself being all greatly wearied returned to the town. It was now nearly night and time to repose, but I gave orders that all the gaps left by the bridges which had been removed should be filled up with stones and bricks lying by, so that the cavalry could freely enter and leave the city: nor did I retire to rest until all these danger points had been well levelled, and so with great precaution and numerous guards we passed the night.

On the morrow now that both the provinces of Mexico and Tenochtitlan were aware that we were in Suchimilco, they came in great force to surround us by land and water thinking that we could not escape from their hands. I mounted one of their idol towers to see where they could attack us and provide for whatever might be moſt expedient. I had finished giving all direċtions when a great fleet of canoes (over two thousand in number I should reckon) bore down upon us, carrying some twelve thousand warriors, and by land such a multitude of people that the whole surrounding plains were covered with them. Their captains who led them bore Spanish swords in their hands, crying out the names of their provinces, and yelling " Mexico, Mexico, Tenochtitlan, Tenochtitlan," and many insulting words, threatening to kill us with the very swords which thėy had captured from us formerly in the city of Tenochtitlan. I had already arranged where each officer was to take up his position, and since the greateſt number of the enemy lay between us and the mainland I rode out againſt them with twenty horse and five hundred Tlascalan Indians. We were divided into three bands, and I gave orders that after breaking through the enemies' ranks we were to rally at the foot of a hill about half a league off, where there were also many of the enemy gathered. On dividing, each squadron pursued the enemy in the direċtion in which it charged, and having put to flight and killed many we met at the foot of the hill, where I ordered certain foot soldiers of my own company who had long served me and were very ſturdy fellows to make an attempt to climb the ſteepeſt side of it. I with all the horsemen would ride round to where the ground was flatter and take them in the middle. So it turned out: the enemy seeing the Spaniards climbing the hill turned tail and fled, as they thought, to safety, but they came straight upon us (we were some fifteen horsemen) and both we and the Tlascalans fell upon them. In this way in very brief time more than five hundred of them were dead and the remainder flying to the shelter of the hills. The other six horsemen pursued the enemy along a broad highway until about half a league from Suchimilco they fell in with an enemy squadron of very fine troops, who were coming up as reinforcements, whom nevertheless they put to flight and killed no small number. The whole of our cavalry had now joined each other at what must have been about ten o'clock in the morning and we returned to Suchimilco, at the entrance to which I found many desiring greatly to know how it had fared with us; they themselves had been in great straits and forced to put forward every effort to repel the enemy of whom they had slain a large number. They gave me two swords which they had recaptured from the enemy and reported that the bowmen had neither arrows nor ammunition left. At this moment before we could dismount a large squadron of the enemy rushed upon us with fierce yells from the mouth of a broad causeway. We immediately flung ourselves upon them, and thrust them with our lances into the water which lined the causeway on both sides. In this manner they were repulsed. Rallying, we returned to the city wearied out, and I ordered it to be burnt entirely save for that part in which we were quartered. We remained thus in the city three days, every one of which was marked by fighting, and finally left it burnt and desolate; and truly it was a sorrowful sight to see, for it contained many houses and idol towers stoutly built of stone and mortar.

THIRD LETTER

(The expedition then completed the circuit of the lakes with continual skirmishing, and finally returned to Tezcuco via Cuyoacan, Tacuba, Coatinchan and Aculman. Considerable losses were inflicted on the enemy, and two young Spaniards were unfortunately captured and could not be rescued. The garrison in Tezcuco greeted them warmly on their return: they had heard nothing of them since their departure and had beaten off numerous attacks on the city. Cortés then continues :)

During our first stay in the capital I had provided, as I informed your Majesty, for certain royal farms to be set up in various provinces, which should produce such things as the locality afforded. Two Spaniards had been sent on such a commission to the province of Chinantla, which was not subject to the Culuans. Other provinces which did owe allegiance to the Culuans killed the Spaniards stationed on the farms when the Culuans rebelled against us, and despoiled the farms of all that they had, so that for almost a year I had no news of my men in Chinantla: for such was the disturbed state of the country that neither could they get news through to us nor we to them. It appeared, however, that being subjects of your Majesty and enemies of the Culuans the natives bade the two Spaniards in no wise to stir out of their country, for they reckoned that after the numerous attacks of the Culuans few of us remained alive. One of the Spaniards, a youth but with an aptitude for war, was made their captain, and led them out to fight against their enemies, being most often victorious. Later, when by God's help we had had some success over the enemy, two Chinantla Indians informed these two Christians that they had heard of Spaniards in the province of Tepeaca and to find out the truth of the matter were willing to send two of their number hither who travelled by night through enemy country, and finally arrived with a letter from him who was the more able man of the two, the tenor of which was as follows:

"Gentlemen, I have written two or three letters to you but know not whether they have arrived or no; and since I have had no reply from them I must be doubtful of receiving one from this. Know, gentlemen, that all the Culuans have rebelled and many times attacked us, yet praise be to God we have ever come off victorious. With the natives of Tuxtepec and other allies of the Culuans we are still in conflict. Those which have remained faithful to your Highnesses and your true vassals comprise seven townships in Tenez. Nicholas and myself remain in Chinantla which is the chief town of them all. I am very desirous of knowing where our Captain is that I may write to him and inform him of what has occurred here. And if perchance you write me from where he is, and should send back twenty or thirty Spaniards with your letter, I would venture to come to him with two native chiefs of this region who are very eager to see and speak with the Captain; for it is now the season to gather in the cacao and the Culuans are hindering the harvest greatly with their warfare. May Our Lord guard the noble presence of your Grace according to your desires.

"From Chinantla, on I know not what date of the month of April, 1521. Your Grace's servant,
"HERNANDO DE BARRIENTOS."

On the receipt of this letter the captain whom I had left in Tepeaca immediately sent it on to me, at the contents of which we were not a little pleased, for while we had always trusted in the friendship of the Chinantla Indians, yet it had occurred to us that if they should have gone over to the Culuans they

THIRD LETTER

would certainly have put those two Spaniards to
death. I wrote to them immediately, telling them
of what had occurred and bidding them hope; for
although they were at the moment surrounded by
enemies on all sides, soon, God willing, they should
find themselves free and able to go abroad in safety.

Having encircled the lakes and reconnoitred many
positions for the siege of Tenochtitlan both by land
and water, I remained in Tezcuco preparing as beſt
I could arms and men and haſtening on the building
of the brigs and a canal which was being cut in order
to bring them to the lake for launching. We had
begun the canal immediately the decks and hulls were
far enough advanced to be floated in a narrow waterway which ran paſt the end of our camp to empty itself
in the lake. More than eight thousand natives from
the provinces of Aculuacan and Tezcuco were employed for fifty days on this work, for the canal was
over twelve foot deep and as many broad, and lined
with ſtakes throughout its length, so that the ships
could be conveyed without difficulty or danger down
to the water, which was certainly a great and marvellous work. The brigs were finally finished and
launched into this canal; and on the 28th of April
of 1521 I held a review of all my men, and found
that we numbered 86 horse, 118 bowmen and musketeers, some 700 foot armed with sword and buckler,
three large iron cannons, fifteen smaller ones of
bronze, and ten quintals of powder. I urged my men
with great earneſtness to keep the ordinances I had
drawn up for aćtive service in so far as was possible,
and bade them rejoice and be of a good heart for they
preceived that Our Lord was leading us to vićtory
againſt our enemies, for they were well aware that
when we entered Tezcuco we had but forty mounted
men, but God had aided us more than we had dared
to think, and the ships had arrived with horses, men

165

and arms, as they themselves had seen. This and above all the knowledge that we were fighting to preserve and spread the true faith, and bring to your Majesty's service all those lands and provinces which had rebelled against him, should give them courage and strength to resolve to conquer or to die. They replied as one man, showing great eagerness and desire in the enterprise. On that day we were very joyful and found ourselves now at last on the eve of the siege and of putting an end to this war, on the result of which depended the whole peace or disturbance of these parts.

On the morrow I sent messages to Tlascala, Guajucingo and Cholula telling them that the brigs were finished and that I and all my men were ready to set out to besiege the great city of Tenochtitlan; wherefore I begged them since their men were already prepared to come with as many and as well armed troops as they could muster to Tezcuco where I would await them for ten days, and that they should in no wise exceed this limit since it would greatly delay my plans. The natives of Guajucingo and Cholula, anxious to come to grips with the Culuans, accordingly gathered at Chalco following my instructions, for our road to the capital passed near by. Likewise the Tlascalan leaders with all their warriors very finely equipped and armed arrived at Tezcuco five or six days before Whitsun which was the time that I had arranged. Hearing that they were near I rode out to meet them with great pleasure and they came in such spirits and good order as could not be better. According to the reckoning of their leaders they numbered some fifty thousand warriors, all of whom were well received and lodged by us.

On Whit Monday I ordered a parade of all horse and foot in the principal square of Tezcuco to give orders and tell off the troops under the three captains who were to proceed to the three cities which immediately surrounded the capital. I put the first company in the command of Pedro de Albarado, giving him thirty horse, eighteen crossbowmen and musketeers and a hundred and fifty foot armed with buckler and sword, together with more than twenty-five thousand Tlascalan Indians, with orders to camp in the city of Tacuba.

The second company I put under Cristóbal de Olid, giving him thirty-three horse, eighteen crossbowmen and musketeers, one hundred and seventy foot and over twenty thousand Indian allies, with orders to camp in the city of Cuyoacan.

The third company I put under the command of Gonzalo de Sandoval, *alguacil mayor*, giving him twenty-four horse, four musketeers and thirteen crossbowmen, and a hundred and fifty light-armed infantry, fifty of them being chosen youths of my own company, together with over thirty thousand natives from Guajucingo, Cholula and Chalco. This force was first to march to Iztapalapa and destroy it and then proceed along the causeway across the lake: it would be supported by the brigs until it joined up with the garrison in Cuyoacan; Sandoval had leave to camp wherever it seemed best to him once I had entered the lake with the brigs.

For the thirteen brigs with which I was going to pass across the lake I told off three hundred men, for the most part used to the sea and very handy; so that there were twenty-five Spaniards in each ship in addition to the captain, government official (*veedor*), and six musketeers and crossbowmen.

The two Captains first named, Albarado and Olid, having received all necessary instructions, moved off with their men on the 10th of May, and went to sleep two and a half leagues away at a little township called Aculmán. The same day I learnt there had been some difference between them concerning lodgings and sent someone that same night to settle it and reprimand them. They proceeded according to orders through three towns all of which they found deserted, and finally on the third day at sunset reached Tacuba which they found likewise empty, and took up their abode in the houses of the chieftain, which are very fine and large. Although it was late the Tlascalans ventured upon two of the causeways leading to the capital and fought for two or three hours very valiantly against the defenders of the city: then as night came on they returned in safety to Tacuba.

Early next morning the two captains joined together according to my orders to cut off the fresh water that was led by pipes into Tenochtitlan; one of them with twenty horse and a few musketeers and bowmen succeeded in reaching the source of the spring about a quarter of a league away and there cut and destroyed the pipes which were built of woodwork and masonry, in spite of the furious opposition of the enemy who resisted him both by sea and land. He succeeded in routing them, however, and concluded what he had set himself to do, which was to cut off all fresh water from entering the city, a very wise stroke to accomplish. The same day the captains repaired several bad bridges and dykes in various places round the lake so that the horsemen could ride easily from one part to the other. Some three to four days were spent in this work which was impeded by numerous encounters with the enemy in which a few Spaniards were wounded and a large number of the enemy killed, to say nothing of the bridges and barricades stormed and gained: there were also challenges and single combats between the Indians of the city and the Tlascalans which were strange enough and well worth the seeing. Cristóbal de Olid then left with his men for Cuyoacan two leagues further on, and

Pedro de Albarado remained in garrison with his men at Tacuba, skirmishing and fighting each day against the Indians. Olid arrived in Cuyoacan at ten o'clock in the morning, found the city deserted, and settled in the chief rulers' houses. Next day he went out to inspect the causeway leading across to the capital with about twenty horse, some bowmen, and six to seven thousand Tlascalan Indians: they found the enemy very well prepared, the causeway broken down in places and many barricades set up. There was some fighting by them on that and on succeeding days. One night at midnight a few of the sentries from the city crept up to the camp and uttered a yell: the Spanish sentries called out "To arms" and everyone turned out, but found not a single enemy, for the Indians had yelled from some distance and had thus put our men in a panic. Meantime the two forces being divided, they looked forward to my arrival with the brigs as they did the salvation of their souls. During this time, however, the two garrisons were quite close to each other and joined one another each day, the horsemen riding through the land and cutting down many of the enemy: they also gathered in large quantities of maize from the hillsides to store in camp. Maize takes the place of bread and food in these parts and is much superior to that found in the Islands.

I myself had been anxious to go by land and arrange the details of our camps, but as the captains were men to be trusted with that matter, and the management of the ships was of paramount importance requiring great nicety and care, I decided to go with them, more especially as the greater risk and adventure were expected on the water. I should add that the chief officers of my company had formally begged me to accompany the garrison forces as they said theirs was the more dangerous job. On Friday the day after the Feast of Corpus-Christi I sent Gonzalo de Sandoval at four o'clock in the morning with his men to make his way straight to Iztapalapa a bare six leagues away. They arrived a little after noon, and began to attack the natives and set fire to the city. The former seeing the number of Sandoval's forces (for he had more than forty thousand of our allies with him) took to the water in their canoes, whereupon Sandoval settled in the city with all his men and remained there that day waiting for further orders and news from me.

Immediately he had left I went on board ship and we set forth using both sails and oars. By the time that Sandoval had begun his attack on Iztapalapa we came in sight of a large rugged peak which rose straight out of the water close to the city and was covered with natives both from the capital and the other towns surrounding the lake, for they knew that Iztapalapa would be attacked first and had gathered there to defend it and attack us if possible. On seeing the fleet they burst into loud cries and sent up large columns of smoke to warn the other lake cities to be on their guard. Accordingly although my intention was to attack that part of Iztapalapa which lies in the water I gave orders to turn back to the peak and leapt on land with about a hundred and fifty men. We began to mount with some considerable difficulty for it was extremely steep and high and finally rushed the barricades which they had built on the top to defend themselves. There we did such execution that not a single one of them escaped save the women and children; twenty-five of my Spaniards were wounded in this fight, but it was a notable victory.

The inhabitants of Iztapalapa having also sent up smoke signals from certain towers where they kept their idols on a hill close by, the Indians in the capital and the other island cities were aware that I had entered the lake with the ships and immediately a great fleet of canoes was got together to oppose our advance and test what manner of vessels our brigs were: so far as we could judge there must have been more than five hundred of them. Seeing them bearing straight for us both I and the men who had accompanied me made haste to embark and I gave strict orders to the commanders of the brigs not to start, so that the canoes might decide to come right up to us thinking that we were afraid to attack them. Accordingly they began to paddle very swiftly towards us. At two bows' length distance, however, they stopped and would come no further. I was eager that our first encounter with them should be very decisive and of such a nature as to fill them with dread of the brigs, for the fate of the whole campaign rested on them, both ourselves and the enemy being in a position to receive most damage from the water. At this moment when we were regarding each other face to face it pleased the Lord that a light breeze should spring up from the land enabling us to close with them. I immediately ordered the commanders to bear down on the fleet of canoes and follow them up right to the walls of the capital: and as the wind was good, although they paddled off as fast as they could, yet we bore right into the middle of them, smashing an infinite number of the canoes, killing and drowning many of the enemy,—the most extraordinary sight in the world. We chased them for three whole leagues until they took refuge within the houses of the capital, and it pleased God to give us a greater and finer victory even than we had prayed or longed for.

The garrison in Cuyoacan could see our advance better than those in Tacuba; they perceived all our thirteen sails sweeping forward over the water urged on by the favourable wind, and then as they afterwards told me, when we fell upon the enemy canoes there was not a sight in the world could have given them greater pleasure. For, as I have said, both garrisons in Cuyoacan and in Tacuba ardently desired my coming, and with good reason, for they were in the midst of a multitude of enemies, and Our Lord Himself kept up their spirits in a truly miraculous way and weakened those of the enemy, so that the latter did not dare sally out and attack their camps, which had they attempted the Spaniards could not have come off without great hurt, notwithstanding that they were always on the alert and determined to conquer or die, like those who find themselves cut off from all human help and can trust alone in God.

As soon as the garrison at Cuyoacan saw us in pursuit of the canoes the greater number of them sallied forth along the causeway leading to the capital and fought very fiercely with the Indians who were guarding it, winning one by one the barricades which they had built. They proceeded to take many bridges, from which the actual planks had been removed, with the help of the brigs which sailed close to the causeway, and both horse and foot passed over. Many of the Tlascalans moreover accompanied them, following up the enemy, slaying many, and casting their bodies over into the inner part of the lake where there were no brigs. They advanced in this way a good league and more along the causeway until they came up to the point where I had stopped with the brigs as I shall proceed to describe.

We had chased the canoes three leagues until they had taken refuge between the houses of the city, and as evening was now drawing on I ordered the brigs to cease the pursuit and gather together close to the causeway. There I decided to land with thirty men to capture a couple of towers containing their idols, small but built on a circular foundation of ſtone and plaſter. As we leapt on to the causeway they attacked us very fiercely in an endeavour to defend the towers: finally, not without some considerable difficulty we captured them, and I ordered three large guns which I had with me to be landed. Since the causeway from that point to the city (which was about half a league) was black with the enemy and each side of it packed with warriors in canoes, I ordered one gun to be trained on them and firing it ſtraight down the causeway it did great damage to the enemy. By the gunner's carelessness, however, in firing that firſt shot he burnt all the powder we had with us, which was little enough. Accordingly that same night I sent one of the brigs to Sandoval in Iztapalapa two leagues off with orders to bring back all the powder he had there. Now although it had been at firſt my intention on boarding ship to go to Cuyoacan and see that they observed every precaution and contented themselves with inflicting as much damage on the enemy as they could, yet having landed on the causeway and captured the two towers, I determined to pitch my camp there, the brigs remaining nearby, and gave orders for half the garrison of Cuyoacan and some fifty of Sandoval's foot to join me on the following day. Having decided this we kept very close guard that night knowing that we were in great danger, and all of the people of the city advanced upon us by the causeway and by the water. At midnight a great multitude of them attacked our camp both from land and the canoes: and of a truth we were in no small fear and dismay, especially because it was at night time and they are never wont to attack at such a time unless very certain of victory. As we were very well prepared we began to fight with them, and the brigs to fire on them, for each one carried a small field gun, to say nothing of musketeers and bowmen. On this they dared not approach nearer nor were their numbers large enough to do us hurt: and so they left us what remained of the night without again attacking.

At sunrise fifteen musketeers, fifty foot with sword and buckler and seven or eight cavalry arrived at the causeway where I was from the garrison at Cuyoacan. The Indians of the city were already engaged with us both on the causeway and in canoes. Their number was such that there was nothing to be seen on land and water but people, and they uttered such yells and shrieks that it was as if the world was coming to an end. We advanced fighting along the causeway and captured one bridge which had been destroyed and a barricade which they had made at its head. What with the guns and the charges of cavalry we did them such damage that we almost forced them back to the first houses of the city. Meanwhile, since on the other side of the causeway where the brigs could not pass there were numerous canoes from which they hurled darts and arrows, I broke down a portion of the causeway close to our camp and ordered four of the brigs to make their way through, which they did, shutting up the canoes within the houses of the city, so that not one dared to come out into the open. On the other side of the causeway the eight remaining brigs attacked the canoes, driving them back amongst the houses, and made their way between them, a thing they had previously not ventured to do, there being many shoals and stakes to hinder them. Finding canals, however, by which they could enter in safety they fought with those in the canoes, captured some of them, and burnt many houses in the suburbs: and in this manner we spent the whole day in fighting.

On the following day Sandoval with those who were with him in Iztapalapa, both Spaniards and Indians, set out for Cuyoacan along the causeway which runs for about a league and a half to the mainland. He had not gone above a quarter of a league when he came to a little town also built on the water but which can be encircled almost completely on horseback, the inhabitants of which began to offer him resistance. He routed them, killed many, and razed and burnt the city. Knowing that the Indians had broken down the causeway in many places, thus preventing our men from passing, I sent him two of the brigs out of which he made a bridge for the foot soldiers to pass. As soon as they had all passed they proceeded straightway to Cuyoacan where they camped and Sandoval with ten horsemen rode on along the causeway to where we were camped and arrived to find us fighting. They immediately dismounted and joined in. Almost at once Sandoval was pierced in the foot by a dart, but although both he and others were wounded that day we did such damage to the enemy with the large cannon, muskets, and crossbows, that neither those in canoes nor those on the causeway dared to come near, and displayed more fear and less pride than they were wont. In this way we continued for six days, no day passing without fighting; the brigs went round the city burning all the houses they could, and managed to discover a canal by which they could enter into the very heart of the suburbs, a discovery of no small importance; they also stopped any onset from the canoes, not one of which dared to show itself within a quarter of a league of our camp.

On the following day Pedro de Albarado who was commanding the garrison in Tacuba informed me that on the other side of the city the inhabitants of the capital were freely entering and leaving the city by means of a little causeway running to several small towns on the mainland, and he thought that if they should find themselves hard pressed they would all leave the city by that way. I should have welcomed such a departure even more than they themselves, for we should have less difficulty in overcoming them on the mainland than within this great fortress which they held on the water. Nevertheless in order that they should be entirely surrounded and unable to receive any help from the mainland I ordered Sandoval although wounded to pitch his camp at a small town at the juncture of one of those two causeways, whereupon he set out with twenty-three horse, a hundred foot, and eighteen bowmen and musketeers, leaving me the remaining fifty foot of my own company. On the morrow he pitched his camp as I had ordered and from that time every causeway leading from the city of Tenochtitlan to the mainland was completely cut off.

I had with me, most powerful Lord, in my camp on the causeway two hundred Spanish foot including twenty musketeers and bowmen, but not counting those on board the ships who must have numbered more than two hundred and fifty more. Since we had now somewhat enclosed the enemy and had large numbers of Indian allies with us, I decided to advance along the causeway to the city as often as possible, the brigs on both sides of it covering our flanks and rear. I also ordered ten of the horse at Cuyoacan to remain at the entrance of the causeway and thus protect us, for several of the lake towns were still in arms against us, but with such a guard and ten thousand Indian allies we should be secure. At the same time I ordered Albarado and Sandoval to attack the city from their camps on that same day since I wanted to capture as much as possible from them. Accordingly we left the camp early in the morning and advanced along the causeway on foot till we found the enemy defending a gap which they had made in it about eight feet wide and as many feet deep. They had made an earth fence on the further side of it and there we fought very valiantly against one another. We finally captured it and continued to advance up to the gate of the city, where there was a tower containing their idols, at the foot of which a large bridge had been removed leaving a broad stream of water flowing through with another breastwork on the other side. As we came up they attacked us very fiercely. But since the brigs were on both sides of the causeway we gained it without difficulty, which we could not possibly have done without their aid. And while some began to tear down the barricade the men in the brigs leapt on land, and our Indian allies who must have numbered more than eighty thousand swam across. Meantime, while we closed up the gap with stones and bricks, the Spaniards had gained another barricade in the principal and broadest street of the city: there was no water to cross there and it was consequently carried with ease. My men then followed the flying enemy along the street until they came to another bridge which had been removed leaving but a single broad plank by which to pass. The enemy once over the water in safety immediately threw this down. At the other end of the bridge they had built up a huge barricade of earth and bricks. We came up to find that our only means of crossing was by throwing ourselves into the water, which was very dangerous, for the enemy fought very valiantly. On either side of the street an infinite number of them were fighting in the stoutest manner from the tops of the flat roofs. Our musketeers and crossbowmen arrived at that moment and discharged two guns down the length of the street doing great damage. Seeing this a few Spaniards leapt into the water and crossed to the other side, but it was two hours before the place was won. Finally the enemy, seeing our men crossing over, abandoned the barricades and the rooftops and took to flight down the street, not a man remaining. I straightway began to close up the bridge and pulled down the barricade. Meanwhile the Spaniards and our Indian allies followed in pursuit down the street for over two bowshots' distance until they came to another bridge which is next to the square containing the principal buildings of the city. This bridge had neither been broken down nor barricaded, for they had not thought that we should capture that day what we did, nor indeed had we ourselves expected to win more than half of it. My men set up a gun at the entrance of the square and thus did great damage on the enemy who more than filled it, and then seeing that there was no water to cross, which was commonly the greatest danger, decided to enter the square. The enemy seeing their decision actually put into effect and even a large number of our allies advancing (of whom in our absence they were not in the least afraid) turned tail and fled before the Spaniards until they gained refuge in the inner part surrounded by a wall of stones and masonry which housed their idols, and which as I have already described, is as large round as a village of four hundred people. From this they were finally evicted and the Spaniards and Indian allies captured it, remaining in possession of the towers for some considerable time. The natives of the city, however, seeing that there were no horsemen returned to the attack and by weight of numbers drove them out from the towers and the whole courtyard contained within the walls, upon which they found themselves in great danger and jeopardy. Setting themselves to rejoin us rather than merely beating a retreat they turned and faced the enemy below the porches of the courtyard. The enemy continued to attack them so fiercely that they forced them back into the central square and further down the street along which they had come, in such wise that the gun which had been placed there was loſt. The Spaniards unable to resiſt the multitudes of the enemy were retreating in very grave danger, and would assuredly have suffered severely had it not pleased God that at that moment three horsemen cantered up and entered the square. The enemy seeing them thought there were more behind and began to fly, upon which they killed several of them and regained the square and walled-in courtyard I have already described. From ten to a dozen of the native chiefs took up their position in the chief and higheſt tower which contains over a hundred ſteps from base to summit, upon which four or five Spaniards mounted it by force, and in spite of a ſturdy resiſtance on the part of the enemy took it and killed them all. Some five or six more horsemen now came up and by means of an ambuscade killed over thirty of the enemy. It was now getting late, and I gave orders for the men to re-form and retire, and so great were the numbers of the enemy pressing on them as they retreated that had it not been for the mounted men there can be no doubt that the Spaniards would have received very many casualties. I had seen to it, however, that all the difficult places both in the ſtreet and causeway, where danger was to be expeɕted, were well filled up and levelled, so that the horsemen might be perfeɕtly free to ride along, and so often as the enemy attacked our rearguard, the horsemen turned upon them and invariably succeeded in despatching some with their lances. The road proved so long that this manœuvre had to be repeated from four to five times. And although the enemy perceived that they were receiving great hurt they ſtill continued to come on like so many mad dogs and could not be prevented in any way from continuing to follow us. The whole of the reſt of the day might have been spent after this fashion had they not retaken many of the flat rooftops which abutted on the ſtreets and thus placed the horsemen in considerable danger. We pursued our way towards the camp without losing a single Spaniard although there were several wounded, and set fire as we went to the greater number of the largest houses in the street so that on re-entering the city we could not be attacked from the rooftops. On this same day Sandoval and Albarado both engaged very fiercely with the natives of the city from their respective camps, and would be about a league and a half and a league respectively from where my men were fighting in the great square. (The city extends over such a large area that I am if anything minimizing the distance.) Our Indian allies who had been sent with them and were almost numberless fought very well and withdrew that day without receiving any hurt.

At this juncture Don Fernando,[17] ruler of Tezcuco and the province of Culuacan, who had been baptized into the Christian faith, made attempts to persuade all the natives of his city and province, especially the chieftains, to join us as allies, for we could not rely on them at that time as we afterwards came to do. Accordingly every day large numbers of smaller rulers and relatives of Don Fernando came to us offering to fight on our side against the defenders of the capital. Don Fernando, being still quite a youth and very friendly with the Spaniards, did all that he could to persuade his vassals to come over to us in this way, and spoke to his brothers, of whom he had six or seven, all well-disposed youths, telling them to command all the people in their districts to come to our assistance. One of them named Istrisuchil, about 22 or 23 years old and a very valiant youth loved and feared by all, he sent as captain. This chief arrived at our camp on the causeway with over thirty thousand warriors very well equipped after their fashion, and some twenty thousand must have gone to the other two camps. I received them gladly thanking them **for** their goodwill and assistance. Your Majesty can well imagine what a very real token of friendship this was on the part of Don Fernando, and what the defenders of the city would feel on seeing themselves attacked by those whom they thought to be their vassals and friends, nay, even relations and brothers, and I will go so far as to say fathers and sons.

Having burnt a large number of houses in the outlying part of the city close to our camp by means of the ships, I considered that seven brigs would be sufficient to ensure the safety of the camp, since no canoe now dared to show its face; and accordingly despatched the remaining brigs three each to Sandoval and Albarado, giving the captains very urgent orders to keep the way open between the two camps, sailing backwards and forwards night and day; for it was the part lying just between the camps which the enemies particularly used, for landing from their canoes with supplies of water, fruit, maize and other provisions. Brigs were also to be used to support troops from either camp whenever they were entering the city in an attack. The six brigs duly left and it proved a wise and fruitful move, for not a day or night passed without their making sudden and unexpected sallies in which they captured large numbers of natives and their canoes.

Having arranged this matter and received the assistance of the neighbouring tribes as I have described, I gathered them together and told them plainly that I was determined to attack the city and enter it within two days, and that I should then know whether they were truly my friends for they would present themselves at that time fully prepared for war, the which they promised to do. Next day I positioned my men and bade them make all ready, and also wrote to the camps and brigs, telling them of my plans and what they had to do for their part.

Early next morning having heard mass and given my officers final instructions, I sallied forth from the camp with fifteen or twenty horse and three hundred Spaniards together with all our allies who were beyond number, and proceeding three bowshots along the causeway found the enemy all ready awaiting us and filling the air with their shouting. It was three days since we had attacked them, and they had consequently undone all our work in blocking up the former bridges, and now held them more strongly than ever. The brigs sailed up on either side of the causeway, and by their aid we succeeded in approaching very near the enemy to whom we did no small damage with guns, muskets and crossbows. Seeing this, some of my men leapt on land and forced both bridge and barricade, upon which we began to cross over in some numbers and pursue the enemy who were proceeding to fortify themselves at the other bridges and barricades which they had made. These two, however, were gained in turn, though with more danger and difficulty than on the preceding occasion, and we finally succeeded in driving them out of the whole of the main street and the square containing the chief buildings of the city. Having got so far I gave orders that no Spaniards should advance further, while I with our allies proceeded to block up with stones and earth all the gaps in causeway and street through which water was flowing, the which entailed so much work that even with the assistance of ten thousand Indians evening was coming on before it was finished. During the whole of this time the Spaniards and our allies continued fighting and skirmishing with those of the city and laying ambushes in which many of them were trapped and killed. I with the horsemen made one reconnoitre of the city, riding along the streets which were not intercepted by waterways and killing with our lances those who attempted to attack us. In this way we forced them to withdraw and they dared no longer venture out on to open ground. Seeing that the defenders were rebellious and displayed such determination to die or to resist I drew two conclusions: the first, that we should regain little or none of the riches we had lost during the "sorrowful night"; the second, that they were bent on forcing us to destroy them completely. I was more concerned about this latter conclusion which grieved me to the heart, and was at pains to think in what way I could terrify them so as to bring them to a knowledge of their sins and the damage that we were in a position to do them. All that I could think of was to burn their houses and the towers in which they kept their idols. Accordingly that day, that they might feel it the more, I ordered the large houses surrounding the square to be set on fire, those houses, namely, in which we had fortified ourselves when we were besieged in the city and which were large enough to contain a native chieftain and some six hundred of his retinue; we also burnt certain smaller ones hard by still more elaborate and very finely worked, in which Muteczuma had been wont to keep all his birds. I was much grieved to do this, but since it was still more grievous to them I determined on burning them. At this the enemy showed no small distress as also their allies from the other cities of the lake, for they had never thought that we should be strong enough to push so far into the city: and this dismayed them not a little.

Having thus set fire to the houses, since it was now late, I gathered my men together to return to the camp. Seeing that we were retreating an infinite number of the citizens rushed out and attacked our rearguard with tremendous fury. But the street was level and without obstacles so that those who were on horseback turned on them and we killed many of them with our lances in repeated charges, which still did not prevent them from continuing to attack and yell in our rear. They were much discouraged that day and plainly showed it, especially on seeing us actually enter their city, burning and destroying, and on finding themselves at grips with Indians from Tezcuco, Chalco, Suchimilco, and the Otumíes, all of whom openly proclaimed where they came from. The Tlascalans, indeed, as also some of the others showed them some bodies of their dismembered comrades whom they said they would sup on that night and breakfast on next day, and so in effect they did. In such fashion we reached our camp to take our rest, for we had toiled hard during the day. The seven brigs which I kept with me had also penetrated into the city by means of the waterways and set fire to many parts. The captains in the other two camps and on board the other six brigs also fought well, but I have not space to recount all that befell them, save only to say that they returned to their respective camps without any casualties.

Early the following day having heard mass I advanced on the city in the same order with all my men, in order that the enemy might have no time to unblock the bridges or erect barricades. Early as we were, however, of the three waterways which cross the road running from our camp to the great square two of them were already open as they had been before, and we only crossed with great difficulty; so much so, that fighting went on from eight o'clock in the morning to an hour after noon, in which time nearly all the arrows, ammunition and cannon balls which the bowmen and musketeers carried with them were used up. And your Majesty may well believe that the danger we ran on every occasion in taking these bridges was beyond all comparison, for to capture each one we were forced to leap into the water and so gain the other side by swimming. And many were either unable or unwilling to venture thus for the enemy resisted us stoutly with knife and lance thrusts to prevent our scrambling up the opposite bank. But they could no longer do us damage from the flat rooftops on either side, and we being but a stone's throw away were continually bombarding them with arrows, so that the Spaniards each day plucked up greater courage and a more fixed determination to get across. They plainly perceived, moreover, that such was my intention and that sink or swim there was nothing else to be done.

It will occur to your Majesty that placing ourselves in such peril as we did over gaining these bridges and barricades, we were negligent in not holding them once they were captured and so avoiding each day the same perils and dangers which beyond a doubt were grave. And certainly so it will appear to those who were not present. But your Majesty must know that the thing was in no wise possible, for to carry it out two things were necessary: either that we should transfer our camp to the square surrounded by the towers containing their idols, or that a guard should be posted during the night. Both these courses would have involved great danger and were in fact impossible. For were our camp within the city, since they were many and ourselves few, every night and at every hour they would have been in a position to attack us; to keep them off would have entailed unbearable toil and they could have attacked us in many different places at once. On the other hand, to have set Spaniards to guard the bridges through the night would have meant that they would have been too tired to fight next day, and thus it was imperative that we should capture the bridges anew each day we entered the city. That day in particular we had taken so long in capturing the bridges and blocking them up behind us that there was hardly time to do more save to take and block up a couple of bridges along the other chief causeway which leads to Tacuba. We also burnt many fine houses in that ſtreet before evening came and the time to retreat, in which we always ran less danger than in taking the bridges. For the sight of our retreat was always certain to imbue the natives of the city with such excitement that anyone would have thought that it was they who had been completely victorious, and we were flying to safety. To retreat, however, it was necessary that the bridges should be thoroughly blocked up so that the horse could cross freely from one side to the other; and so as we retired and they came burſting with eagerness in pursuit we sometimes feigned to fly and then the horsemen suddenly wheeling round usually managed to catch a dozen or so of the moſt headſtrong. With these and certain ambushes which were practised on them they never failed to come off the losers, and yet it was aſtonishing to see the way they rushed on. For no matter how certain the hurt and damage which they knew they would receive during our retreat, yet they never ceased to pursue us until we were beyond the city wall. In such fashion we returned to our camp where I heard from the two other captains that all had gone well with them, and they had succeeded in killing many both by land and sea.

Albarado in particular wrote me from Tacuba saying that he had gained two or three bridges, for as he was proceeding along the causeway leading from the central market to Tacuba the three brigs which I had sent him could sail up the side of the causeway and so assiſt him more than in the preceding days. There were of course more bridges and gaps in the causeway, but fewer of the flat rooftops on either side.

During all this time the natives of Iztapalapa and several other towns which lie as I described before on the shores of the fresh water lake had steadily refused to sue for peace though at the same time abstaining from attacking us in any way. The Chalco Indians accordingly, being very loyal vassals of your Majesty and seeing that we had our hands full with the natives of the capital, united with several other townships round the lake and inflicted all the damage they could on the fresh lake dwellers. These, seeing that each day brought us fresh victories against the Mexicans and that they were like to receive great harm from our allies, decided to come to our camp, and begged me to forgive them for what had been done in the past and order the Chalco Indians and their neighbours to do them no further hurt.

I replied that I was prepared to do so and was not angered with them but only with the inhabitants of the capital: and to prove the sincerity of their friendship I requested them (since I was determined not to strike camp until the city had surrendered either peaceably or by force) to aid me with their canoes of which they had a large number, fit them out with as many fighting men as they could muster and come to my help over the water. I also requested them, since the huts of the Spaniards were few in number and those very dilapidated and there was much rain, to build as many huts in my camp as they could, bringing bricks and wood in their canoes from the houses in their city which lay nearest our camp. They replied that the fighting men and the canoes were ready at any moment, and as to building houses they set to work so well that they had soon completed two lines of them on either side of the causeway which must have stretched from first to last a distance of some three to four bowshots from the towers where we were encamped. And your Majesty must consider that this causeway which runs across the deepest part of the lake is yet so wide that notwithftanding the houses on either side a broad ftreet remained down the middle along which both horses and foot soldiers could freely pass backwards and forwards. Moreover in the camp itself there were continuously lodged more than two thousand persons, counting Spaniards and the Indians who acted as their servants: all our native allies lodged at Cuyoacan about a league and a half away, and both this town and others provided us with certain ftores of which we ftood in great need, especially fish and cherries, of which they have such abundance that in the five or six months in which they are in season they could feed twice as many people as there are in this land.

As we had entered the city from the side of our camp for two or three days running (not to mention three or four times before) and had been unfailingly victorious and were killing such infinite numbers of them with our crossbows and muskets, we thought that at any moment a move would be made towards peace, which we desired as we did our own salvation. But nothing seemed able to bring them to this pass. Accordingly to put them in greater ftraits and see whether I could not force them to ask for peace I proposed to continue to enter the city daily and attack them in three or four places. To this end I summoned all our allies from the various lake cities so that that morning there were more than a hundred thousand men in our camp. I gave orders for the three brigs with half the canoes, which would be some hundred and fifty, to advance one side, and the other three brigs with a like number of canoes to go by the other and so encompass a greater part of the city, burning and doing all the damage they could. I myself proceeded along the main ftreet to find it free of obftacles as far as the large houses in the central square, not one of the bridges having been torn down; we therefore advanced as far as the causeway leading to Tacuba, in which there were some seven or eight bridges. Arrived there I ordered one officer to enter another street with sixty or seventy men and seven horsemen to protect their rear, and ten or twelve thousand of our Indian allies in addition: a second officer I ordered to proceed in like manner down another street, and I with the remaining men advanced along the Tacuba road. We captured three bridges which we blocked up, and owing to the lateness of the hour left the others which could be better won on the morrow; for I was very eager to gain possession of the whole of that street so that the men in Albarado's camp could communicate with ours and pass freely from one camp to the other, as also the brigs. The day was thus eminently successful both on sea and land, and some small booty was taken from the defenders: Sandoval and Albarado were likewise equally successful.

On the following day I again entered the city in similar fashion and God gave us such good success that where I was with my men it seemed as if no resistance was offered to us. The enemy retreated so vigorously that we seemed to have captured three quarters of the whole city. Those from Albarado's camp likewise made good headway, and certainly after the work of those two days I felt that peace could not be very far off, for at no time either with victories or otherwise did I cease from giving every sign of desiring peace that I could. Yet in spite of all we observed no answering signals, and that day we returned to camp with much contentment for what had been achieved, though heavy at heart to see the citizens so determined to die.

During these days Pedro de Albarado had captured many bridges and in order to hold them had placed sentinels both on horse and on foot to guard them during the night, the rest of his men going back to their camp some three-quarters of a league off. This labour of keeping guards becoming too great to be borne, he decided to move his camp to the end of the street leading into the chief market of the city, a square rather larger than that of Salamanca, and entirely surrounded by arcades; to do this he had only some two or three more bridges to gain, but they were exceptionally deep and presented numerous difficulties; he fought thus for several days with this object and was uniformly successful. On that day which I have already described when our enemies displayed such cowardice and we attacked them very fiercely and continuously, Albarado somewhat intoxicated with the savour of victory and the many bridges he had captured, decided to make an attempt to gain an exceptionally wide one at a spot where more than seventy feet of the causeway had been torn up giving place to water about nine feet deep; they attacked it accordingly that same day and with the very considerable assistance of the boats passed the water and gained the bridge-head, continuing even further in pursuit of the enemy who fled before them. Pedro de Albarado made great haste to block up the gap so that the cavalry might pass across, and also because there was no day on which I did not warn him both in writing and by word of mouth not to capture so much as a hand's breadth of land without securing it so that horses could pass over it safely, for it was on the horses that the fortunes of war depended. On this occasion the natives of the city, seeing that there were only some forty or fifty Spaniards on their side of the gap together with a few of our allies and that the horse soldiers could not yet pass, charged back on our men with such fury that they were forced to turn and leap into the water: three or four Spaniards were taken alive and afterwards sacrificed and several of the allies were killed. Finally Pedro de Albarado retreated to his camp. When I returned to our camp that day and heard of this I was more grieved than at anything else which could have happened, for it was just such as would hearten our enemies and give them cause to think that we should not dare to penetrate into the city. The reason for Albarado being so eager to take that difficult bridge was, as I have said, the great success he had already had and the weakness displayed by the enemy, but principally because the soldiers in his camp worked on him to capture the market, for that gained (they said) the whole of the city was practically ours, since it was there that the natives placed all their hope and strength. Moreover, Albarado's men seeing that I continued to attack the city from my side without a break feared that I should capture the market place before them, and as they were originally nearer it than we ourselves they held it as a point of honour to be the first to capture it. In this way Pedro de Albarado was won over to do what they wanted; the same attempts had been made upon me in my own camp; for all my men begged me earnestly to give the order to advance by one of the three streets leading to the said market place, since we were meeting no resistance and that place once gained our labours would be lessened. I prevaricated, however, in every way I could, urging reasons for not attempting it although concealing the real cause, which was simply the inconveniences and dangers which I plainly saw would follow; for in order to enter the market place there were innumerable rooftops, bridges and broken-down causeways to be captured, in such wise that almost every house which we should have to take was like a little island surrounded with water on all sides.

I had heard the news of Albarado's setback on returning to my camp in the evening and accordingly next morning set out for his camp to reprimand him, examine what had been gained and the new position of his camp, and advise him as to the best means for ensuring his safety and renewing the attack on the enemy. Coming to his camp I was really amazed at the distance he had advanced it into the city and the perilous gaps and bridges which he had captured; so much so that I could not blame him as I had thought to do before, and after discussing what was to be done, I returned to my camp the same day.

After this incident I continued making attacks into the city in the same parts that we were wont to do, the brigs and canoes being engaged in two places and myself within the city in another four places; we were always successful and killed many of the enemy, for every day innumerable fresh troops came to join us. I still hesitated however to pierce further into the city, both to see whether the natives would not come to terms and because such an entrance could only be made with considerable danger, since the enemy were a united body, strong, and quite determined to die. The Spaniards, seeing this delay (for they had attacked in this manner without advancing for over twenty days), importuned me anew very earnestly to penetrate further and attack the market place, where the enemy would be left with but a small place in which to defend themselves, and should they refuse to surrender would die of hunger and thirst, for they had nothing to drink save the salt water of the lake. I was arguing against it when your Majesty's treasurer spoke up saying that it was the opinion of the whole camp and that I must perforce put it into operation: upon which I replied to him and other gentlemen of importance there present saying that his plan and intentions were alike excellent, and that I desired to follow it more than anyone, but that I had abstained from doing so for a reason which I was loath to declare, but which was that while (I knew) he and others would bear themselves as valiant men, yet since the enterprise was one of much danger, there would be others who would not. Finally, however, they persuaded me to agree to go forward with the scheme so far as I was able, firſt consulting with the other two camps.

On the following day, in conjunction with several of my chief officers, we agreed to inform Sandoval and Albarado that we should enter the city the next day and make an attempt to reach the market place, and I set down in writing what they were to do from the Tacuba side. In addition to writing, to make more certain, I dispatched two of my servants to acquaint them with the whole business: their orders were that Sandoval should come immediately with ten horse, a hundred foot and fifteen musketeers to Albarado's camp, leaving ten horsemen and all the reſt behind in his own. On the following day, being that of our attack, the men he left were to ambush themselves behind some houses, carrying off all the baggage as if they were ſtriking camp: the natives of the city would then rush out after them and would be caught in the rear. Meanwhile Sandoval with the three brigs which he had himself and the other three of Albarado would capture the difficult gap where the latter had been defeated, and would immediately set to to block it up. They could then advance further taking care all the while never to pass on beyond a bridge which had not firſt been filled up and levelled. If they could without great risk win to the market place they should make every effort to do so and I would do the same: but they should underſtand these inſtructions as urging them not to take so much as a single position which should put them in danger of a reverse; I warned them in this way because I knew from what manner of men they were that they would venture their persons wherever

I should bid them even though they knew that they would lose their lives by it. The two servants were thus dispatched as I have said and informed Sandoval and Albarado of all that we had agreed; and since they had only to attack in one place whereas I was attacking in many I requested them to send me seventy or eighty foot to assist me; these accordingly returned with my two servants that same night and slept in our camp.

All being ready, on the following day after mass the seven brigs left our camp together with over three thousand canoes of our allies. I with twenty-five horse and all the foot (including seventy from the Tacuba camp) advanced along the causeway into the city, where on arriving I divided my men up in this manner. There were three streets all running from the one we had already gained to the market, called by the Indians *Tianguiz*; one of these is the principal and largest. I ordered your Majesty's treasurer and *contador* to advance along this one with seventy of our own men, some fifteen to twenty thousand of our allies and seven or eight horsemen in the rear; they were to block up all bridges and break down barricades so soon as they had taken them, and had some dozen Spaniards and also natives with picks to see that this job was done. The two other streets branching off from the road leading to Tacuba are narrower and more cut up by bridges and waterways. I ordered two captains to advance along the broader of the two with eighty Spaniards and over ten thousand of our allies, and at the beginning of the road leading to Tacuba I placed two heavy guns with eight horsemen guarding them. I myself with eight horsemen and about a hundred foot (among whom there were over five and twenty musketeers and bowmen) proceeded to advance along the narrowest street with what haste we could. At the very mouth of it I halted the horse-

194

men and gave them strict orders not to move from
there or attempt to come after me unless I should
send them word. Upon this I dismounted and advanced to the barricade which they had made at the
end of a bridge. By the aid of a small field gun and
the musketeers we gained this and advanced again
along the narrow street which was entirely broken
down in two or three places.

In addition to these three carefully planned attacks
in which we were engaged, our native allies who were
entering the city on their own and taking rooftops
and other places were so numerous that there seemed
to be no point at which we could be taken off our
guard. We ourselves captured two bridges and
barricades ahead of us and the road between, and our
allies forthwith advanced up the street without any
Spanish troops to aid them. I was left with some
twenty Spaniards on a sort of little island and saw our
friends engaged with the enemy in front; several
times they were driven back and some of them thrown
into the water, but with our assistance they returned
to the attack. In addition to this we were on our
guard to prevent any of the enemy from cutting across
the side streets and catching the Spaniards, who had
advanced up the other streets, in the rear. These
sent me a message at this moment to say that they
had made a lot of ground and were not far from the
market square; they were eager to press on at all
costs since they could hear the noise of the attack
which Sandoval and Albarado were delivering from
their side. I sent to them telling them in no wise
to advance further without first seeing that the bridges
were thoroughly blocked up, so that if it should
become necessary to retreat to the lake there should be
no difficulty or disturbance, for they knew that it was
there that danger lay. They sent back another message
to say that all that had been won was well repaired,

and that I might go through and see that it was so.
I, anxious lest they should go astray and neglect due
precautions in blocking up the bridges, accordingly
made my way there, and found that they had passed
one gap in the road some ten to twelve yards broad,
through which flowed water over twenty foot deep.
To pass it they had jammed up the gap with pieces
of wood and common reed grass, and since they had
crossed one at a time and with care the wood and
reeds had remained above the water; so that drunk
with victory they thought it was very secure. But as
chance would have it at the very moment that I arrived
at that accursed bridge it was to see the Spaniards
and many of our allies flying back in retreat, with
the enemy like so many hounds at their heels. Seeing
the disorder I immediately yelled out "Take care,
take care." The next moment as I came to the edge
of the water I found it full of Spaniards and Indians
so that it seemed as if not so much as a straw had
been thrown into it. The enemy rushed on in such
numbers that, bent on killing the Spaniards, they
threw themselves into the water after them: meanwhile the waterway filled up with enemy canoes who
captured our men alive in the water. The whole
business was so sudden, that seeing what numbers
of my men were falling, I determined to take my
stand there and die fighting. The best that we could
do, I and those who were with me on the near side,
was to stretch out our hands to a few of the unfortunate men who were drowning and help them on to
the land: some thus escaped from the water wounded,
others half-drowned, others again without their arms,
all of whom I dispatched back to the rear. The
enemy was so numerous that already I and the twelve
or fifteen who were with me found ourselves surrounded
on all sides.

I myself was so intent on saving those who were

drowning that I saw and thought nothing of the danger in which I was in: certain of the enemy were just about to seize me and would have borne me off had it not been for the captain of fifty foot who always accompanied me, and a youth in his company, who, after God, was the chief instrument in saving my life: and saving me, like a valiant man he lost his own. In this pass the Spaniards who got over the bridge pursued their way back along the street, which was small, narrow and bounded by water on both sides: (this the dogs had specially designed). Many of our allies were also fleeing pell mell down it so that there was little wonder that the road was soon blocked up with people who took so long to make any headway that the enemy had time to get into their canoes and come round on both sides of it on the water where they captured and killed at their pleasure. The captain who was with me and whose name was Antonio de Quiñones said to me: "Let's get out of here and save your person for you are well aware that without you not a single one of us will escape alive," but he could not succeed in persuading me to abandon the place. Seeing this he seized me in his arms to compel me to retreat, and although I would at that moment have welcomed death rather than life, yet at the importunities of that man and other comrades who were with me, we began to retire fighting with swords and bucklers against the enemy who struck fiercely at us. At this moment one of my servants arrived on horseback and cleared some space around us, but almost immediately an Indian standing on one of the low flat roofs gave him a spear thrust in the throat which forced him to retreat. We continued to fight thus desperately, waiting until the men should pass the narrow street and gain a place of safety while we held back the enemy, when a youth, one of my own special company, made his way back to us leading a horse for me to ride, for the mud was such in the narrow street from those who had fallen into and escaped from the water that it was as much as one could do to stand, especially with the pushing and shoving that went on from our men trying to escape. I mounted, but not to fight, for it was impossible to do so on horseback: at an earlier point in the causeway we had come across the eight horsemen whom I had left cut off on a kind of island and all that they had been able to do was to retire along the causeway: even retiring was so dangerous that a couple of mules ridden by two of my servants fell from the roadway into the water, the Indians killing one and the other being saved by some of the foot soldiers. Another youth of my own company, named Cristóbal de Guzman, mounted a horse given to him by one of the eight left on the island to bring to me so that I could escape, and both horse and rider were killed by the enemy. The death of this youth filled the whole camp with such sorrow that even now the grief of those who knew him is still fresh. And now after all our labours it pleased God that those who remained to us should finally come out into the Tacuba road which was very broad, where rallying my men I again proceeded, myself and nine other horsemen forming the rearguard. The enemy still came on with such spirit and certainty of success that it seemed as if not one of us would escape with his life. Withdrawing thus as best I could, I sent to the treasurer and *contador* to tell them to fall back on the great central square in close order; I sent the same message to the other two captains who had entered the street leading to the market. Both forces had fought very valiantly and gained many barricades and bridges which they had thoroughly blocked up, on account of which they received no damage when retreating. Even before the treasurer and *contador* began to retire the inhabitants of the city had tossed two or three white men's heads at them over the barricades which they were defending, the besiegers not knowing whether they came from Pedro de Albarado's camp or from ours. We were all gathered in the central square when from all sides such numbers of the enemy charged out upon us that we had our hands full in beating them off, and that in places where before this setback they would not have dared to attack three horsemen and a dozen foot. Suddenly from one of their lofty idol towers which stood near the square they set fire to a mass of perfumes and gums which are found in this land and are very similar to myrrh, the which they offer to their idols as a signal of victory; and although we had been glad to prevent it, yet we were not able to do so, for all the men were already making their way back to camp as fast as they could.

In this defeat the enemy killed from thirty-five to forty Spaniards and more than a thousand of our Indian allies; they wounded more than twenty of us, I myself receiving a wound in the leg; the small field gun which we had taken with us in our advance was lost, together with many crossbows, muskets and other arms. The citizens, so soon as they had gained the victory and in order to dismay Sandoval and Albarado, carried all the Spaniards they had captured, both living and dead, naked, up to certain lofty towers near the market place, and there sacrificed them, cutting open their breasts and tearing out their hearts to offer them to their gods. This the Spaniards under Albarado could plainly see from where they were fighting, and from the whiteness of the naked bodies they knew that they were Christians who were being sacrificed; at the which they were seized with great sadness and dismay and retreated to their camp. Nevertheless they had fought right well that day and had gained almost to the market place, which place indeed would have been taken had God for our sins not permitted so great a disorder. We ourselves returned to camp in very low spirits somewhat earlier than we were wont to do, for we heard news in addition that the brigs had been captured and the enemies' canoes would be taking us in the rear, although thanks be to God such was not the case. Nevertheless the brigs and our allies' canoes found themselves in a tight corner, so much so that one brig was very near being loſt, and its captain and maſter were badly wounded, the latter dying a week later.

The next day and night those within the city made great rejoicings with drums and trumpets, so that it seemed as if the very walls would collapse; all the waterways and bridges were reopened as in the beginning, and the enemies' fires and sentries advanced to within a couple of bowshots of our camp. We ourselves were so battered and wounded, many having loſt their arms, that it was essential to obtain reſt and time for repair. The citizens took advantage of this respite to send messages to many subject provinces, saying that they had been victorious, had killed many Chriſtians and would soon make an end of us, and were resolved in no wise to discuss terms of peace with us. As proof of what they said they sent a couple of horses' heads and certain heads of Chriſtians which the messengers went about to show to all whom they thought fit, and thus ſtrengthen more than ever the rebels in their obſtinacy. With all this, however, so that our enemies within the city should not become too proud nor perceive our weakness there was no day on which a few Spaniards both on horse and foot together with large numbers of our allies did not advance to attack the city, although they could never gain more than a few of the bridges in the firſt ſtreet leading to the central square.

Two days after this reverse, news of which had

THIRD LETTER

already spread over the whole countryside, the natives of a town known as Cuernabaca who were subjects of the Mexicans but had come over to our side came to the camp to tell me that the inhabitants of Malinalco, a neighbouring town, were doing much damage and destroying their land, and were now leaguing themselves with the province of Cuisco (which is very large) to attack them in force and kill them for having surrendered themselves as vassals of your Majesty and our friends: after they had destroyed them, said they, they would come and attack us. Now although our setback was so recent and we were in need of help rather than in a position to give it to others, yet since they begged me very earnestly I determined to assist them; and so in spite of great opposition from some, who said that I should destroy us all by depleting the numbers in our camp, yet I sent back with them eighty foot and ten horsemen under the command of Andrés de Tapia, whom I charged very gravely to do what might be most expedient to your Majesty's service and our own security, for he could well see the danger in which we lay, and he was to return within ten days. He accordingly set off and arriving at a little town between Malinalco and Cuernabaca found the enemy waiting for him; he with the natives from Cuernabaca who accompanied him immediately offered battle in the open field and our men fought so well that they broke up the enemies' ranks and pursued them right up to the walls of Malinalco, which is perched on a very lofty peak too steep for the horses to climb; seeing this they destroyed what buildings there were in the plain and returned victorious to our camp before the ten days were out; within the city at the top of the peak (they reported) there were many springs of excellent water producing a very fertile vegetation.

Meanwhile, as I have already described, some of

our men on horse and foot together with our allies were daily entering the city to combat the natives and advancing nearly to the large houses surrounding the great square; they did not succeed in progressing further, for the inhabitants had opened a very broad and deep gap in the causeway at the mouth of the square and had erected an exceptionally high and strong barricade on the further side. They fought thus till night overtook them.

A native ruler in the province of Tlascala known as Chichimecatecle, whom I have already mentioned (he who brought the decking of the ships built in his province), had from the beginning of the attack taken up his quarters in Albarado's camp with all his men, and seeing that after the recent setback the Spaniards did not fight as they were wont to do, he determined himself to enter the city with his own men, posting four hundred native archers at a dangerous gap in the causeway which he had captured from the citizens though not without our help. He accordingly advanced at the head of his men with a great deal of noise, all shouting out the names of their country and their ruler, and fought very fiercely that day so that on both sides there were many wounded and killed. The inhabitants of the city, however, were well assured that they had their adversaries in their power, for it is their nature when their opponents retreat, whether they themselves be victorious or not, to follow on their heels with great determination; and so they thought on this occasion when their opponents came to cross the water, an operation always fraught with danger, that they would take full revenge on them. It was for this reason that Chichimecatecle had left his four hundred archers at the bridge-head; for now as they began to retreat the citizens charged down on them with fresh fury, upon which the Tlascalans threw themselves into the water and protected by the archers passed safely across, while the enemy finding this unexpected resistance halted, not a little terrified at the daring nature of the Indian chief's attack.

Two days after Andrés de Tapia's return from Malinalco ten of the Otumíes Indians, who had been enslaved by the Mexicans, arrived in our camp saying that the rulers of the neighbouring province of Temascalcingo were making war on them, had burnt one town and carried off some of its inhabitants, and were now advancing, destroying as much as they could, with the intention of reaching our camp and falling upon us, so that those within the city could sally out and dispatch us. We were the more willing to give credit to this tale since but a few days before as we entered the city the inhabitants had threatened us with news of aid from Temascalcingo of which we knew little, save that it was a large province lying some twenty-two leagues from our camp. These Otumíes now begged us for aid; and although the request came at so grim a time, yet trusting in the help of God, and somewhat to break the spirit of those within the city who were now daily threatening us with help from this quarter and showed plainly that they were building upon it (for there was no other quarter from which help could come), I decided to send Gonzalo de Sandoval, *alguacil mayor*, thither with eighteen horse and a hundred foot (including but a single crossbowman), who accordingly left soon afterwards taking a number of Otumíes in his company. God knows the peril in which all went and also that in which we ourselves remained; but as it behoved us to display more courage and spirit than ever and die fighting if need be we concealed our weakness alike from our friends as from our enemies. Nevertheless not one but a thousand times my men declared that if it should please God to grant them their lives and to be victorious against the inhabitants of the capital even although they should gain no other advantage or reward in the city, nay, in the whole land, they would ask nothing more; from which may be understood the extremity of peril and want in which we had placed our persons and our lives.

Sandoval slept that night at a frontier town of the Otumíes facing the province of Malinalco, and rising very early next morning came to some farms belonging to the Otumíes which he found deserted and in large part burnt; riding further across the plain on the bank of a little stream he found a large band of enemy warriors, who had just finished burning another town. Seeing the Spaniards they began to fly, and our men pursuing them came across many bundles of maize dropped in the road together with the roasted bodies of children which they were carrying with them as provisions. After crossing the river they perceived the enemy rallying further on in the plain, upon which Sandoval and his horsemen charged and routed them, following up their flight straight to the town of Temascalcingo which was some three leagues off. The horsemen thus pursued them until they were actually within the gates of the town, when they waited for the foot and Indian allies to come up: these latter had occupied themselves in killing those whom the horsemen had overtaken and left in their rear, in such wise that over two thousand of the enemy perished in this pursuit. As soon as the foot arrived together with the Otumíes, numbering now some seventy thousand, they made a rush on the town where the enemy resisted them while the women and children together with their household belongings reached a place of safety in a stronghold perched on a very lofty peak nearby. But such was the fury of the attackers that the men were forced also to retire to the stronghold which was exceptionally rocky and difficult to approach, and in a very short space of time they had pillaged and burnt the town. It was now late and Sandoval decided not to attack the fortress, for they were all very weary, having fought all day. The enemy spent the greater part of the night in wild shouting and a great din of drums and native trumpets.

Next morning Sandoval with all his men began to ascend the hill in order to capture the fortress, although not without fear of finding themselves in difficulties in case of resistance, but on their arrival not a single one of the enemy was to be seen; certain of our Indian allies met them coming down from the top to say that there was nobody there and that all the enemy had left a little before dawn. As they were thus talking looking down they suddenly perceived the whole plain below them filled with people who were actually Otumíes; but the horsemen thinking them to be the enemy charged down on them and killed three or four with their lances; and as their language is different from that of the Mexicans they understood nothing more than that they were throwing down their arms and approaching them: even on this some three or four more were killed; but they afterwards entirely understood that it was a mistake. Since the enemy had not awaited their coming the Spaniards decided to turn upon another town belonging to them which was also at war with the Otumíes. The inhabitants, however, seeing such great numbers advancing against them, immediately came out with offers of peace; Sandoval held converse with its ruler, telling him that I received kindly those who came to offer themselves as vassals to your Majesty even though guilty of grave crimes, and requesting him to speak with those of Temascalcingo and urge them to come to me, the which he promised to do and also bring the natives of Malinalco in peace: this done Sandoval retired to his camp.

That day certain Spaniards from my camp had advanced as usual to attack the capital and a request was brought back that our interpreter should approach because the citizens wished to discuss terms of peace. This, it afterwards appeared, they wanted only on condition that we should evacuate the entire country. The proposal was put forward simply to obtain a few days' breathing space in which they would have time to furnish themselves with various things they lacked, for we never succeeded by any such hardships in changing their intent to continue the fight against us. While they were thus conversing with our interpreter, but a short distance from our men, with only a demolished bridge between them, an old warrior in the sight of everybody leisurely took out of his knapsack a few eatables which he ate, so as to give us plainly to understand that they were not in need of food, as a reply to our men who told them that they would die of hunger. Our Indian allies told us that these attempts at peace were foils, and urged that they should attack them; however, there was no further fighting that day as the chiefs begged the interpreter to speak with me as to what they had proposed.

Four days after Sandoval's return from Temascalcingo, the chiefs both of that province and of Malinalco and Cuisco, another very large province which had rebelled, arrived at our camp, asking forgiveness for the past and offering to serve us faithfully in the future, the which they have done up to the present.

During Sandoval's absence at Temascalcingo the inhabitants of the capital planned to make a night attack on Albarado's camp, and appeared suddenly an hour before dawn. The sentries both on horse and foot hearing them yelled out "To arms!" and those who were near threw themselves upon the enemy, who when they found mounted men fighting against them cast themselves into the water. In the meanwhile the main body of Spaniards came up and fought very fiercely for some three hours. We heard from our camp the noise of one of the field guns being fired, and anxious lest they should be defeated I ordered my men to arm themselves and advance upon the city so as to weaken the enemies' attack on Albarado. The inhabitants, however, finding the resistance of the Spaniards so determined finally retired into the city, and during the day which followed we attacked them anew.

By this time those of us who had been wounded in our defeat were recovered. A ship belonging to Juan Ponce de León had arrived in Vera Cruz having met with rough treatment on the coast of Florida. With this news from Vera Cruz came a certain amount of gunpowder and crossbows of which we were in very urgent need. And by now, thanks be to God, the whole land about us had declared on our side. Yet, seeing how rebellious the inhabitants of the city still were and as plainly determined to die without surrender as was ever any race of men, I knew not by what means to save ourselves so much peril and toil, and at the same time avoid destroying utterly both them and their city, which was one of the most beautiful sights in the world: for it profited us nothing to assure them that we were resolved never to strike camp, that the ships would continue to make war on them by water, that we had conquered the tribes of Temascalcingo and Malinalco, and that in all the land there was none to help them, nor any place from which they might obtain maize, flesh, fruit, water, or any· other kind of nourishment. The more we spoke to them of such things, the less of weakness we perceived in them: rather in fighting and attacking we found them yet more spirited than before. Seeing then that the matter stood in this wise and that the siege had already lasted over forty-five days, I determined to adopt a method which should contribute to our safety and place the enemy in closer straits, namely, that as we proceeded slowly to gain the streets of the city we should raze to the ground every house that we came to on either side of the street: so that we should not advance so much as a step without leaving everything desolate behind us, blocking up every single waterway, no matter how slow our progress should be. To this end I called together all the rulers and chief men of our allies and told them what I proposed; they accordingly summoned a large number of their labourers who brought their hoes, a kind of shortened stick, which they use very much as peasants do their spades in Spain. They told me they would carry out my instructions very willingly and thought them very prudent. The work pleased them not a little, for it seemed to them a means by which the city should be made utterly desolate, the which they desired more than anything else in the world.

Three or four days were occupied in making these arrangements. The inhabitants were certain that we were planning some new attacks on them. They themselves, as it afterwards appeared, were ordering what they could for their defence, as we likewise guessed at the time. Having agreed, therefore, with our allies to attack both by land and water, we heard mass early the next morning and forthwith took the road to the city. On our arrival at the demolished bridge and barricade close to the large houses in the great square, the inhabitants bade us cease from fighting for they desired peace. I immediately gave orders to my men to stay their hands, and requested the ruler of the city to come and speak with me to arrange conditions of peace. They, saying that they had already sent for him, delayed us more than an hour;

in truth they had no desire for peace and were not long in showing it, for as we ſtood quietly by they began presently to pelt us with arrows, darts and ſtones. Seeing this we immediately began to ſtorm the barricade and capture it. On entering the square we found it littered with large ſtones to prevent the horsemen from riding through it, since it is they who are the deciding factor in battle: we likewise found a ſtreet walled up with loose ſtones and another scattered with them to prevent the advance of cavalry. That day we blocked up the waterway immediately outside the square in such fashion that never afterwards did the Indians succeed in opening it. From that time onward we began to demolish the houses one by one and close up with extreme thoroughness all the bridges we captured, and since on that day over a hundred and fifty thousand warriors marched with us, not a little was accomplished. So we returned to our camp; the brigs and canoes of our allies had likewise done much damage in the city, and returned also to reſt their crews.

On the following day and in the same order we entered the city, and arriving at the large enclosure surrounding the towers of their idols, I gave orders to my officers that their men do nothing before blocking up the waterways and making smooth the rough places which we had already gained. Our allies were in part to burn and demolish the houses and in part to advance and engage the enemy in those ſtreets in which we were wont to fight, being protected in the rear by our horsemen. I myself mounted the loftieſt of the towers where the Indians could see me (which I was aware would grieve them) and thence I encouraged our native allies and sent help to them when necessary; for fighting as they did without ceasing, at times the enemy gave way, at times our friends, who were then reinforced by some three or four horsemen, the which encouraged them mightily to attack their enemies anew. In this fashion we entered the city some five or six days running, and always on retiring we sent our allies on in front, a few Spaniards ambushing themselves in certain houses and the horsemen remaining behind so as to spring out on our enemies suddenly and catch them in the open square. Thus with the ambushes of both horse and foot we always succeeded in striking down a good number with our lances. One day in particular seven or eight horsemen were waiting in the square for the enemy to come out into the open: seeing that the enemy did not come they made as if to retreat; but the enemy fearing to be struck down by the lances of the cavalry when they turned suddenly, as had happened before, placed themselves on certain walls and low roofs of which there were an infinite number; and when the eight or nine horsemen turned on them they fled down a narrow street whose mouth they held and whither they could not be pursued. Upon this the horsemen were forced to retreat to the main body. The enemy, encouraged by this, came on again very intent on doing them mischief, but cautiously, perching themselves on walls and the like where they could not be hurt themselves, but where they could inflict damage on the horsemen who had to retreat. They thus succeeded in wounding two horses. This gave me the opportunity of devising an excellent trap as I shall recount to your Majesty. We returned to our camp that evening leaving all that we had captured very secure and open, and those within the city very boastful, thinking they had compelled us to retire through fear. That night I sent a message to Sandoval bidding him be at my camp before dawn with fifteen of his own horsemen and the same number of Albarado's.

Sandoval accordingly arrived with fifteen horse. I

had another twenty-five from Cuyoacan, which made forty in all. Ten of them I ordered to accompany the rest of the troops in the morning and together with the brigs fight in the same order that we had observed on previous days. Many bridges had been gained within the city and the ground levelled: they were therefore to charge the natives as often as they could so as to coop them up as much as possible within their strongholds, and keep them so until it was time to retire. I myself would then enter the city with the other thirty horse, and without being seen we would place ourselves in certain large houses hard by the central square. My men did as I had commanded and an hour after noon I took the road leading to the city with my thirty horse; arrived there, I left them in the houses indicated, and mounted the high tower as I was wont to do. There, as it chanced, some Spaniards opened up a grave and found within golden ornaments to the value of more than fifteen hundred *castellanos*. The hour for retreat was come: I ordered them to begin to retreat in close order, and that the ten horsemen on arriving in the square should pretend to make an attempt at charging but seem not to dare accomplish it. This they did when there were large numbers of the enemy near by the square and actually in it, and my men in ambush were already longing for the moment to arrive, for they were eager to acquit themselves well and were weary of waiting. I joined them: already the Spaniards on horse and foot as well as our Indian allies who had been informed of my plan were retreating through the square. The enemy was darting forward with such shouts that you might have thought they had been entirely victorious, and the horsemen turned and made as if to charge them across the square and then suddenly drew back. They had done this twice and the enemy came on so enraged that they were close on the haunches of their horses at the very mouth of the street where we lay. We saw the Spaniards pass along the front of us and at the same instant heard a musket shot which was the signal, and knew that the moment had come. With the cry of " *Santiago* " on our lips we suddenly burst upon them, and charged straight across the square spearing, striking down, and passing over many who were killed by those who followed us; in such wise that in this ambush more than five hundred fell, including all their principal men and those the most hardy and valiant. That night our native allies dined well enough, for all those that we killed they cut to pieces and took off with them to eat: and such was the terror and astonishment of the enemy in finding themselves thus suddenly put to rout that during the whole of that evening they uttered not so much as a word or yell and hardly dared show themselves in the streets or on the rooftops, save it were in some very secure position. It was now almost nightfall when we retired and it seems that those within the city ordered certain slaves to spy out whether we were really retiring or what we were doing. And as they peeped out at the end of one street ten or twelve of our cavalry whirled round on them and pursued them so that not a single one escaped. At this fresh success the enemy took such fright that never again during the whole siege did they dare enter the square while we were retreating, even although but a single horseman were there, neither dared they attack so much as one of our foot soldiers or allies, thinking that some ambush would spring out at them from their very feet. This victory, in short, which our Lord God vouchsafed to us was the very principal cause by which the city was more swiftly gained, for the inhabitants were much dismayed at it whereas it redoubled the spirits of our allies; and so we returned to our camp intending to end the siege as rapidly as possible letting no day pass without entering the city. We suffered no casualties that day except that in bursting out of the ambush some of the horsemen came into collision and one fell from his mare which fled straight for the ranks of the enemy, but being received by arrows and badly wounded rushed back to us but died that same night: and although we were grieved at this, for on the horses our lives depended, yet we were relieved that it had not died in the hands of the enemy as we thought had like to happen, for had such occurred their pleasure at its death would have been greater than their grief at the death of their comrades whom we had killed. Likewise our brigs and our allies' canoes made great slaughter in the city that day without receiving any hurt.

We knew that the Indians within the city were panic-stricken and we now learnt from two of them who left the city at dead of night and came to our camp that they were dying of hunger; they were forced to come out at nightfall and fish in the water running between the houses of the city, and were going about the part which we had won from them seeking wood and weeds and roots to eat. We had already blocked up a number of broken-down bridges, and smoothed several rough places, so that I now decided to enter the city before dawn and do all the damage that we could. The brigs left their moorings before daybreak, and I with twelve to fifteen horse, a few foot and some of our allies entered swiftly and immediately put certain spies on guard. Directly it was day they signalled to us in ambush to rush out and we fell upon an infinite number of people. They were for the most part the most wretched of the citizens who had come out to look for food, were nearly all unarmed, and principally women and children: we inflicted such slaughter on them in all the streets open to our horses that prisoners and killed must have amounted to more than eight hundred, and the brigs in addition captured many prisoners and canoes who were out fishing and did great slaughter. The captains and chief men of the city seeing us attack them at so unaccustomed an hour were as panic-stricken as when we had ambushed them, not one of them daring to advance and fight against us: in such fashion we returned to our camp with no small booty for ourselves and victuals for our allies.

Again next day we entered the city: our allies seeing the steady progress we were making towards its destruction were swelling daily to such an extent that they could not be counted. We gained the whole of the Tacuba road and blocked up all dangerous places in it, so that those in Albarado's camp could communicate with us by way of the city; in the principal road leading to the market two more bridges were captured and securely blocked, and the palace belonging to the ruler of the city (the second since Muteczuma's death), a youth of some eighteen years known as Guatimucin, was burned; the palace in question had been very strongly fortified and surrounded by a moat of water. Several other bridges were gained and secured so that three-quarters of the city had now been captured, and the Indians were forced to withdraw to the strongest part which comprised those buildings standing farthest out into the waters of the lake.

On the day of Saint James following we again entered the city in the same order and passed along the principal street leading to the market, capturing only after some time and at great danger an exceptionally wide waterway which they thought quite secure; there was not time, however, to block this up completely, and as we remained on foot on the further side and the Indians saw that the horses were unable to cross they charged us afresh, many of those who charged being outstanding warriors. We resisted them stoutly and being supported by a number of crossbowmen forced them to retreat behind the palisades again though not before they had received a goodly volley of arrows. My men also bore pikes which I had ordered to be made after our reverse and which proved extremely useful. That day on either side of the principal street there was little to be seen or heard save the burning and demolishing of the houses which indeed was pitiable to see: yet since there was no other way to achieve our end we were forced to do it. The inhabitants seeing such damage cheered themselves by telling our allies that in any case they would have to turn to and rebuild them, for if they themselves were victorious they could be quite assured of that, and if so hap we were it would be just the same: which latter, thanks be to God, was what occurred, although it is they and not our allies who are rebuilding them.

Early next morning we found the gap in the main street closed just as we had left it the day before, and forthwith advanced two bowshots further, capturing two dykes they had made in the very middle of the street, and arriving at a small idol tower where we found the heads of certain Christians whom they had killed, the which grieved us not a little. From that tower one turning to the right led to the causeway on which Sandoval had pitched his camp; another to the left led to the market-place and was broken by but a single canal which they defended furiously; that day we advanced no further though fighting long and bitterly with the Indians. But as each day our Lord God vouchsafed us victory, the enemy had ever the worst of it; finally, as it was growing late that day, we retired to our camp.

At nine o'clock the next morning when we were preparing to enter the city we observed from our camp smoke coming from the two high towers in the market-place which we were at a loss to account for, but as it seemed too thick for the burning of incense, such as the Indians did before their idols, we wagered that Albarado's men had succeeded in penetrating there, the which though it afterwards proved true yet we could hardly believe at the time. And in truth Pedro de Albarado and his men fought right valiantly that day, for we had still many bridges and barricades to capture and at each attack practically the whole body of the city rushed to defend them. But he, seeing that on our side we were sorely besetting the enemy, did everything in his power to force an entrance into the market, for that was their stronghold; he only succeeded, however, in coming within sight of it and capturing those towers from which we had seen the smoke and many others close to the market square, which indeed comprise practically the whole circuit of the idol towers of the city, and they are not few. The horsemen found themselves, however, in considerable difficulty and were obliged to retreat, in which retreat three horses were wounded. Pedro de Albarado accordingly drew off his men to their camp, and we abstained from capturing a broken bridge and canal which alone stood between us and the market, contenting ourselves with levelling bad patches of road and blocking up bridges. On retiring for the night they followed us furiously although it was to their cost.

The following morning we immediately attacked the remaining waterway and barricade which lay close to a small tower. An ensign and two or three other Spaniards leapt into the water, upon which the inhabitants abandoned the defence, and we immediately set to blocking up the bridge and levelling the ground so that the horses could pass over. At that moment Pedro de Albarado rode up with four other horsemen, which was a cause of infinite rejoicing both to our men and his own, for by this union the siege would soon be over. Albarado had left men both in the rear and on his flanks to guard what had been captured as also to defend their comrades, and the bridge now being ready I crossed over with a few horsemen and rode forward to view the market-place, ordering my men not to advance beyond the bridge-head. We proceeded into the square observing the arcades which surrounded it, whose low flat roofs were full of the enemy, but as the market-place was large and they saw that we were on horseback they did not dare attack us. I then mounted the huge tower which ſtands close to the market-place and found both there and in other towers the heads of Chriſtians ſtuck up in front of the idols to which they had been sacrificed as also the heads of our Tlascalan allies who are old and very bitter enemies of theirs. From the top of the tower I examined how much we had won of the city which could not be less than seven-eighths, and considering to myself that so large a number of people could not possibly maintain themselves in such narrow squares, especially since the houses which remained to them were small and built right upon the water, and moreover that they were like to perish with hunger (for in the ſtreets we found the roots and even the bark of trees gnawed off), I decided to desiſt from fighting that day and attempted to make some treaty to save so great a multitude of people from being deſtroyed. For in very truth the damage that was done on them gave me such grief and pain that for that cause alone I did not cease at any time from making overtures of peace. But they always replied that they would in no wise surrender; even if but a single man were left alive he would die fighting; moreover, nothing of all their treasure would fall into our hands for they would burn it or throw it into the water where it could not be found. Being determined not to repay evil by evil I flattered their hopes by refraining from attacking them.

Since our powder was running very short we had spoken over a fortnight before of making a catapult: and although we had no engineers really competent to undertake it, yet some carpenters offered to make a small one, so that though I had no great hope of success in the matter, I had consented that they should try their hand. It was now finished and brought to the market-place and set up on a kind of raised platform in the middle, the platform being made of stones and mortar, about fifteen feet high and some thirty yards square. It was wont to be used by the inhabitants at feasts and games when the actors and dancers would place themselves upon it so that all the people in the market-place and those both within and on top of the arcades could see what was going on. The catapult took some four days to put into position even after it appeared in the square. Meanwhile our Indian allies were proclaiming to those in the city in what a marvellous manner we were going to kill them all. And though there had been no other fruit, as indeed there was not, yet the terror which was inspired by it, which was like to have made them surrender, was real enough. Both hopes however were doomed to disappointment, for neither did the carpenters succeed in working their engine, nor did the inhabitants though frightened make any move towards surrender, so that we were obliged to cover up the failure of the catapult by saying that moved by compassion we were unwilling to kill them all.

The day following this misfortune we again entered

the city, and as we had not attacked for three or four days found the streets full of women and children and other wretched beings half dead with hunger, and moving about listlessly outside their defences in the most pitiable manner. I gave orders to our native allies not to harm them. Not a single warrior had advanced into the open, but we saw them sitting wrapped in their mantles on the flat tops of the roofs and without arms. I again offered them peace through the mouths of my interpreters, to which they gave nothing but deceitful answers. Thus they wasted a great part of the day, whereupon I sent to say that I intended to continue fighting, and that they should withdraw their people from the streets or I would give our allies permission to butcher them. They replied that they desired peace. To this I made answer that I saw no chief there with whom I could treat, but that if he would come to me I would give him every security and we would discuss terms of peace. We then saw that they were but tricking us and were still prepared to fight, upon which having repeatedly warned them, in order to put them in yet greater straits I ordered Albarado with all his men to enter one quarter still held by the enemy and containing more than a thousand houses, and I myself entered another on foot with my own men, for the ground would not permit of riding. So fierce was the fighting between us and the enemy that we captured the whole quarter, and such was the mortality among the enemy that more than twelve thousand of them were killed or captured, whom indeed our allies used so cruelly that they would not spare the life of so much as a single one of them, notwithstanding our repeated warnings and rebukes.

On entering the city next day I gave orders that our enemies should not be attacked in any way. Upon this, seeing the multitude of people coming against them, and realizing that their own vassals and former subjects were coming to kill them, knowing also their extreme necessity and that they could not so much as move except on the dead bodies of their comrades, and being eager to see themselves delivered from so great straits, they called out asking why we did not dispatch them, and soon begged me to be sent for as they wished to speak with me. The Spaniards, all of whom desired greatly to make an end of the siege and were truly grieved at the damage and hurt that we had done, rejoiced much at this, thinking that the Indians were desirous of peace. They thus came to me very joyously to beg me to approach the barrier where were several native chiefs. Though aware that my going would little profit the matter I yet decided to go there, for I knew well that the decision to hold out depended solely on the ruler and three or four of the chief men of the city, the common people desiring to see themselves whether dead or alive out of that pass. Arrived at the barrier they told me that since they held me for an offspring of the sun, which so swiftly in but a day and night revolves round the whole earth, why did I not with equal swiftness finish the business of killing them and put them out of so great misery, for they were eager to die and go to heaven where their God Huitzilopocthli (that idol whom they hold in greatest veneration) was waiting to refresh them. I brought forward many arguments to persuade them to surrender, but had no success, although they received from us, now that we were victorious by the aid of God, more offers and signs of peace than had ever been given to us when we were on the losing side.

Our enemies were now in the most desperate straits, as may be gathered, and to wean them from their evil determination to die where they stood, I spoke with one of their chief men who had been captured some three or four days before, and although badly wounded offered him the chance of returning to the city, which he accepted. Next day accordingly I sent him under the charge of certain Spaniards to be handed over safely to the inhabitants: I had previously told him to speak with the ruler and other chieftains about peace and he had promised to do all that he could in the matter. The inhabitants received him with great respect as an important chief; but (it was reported to me later) on being brought before Guatimucin, his ruler, and beginning to speak of peace, he was straightway ordered to be killed and sacrificed to the gods; and the reply which we were expecting they gave us by advancing with tremendous shouts, flinging darts, arrows and stones, and beginning to attack us with terrific fury; so much so indeed that they wounded one horse with a long spear which one of them had made out of one of our swords; but it cost them dearly in the end, for great numbers of them fell: and so we returned to our camp.

On again entering the city we found the enemies' forces so much reduced that large numbers of our allies had ventured to remain within the city all night: and on coming within sight of the enemy we were unwilling to fight but passed to and fro in the city, thinking at every hour, at every moment, that they would come out to treat with us. And the more to incline them so to do, I rode up to the barricade which they held very strongly fortified and called out to certain chiefs behind it whom I knew, asking them since they could see that they were lost and knew that if I wished within an hour not one of them would remain alive, why did not Guatimucin, their lord, come and speak with me, for I promised to do him no harm, and on his surrender and their sueing for peace they should be very well received and well treated by me. Other arguments I advanced at which they wept unrestrainedly; and still weeping replied to me, saying that they well knew that they had erred and were in truth lost, and were willing to go and speak with their lord whose answer they would straightway bring me if I would stay there. They went off and came back after some time saying that their lord was not come with them because it was so late, but that at midday on the morrow he would surely come and speak with me in the market square; and so we went back to our camp. I gave orders that a trestle table should be set up on the high platform in the market-place for the ruler and chief men of the city, such as they were accustomed to use, and that food should be provided ready, all of which was done.

On the morrow I warned my men to be on the lookout so that if any of the citizens attempted any treachery they should not find us unprepared; I likewise warned Pedro de Albarado who was also present. On coming to the market-place I sent to acquaint Guatimucin with the manner in which we were awaiting him, but he, as it appeared, decided not to come himself and sent in his place certain five of the principal men of the city. They informed me that their lord requested my pardon for not appearing, but that he was very fearful of coming before me and was not well and that these men were come for him: he would see that they obeyed whatever I should command. Thus although the ruler did not come in person we rejoiced greatly at the arrival of the chieftains considering it a means of giving a speedy end to the business. I received them cheerfully and immediately ordered food and drink to be set before them; in devouring which they plainly showed their appetite and need for it. After they had fed I told them that they were to inform their lord that he need have no fear, and that I promised him that on coming before me no indignity should be put upon him nor would he even be detained, for without his presence nothing could be definitely decided. After this I ordered them to be given certain refreshment which they took away with them. They promised me to do all that they could in the matter and so departed. In two hours they returned bringing a few well-woven cotton mantles such as they wear and told me that for no consideration was Guatimucin willing to present himself before me, and begged to be excused from further parley. I again repeated that I could not understand why he refused to come to me since he saw that they, whom I well knew to be ringleaders in the stirring up and carrying on of the war, were free to come and go without harm; I begged them to speak with him again and urge him to come, since it was fitting he should do so and I proposed it for his own advantage; they replied that they would do this and would return with his answer on the morrow, upon which we both retired to our respective camps.

Very early next morning the chiefs arrived in my camp with the message that I should repair to the market-place where their lord would speak with me; I, thinking they spoke truth, rode there and waited some three or four hours without his putting in an appearance. Finally, seeing that I was tricked and that it was growing late without either the messengers or their master having arrived, I sent for our Indian allies: they had remained at the entrance of the city almost a league from where we were with orders to advance no further, for the inhabitants had requested that while peace was being arranged none of them should remain within the city. On receiving my message they waited not a moment, nor did Albarado's men, but immediately came up and began to attack a few barricades and bridge-heads which they still held and which was all that remained to them. These we captured, and as many of our men and of our allies as cared to, crossed them. On leaving camp I had given Sandoval orders to force his way with the brigs between the houses on the other side where they were still in possession, in such a way that we should encircle them, but that he was not to begin fighting until he saw that we were engaged. They were thus hemmed in closely on all sides and could only move by treading on the bodies of their dead on the tops of the few roofs which remained to them. They had neither arrows, darts nor stones with which to resist us, and they were fighting against our allies armed with swords and shields. Such was the mortality among the enemy by land and water that on that day more than forty thousand souls were either killed or taken; and such was the shrieking and weeping of the women and children that there was no one whose heart did not bleed at the sound of it. We ourselves were already more engaged in preventing our allies from slaughter and insensate cruelty than in fighting against the enemy: and surely the like of such cruelty was never seen before in any generation, nor so unnatural as was seen in the natives of these parts. Our allies took also much booty that day, which we could in no way prevent since we numbered but some nine hundred Spaniards and they were all told more than a hundred and fifty thousand, whom no precaution nor diligence could have kept from robbing, although on our part we did all that we could.

One of the reasons why I had during the preceding days attempted to avoid such violence with the inhabitants was that in reducing them by force they would naturally throw all that they had into the water, and even if they failed to do this our allies would inevitably carry off all that they could find. On account of this I feared that there would remain but little part for your Majesty of the riches which the city once contained, and which I had once held in truſt for your Majeſty. It was now late, and unable to bear the ſtench of the dead bodies which had lain in the ſtreets for many days and than which there is no smell more peſtilential, we retired to our camps. That night I arranged that on the morrow three heavy cannons should be dragged into the city, for I feared that the enemy, massed together as they were and without room to move about, on our attempting to break them by force, might without any actual fighting, as it were, swallow up the Spaniards in their midſt. I therefore hoped to do them some damage with the guns so as to persuade them to rush upon us. I also gave orders to Sandoval to be prepared to enter the city with the brigs as on the previous day and make for a large ſtretch of water lying between the houses where all the city's canoes were gathered together: for they were now forced to such shifts for room that the ruler of the city had taken up his quarters in a canoe with chieftains, not knowing where else to put themselves.

As soon as day broke I assembled all my men, having previously ordered Albarado to wait for me in the market-place and not to attack until I arrived, and when we were all together and the brigs had taken up their position on the further side of the houses which the enemy ſtill occupied I gave orders to my men that on the sound of a musket shot they should attack the small portion which remained and force the enemy to throw themselves into the water at the very place where the brigs were; I warned them to keep a sharp look-out for Guatimucin and to make every effort to take him alive, for that done all fighting would cease. I myself went up to one of the roof-tops and before the combat spoke with several of the enemy chiefs whom I knew asking them why their lord was unwilling to come to me in person; for since they were in such ſtraits they would do well to avoid acting in such a way that all must perish, and should bid him come forward without fear; upon this two of the chiefs seemed to depart and speak with him. In a short time one of the most important of all the chieftains returned with them, by name Ciguacoacin, the captain and governor of them all, whose advice was taken in all things pertaining to the war. I greeted him kindly to reassure him, and finally he told me that their ruler was utterly determined not to come to me and would rather die in the city, the which grieved me much. Seeing therefore his determination I bade him return to his men and bid them prepare themselves for battle for I intended to attack them and kill them all: and on this he departed. More than five hours were thus spent in these bargainings. Those left in the city stood and walked on piles of dead bodies, others were already in the water either attempting to swim or drowning in the great lake where their canoes were; such in a word was the affliction which they were in that it was beyond the wit of man to understand how they could endure it: all the time an infinite number of men, women and children were making their way towards us: and in order that they might escape the quicker many were jostled into the water and drowned amidst that vast multitude of corpses; for as it afterwards appeared, the drinking of salt water, hunger and the stench of dead bodies had worked such havoc upon them that in all more than fifty thousand souls had thus perished. And in order that we should not realize their plight these bodies were neither thrown into the water where our brigs would have come across them nor taken out of doors and exposed in the streets where we should have been able to see them. I myself visited some of the streets which remained to them and found the dead heaped one upon the other, so that one was forced to walk upon them. As the inhabitants of the city were now coming out of their own accord towards us, I provided that there should be Spaniards posted in every street to prevent our allies from killing the wretches who thus abandoned their city, and who were too numerous to count. I likewise warned the leaders of our allies that none of these people was to be killed; yet the numbers were such that it was impossible to prevent them and some fifteen thousand must have lost their lives that day: yet the chieftains and warriors still remained in certain corners, roof-tops and boats, where no kind of dissimulation could longer profit them, since their ruin and helplessness were only too plain. Seeing that night was drawing on and that they still refused to surrender I trained two guns on them to see if that would move them, for to have permitted our allies to attack them would have caused greater suffering than the guns, which in effect did them some damage. But this profiting nothing, I ordered the musket to be fired and almost immediately the corner which they held was rushed and taken and those that remained were thrown into the water: others surrendered without striking a blow; the brigs immediately entered the inner lake and broke right into the middle of the fleet and canoes full of warriors who no longer dared to fight: and by the mercy of God a captain of one of the brigs took up the pursuit of a canoe which seemed to contain people of importance, and having two or three bowmen on board ordered them to aim at its occupants: upon this the natives made a signal that they should not fire as their ruler was on board, whereupon the sailors in the brig soon came up with them and took prisoner Guatimucin, the ruler of Tacuba and other chieftains. On his coming before me I bade him be seated, unwilling to show him any incivility; he told me in his own tongue that he had done all that it was his duty to do to defend himself and his people until they were come to this grievous state, and now let me do what I would with him; he then drew a dagger which he had in his belt, bidding me dispatch him with it at once. I told him to be of good courage for he had nothing to fear. And so immediately this lord was taken prisoner all fighting ceased, which it pleased God to fall on Tuesday, the day of Saint Hippolitus, the 13th of August in the year 1521. Thus the siege which had started on the 30th of May in the same year had lasted seventy-five days, during which your Majesty will have seen the perils, misadventures and difficulties which your vassals suffered, and in which they constantly ventured their lives as is plainly shown by the deeds which they accomplished.

And of all those seventy-five days of siege not one passed without some fighting with the inhabitants of the city either more or less. On that last day having taken what spoil we could, we returned to our camp, giving thanks to God for his signal mercy and the victory we had so long desired. I remained three or four more days in camp seeing to the arrangement of various matters and we then left for this city of Cuyoacan, where I have since been busied in the restoration of good order and government, and the pacification of these parts. The gold and other objects obtained were pooled with the consent of your Majesty's officials and amounted to over a hundred and thirty thousand *castellanos*, of which a fifth was handed over to your Majesty's treasurer, exclusive of other due claims of your Majesty with reference to slaves and the like, as will be seen set out in detail in a separate account signed with our names. The gold which remained was divided amongst myself and my men according to the merit, service and rank of each; there were also certain jewels and ornaments, of which a fifth part of the most precious was handed over to your Majesty's treasurer.

THIRD LETTER

Among the other booty taken from the city were many golden shields, crests and plumes, and other such marvellous things that they could not be described in writing nor comprehended unless they were actually seen; so that it seemed fitting to me that they should not be divided but rather that they should be presented as a whole to your Majesty; to which end I assembled all the Spaniards and asked them whether they thought it good that all these marvels should be sent as proof of our loyalty and including both their portions and my own; they replied that they were delighted and would gladly subscribe to it, so that the representatives sent by the councils of New Spain will bear this our service to your Majesty.

The ruler of the great province, by name Michoacan, whose seat is some seventy leagues from Tenochtitlan, hearing of our capture and destruction of the capital, and thinking that since we had done this nothing could be impossible to us, sent in fear certain messengers to tell me that he had heard that we were vassals of some mighty lord, and (if I should think it good) both he and his people desired to become vassals of that lord and dwell in friendship with us. I replied that we were in sooth such vassals of your Majesty and that it was our business to make war on all such as refused to become so, for which reason he and his people had done well. And as, but a short time before, I had heard news of a southern sea, I enquired of them whether it could be reached by way of their land, to which they replied, yes. And thereupon in order that I might inform your Majesty of this sea and of their province, I requested that two Spaniards might accompany them back to their lord, to which they agreed with pleasure, but added that to reach the sea it was necessary to pass through a land ruled by a lord with whom they were at war, so that at the moment it was impossible to pass. During the three or four days that those messengers stayed with me I ordered the cavalry to skirmish in front of them, that they might carry news of this wonder to their own land; after which, having given them certain jewels I dispatched them with two Spaniards to Michoacan.

I had heard, as I said, of a sea lying to the south, and in some places not more than twelve, thirteen or fourteen days' march distance, at which I rejoiced greatly, knowing the common opinion of learned men that islands rich in gold, pearls, precious stones and spices, together with many other secret and marvellous things, are to be found there, and desiring to do your Majesty such signal and memorable service I dispatched four other Spaniards to make their way two and two through different provinces, providing each party with guides and an indication of the roads that they would have to follow. I ordered them not to halt until they should reach the sea, when they should take full and royal possession of it in the name of your Majesty. After certain days one party returned, reporting that they had proceeded south some hundred and thirty leagues through various fertile provinces without receiving any check, and on coming to the sea had duly taken possession of it planting crosses on the shore as a sign to others. They brought with them several natives from the coast and in addition a very fine sample of gold from mines which they found in the provinces through which they passed, the which I am now sending together with other samples to your Majesty. The other party was somewhat longer in returning, having marched some hundred and fifty leagues to the south and likewise discovered the sea and taken possession of it. They also brought certain of the natives back with them, all of whom I received very kindly, and having informed them of the great power of your Majesty and given them a few presents I sent them back to their lands.

(The various tribes who with the Culuans had thrown off the Spanish yoke after the retreat from the capital had now for the most part been forced to return to their allegiance. A few provinces some fifteen to thirty leagues to the north were, however, still rebellious, and Sandoval was dispatched with a small force to overcome them. At the same time, the officer whom Cortés had left in charge of the garrison of Segura de la Frontera was sent south to subject the province of Oaxaca, which he had already explored in part during the absence of his master. Both officers left Cuyoacan on October 30th 1521. Nearly a month later letters from Sandoval reached Cortés telling of his success in the north. Cortés replied, assenting to his plan for settling the district and bidding him found a town in the province of Tuxtepec, to be called Medellín : he enclosed a list of the officials, justices, councillors and the like, whom he proposed. The Governor of Segura was equally successful and sent back with his report a sample of gold obtained from the mines in the province. Meanwhile the city of Mexico was being rebuilt ; Spaniards were directing the work, and hopes were held that it would once again take its place as the pride of New Spain. Ambassadors from other tribes to the south came in bearing presents and were well received. Another expedition was also sent to pacify the natives on the banks of the Pánuco river and to found a town there if it seemed feasible. Cortés then proceeds :)

At this time I received letters from Vera Cruz saying that a ship had arrived bearing one Cristóbal de Tapia, imperial overseer (*veedor*) of the metal castings in Hayti; the next day I received a letter from him in person acquainting me that his coming to this land was for the purpose of taking over the government of it by order of your Majesty, for which he bore royal warrants, which he would present to me in person but to none other beforehand: this he hoped would be soon; but as his horses were wearied from the sea journey he had not yet set out, and begged me say whether it were best I should go to him or he come to me. I replied straightway that I rejoiced greatly at his coming, and that there was no one coming with royal warrant to take over the government of these parts whom I should have been more pleased to see, on account of our old acquaintance, in the days when we had lived as close neighbours in Hayti. And since the pacification of these parts was not yet so complete as I could have wished and any new arrangement would only unsettle the natives, I requested Father Pedro Melgarejo de Urrea[18] very urgently to undertake the work of seeing Tapia and examining the royal warrants. This friar had taken part in all our toils and was very well informed as to how matters stood with us. (Indeed your Majesty was very well served by his coming and we ourselves greatly benefited by his teaching and counsel.) He was therefore in a position to know better than anyone what was expedient for your Majesty's service and the good of these parts. I accordingly gave him leave to come to an arrangement with Tapia as to what had best be done, for he had instructions from me which he was not to exceed by a hair's-breadth; and this conversation took place between us in the presence of your Majesty's treasurer who likewise urged him to undertake the commission.

Upon this he left for Vera Cruz, and in order that Tapia might be received and welcomed with all hospitality both there and in other towns, I dispatched two or three trustworthy persons from my company with the friar. I remained at Cuyoacan, making certain preparations to come to the coast myself, and in the meantime seeing to several matters in your Majesty's interest in connection with the pacification and subjection of these parts, and so awaited the reply which arrived some ten or twelve days later. In it the justices and council of Vera Cruz informed me that Tapia had presented the warrants which he bore from your Majesty and the Governors of the Indies in your Majesty's name, which they had received with due reverence, but as to fulfilling them they had replied that they must inform the other members of the municipality who were for the most part with me in Cuyoacan, and they would then do and fulfil all things which should be to the service of your Majesty and the good of this land. At this reply, they reported, Tapia had been not a little disgruntled, and had even attempted certain scandalous things. While much grieved at this, I replied to them urging them strongly to endeavour to appease Tapia, looking always in the first place to the interests of your Majesty, and to avoid any occasion for disturbance: I myself was on the way to see him personally and carry out all that your Majesty commanded and was most in your Majesty's service. I had already set out and countermanded the orders of the captain and men who were going north to the Pánuco river (for in my absence it was necessary that a strong garrison should remain in Cuyoacan), when the procurators[19] of the various councils of New Spain sent to me with many and earnest protestations against my leaving Cuyoacan, saying that all these provinces of Mexico had been but so lately pacified that if I went rebellion would be certain to break out, causing great disservice to your Majesty and commotion in the land. Many other reasons they gave for my continuance in Cuyoacan and finally declared that with the consent and approval of the councils, they would proceed to Vera Cruz where Tapia still was, see the royal warrants and do all that was fitting in the service of your Majesty. I accordingly sent a message by them to Tapia acquainting him with what was being done and telling him that Gonzalo de Sandoval, *alguacil mayor*, Diego de Soto, and Diego de Valdenebro who were all in Vera Cruz were empowered to speak in my name, and were together with the council of Vera Cruz and the procurators of the other city councils to see that everything was done in your Majesty's best interests and those of the country, for they were and are very proper persons to deal with such matters. Meeting Tapia on the road, accompanied by Friar Pedro, they requested him to return, and all repaired to the town of Cempoal, where Tapia again presented the royal warrants, which were received by all with the respect due to your Majesty; and as for putting them into effect, they replied that they would petition your Majesty directly, for so would your Majesty's interests best be served, as should appear by the various causes and reasons to be set out in the petition and which was afterwards done; this petition which is to be presented to your Majesty by representatives of New Spain has been signed by a public notary. Finally, other agreements and requisitions having passed between Tapia and the procurators, he embarked again in the ship which had brought him, as he was requested: for his sojourn here and the fact that he had given out that he was coming as Governor and Captain General of these parts had already provoked several risings; and indeed the natives of Mexico, including the capital city, had agreed with the natives of these parts to rebel and join in such an act of treachery as had it succeeded would have been worse than the former one: in such wise that the coming of Tapia and his lack of experience of the land and its people caused considerable disorder, and his longer stay would have done much harm had God not remedied it. He had done better service to your Majesty by remaining in Hayti and first consulting your Majesty and acquainting him with the condition of these parts, which he must have known from the ships which I had sent to that island asking for help, and he obviously knew that we had by now settled the disturbance which was thought likely to follow and did indeed follow the arrival of Pánfilo de Narváez's fleet, which, it should be noticed, was fitted out for the most part by the Governors and Royal Council of your Majesty in the Indies; more especially should he have delayed his coming since the Admiral, judges and officials of your Majesty in Hayti had urged him many times not to visit this land before informing your Majesty very fully of all that had occurred here, in default of which they laid certain penalties upon his coming. He, however, regarding rather his own interest than the true interests of your Majesty, succeeded in winning them over to withdraw their resistance to his visit. I am only now making an account of the whole matter to your Majesty; the procurators and myself abstained from doing so when Tapia left because we considered that he would not have been a faithful bearer of our letters: but I trust that now your Majesty may see and believe that by our refusing to receive Tapia your Majesty was truly served, as can and shall be proved at greater length whenever and at any time it may be necessary.

I have already mentioned that the captain sent to conquer the province of Guaxaca had pacified it and was awaiting my instructions. This officer, being the chief justice and deputy Governor in Segura de la Frontera, was now wanted, and I accordingly sent

Pedro de Albarado south with fresh troops to join the
men who were there (some ten horse and eighty foot)
and conquer both the province of Tatutepec some
thirty leagues further to the South close to the sea,
whose inhabitants had done much damage in fighting
against those who had become vassals of your Majesty,
and that of Tecoantepec who had permitted us to
pass through their land to the southern sea. Albarado
left this city accordingly on the last day of January
of this year having under him (including those who
would join him in Guaxaca) forty horse and some two
hundred foot, among whom were forty musketeers
and bowmen and two small field guns. Three weeks
later I heard from him that he was now on the road
toward Tatutepec and had captured certain enemy
spies, from whom he learnt that the ruler of the
province was drawn up with his men in the field; he
himself was resolved to do his utmost to pacify the
land and was consequently taking along with him in
addition to the Spaniards a large number of native
warriors. I was very anxious to hear further of the
business, but his next letter did not arrive until
March 4th. He informed me that on his entering
the province three or four towns had attempted to
resist him but had not persevered in it. They had
continued to advance and had entered the town of
Tatutepec where they were apparently well received.
The ruler had bidden them lodge in certain large
thatched dwellings, but since the ground was somewhat too rough for the horses they had preferred to
pass the night in a lower and flatter part of the city:
he was not long in finding out, moreover, that the
inhabitants were planning to kill him and all his men
in this way, to wit, in the middle of the night when all
the Spaniards were asleep in the houses, which were
very large, they were to be set fire to and completely
burned. God discovered to him this business, and he

had consequently dissimulated with the chief and persuaded him with his son to visit the lower parts of the city, where they were detained and kept as prisoners, on which they had given him gold to the value of twenty-five thousand *castellanos*. He believed according to what the common people said that this lord possessed great treasures. The whole province was now thoroughly pacified; merchandising and commerce went on as before. The land was very rich in gold mines, a sample of such gold having been shown to him which he now sent me. Three days before, he had penetrated to the sea and taken possession of it in the name of your Majesty; there he had seen some pearls such as they are wont to find there which he likewise sent me. Both these I am herewith sending on to your Majesty.

Our Lord God was advancing this business and fulfilling the desire which I have to serve your Majesty in so notable an undertaking as this of the southern sea. I have therefore been at great pains to set men to work, in one of the three places where we have reached the sea, to making two caravels of moderate size and some brigs: the first for the purpose of further discovery and the second for surveying the coast. To this end I have sent some forty Spaniards under a capable man, including in their number master carpenters, shipwrights, sawyers, blacksmiths and seamen: from Vera Cruz I have obtained nails, sails and other necessary gear, and all possible haste is being used to finish and launch them; which done, your Majesty may be assured that it will be the greatest happening and one from which the most profit will redound to your Majesty since the Indies themselves were first discovered.

When we were in the city of Tezcuco before advancing to lay siege to the capital, preparing and furnishing ourselves with whatever was necessary, and little thinking what certain persons were plotting, one of those who were in the plot came to me and informed me that certain friends of Diego Velázquez in my company were treacherously planning to kill me, and had already elected a captain, a chief justice, *alguacil* and other officials among themselves. He begged me to intervene for he now saw plainly that in any case, apart from the disturbance which would follow my death, it was plain that if we turned against one another not a single one of us would escape with his life, for we should find not only the enemy forewarned but even those whom we held as friends would do everything in their power to dispatch us all. When I saw that by the mouth of this man so great a treachery had been revealed to me I gave thanks to God, for in my knowledge of the plot lay the remedy. I immediately arrested one who was the principal man concerned, and he confessed voluntarily that he had plotted with many persons whom he named in his confession, to take or kill me, and assume the government of the land on behalf of Diego Velázquez; it was true that the new captain and chief justice had been elected and that he himself as *alguacil* had the job of capturing or killing me. There were many people concerned in this whose names were set down in a list which was later found torn up into small pieces in his lodgings. This plot had not only developed in Tezcuco but had been discussed and arranged in the midst of the fighting which took place in the province of Tepeaca. Having made this confession and certified his own part in the plot, the man, whose name was Antonio de Villafaña, a native of Zamora, was condemned by a justice and myself to death, and the sentence was duly executed on his body. And despite the fact that in this crime I discovered others very guilty, I dissembled with them and continued to treat them in a friendly manner, for since the matter pertained most directly to me, although touching your Majesty very closely, I was unwilling to proceed against them with extreme rigour. My forbearance has not borne much fruit, however, for since that time several of Diego Velázquez's partisans have laid many a snare for me, secretly stirring up numerous alarms and scandals against which I have had to be on my guard even more than against the enemy. Yet our Lord God has ever guided the matter in such wise that without punishing them I have been at all times able to maintain entire peace and tranquillity; and should any other such plot arise in the future it must be dealt with according to the law.

I informed your Majesty in my previous letter that close to the provinces of Tlascala and Guajucingo there is a circular very lofty peak from whose summit a continuous stream of smoke rises as straight as an arrow into the air. The Indians gave us to understand that it was a very evil place and that they would die if they ascended there. I accordingly dispatched certain Spaniards to climb the mountain and examine its upper slopes. At the time of their ascent the smoke was being ejected with such a rumble that they neither dared nor could arrive at the mouth of the crater; and later I sent other Spaniards who twice climbed right up to the mouth of the crater from which the smoke emerges; they found it measured some two bowshots across and some three-quarters of a league in circumference: it was so deep that they could not see the bottom of it: they found, however, a certain amount of sulphur lying nearby, which is expelled by the force of the smoke. On one occasion while they were there they heard a great rumbling noise and made haste to descend, but before they were half way down an infinite number of stones began to rain down on them which put them in no slight danger. The

Indians considered it a great enterprise to have dared to go where the Spaniards did.

I have likewise informed your Majesty that the natives of these parts are of much greater intelligence than those of the Islands; they seem to us indeed to possess sufficient intelligence to conduct themselves as average reasonable beings. On this account it seemed to me a very serious matter to compel them to serve the Spaniards in the same way as the natives in the Islands; yet without this service the conquerors and settlers of these parts would not be able to maintain themselves. In order, therefore, not to enslave the Indians at that time, and yet to assist the Spaniards to settle, it seemed to me that your Majesty might order a certain portion of the royal revenues accruing to your Majesty from these parts to be appropriated to the expenses and maintenance of the colonists, as I explained very fully to your Majesty. Since then, however, bearing in mind the many and continued expenses of your Majesty, and the fact that we should seek in every way to increase your Majesty's revenues rather than diminish them, and seeing, moreover, the long time that we have spent in fighting against the natives and the hardships and loss which we have been put to on that account, together with the delay which your Majesty might for that reason command; above all, on account of the many importunities of your Majesty's officials and all my men, which there was no means of resisting, I found myself practically forced to hand over the rulers and natives of these parts to the Spaniards, taking into consideration when doing so their estate and the services which they have rendered your Majesty in these parts, so that until your Majesty shall make some fresh arrangement or confirm this one, the aforesaid rulers and natives will serve and provide the Spaniards, to whom they were respectively allotted, with whatever they may need to sustain themselves. All this was done with the approval of persons who have great knowledge and experience of the country. No better course could have been taken, nor one which contributes more both to the proper maintenance of the Spaniards, and the conservation and good treatment of the Indians; of all this the procurators now proceeding to your Majesty from New Spain will give your Majesty a long and complete account. Your Majesty's farms and granaries have been placed in the best and most convenient cities and provinces. I beseech your Majesty to approve this and order in what way the royal interests may best be served.

Most Catholic Lord: Our Lord God conserve the life, the very royal person and powerful state of your cæsarian Majesty, and increase it with many kingdoms and dominions such as your royal heart desires. From the city of Cuyoacan, in this New Spain of the Ocean Sea, the 15th of May, in the year 1522: Your Majesty's most humble servant and vassal who kisses your Majesty's royal hands and feet.

HERNANDO CORTÉS.

THE FOURTH LETTER

Sent by Hernando Cortés, Governor and Captain-General of New Spain to the Emperor, Don Carlos.

Most Lofty Powerful and Excellent Prince, very Catholic and Invincible Emperor, My Lord and King:

At the time when the city of Tenochtitlan and surrounding country were recovered for your Majesty two other provinces became subject to the imperial crown, lying forty leagues to the north on the borders of the province of Pánuco, by name Tuxtepec and Metztitlan. Their country is strongly defended and they are well used to arms, as is shown by the past history of this tribe in conflict with their enemies, by whom they are almost entirely surrounded. As nothing now hindered your Majesty's cause they sent me messengers offering to become your Majesty's vassals, in which capacity I received them in your Majesty's royal name, and so they remained until the arrival of Cristóbal de Tapia. In the turmoil and distrust which he sowed among these people, however, they not only ceased to pay that obedience as of old but even assaulted neighbouring tribes who were vassals of your Majesty, burning many towns and killing many people. At that time of crisis I had few troops to spare for they were much divided, but considering that to make no move in this matter would be highly dangerous, since the neighbouring tribes might for very fear of further damage join with the rebels, I sent an officer with thirty horse and a hundred foot, including bowmen and musketeers, and a large number of our allies thither; they had several encounters

243

with the enemy in which a certain number of our Indian allies and also two Spaniards lost their lives. But it pleased God that they should ask for peace of their own accord, and I accordingly pardoned their chiefs who came to speak with me of it, in that they had come of their own free will without being taken in battle. Later, when I was in Pánuco, a rumour was spread in those parts that I had gone back to Spain, which caused no small commotion. Tuxtepec rebelled again, and the ruler of the province marched down with a large following and burnt more than twenty townships belonging to our allies, killing and capturing many of them.

Accordingly on my way back from Pánuco I turned aside to subdue them: and although on first entering the province several of our allies who remained too far in the rear were killed, and ten or a dozen horses died as the result of hardships endured in crossing the mountains, yet the whole province was finally conquered, and its ruler, his son, and a leading border chief, taken prisoner. The ruler and the chief were subsequently hanged, and all those who had taken part in the war enslaved, to the number of some two hundred persons. They were branded and sold in the public auction, the remainder, after the royal fifth had been set aside, being divided among those who had taken part in the fighting. The sum did not suffice, however, to pay for the thirty horses which had been lost, for the land being barren there was no other booty. The province has since been at peace, with the brother of the dead ruler now on the throne. Up to the present, however, it has been of neither service nor profit, the land being so barren, as I have said; nevertheless our allies are safe from being disturbed and for greater security I have even settled some natives of this province there.

At this time a small brig arrived at the harbour

and town of Espíritu Santo (which I have already mentioned) bound from Cuba and bearing one Juan Bono de Quejo, who had commanded one of the ships which Pánfilo de Narváez brought with him. According to the dispatches which he bore he came on behalf of Don Juan de Fonseca, Bishop of Burgos,[20] evidently thinking that Cristóbal de Tapia who had been sent by the Bishop to take over the governorship of this land was still here.

He sent him to Cuba to report to Diego Velásquez, which he did, and the latter provided him with a ship in which to sail hither. This Juan Bono carried with him as many as a hundred letters[21] all in the same strain, signed by the Bishop, which he was to give to such persons as seemed to him good, declaring to them that by receiving Tapia as Governor they would be doing great service to your Majesty and on that account he promised them very substantial favours to come; they should know that they had taken service in my company against the wishes of your Majesty, and many like passages sufficiently calculated to stir up strife. He sent me a separate letter in the same terms, telling me that if I would be obedient to the aforesaid Tapia he would procure very special favours for me from your Majesty, but that if I refused I might regard him as my mortal enemy. The arrival of this Juan Bono and the letters affected the men of my company so much that I can assure your Majesty that I was hard put to it to pacify them, telling them the reason of the Bishop writing such a letter, and bidding them disregard his threats, for the greatest service they could do your Majesty and that from which they might hope to reap most reward, was to prevent the Bishop or any of his creatures from interfering in these parts, since it was his intention to conceal the true extent and nature of them from your Majesty and request grants of land in reward, without

your Majesty knowing what he was thus bestowing.
In particular I was informed, though I feigned to be
ignorant of it at the time, that it had been suggested
by several, since the only reward of their services
were continual suspicions, that it would be well to
set up a local municipal government (a *comunidad*) as
was done recently in Castile, until such time as your
Majesty should be informed of the true state of affairs;
for the Bishop wielded such power in this matter that
he prevented their letters from reaching your Majesty
(having, as in very truth he had, the officials of the
Indies house in Seville under his thumb, in which place
messengers sent by the settlers were ill-treated, their
reports, letters and money taken away from them and
reinforcements of men, arms or provisions thus prevented from ever setting sail). On my acquainting
them of all this, however, which as I told them your
Majesty was ignorant of (for they could be very sure
their services when made known to your Majesty
would be amply repaid as befits good and loyal vassals
who have truly served their lord as these have done),
they were reassured, and according to the use which
your Majesty graciously bade me make of the royal
provisions, they have been and remain contented
and serve with a good will, to which the fruit of their
services may testify. And on that account they do
deserve that your Majesty should grant them certain
favours which for my part I humbly beg your Majesty
to do, since I shall be no less grateful for favours
vouchsafed to anyone of them than if they had been
vouchsafed to me in person, since without them I
could not have served your Majesty as I have done.
In particular I beg your Majesty very humbly to
write to them, acquainting them that your Majesty
recognizes the toils they have undergone in your
Majesty's service and offering certain rewards; for in
addition to discharging a debt your Majesty will

hearten them so that henceforth they will serve him with still greater will.

(Natives had come from the province of Pánuco in the north to request Cortés's help against their enemies. They admitted having killed two parties of white men, one commanded by a Lieutenant of Francisco de Garay, but excused themselves by saying that they had done it because they knew that these men were not of Cortés's company, and they had been ill-treated by them. They feared, however, that other white men would return. Cortés had no men to spare at the time, but promised to do what he could as soon as possible. A few days later the natives were back again urging that since Cortés was settling various parts of the country he should send Spaniards to settle in their land. Upon this, and knowing moreover that there was a good harbour on the Pánuco river, Cortés ordered one of his officers to set out north. Cortés then proceeds :)

At the very moment of his departure, however, I learned from the boat newly arrived from Cuba, that the Admiral Diego Colón, and the Governors, Diego Velázquez and Francisco de Garay, were planning to land at Pánuco as my enemies to do me all the harm that they could; and in order that their evil intent might not have effect and to prevent any such disturbance as followed the arrival of Narváez I determined to leave the best guard I could in this city of Tenochtitlan and go north in person, so that if all or any of them should land I should be the first one they would meet and thus be better able to avoid all damage. I left accordingly with 120 horse, 300 foot, and some artillery, and as many as 40,000 native warriors from this city and the neighbourhood. On coming to the confines of their land some good five and twenty leagues before the port, at a large town

known as Coscatlan, a great multitude came out
against me and we fought together. But since my
Indian allies were as numerous as our opponents and
the ground was flat and well suited for the horses,
the battle lasted not long; and while they killed a few
horses and a few Spaniards together with some number
of our allies, yet they were in worse case for a very
great number of them were routed and slain. I
remained in the town some two or three days both to
look to the wounded and to receive those natives of
Pánuco who had already visited me offering to become
vassals of your Majesty. They accompanied me from
that place to the port, from that time forward serving
us in every way they could. I was several days on
the road, but had no encounters with the natives. On
the contrary those through whose villages we passed
came out to ask pardon for their fault and offer themselves in your Majesty's royal service. On arriving
at the port and river of Pánuco I camped in a town
five leagues from the sea by the name of Chila which
was deserted and burnt, for it was there that they had
repulsed the captain and men sent by Francisco de
Garay. From there I sent messengers to the other
side of the river and through the various lakes which
were all fringed with large towns bidding them have
no fear for what had been done in the past, for I
intended to do them no hurt, knowing well that they
had risen against the white people on account of the
evil treatment they had received and were therefore
not to blame. In spite of this they steadily refused
to come to me and even maltreated my messengers,
killing one or two of them. Moreover, since the
water on the other side of the river was sweet we took
our supplies from there, and they concealing themselves leapt out and attacked our men who had gone
to fetch it. I remained thus for fifteen days thinking to bring them over to us by peaceful means, since

when they saw how well those who had surrendered were received by us, I thought they would come in likewise; but they had such confidence in the strength of the lakes on which their towns were built that they would not submit. Seeing that fair deeds were of no avail I began to seek another remedy, and adding a considerable number of canoes to those we had there already, I set about ferrying a certain number of horses and men one night across the river. When dawn came a considerable force of men and horses had reached the other side without being seen and I then crossed over myself, leaving strict guard in my camp. As soon as they perceived us a large number of the enemy attacked with such fury as I have not seen equalled in the open field during all the time that I have been in these parts. They killed two of our horses and wounded ten more so badly that they could not go on. That day, however, by the help of God they were routed and pursued nearly a league, suffering heavy casualties. With about thirty horses and a hundred foot I advanced steadily and slept that night in a town three leagues from the camp. The town was deserted and in the temples we found many articles belonging to the Spaniards of Francisco de Garay's party who had been killed. Next day I continued along the shore of the lake seeking for some neck of land that should enable us to get to the other side where townships and natives were to be seen, but the whole day passed without our coming to the end of the lake or any place where we could cross. At dusk we came in sight of a very fine town towards which we directed our steps, still marching along the shore of the lake. It was late when we approached and still there was no sign of the enemy. For greater safety I ordered ten horsemen to enter the town by the main road and I with ten more skirted round it towards the lake; the remaining ten acting as rearguard had not yet come up. As soon as we entered the town we discovered a vast quantity of people hiding in ambush behind the houses intending to take us unawares. They fought so furiously that they killed one horse, wounded almost all the rest, and many Spaniards. They displayed such tenacity that the fight went on for a long time, and although three or four times broken by our charges yet they re-formed for the attack. Drawing up in a circle they knelt with one knee on the ground and awaited us in this manner without a word or cry such as they are wont to utter: not once did we get amongst them without receiving a plentiful flight of arrows, so many indeed that had we not been well armed they had taken no small stock of us and I believe not one of us had escaped alive. It pleased God, however, that a few of the enemy who were close to the river flowing nearby (and which emptied itself into the lake which we had been skirting all day), should begin leaping into the water, upon which others began to fly to the same river, and in this way their ranks were broken, although once they had crossed the river they ceased to flee. We thus remained ourselves on the one side and they on the other until nightfall, for the river was so deep that we could not cross over to them; yet indeed we were not sorry to see them pass over. In this fashion we returned to the town, which would be about a sling's throw from the river, and there passed the night with the best guard we could; the horses that they had killed served us for supper, for we had no other food. On the morrow we took the road again, there now being no sound of our late opponents, and came upon three or four towns, deserted alike of people and provisions, save for certain stores of wine such as they are wont to make which was contained in a considerable number of earthen jars. We passed the whole of that day without falling in with any of the enemy and slept the night following in the open, for we came upon some maize fields where both men and horses broke their faſt. In this manner I marched on for two or three days, seeing no one, although coming across numerous towns. We were finally so much in need of provisions, for during this time there were not more than fifty pounds of bread between the lot of us, that we returned to camp, to find the men I had left there in very good fettle, having had no encounter with the enemy. Forthwith, concluding that all the natives were keeping to the other side of the river where I had been unable to pass, I conveyed men and horses rapidly across one night in canoes, and ordered musketeers and cross-bowmen to proceed up the lake by water while the others took their way by land. In this order they attacked a large town where the inhabitants were surprised and many killed. This success so terrified the natives, who perceived that although surrounded by water they had yet been caught unprepared, that they began at once to come in to us asking for peace. About four weeks later the inhabitants of the whole province had submitted and offered themselves as vassals to your Majeſty.

Now that the land was at peace I sent persons to visit every part of it and bring back news of its towns and people. This ascertained, I sought out the beſt position I could and founded a town there, to which I gave the name Santiſteban del Puerto. I appointed certain native townships in your Majeſty's name and provided for such of my men as were willing to settle there. *Alcaldes* and *regidores* were elected; I left my lieutenant governor in charge, and there remained with him some thirty horsemen and about a hundred foot. I left them also a ship and a small rowing boat, which had come from Vera Cruz with ſtores. At the same time one of my servants sent me from the same port a ship laden with meat, bread, wine, oil, vinegar and other provisions, which struck on a small island some five leagues from land and was lost entirely. Three of the crew managed to reach the island, and when later I could send a boat to them they were still alive, having fed on seals which they found in great quantities and a fruit which they said was not unlike our Spanish fig.

I can assure your Majesty that this expedition cost me personally over thirty thousand *pesos* of gold, as your Majesty may be pleased to see from an examination of the accounts: and those that went with me were forced to spend money on horses, stores, arms and harness, which were at the time worth their weight in gold or twice their weight in silver. Yet that your Majesty might be served in that venture not one of us but would have eagerly spent both that and more. For in addition to bringing the Indians under your Majesty's imperial yoke the expedition accomplished more. Not long afterwards a ship carrying many men and an abundance of provisions was forced to make for that coast, and had the land not been at peace not a single one would have escaped, but would have been killed like those of the former party, the skins of whose faces we found spread and dried like masks in the Indian temples and so preserved that many of them could be recognized. Again, when Francisco de Garay came to this land, as I shall describe to your Majesty, it happened that they touched land some thirty leagues this side of Pánuco river, and after losing several of their boats finally landed in great disorder; it was therefore fortunate that they found the natives at peace, for had they found them at war all the newcomers would have lost their lives: actually the Indians did them good service carrying them in litters until they had reached the town settled by the

Spaniards. The pacification of the land thus brought very real benefits.

(*An officer in command of about one hundred Spaniards, horse and foot, was now sent south to conquer the province of Impilcingo. This was accomplished with partial success, the ruggedness of the country preventing a complete subjection on the part of the Spaniards. He then proceeded to the town of Zacatula, and with additional reinforcements marched eastwards to the province of Colimán, a journey of some seventy leagues. After one stiff encounter the province as a whole submitted, together with various neighbouring tribes. A town, named Colimán, was founded, and news of the harbour sent back to Cortés. News was also sent of an island which, so they reported, was entirely inhabited by women.*)

At certain times men come over from the mainland with whom the women have intercourse; and those who become pregnant if they bear female children are kept, but if men children they are cast forth from their company. The Island, they say, is ten days' journey from this province and many have been and seen it. They report, moreover, that it is very rich in pearls and gold; of all of which I shall endeavour to learn the truth and give a full account of it to your Majesty.

(*Cortés was about to dispatch two expeditions commanded by Pedro de Albarado and Cristóbal de Olid to Guatemala and Honduras respectively when, at the very moment of departure, a messenger arrived from Santisteban del Puerto, a town recently settled on the Pánuco. Cortés then continues:*)

By this messenger the *alcalde* informed me that Francisco de Garay (the Lieutenant Governor of

253

Jamaica) had arrived in the Pánuco River with 120 horse, 400 foot and many guns, calling himself the governor of that land, as he ordered to be proclaimed by the native herald. He declared he would avenge the wrongs which they had suffered at my hands in the late fighting, and bade them join him in expelling those Spaniards whom I had left there and any others that I should send, in all of which he would help them, and other such-like matters of scandal. The natives had been not a little disturbed by these words. As further proof of my suspicion that he was plotting in concert with the Admiral and Diego de Velázquez, within a few days a ship arrived from Cuba bearing certain dependents and friends of Velázquez and a servant of the Bishop of Burgos who (they said) had already been made imperial overseer (*factor*) of Yucatán, and thus made up almost the entire company. On hearing this news, although at the time I was lying in bed with one arm useless by reason of a fall from a horse, I determined to go there in person in order to prevent disturbance, and immediately dispatched Pedro de Albarado to go on ahead with all the men who were to have accompanied him on his expedition. I myself would follow in two days' time. We were already on the road, I still on my bed, and had gone some ten leagues from this city to the place where we were to sleep, when close on midnight a messenger arrived from Vera Cruz bringing me letters from the ship newly come from Spain. Among them was a decree signed with your Majesty's royal name, ordering Francisco de Garay not to land on the Pánuco nor to attempt to interfere with any part which I had already settled, for your Majesty was well pleased that I should hold it in his royal name: for which decree I most humbly and gratefully thank your Majesty. On receiving it I halted immediately. This was not a little advantageous to my health for I had not slept for two months, and was utterly worn out, so that had I gone on at that time I had been near to losing my life. But all such considerations I put aside, holding it better to die on that venture than by preserving my life give cause to such scandalous disturbances and murders as were then notorious. I further dispatched Diego de Ocampo, *alcalde mayor*, with the royal decree, to overtake Albarado, and gave him a letter bidding Albarado on no account to advance too near Garay's men for fear of disturbances. I ordered the *alcalde mayor* himself to inform Garay of the terms of the decree and to bring me back his reply without delay. De Ocampo accordingly went on as fast as he could and arrived in the province of the Huastecos where he learned that Albarado had been there before him. He was further informed that Albarado had had news of a certain captain of Garay's named Gonzalo Dovalle who was riding through the towns of that province with twenty-two other horsemen pillaging and stirring up the natives: he even went so far as to place outposts on the road which Albarado would have to take. At this (it was reported) Albarado was very wrath, thinking that Dovalle wished to do him harm, and immediately gathering all his men together marched on the town of Las Lajas where he found Dovalle encamped with all his men. On coming up he succeeded in getting speech with Dovalle and told him that he had learnt of his behaviour, at which, he said, he wondered greatly; for it was not the intention of the Governor or his officers (nor had it ever been) to attack them or do them any harm: on the contrary, he had ordered that they should be well received and provided with everything they lacked; and since the matter stood thus, he begged him, until such time as they could be certain that there would be no scandal or disturbance between the two parties, that he would consent to his men laying down their arms until the affair should be settled. Dovalle disclaimed all guilt saying that the facts were not as he had been informed, but that he was willing to do what he asked. The two parties accordingly joined in eating and making merry together, both the captains and all their men, without any bitterness or rancour between them. Immediately the *alcalde mayor* heard of this he ordered one of my secretaries who was with him, Francisco de Orduña by name, to make his way to the two captains, with authority to restore both arms and horses to Dovalle's men, giving them to know that I desired to treat them well and help them in whatever they might lack, providing they ceased to stir up the country. He also sent a separate messenger to Albarado bidding him treat them with all civility and see that none of their belongings was touched nor themselves annoyed in any way: the which he did.

During this time, most powerful Lord, Garay's ships were lying at the mouth of the river Pánuco, as if ready to attack the inhabitants of Santisteban, a town I had founded some three leagues up the river, and where all the ships arriving at that port usually anchored. Accordingly Pedro de Vallejo, my lieutenant in the aforesaid town, in order to prevent the danger which he anticipated from a rising on the part of the crews, issued certain orders to their commanders requiring them to sail up to the port and there anchor in peace; by this means the land would receive neither disturbance nor hurt. And moreover if they possessed any licence from your Majesty to enter or settle the land, or of any other nature, he required them to produce it, promising that once produced, it should be faithfully carried out according to the exact terms of the licence. To this the commanders replied in vague words, whose effect was that they refused to obey anything that my lieutenant ordered them. On this the lieutenant issued a second edict of the same nature attaching certain penalties to its non-compliance; to this they made the same reply. Matters remained in this condition for over two months until the commanders of the ships perceived that their long stay in the mouth of the river was causing disturbances not only among the Spanish residents of the town, but also among the natives of the province; upon this two of their number, a certain Castromocho and Martin de San Juan, sent messengers secretly to the lieutenant, declaring that they were desirous of peace and were ready to obey the law of the land: they begged him to come aboard their ships when they would receive him and carry out all his orders, adding that they had prepared the way for the other ships likewise to surrender peaceably and carry out his commands. The lieutenant accordingly decided to visit the ships accompanied by no more than five followers and was received well by the aforesaid captains. Further he sent to the commanding officer, Juan de Grijalba, who was at that time on board the flag ship, requesting him to fulfil the orders and requirements which he had already communicated to him. The commander not only refused to obey but commanded the other ships to join him and when they had all come up gave orders to their various captains to fire on the two ships which had surrendered and send them to the bottom. As soon as this order was made public to all present, the lieutenant in his own defence ordered guns on board the two ships to be got ready. Meanwhile the commanders of the other ships showed themselves unwilling to carry out Grijalba's order, and Grijalba himself sent a notary, Vincente Lopez by name, to speak with the lieutenant. He gave his message, and the lieutenant replied justifying his orders and declaring plainly that his intervention was solely in the cause of peace and to avoid such scandals as were inevitable if the ships

refused to come up-stream to the usual landing-place
and remained in their present suspicious place like
pirates ready to make a sudden landing on your
Majesty's domains: all of which gave a very bad
impression. He brought forward other arguments
with such effect that the notary carried back his reply
to Grijalba and succeeded in persuading the commander
to obey, since the lieutenant was plainly acting as
your Majesty's justiciary in that province, and Grijalba
was well aware that up till then neither he nor Francisco de Garay had presented any royal licences such
as the lieutenant and inhabitants of Santisteban would
be bound to observe, and that his lying there with his
ships like so many pirates off your Majesty's coast
was an ugly business. Moved by these considerations
Grijalba and the other captains offered to obey the
lieutenant and came up-stream to the usual landing-
place. As soon as they had come into harbour, for
the disobedience shown to the lieutenant's orders, Juan
de Grijalba was ordered to be arrested. But on news
of this reaching Diego de Ocampo, my *alcalde mayor*,
he immediately gave orders that Grijalba was to be set
free on the morrow and treated with all respect, as
were all his companions, none of their property to be
interfered with: the which accordingly was done.

De Ocampo likewise wrote to Francisco de Garay,
who lay in another port some ten to twelve leagues
away, informing him that I could not come to him in
person, but that I sent him with my full authority to
decide as to what was to be done, examine mutually
each other's royal licences and determine in what
way your Majesty could best be served. As soon as
Garay received this letter he marched to where the
alcalde was, and was very cordially received, both he
and his men being supplied with everything they
needed. There, after conversation and examination
of the royal warrant which your Majesty graciously

sent me, Garay at the instance of the *alcalde* acknowledged it, and declared himself ready to fulfil it, to
which end he was desirous of re-embarking with his
men and departing to settle in another part of the
land outside that disposed of by your Majesty's
warrant. I was eager to serve him and ordered the
alcalde to assist him in rallying his men, for many
who had accompanied him wished to remain in these
parts, and others had deserted; likewise the *alcalde* was
to provide him with stores which he lacked both for
his ships and crew. De Ocampo forthwith set to work
to provide all that he asked, and it was immediately
published in the town of Santisteban where the majority
of my men and Garay's now were, that all who had
come in Garay's fleet should join him, under pain of
losing his arms and horses if he were a gentleman,
and of a hundred lashes if a foot soldier in the ranks:
in either case the offender was to be handed over to
Garay as a prisoner.

Some of these men had sold their arms and horses
both in the town and port of Santisteban and in
various parts of the district, and Garay requested that
they might be restored, since without them they would
be useless. The *alcalde* made extensive enquiries to
find out where such arms and horses might be, and
ordered all which had been bought in this way to be
restored to Garay. Likewise, the *alcalde* had guards
placed on all the roads to arrest any who attempted
to flee and bring them in as prisoners: many were
captured in this way. The same declaration was
made in the town part of Santisteban and both men
and horses were brought to Garay. All this was
carried out with much diligence. Garay went down
to the harbour to embark, the *alcalde* remaining some
six or seven days to see that all was carried out as I
had ordered: and as there was a shortage of provisions
he wrote to Garay asking him in what way he could

command him, for he himself was returning to the city of Mexico, which is where I resided. Garay thereupon made him the bearer of a message to me in which he said that he had not the requisite tackle to allow of his departure, the missing boats (six in number) had not yet been found, and the remainder were unfit. He was busy drawing up a report dealing with this matter and exposing why he was unable to leave the land. He likewise informed me that his men were at loggerheads with him saying that they were not obliged to follow him and appealing against the orders of my *alcalde mayor* on sixteen or seventeen points. One such reason was that several persons in his company had died of hunger: others were more insolent and directed against him personally. It was pointed out at the same time that all attempts to prevent men leaving him were futile, for if they were there at night they were gone by morning, in such wise that those brought in to him captured one day were set at liberty on the morrow, and he would thus lose as many as two hundred men in a single night. He therefore very earnestly begged the *alcalde* not to depart until he had arrived, for he wished to visit me at this city, and was like to die of weariness if left in idleness in his ships. Two days later he came up with the *alcalde* who had waited for him, and a messenger was dispatched to me saying that Garay was making his way towards Mexico and was then approaching Cicoaque (a town on the borders of these provinces) by short stages, where he would await my reply. Garay also wrote to me telling me of his misfortunes and expressing the hope that I should be able to fit him out with rigging and men for he was well aware that none other could help him: he had accordingly made up his mind to come and see me, and offered me his eldest son with all that he possessed in marriage to my infant daughter. Meanwhile the *alcalde mayor* discovered that several highly suspicious persons had accompanied Garay's fleet, had shown themselves very hostile to my plans, and plainly intended to do no good in the province but rather to cause disturbances; accordingly he ordered them to leave the land in accordance with the royal warrant sent me by your Majesty. The said persons included Alonso de Mendoza, Antonio de la Cerda, Juan de Avila, Lorenzo de Ulloa, Taborda, Juan de Grijalba, Juan de Medina and others. This done, the *alcalde's* party came to the town of Cicoaque where my reply to the letters they had sent me reached them. I wrote that I was delighted at Garay's arrival, and on his coming to this city I would very readily agree to all his proposals, and that his expeditions should be well fitted out as he desired. At the same time I provided that he should be well looked after on the road, ordering all chiefs of townships to give him freely whatever he lacked. On his finally arriving at this city I received him with all the good will and good works that were fitting or that I could do him, indeed as I would have received my own brother; and since in truth I was greatly grieved at the loss of his ships I frankly offered to do everything in the matter that I could. Garay was very eager that the marriage which he had suggested in his letter should be carried out and begged me repeatedly to conclude it. I, to do him pleasure, agreed to his request which he put forward so insistently, upon which with great ceremony and oaths on both sides certain agreements were signed concluding the marriage, and stating the obligations of either party (in which above all else the interests of your Majesty were consulted); in such wise that in addition to our ancient friendship this contract and agreement now existed between us, together with the obligation which we incurred on both of our children, and we were now of such one mind and wish that there was nothing in our mutual agreement which was not to the advantage of either and especially to that of Garay.

I have already described, most powerful Lord, the great efforts of my *alcalde mayor* to rally Garay's men, but great as they were they had not sufficed to remove the discontent of the men with their commanders: for hearing the terms of the proclamation and thinking that they would be forced to go with him, they penetrated inland into various parts in small bands of three or half a dozen, and thus hiding themselves so that they could not be taken and brought back they were the principal cause of the Indians rising in that province; not only because they saw the Spaniards thus scattered all over the land but on account of the many perils which they caused with the natives, carrying off their women and food by force, with other like disturbances, which resulted in the whole district rising in rebellion. For the Indians believed that there was dissension among the Spaniards (as Garay had proclaimed by the native interpreter), and accordingly with great cunning, first finding out where and in what strength the Spaniards were, they attacked them by day and night in all the townships amongst which they were scattered; and thus coming upon them unprepared and unarmed they killed many, until their daring reached such a pitch that they approached the town of Santisteban, which was founded in your Majesty's name, and attacked it so fiercely that they reduced its inhabitants to great distress, so that they thought they were dead men and would have been so had they not been prepared and united, and thus able to resist their enemies, sallying out and fighting with them in the open until they forced them to retreat.

I came to hear of what had happened by a messenger who fled on foot from one such defeat; he told me that the whole province of Pánuco was in revolt, and many of Garay's men killed together with certain inhabitants of the settlement there. At the news of such disaster I thought that not one of the Spaniards now remained alive, at which God knows what was my grief; for I perceived that no novel event takes place in these parts without causing much hurt and all but the loss of the whole province. Garay was so much affected by this news, both because he felt himself to be the cause of it as because his son had been left behind in Pánuco, that he fell sick of his great grief and of this sickness passed away in three days.

And that your Majesty may be better informed of all that occurred after the first news which reached me, your Majesty must know that the Spanish messenger gave no further account of the rising of the natives in Pánuco other than that he with three horsemen and one on foot had been set upon in the village of Tanjuco by the natives, who had killed two of the riders and him on foot and the horse of the third rider; two of them had then succeeded in escaping under cover of night; moreover, they saw later the building where the lieutenant with fifteen horse and forty foot was to have awaited them, burning, and as it seemed to them, all must doubtless have lost their lives. I waited six or seven days to see whether any further news would come in, and during that time a message arrived from the said lieutenant informing me that he had been waiting in the city of Tantoyuca with fifteen horse and forty foot to be joined by certain other troops who had crossed the river to pacify some Indian tribes still in rebellion. Just before dawn they were surrounded by large numbers of the enemy who set fire to the building in which they were in. They immediately rode off in great haste, yet being unprepared (for they had thought the natives to be as peaceably inclined as they had ever been) they were pursued and all of them killed save only he and two others on horseback who escaped. He himself, however, had lost his horse and was forced to mount behind his comrade; two leagues further on, moreover, they had fallen in with the *alcalde* of the town with certain soldiers who assisted them, although even with these reinforcements they did not hold out long, but straightway fled out of the province. Of those who had stayed in the town or of the rest of Francisco de Garay's men who were scattered in various parts they had had no news and believed that not one of them remained alive. For as I have already informed your Majesty, after all that Garay had told the natives on his first arrival, encouraging them to drive out all my men from the province and the like, they were of a mind never to serve a Spaniard again. They had indeed murdered several whom they met with on the roads; it was thought therefore that they had planned this rising in concert, and that just as they had attacked the lieutenant and his men, so they must have fallen upon the inhabitants of the town and all other Spaniards in the various villages, all of whom were totally unprepared for any such outbreak, seeing how willingly they had served them up till then. Being thus better informed of the rebellion in Pánuco I immediately dispatched fifty horse and a hundred crossbowmen and musketeers on foot, with four guns and much powder and shot, all under a Spanish officer, accompanied by two native chiefs of this city with fifteen hundred men each. I ordered the officer to make for the province with all possible haste and endeavour to enter it without delaying in any place save for the most urgent need, until he should arrive at Santisteban del Puerto, where he was to find out news of those who had remained in it, since they might be besieged in some place, and if so he was to assist them. The said officer proceeded north accordingly with all possible speed, entered the province and fought two battles with the natives in which God gave him the victory. He finally arrived at Santisteban where he found twenty-two horse and a hundred foot besieged there, who had already engaged the enemy six or seven times and with the help of a few guns which they had there had succeeded in defending themselves. They could not have defended themselves, however, much longer and were by that time in no small danger, in such wise that had the officer whom I sent arrived three days later not one of them would have remained alive, for they were all dying of hunger. They had already sent one of the brigs (brought thither by Garay) to Vera Cruz, in order thus to get news through to me, there being no other way open, and to bring back provisions to them, which indeed arrived after they had been succoured by the men I sent. They learnt there that another party some hundred strong of horse and foot, left by Garay in a town known as Tamuy, had all been killed, save only for one Jamaican Indian who had escaped through the woods and brought the news how they had been suddenly attacked by night. It was found that of Garay's men in all 210 had been killed, and of the inhabitants, all settlers, whom I had left in Santisteban, 43, being those who had scattered through the various villages; the numbers of Garay's men may have been even larger for not all their names were recorded. The men whom my officer took with him, together with those of the lieutenant and the *alcalde* and those found in Santisteban, now numbered in all some eighty horse; they divided into three bands and waged war on the natives to such effect that as many as 400 chieftains and headmen were captured (without counting common people). These they tried and burnt, after they had confessed to being the prime movers of the rebellion and to being each one of them either concerned with or actually responsible for the death of the Spaniards. This done, the other prisoners were released and the natives returned to the villages. An officer in the name of your Majesty appointed as new rulers in the various townships such persons as were entitled to succeed according to their customs. I now received letters from the officer and others reporting (for which our Lord be praised) that the whole province was again pacified and settled, the natives serving with a good grace, which I think they will continue to do throughout the years to come when the present rancour is past.

I can assure your Majesty that the natives of these parts are so warlike that any disturbing appearance or novelty moves them to rebel, for so it was their custom to rise against their former lord; and no occasion for such rebellion passes without their taking advantage of it.

I mentioned that at the time of Garay's arrival in the Pánuco I was on the point of sending an expedition by sea to the point of the Hibueras and the causes that led me thereto. This was interrupted by Garay's appearance. When the disturbance had finished, however, in spite of the fact that it involved me in no little expense for sailors' wages and provisions for the ships and men to sail in them, yet considering that such an enterprise was much to the profit of your Majesty I pursued my plans and bought additional ships, so that my fleet now contained in all five large ships and one brig, carrying 400 men with sufficient guns, shot and arms, and other provisions and victuals. In addition I sent by the hand of two of my servants eight thousand *pesos* of gold to Cuba to buy horses and stores, both to take with them on this first voyage and to have ready on their return to load up the ship, so that they might leave nothing for which I sent them undone on account of hunger; in particular I desired that they should not weary out the natives of the land through lack of provisions themselves, but should rather give of what they carried with them than take from the natives. In this order they left the port of Vera Cruz on the 11th of January 1524 bound for Habana (at the western extremity of Cuba), where they are to take on board anything they lack, especially horses, and gather the boats together, and whence with the blessing of God they are then to follow their route to the aforesaid land of Hibueras itself. Once arrived there, at the first harbour they are to land, taking all men, horses and provisions on shore, fortifying themselves with their guns (of which they have many and goodly ones) in the most suitable spot that may appear, and there found a town. They are then to send the three largest of their ships back to Cuba to the harbour of the town of Trinidad (that being most conveniently placed for them) and there one of my servants is to await them with a cargo of such things as may be necessary to them and requested as such by the captain. The smaller ships and the brig under the command of the chief pilot and a cousin of mine, by name Diego de Hurtado, are to coast southwards along the Bay of Ascension seeking for the strait which is said to exist there, and to leave nothing unexplored, after which they are to return to wherever the captain, Cristóbal de Olid, may be, and thus send me news by one of the ships of whatever they may have found, and of what Olid may have learnt of the land and aught that has happened in it, to the end that I may send a long and detailed account to your Majesty.

I also mentioned that I proposed sending Pedro de Albarado in command of a party of citizens to Ucathlan and Guatemala and the provinces of which I have had news lying beyond them. Accordingly in spite of the large expense I had been put to, in horses, arms, guns and munitions as well as in actual money, and considering that God and your Majesty are greatly to be served by such an expedition, since from the reports I have heard I am like to discover many rich and splendid lands inhabited by new and different races, I determined to carry out my original plan and set to fitting out Albarado's party, whom I dispatched from this city on the 6th of December 1523. He took with him 120 horsemen with spare mounts sufficient for 170, and 300 foot including 130 crossbowmen and musketeers; in addition he had four guns with good supply of powder and shot, and several chieftains both of this city and neighbouring cities with certain of their men (though not many, the way being long) accompanied him.

I have had news of them; on January 12th they had reached the province of Tecouantepec and were progressing well. May it please God to guide both them and the other party that He may be truly served, for I firmly believe that going as they are on His service and in the name of your royal Majesty they cannot fail to prosper.

I likewise commanded Albarado to take especial care to send me a long and detailed account of everything that happened to him that I might acquaint your Majesty with the same. And I am persuaded according to the reports and configuration of the land that Albarado and Olid are bound to meet and join forces, providing there be no strait between them.

Many roads would have been opened up in the land and many of its secrets already discovered had I not been hindered by the expeditions coming to these shores. And I can assure your Majesty that great disservice has been done him both in that lands have not been discovered and that great store of pearls and gold have thus been prevented from reaching the royal treasury: but from now onwards in the absence of further expeditions I shall endeavour to restore what has thus been lost. Nor shall I spare either my own person or my private fortune in this work, though I can assure your Majesty that in addition to spending all that fell to my lot I owe some 70,000 *pesos* of gold to your Majesty to pay my men, which I have taken from the royal revenue, to say nothing of a further 12,000 *pesos* which I have borrowed from private individuals to meet the expenses of my household.

(*On December 8th* 1523 *an officer was sent east to the town of Espíritu Santo to subjugate the natives of that province who had rebelled. A certain* Rodrigo Rangel, *alcalde of Tenochtitlan, was also sent to subdue two tribes, the Zapotecas and the Mixes, dwelling in the mountainous country surrounded by Tecouantepec, Chinanta, and Guasacualco, who were very warlike. Two expeditions were necessary before the natives were finally quelled; and as a punishment for their obstinacy they were enslaved and divided among the Spaniards of the party. Each of these expeditions, Cortés says, cost him at the least* 5,000 pesos *of gold, and those of Olid and Albarado something more than* 50,000, *not counting certain incidental expenses:* "But since it is in the service of your Majesty," *writes Cortés,* " I should count it yet a greater favour to spend my life itself; and should such opportunity arise I shall not hesitate to take it." *He then continues:*)

I have mentioned the four ships which I had building on the Southern Sea, and lest it should appear that I have been tardy in not completing them before now I will give your Majesty the cause of the delay. The Southern Sea, or at any rate that part of it where I am building the ships, is something over 200 leagues from the harbours in the north where all stores arriving in New Spain are landed, and the road between lies through very rocky mountain passes and across large and rapid rivers, in such wise that goods are carried only with the greatest difficulty across land from the north to the south. To top all, when I had gathered in a warehouse on the harbour where the ships were being built all the stores and implements needed,— sails, ropes, rigging, decks, anchors, pitch, tallow, oakum, bitumen, oil, and the like,—a fire broke out one night and burnt everything, the anchors alone being saved since they could not burn. I have now begun to collect stores again, it being four months since the ship arrived from Castile bringing everything necessary for the ships, for fearing what did actually occur I had provided for it and sent to Spain in readiness. I can assure your Majesty that even before the ships enter the water they will have cost me over 8,000 *pesos* of gold, exclusive of certain special expenses: but they are now, God be praised, in such way that by Whitsun or Saint John's day in June, they will be ready to be launched, provided bitumen be not lacking: for as all the previous store was burnt I have been unable until now to obtain more, but I am hoping to obtain some from this country, and have made provision that it shall be sent me. I am reckoning on these ships more than I can say, for by them I am strongly persuaded that if it please God your Majesty will be made ruler of more kingdoms and dominions than all those of which our nation yet has knowledge. May it please Him to direct us that He may be served and your Majesty so prosper, when I think there will be nothing wanting to make your Majesty the monarch of all the world.

After it had pleased God that we should capture the great city of Tenochtitlan it seemed to me unwise for the time being to reside in it on account of many inconveniences, and I took up my residence with all my company at Cuyoacan, a town lying on the shore of the lake which I have already mentioned. I was always desirous, however, that the city should be rebuilt considering its great and marvellous site, and endeavoured to recall all its inhabitants who had fled to various parts when the fighting was over. I have long kept its governor, Guatimucin, a prisoner, but now entrusted the work of repopulating it to a young native captain whom I had known while Muteczuma was still alive. And that he might have more authority I gave him the same position which he had held under the native ruler, that is to say *ciguacoat*,—a kind of lieutenant governor. Other natives whom I had known I likewise entrusted with offices such as they were used to have. To this *ciguacoat* and the rest I gave lordships with lands and followers on which to live, although not so large as they had held before nor such as would enable them to rebel at any time. I have since taken every opportunity of showing them respect and favour, and they have worked to such good purpose that there are now more than 30,000 inhabitants within the city, and the same good order is observed in the market-places and in their tran-sactions as in former days. I have granted them such liberties and exemptions that many flock into the city daily and they live in great freedom, those versed in the mercantile arts, for instance, working as day labourers for the Spaniards: these comprise car-penters, masons, stone-cutters, silversmiths, and like craftsmen. The merchants open their stalls in safety and sell freely: the rest live either by fishing,—a flourishing trade in this city,—or by agriculture, many of them having their own plots, in which they grow all those of our native plants of which we have been able to obtain seedlings.

And I can assure your Majesty that if plants and seeds from Spain were to be had here, as I requested in my last letter that your Majesty might be pleased to order to be dispatched, the natives of these parts show such industry in tilling land and planting trees that in very short time there would be great abundance, from which I think no little profit would redound to your Majesty's imperial crown, for by this means the fruitfulness of these parts would be secured, and your Majesty would draw from them greater revenue and dominions than in all those regions which in the name of our Lord your Majesty now possesses; for which reason your Majesty can be very certain that he will not find me lacking in such a scheme but rather that I will do everything in my power to forward it.

After the capital was taken I put in hand the building of a fortress in the water where the brigs could be safely anchored and yet from it attack the whole city if need arose, in such wise that I should command all the entrances and exits of the city; and this was done. I have seen other fortresses and arsenals but not one to equal it; others of a wider experience report the same. The manner of its building is this: on the side exposed to the lagoon there are two very strong towers with embrasures where necessary. Each of the towers juts out beyond the side-wall, which it can thus cover with its guns. Between these two towers the main building extends backwards from the lagoon; it is triple-aisled, and has a gate by which the brigs can pass in and out. The whole of this building is likewise heavily embrasured, and has at its further end toward the city another large tower together with various quarters for the men, also provided with defensive and offensive fortifications. I am sending your Majesty a drawing of it and will therefore give no further details, save to say that so long as we hold it, and guard it with the same number of ships and guns as we now have there, the decision as to peace or war lies in our hands. Once this building was completed, I considered that it was safe to proceed with my plan, which was to repeople the city, and therefore took up my quarters with all of my company within it. The various plots of land were divided out among the inhabitants and to each one of the " Conquerors " I gave in your Majesty's name a plot for which he had laboured in addition to that which he was entitled to receive as a settler and an inhabitant, and those who have settled have worked so rapidly to build themselves houses that many of them are already completed and others are well on their way. Moreover there is such plenty of stone, lime, wood and bricks made by the natives, and they are building such large and comely houses that your Majesty may be certain that within five years' time it will be the noblest and most populous city in the world and the best built. The district in which we Spaniards have settled is apart from that of the natives, being separated by a waterway which is spanned nevertheless by numerous wooden bridges, thus allowing commerce from the one side to the other. The natives have two great market-places one in their own quarter and one in the Spanish quarter. In these are to be found all such manner of produce as is grown throughout the land, for there is nothing which is not brought there for sale; and the variety of merchandise is not less than in the former days of prosperity. It is true that there are now no ornaments of gold or silver, nor featherwork, nor other treasures as there were wont to be; a few small pieces of gold and silverwork appear, but not in the quantity as before.

Owing to the differences which Diego Velázquez has had with me, and the ill-will which Don Juan de Fonseca, Bishop of Burgos, has ever borne toward me, being roused up in that by the said Velázquez, I have not been provided with the guns and arms which I badly needed, although constantly sending money for them. For by the Bishop's intention and orders the officials of the imperial provision house in the city of Seville were set against me and in particular one Juan López de Recalde, the *contador*, upon whom during the Bishop's term of office there everything depended. Yet since necessity was ever the prime sharpener of men's wits and I now found myself in such sore straits without hope of remedy (for the officials I knew would keep such information from your Majesty's ear) I set myself to finding a means by which that which had caused us such toil and peril to win should not be lost to your Majesty, which disaster would indeed not only cause great disservice to God but great danger to all such of us as remain here. I therefore hastened to dispatch messengers through all the neighbouring provinces in search of copper which we bartered with the natives for a high price that we might obtain it the more readily. Much was thus brought in, and I set a master gunsmith who luckily was to be found here to the work of casting cannon. In this way I had two moderately large culverins made, with such success that for their size they could not have been beaten. I had now copper, but tin was still lacking, without which guns could not be made; it had been difficult to find enough for these two and I had had to pay heavily to people who had dishes and other plate made of it, but more could not be had either cheap or dearly. I began to enquire therefore in all parts whether there was anywhere any to be had, and by the grace of God, who has ever been swift to supply us with what we lack, I discovered certain small pieces of it being used as coins among the natives of a province of Tazco. Proceeding further in my search I found that in both this province and in others it was commonly used as money. Finally I learnt that it was mined in the province of Tazco some seven-and-twenty leagues from this city; upon which, having discovered the situation of the mines, I sent Spaniards with mining tools and they brought me back samples of it. I have since given orders for all the necessary tin to be mined there and this has been done although with no small labour. Those who went to seek for tin, however, came upon a vein of iron which according to experts is of exceeding richness.

Since finding this tin I have continued to cast guns at regular intervals, and five in all have been finished up to the present, consisting of two medium-sized culverins, two slightly smaller and a small cannon; I have also two other small cannon which I brought with me to these parts and another medium-sized culverin which I bought from the effects of the governor Juan Ponce de León. From the ships which have come to these shores I have in all thirty-five pieces of cannon in bronze of all sizes from falconets upwards, and in iron as many as seventy pieces, including lombards, small bore culverins and the like. Thus, God be praised, we can now defend ourselves. God provided us no less with powder, for we found such good store of saltpetre and of so excellent a quality, that we could provide for other needs had we but suitable vessels in which to heat it, although we certainly consume a large quantity in our various expeditions. As for sulphur, I have already described to your Majesty the mountain in this province from which rises a great column of smoke. A Spaniard was let down into the crater some seventy or eighty furlongs on the end of a rope, and succeeded in gathering sufficient for our needs up to the present: in the future this method of procuring it will be unnecessary: it is certainly dangerous and I am continually writing to Spain to provide us; your Majesty has been pleased to see that no Bishop can now prevent its reaching us.

(Before moving his quarters to the capital Cortés had visited Vera Cruz and Medellín to inspect them and arrange certain matters. It now became plain that the situation of the old Rica Villa de Vera Cruz was no longer very convenient, and a new site was chosen some two leagues east. The inhabitants of the township of Medellín twenty leagues inland were moved to this new town and port, and the work of clearing trees and building houses was immediately set in hand. Boats would be able to sail right up to the quays and the town would thus form a general warehouse of stores for the whole of New Spain.

Work on the road from the new town to the capital has begun and the journey will thus be shortened by a whole day.

Cortés has also decided on certain plans for the future. He intends sending an expedition to explore the coast north of the Pánuco to Florida, and so on as far as the Bahamas itself, it being generally held, he says, that in this coast there must be some strait giving access to the Southern Sea. The advantages accruing from such a discovery are so great that although in debt and burdened with the cost of various other expeditions by sea and land, he has determined to dispatch three caravels and a couple of brigs on this adventure, notwithstanding that it will cost him over 10,000 pesos. "Even if no strait be discovered," *says Cortés,* "it is impossible but that many great and rich lands will be opened up by which your Majesty will be well served." *In July of* 1524 *he also hopes to dispatch three ships from the port where they have been a-building to look for a strait; if they do not find it they will at least follow the coast as far as the point which Magellan had already reached from the south. The question whether there be a strait either to the north or south will thus be definitely settled. Cortés then proceeds :)*

276

FOURTH LETTER

The officials sent by your Majesty to audit the royal accounts and revenue have arrived and have begun their work with those whom I had appointed in your Majesty's name to hold this office. They will give your Majesty an account of all the provisions that have been made in this respect: I will therefore waste no time in giving a particular report of it to your Majesty, and will simply refer to that which they are sending, which I think will be such as will make clear to your Majesty the care and watchfulness I have expended on everything attaching to your Majesty's service; and although the labour of carrying on wars and pacifying the land has been great, as is amply shown by the result, yet I have not on that account neglected any effort to preserve and gather in everything belonging to your Majesty upon which I have been able to lay my hands. It appears from the account which the officials are sending your Majesty, and which your Majesty will see, that in the pacification of these parts and the expansion of those dominions which your Majesty holds here, I have spent some 72,000 *pesos* of the royal revenue. It is well that your Majesty should know that I could do nothing else, for I only began to encroach on the royal revenue when I was left with nothing to spend of my own and indeed owing some 30,000 *pesos* to private persons: thus since there was no other course to take and what was necessary in your Majesty's service could not otherwise be undertaken I was obliged to spend the money. Nor do I think that the gains have been or will be small, for they will hardly be less than a thousand per cent. of the sum invested. But since your Majesty's officials when I stated that the sum was spent in your Majesty's service were yet unwilling to enter it in their accounts saying that they had neither commission nor power to do so, I beg your Majesty (if it appears well spent to him) to credit me with the amount and pay back to me in addition some 50,000 *pesos* which I have spent of my own substance or borrowed from my friends; for failing such repayments I should be unable to meet my creditors and should find myself in great embarrassment. This I think your Majesty will not permit, but rather in addition to this repayment will grant me many and signal favours; for besides that your Majesty is so catholic and christian a Prince, my services for their own part merit no less, and of these their fruit will bear sufficient testimony.

From the officials and others in their company I learn that what I dispatched to your Majesty by the hands of Antonio de Quiñones and Alonso de Avila, as representatives of New Spain, did not arrive in Castile, but was captured by the French by reason of the insufficient forces sent by the Indies House in Seville to accompany the treasure ships from the Azores [22]. I was much grieved at the loss, for the things were so rich and strange that I desired greatly that your Majesty should see them, and in addition they had made my services more manifest. Yet I was also well content that they should be thus lost, since it is but slight lack to your Majesty, and I shall endeavour to send others yet more rich and strange, having heard news of provinces which I have but lately sent to conquer, and still others to which I shall send expeditions so soon as I have men to spare. Moreover the French and other princes to whom these new discoveries were well known will now perceive why they should subject themselves to your Majesty's imperial crown, for over and above the many and great kingdoms and lordships which your Majesty possesses in these distant parts, they will see that I, the least of your Majesty's vassals, am yet able to render such great and signal services. And as the first fruits of my offering I am now sending by Diego de Soto, my servant, a

few things which were then put aside as unworthy
to accompany the others, and certain others which I
have since had made, and which, although as I say,
were put aside, have yet something to commend them.
I am sending in addition a silver culverin caſt from
$24\frac{1}{2}$ hundredweights of silver, which coſt me some
24,500 *pesos* of gold for the metal, and some further
3,000 *pesos* for engraving, carriage to the port, and
the like. Yet considering that it was so rich and
marvellous a piece of work and worthy to go before
so mighty and excellent a Prince I resolved to complete the work and spend the money. I beg your
Majeſty to receive this slight service and see in it
a token of my great desire to do him greater services
if fortune so aid me. For though in debt, as I said
to your Majeſty before, yet I was well content to
increase my indebtedness in my eagerness that your
Majeſty should know the desire that I have to serve
him; for my ill-luck has been such that up to this
present I have preferred so many plaints before your
Majeſty that they have obscured my desire to do your
Majeſty some service.

I am sending at the same time to your Majeſty
70,000 *pesos* of gold as part of the royal revenue, as
your Majeſty will see from the accounts which both
I and the royal officials are sending. Moreover, we
have ventured to send such a large sum entire both
on account of the need which we are informed your
Majeſty muſt have of it to carry on his wars and other
matters, and that your Majeſty may not grieve over
the loss of the former packet. In future every opportunity will be taken of sending home as much gold
as is possible. For your Majeſty may reſt assured
that as things are tending at present and the kingdoms
and dominions of your Majeſty continue to grow, he
will draw revenues from them more safely and at less
expense than in all his other lands, provided that no

further disturbances hinder us as they have hindered us in the past. I mention this because but two days since, Gonzalo de Salazar, your Majesty's *factor*, arriving at the port of San Juan in New Spain, informed me that he was told in Cuba that Diego Velázquez, Admiral's deputy, had come to an agreement with Cristóbal de Olid, whom I sent to settle the Hibueras in your Majesty's name, that he should seize the land on behalf of Diego Velázquez. And although of a truth the matter is so ugly and of such disservice to your Majesty that I could hardly believe it, yet knowing the wiles that Diego Velázquez has ever used to injure me and prevent me from doing your Majesty some service I am led to think it true. For in default of all else, Velázquez endeavours to stop men from coming over to us, and as he is in command of the Island he takes such as wish to do so and persecutes them, despoiling them of much of their gear, and finally bargains with them for their freedom, to gain which they do and say anything that he requires. I will inform myself of the truth of the matter and if I find it to be thus I propose to send a force over to Cuba, arrest Diego Velázquez and send him as a prisoner to your Majesty; for once the root of all evils has been cut, and truly this man is such, all the other branches will wither, and I shall be enabled without hindrance to carry out enterprises both already begun and those which I hope to undertake in your Majesty's service.

In no letter that I have written to your Majesty have I failed to point out the opportunity that exists to convert certain of the natives in these parts to our holy Catholic Faith, and I have begged your Majesty to dispatch religious persons of saintly life and character for that purpose. However, few, if indeed any, have arrived up to this present, and since it is certain that they would reap a great harvest I am again bringing the matter to the notice of your Majesty begging him to dispatch priests as speedily as possible, by which our Lord God will be mightily served and the desire of your Majesty as a true Catholic will be fulfilled. In the letter which Antonio de Quiñones and Alonso de Avila carried to you as our representatives, the town councils of New Spain and I begged your Majesty to provide bishops and other dignitaries for the administration of the sacred offices of our religion, and so it seemed to us good at that time. But now considering the matter well, it occurs to me that your Majesty will do better to make different provision to the end that the natives of these parts may be more speedily converted and instructed in the mysteries of our holy Catholic Faith, to wit, that your Majesty should dispatch to these parts many religious persons, as I have said, eager for the conversion of these people, and that they should build houses and monasteries throughout the provinces such as seem to us most suitable, and should receive the tenths of the charge in order to make their homes and maintain themselves, any remaining sum to be expended on churches and their decoration in townships where Spaniards are settled and on the priests who minister to them. These tenths should be collected by your Majesty's officials who should render an account of them and share the sum out among the monasteries and churches, which indeed would suffice for all and more than all that could be done in this matter in your Majesty's service. I beg therefore that your Majesty may appeal to the Pope, to grant him the tenths for this purpose, giving him to understand the service which will be rendered to our Lord God by the conversion of these people, and that the object can be attained in no other way. For should we have bishops and prelates here they would not put off the custom (which for our sins they now have) of wasting the goods of the church in pompous ceremonial and like evils, and of gathering together estates to leave to their sons or kinsmen. Indeed the evil would be yet graver in that the natives of these parts used commonly to have priests learned in their rites and ceremonies who withdrew so much from the world both in honesty and chastity of life, that were one of them suspected of anything of this nature he was put to death. And should they now see those things which concern the church and the service of God in the hands of canons and other such dignitaries, and learn that they were ministers of God, seeing they indulge in those vices and profanities which at this day are common in Spain, they would despise our Faith and deem it but a jest. The danger of this would be so real that I doubt whether any subsequent missionary effort could succeed in converting them. Since, then, so much depends upon this, and the conversion of these people is and must ever be the principal intention of your Majesty, which we must follow in our dealings with those among whom we have settled, taking as Christians especial care of them, I venture to advise your Majesty on this point and give him my opinion, which I beg your Majesty may receive as from his loyal subject and vassal; for just as I labour and shall labour with all my bodily force to extend the dominions of your Majesty in these parts and publish his royal name and power among these peoples, so also I am eager to labour in spirit that your Majesty may command our holy Faith to be sown in these parts by which deed he may reap the reward of eternal life. Moreover since it will be difficult to send for bishops from other parts for such matters as the admission to religious orders, the consecration of churches, vessels, oils, and the like, it will be necessary for your Majesty to persuade the Pope to delegate his power to the two chiefs of the religious orders who shall settle in this country, the one of the order of Saint Francis the other of Saint Dominic, who together will enjoy (it is to be hoped) the largeſt powers that your Majeſty can grant. For these lands are so widely separated from the Roman church, and we Chriſtians who reside and will reside here so cut off from all external aid to conscience, yet like all men so apt to fall, that it is essential that the Pope should ſtretch a point in this matter and endow these officials with powers beyond the ordinary: such powers to reside in the persons aĉtually living in these parts, whether it be the general of the order for this region or in the provincial official of each one of these orders.

I have likewise heard, moſt Catholic Majeſty, from ships but lately come from the Islands that your Majeſty's judges and officials in Cuba have publicly proclaimed that neither from that Island nor from any other shall mares (or other creatures that can multiply) be shipped to New Spain under pain of death. This they have done that we may always be forced to buy their beaſts and cattle, for which they charge us excessive prices. These things ought not to be, for it is common knowledge what great disservice is done to your Majeſty in preventing the settling and pacification of this realm. They know our need of horses, and yet hinder us both in holding what we have won and in gaining more, in spite of the great assiſtance and treasure that the Islands have received from these lands of New Spain. And since they have little enough need of what they deny us, I beg your Majeſty to send his royal decree to the Islands proclaiming that all who wish to ship animals out of the country are at liberty to do so without let or hindrance; for without them we can do nothing here in the way of further conqueſt or even of holding what we have won, with which indeed I had been well content.

They took great delight in spreading their proclamations abroad: though had I issued another to the effect that nothing brought from the Islands should be allowed to be unloaded in this country save only what they denied us, they would soon be ready to bring us animals in order that we should receive other cargoes, for their only means of wealth consists in trade with this land. Indeed, before such trade was carried on there was not a man in the Islands who owned a thousand *pesos* of gold, and now they possess more than they ever did before. Yet to give no occasion of railing to those who desire to speak ill of me I have refrained from any such action before discovering the matter to your Majesty, that your Majesty may order it as is most proper for the royal service.

I have also informed your Majesty of the necessity of sending plants of every kind to this land and of the opportunities that exist for agriculture of the most varied sorts: and since till now nothing has been done in this matter I once more beg your Majesty, since it will be greatly to his profit, to give orders to the provisioning house at Seville that every ship bound for these lands shall carry a certain number of plants, without which it shall not be allowed to set sail, the which will be of great service in the settlement and prosperity of this land.

It behoves me to seek every means possible for the settling of these lands, that both Spaniards and natives may maintain themselves and multiply, and our holy Catholic Faith take root, with which task your Majesty graciously charged me, our Lord God being pleased to make me the instrument by which He should be made known, and I have therefore made and proclaimed certain decrees in your Majesty's imperial name, a copy of which I am sending to your Majesty.

I will therefore say nothing further of them, save only that so far as I have been able to ascertain up to the present it is highly expedient that the said decrees should be carried out. With some of them the Spaniards in these parts are not too well pleased, especially with those which recommend them to settle and ſtraightway take root on the land. For all or the greater number of them have notions of using towards these lands as they used towards the Islands before them, that is to say, impoverishing them, deſtroying them, and then abandoning them. And since it seems to me we should be greatly to blame did we not profit by the experience of the paſt to remedy the present and the future, providing againſt those causes through which it is common knowledge the Islands have been ruined (more especially considering the great extent and riches of these lands as I have many times declared to your Majeſty, in the which our Lord God can mightily be served and your Majeſty's revenues increased) I beg your Majeſty to consider these decrees, and inform me as to what line I should take, both in the keeping and carrying out of these decrees as of all those by which your Majeſty may be the better served. I shall ever be at pains to issue such other orders as may seem to me beſt, for the extent and diversity of the lands which are daily discovered and the secrets which thus become apparent are such that for each new matter new decisions and new orders are necessary; so that should I seem to contradiᨢt paſt orders in those which I now report or shall report to your Majeſty, your Majeſty may believe that a new problem has led me to a new decision.

Invincible Cæsar, our Lord God watch over the imperial person of your Cæsarian Majeſty, and keep and prosper him with the increase of yet greater kingdoms and dominions for many years, together with all else that can be desired for your royal Majesty. From the great city of Tenochtitlan in New Spain, the 15th day of October 1524. From your Majesty's most humble slave and vassal, who kisses your Majesty's royal feet and hands.

HERNANDO CORTÉS.

THE FIFTH LETTER

Sent to the Emperor from the City of Tenochtitlan on the 3rd of September 1526.

Sacred, Catholic, and Cæsarian Majesty:

Having given orders for all things concerning Cristóbal de Olid, as your Majesty was informed, I bethought me that my own person had now long been idle, attempting no new matter in your Majesty's service by reason of my broken arm, and although not wholly recovered from it I thought it well to undertake something. Accordingly on October 12th in the year 1524 I left this city of Tenochtitlan with certain men on horseback and on foot, which were no more than those of my own household and of a few friends and relatives, together with Gonzalo de Salazar y Peralmírez, and Chirinos, *factor* and *veedor* of your Majesty. I likewise took with me the chief natives of the land, leaving the administration of justice to the Government in the hands of your Majesty's treasurer and *contador* together with the licentiate Alonso de Zuazo[23]. In the capital itself I left great store of guns and ammunition and sufficient troops; the forts likewise were well furnished with guns and the brigs in excellent repair. The city with its *alcalde* was well prepared in every way for defence and even for attack if need be.

I accordingly left the capital in this order and arrived at the township of Espíritu Santo in the province of Coazacoalco, 110 leagues off. Here, while ordering certain matters within the city, I sent to the provinces of Tabasco and Xicalango informing the native rulers of my visit to these parts and bidding them to come to hold speech with me or send persons whom I could

287

instruct as to what they were to do, the which they did, receiving my messengers very warmly and sending me seven or eight persons of lofty rank (as they were wont to do) who informed me that on the other side of Yucatán close to the coast near the Bay of Ascension there were certain Spaniards who were doing them much ill. Not only had they burnt many villages and killed certain natives, on which many had deserted their homes and fled to the woods and mountains, but they had injured merchants and traders even more severely; in such wise that all traffic with the coast which had been considerable had now ceased, and as eye-witnesses they gave me an account of practically all the townships along the coast down to where Pedro Arias de Avila, your Majesty's Governor, is stationed: they drew the map of the whole coast on a piece of cloth from which I reckoned that I could journey the greater part of it, in particular as far as that place which they pointed out as being occupied by the Spaniards. I was glad to find such good news of a road by which I could put my plan into execution and thus bring the natives of the land to the knowledge of our Catholic Faith and the service of your Majesty, for on such a lengthy journey I was certain to pass through many and various provinces and peoples, and should be able to discover whether these Spaniards of whom I heard belonged to the expeditions which I had sent under Cristóbal de Olid, Pedro de Albarado or Francisco de las Casas. And to order all those things aright it seemed to me expedient to your Majesty's service that I should go forward in person, especially seeing that it was inevitable but that we should discover many lands and provinces previously unknown and might succeed in pacifying many of them, as indeed afterwards happened. Whereupon, conceiving in my mind the results likely to follow from my visit, I determined, putting aside all possible toil and expense, to follow that road, as indeed I had decided upon before leaving the capital.

Before arriving at Espíritu Santo I had two or three times received letters on the way from the capital, both from those whom I had left as my lieutenants and from other persons. Your Majesty's officials who were of my company likewise received them. I learnt that there was not that harmony between the treasurer and *contador* so necessary for all things pertaining to their office and the charge which I had laid upon them in your Majesty's royal name. I did that which seemed to me best, to wit, wrote them in the strongest terms of rebuke, and even warned them that unless they made up their differences and behaved themselves very differently from that time on, I should make such provisions as would be very little pleasing to them, and would even make report of the matter to your Majesty. Later, since my arrival in Espíritu Santo further letters from them and other persons arrived, in which I learnt that their disputes still continued and indeed increased, so much so that on one occasion swords had been drawn on either side. This caused such scandal and disturbance that not only did the Spaniards arm themselves on both sides, but the natives of the city were induced to fly to arms saying that the tumult was directed against them. Seeing then that my rebukes and warnings were useless and that short of abandoning the expedition I could not return in person to put an end to the matter, I thought it good to send the *factor* and *veedor* with equal powers to those held by the *treasurer* and *contador*, to see where the fault lay and restore order. I further gave them secret powers by which if the culprits proved unamenable to reason, they should have authority to remove them from the charge which I had laid on them, and should occupy it themselves together with the licentiate Alonso de

Zuazo. They should also punish the guilty persons. The matter being thus arranged the *factor* and *veedor* left and I held it as very certain that their return would produce much fruit and prove an effectual remedy to calm the passions which had been aroused; and with this my mind was somewhat set at rest.

(Cortés then set off. He had about 140 *men, of whom* 93 *were mounted, and there were some* 150 *horses. He commandeered a brig which was lying in the port of the Villa del Espíritu Santo having sailed thither from Medellín with supplies for him, and sent it on to the Tabasco river with the supplies that remained, four guns and a considerable amount of ammunition. Cortés then wrote to his agent at Medellín to load two caravels and a larger ship with provisions and send them after him. He also wrote to Rodrigo de Paz bidding him send him five or six thousand pesos of gold to buy stores. He even wrote to the treasurer at the same time asking him to lend him the money, which he did, and the ships duly arrived at the mouth of the Tabasco.*

Cortés now proceeded eastwards along the coast. The land was very marshy and frequently intersected by small streams. There were also three large rivers to cross : the first two the horses managed to swim, their bridles being held by men seated in the canoes, but to cross the last it was necessary to build a bridge which was no less than 934 *paces long, a thing as Cortés remarks,* "very marvellous to see." *They found abundance of fruit, particularly the cocoa nut, in this province of Cupilco, as also of fish. There were some ten or twelve fair-sized towns and the natives remained quiet although somewhat overawed at the Spaniards whom they saw now almost for the first time. From the last town in the province, Anaxuxuca, Cortés sent on a few Spaniards and Indians to spy out and open up a road, and they reported many mountains and swamps ahead.*

The Guaxala river lay immediately in front of them and was crossed in rafts with but a single Indian casualty. While they were doing so the boats with provisions arrived from the mouth of the Tabasco. One of the scouts had made his way up this river and reached the town of Zaguatán itself. He now sent word back by means of some of the natives. The following night in the midst of a violent rainstorm he arrived where Cortés was encamped on the further side of the river with some seventy Indians who had come with him to open up the road. On the day following the main body succeeded in reaching the town, only to find it deserted; even the seventy Indians who had assisted them had fled. For four days Cortés remained in the town thinking they would return when their fears were past, but finding they did not do so sent out parties of Spaniards who captured two native men and a few women. They could or would say nothing as to where all had disappeared, but pointed to a range of hills some ten leagues off where, they said, the chief town Chilapán was to be found on the further side of a great river, which flowed into the Zaguatán and thence into the Tabasco. They also declared that higher up the river was a town called Ocumba.

Cortés remained twenty days longer in this town. It seemed to be entirely surrounded by fearful marshes, and finally in desperation, since food was running short, a large bridge was built and the company set out in the direction of Chilapán. A smaller boat was at the same time dispatched to Ocumba. Here again the natives fled. A few men and women who were captured guided the Spaniards to Chilapán, where they arrived late the next day to find it also burnt and abandoned. Proceeding to Topetitán they found it in like state. They were already extremely short of food and found but little at Topetitán to relieve their want. The advance party was sent on to Istapán with orders to send back word as to the road, until which time the main body would remain in the city. "And so," *says Cortés,* "they set off."

But two days later having received neither letter nor any other news of them I was forced to set out also on account of lack of food, and follow them with only their track through the marshes to guide us along a terribly bad road; for I can assure your Majesty that even on the highest ground the horses sank up to the saddle girths and that although their riders were not in the saddle but leading them by the bridle. I proceeded thus for two days following the track, without news of our comrades ahead and in no little perplexity as to what I should do next; for to retrace our steps was impossible and yet I had no certainty as to what lay in front of us. It pleased God, however, Who in our greatest need is wont to succour us, that as we lay encamped greatly downcast in mind thinking that we must all perish there without hope of aid, two of my native Mexicans arrived with a letter from the Spaniards saying that they had reached Istapán. On approaching the town they found that it stood on a neck of land between two streams: the women and chattels had been already moved to the furthest bank. The men, however, remained in the town itself thinking that the Spaniards would be unable to cross the broad creek that separated them: but seeing them begin to swim it holding on to the saddle-bows of their horses, they set fire to the town and fled across the river, some in canoes and some swimming.

Many were drowned in their hurry. The Spaniards arrived before the town was wholly burnt, and took seven or eight prisoners, among whom there was one who appeared to be the chieftain, intending, as they wrote, to keep them until my arrival.

It would be impossible to describe to your Majesty the joy of my men on hearing this letter, for, as I have said, they had almost given up hope. Early on the morrow we continued our march having the two Indians as guides, and late that night arrived at the town where I found all the men of the advance party in good spirits, since they had found many small maize fields, together with *yucas* [24] and red pepper, a food commonly used in the Islands and not unpalatable. I ordered the prisoners to be brought before me and asked them by an interpreter why they burnt and fled from their own homes and villages since I had done them no harm, but on the contrary gave presents to those who received me. They replied that the ruler of Zaguatán had come through there in a canoe and frightened them greatly, persuading them to set fire to their town and abandon it. I confronted this chief with all the natives who had been taken in Zagatuán, Chilapán, and Topetitán, and in order that the natives of Istapan might see how evilly he had lied to them, I desired the others to declare whether I had done them any wrong or whether they had been well treated in my company: the which they declared, weeping and saying that they had been deceived, showing themselves truly sorry for what they had done. Accordingly, the more to reassure them I gave all of them permission to return to their homes together with certain trifles and a letter for each one of them which I ordered them to keep in their villages and show to any Spaniards who might pass that way. They would thus be secure. I bade them tell their chiefs the fault they had committed

293

in burning and deserting their towns and to abstain from it in future, for they might remain securely at home since no hurt or damage was done them. Upon which they departed very contented, and all this being done in the presence of those of Istapán went no small way towards pacifying them also.

This business finished I spoke at greater length with what appeared to be the head man among the captives, telling him that I was come not to harm them but to instruct them in many things that it behoved them to know both for the security of their persons and goods as for the salvation of their souls. I therefore earnestly begged him to send two or three of his fellows (to whom I would add as many Mexicans) to seek out their ruler and tell him to have no fear, for I was certain that it would be greatly to his advantage to come to see me: to this he agreed and on the morrow the messengers returned and the ruler and some forty men with them. He told me that he had burnt his town and fled at the bidding of the chief of Zaguatán who had said that I should burn and slay all that I met, but that he was now aware that he had been misled. He was sorry for what was past and begged me to pardon him, promising to do all that I bade him from that time on. He also asked that certain women taken by the Spaniards on their first arrival should be restored, upon which as many as twenty were found whom I handed over to him, to his great content.

It happened that a Spaniard found a Mexican Indian of his company eating a portion of the flesh of an Indian who was killed when we took the town. He reported this to me and I ordered the Indian to be burnt in the presence of the chief of Istapán giving him to understand the reason, to wit, that he had killed an Indian and eaten him, the which was forbidden by your Majesty and had been publicly so proclaimed by me in your Majesty's name, for which crime he was to be burnt. For I desired that they should kill no one, but rather according to your Majesty's commands was set on aiding and defending them, both their persons and property. They should know also that it was their duty to hold and worship one true God, Who is in heaven, Creator and Maker of all things, by Whom all creatures live and are maintained, and to lay aside all those idols and heathen rites which they had hitherto held, inasmuch as they were lies and snares devised by the devil, enemy of the human race, to deceive them and bring them to eternal damnation in great and terrible torments, dividing them from the knowledge of God that they might not save themselves and partake of the glory and blessedness promised and prepared by God for those who believe in Him, the which the devil lost by his own malice and wickedness.

I was likewise come to acquaint them of your Majesty, whom divine providence has willed that the whole world should obey and serve. They also must bow under the imperial yoke and do that which we as your Majesty's ministers should in your Majesty's royal name command. Doing which they would be well treated and their rights both of person and of property upheld: but failing so to do they would be proceeded against and punished according to the law. I dwelt on many other matters with which I will not trouble your Majesty as being too long. To all he agreed very readily and sent off a few of his men to bring further provisions which they did. I gave him certain trifling gifts of Spanish ware which he greatly prized and he remained with me all the time I was there.

Our road lay through Tatahintalpán: and since there was a deep river to be crossed he ordered a road to be made and a bridge built. I sent a party of

Spaniards down to my ships in the Tabasco to order them to sail round the point of Yucatán and anchor in Ascension Bay where they would either meet me or receive fresh orders from me: the party was then to return bringing as many provisions as they could and following up a large creek until they met with me in the province of Acalán forty leagues off where I would wait for them. On the departure of these men I asked the ruler of Iſtapán to let me have three or four canoes and send in them a party of Spaniards and a native chief up-ſtream to allay the fears of the natives that they might not burn or desert their towns. To this he agreed very willingly, and the projeĉt bore no small fruit as I shall proceed to show your Majeſty.

Iſtapán is a fine large town and is situated on the bank of a magnificent river. There are rich grazing grounds on either side and also good farm land. It possesses in addition a fine ſtretch of cultivated ground.

(After residing for a week in Iſtapán Cortés again set out. Owing to the winding of the river he reached the firſt village before the canoes and found it burnt and deserted. Thence he continued his way to Signatecpán, the next large town marked on his map. Some kind of a road had to be made through swamps and over mountains and rivers; finally after two days of ſtubborn labour spent in cutting a way through dense foreſt the guides confessed themselves loſt. Cortés ſtaked everything on his ship's compass, ordered leaders to press on in a ſtraight line to the north-eaſt and was rewarded by coming upon Signatecpán at nightfall. The town itself was burnt, but a large amount of maize had been left behind and there was good grazing for the horses. Nothing was to be seen of the advance party save a single arrow buried in the ground

near the town ; Cortés was greatly cast down at this, thinking that they had fought with the natives and all lost their lives. On crossing over the river, however, the whole body of natives was discovered who greeted the Spaniards quite fearlessly and confessed that they had been induced to burn their town by the chief ruler of Zaguatán, but that certain Spaniards had arrived in canoes together with natives from Istapán who had reassured them. The Spaniards had stayed two days there and then gone on up-river : Cortés immediately sent word after them, and on the evening of the following day they returned with news of success and four native canoes accompanying them. They had pacified several towns and villages and sent messengers on to three which they had been unable to reach.

Seven or eight further canoe-loads of natives arrived bearing some food and a little gold as gifts to the strangers. Cortés received them graciously, impressing on them their duty to God and to his Catholic Majesty, and some of the idols in Signatec-pán were publicly destroyed.

Finally, after carefully enquiring which was the best road and getting very contrary answers, Cortés set out for the province of Acalán, leaving the natives very quiet and contented. He crossed one river with some slight loss, and pushed on for three days through thick jungle, following a very narrow path. From this he came out on to the bank of a great river over five hundred yards wide, and attempted to find a ford both above and below, but was unsuccessful. The guides told him that it was vain to look for one this side of the mountains which were a twenty days' journey up-stream.)

I was more cast down, says Cortés, at the sight of this arm or inlet of the sea than I could possibly describe. To pass it was impossible on account of its width and the lack of canoes, but even had we had them for the men and baggage the horses would have been unable to get across; for lining either bank were great marshes and large tree roots surrounding them, so that for this and other reasons any idea of getting them across was quite impossible. Yet to attempt to retrace our steps would, it was obvious, mean the death of us all, on account of the wretched roads we had followed and the heavy falls of rain that had since taken place. For we were aware that the river in its rise must have swept away all the bridges we had made, and to build them again would be a matter of tremendous difficulty since the men were now all wearied out: in addition we bethought us that we had now eaten all the stores to be had on the road and should we return would find nothing more to eat; for I had many men and horses with me, including in addition to the Spaniards more than 3,000 native Mexicans. Yet the obstacle to our further progress remained, as I have described to your Majesty, and so formidable a one that the wit of man was powerless to remedy it, had not God, Who is the true remedy and succour of those in affliction or want, put it into my mind. I took the little canoe which the Spaniards whom I had sent on ahead had used and had the river sounded from one bank to the other, when it was found that there was an average depth of four arms' length. I ordered lances to be tied together to examine the bottom and another two arms' length of mud was discovered, so that the total depth amounted to six arms' length. Accordingly as a desperate remedy I determined to make a bridge over it. I immediately ordered wood to be got to those measurements, of some nine to ten arms' length, allowing for what would rise above the surface of the water. I ordered the Indian chieftains who had accompanied me to cut and bring wood of this length, each one according to the number of his followers. Meanwhile the Spaniards and I began to drive in the stakes, using rafts and the small canoe with two others which were found later, but to all the task seemed impossible to accomplish. Some even whispered behind my back that it would be better to turn back before all the men should be worn out and unable through weakness and hunger to do so. Indeed the murmur grew so loud among my men that they almost dared to say it to my face. Upon this, seeing them so discontented (and in truth they had reason to be since the task was truly overpowering and they had nothing now to eat but roots and herbs) I ordered them to abandon work on the bridge, saying that I would complete it with the help of the Indians. Forthwith I called all the native chieftains together and bade them consider in what plight we were, that we must either pass over or perish. I therefore begged them very earnestly to urge on their people that the bridge might be finished, and once crossed we should enter upon a great province called Acalán where there was great abundance of provisions and where we could encamp: moreover, I reminded them that in addition to the stores to be found in that land I had ordered stores to be brought up to us in canoes from the ships and that therefore in that province we should have abundance of everything; in addition to all this I promised them that when we returned to Mexico they should be very fully rewarded by me in your Majesty's name. They promised me they would undertake the work, and began forthwith to divide it out among themselves, working at it with such skill and speed that in four days they had finished it and all the horses and men were able to pass over it. Moreover it will take more than ten years to destroy it, provided it is not interfered with by the hand of man; and even so almost the only method would be to burn it, for it contains more than a thousand stakes the smallest of which is about the thickness of a man's body, to say nothing of smaller logs which are beyond number. And I can assure your Majesty that I think there is no man who could rightly declare after what plan or fashion the natives built this bridge; all that one can say is that it is the most extraordinary thing one has ever seen.

No sooner had the men and horses reached the other side than we came upon a great marsh full two bowshots broad and the most frightful thing that ever my men set eyes on. All the horses, riderless as they were, sank up to the saddle-cloths, nothing else appearing above the slime. To attempt to urge them on was but to make them sink the deeper, in such wise that we lost all hope of being able to get a single horse across and thought that they must all perish. Nevertheless we set to and placed bundles of grass and large branches underneath them on which they were borne up, and no longer sank, matters being thus somewhat relieved. Then as we were busy going hither and thither in our task a lane of water and slime opened up in the middle so that the horses could swim a little, by which help it pleased God that they should all escape without injury, although so fatigued and utterly worn out that they could hardly remain on their feet.

We returned thanks to God for his great mercy towards us, and while we were so doing the Spaniards whom I had sent on to Acalán arrived with some eighty natives of that province loaded with stores of maize and birds, at which sight God knows how we rejoiced, more especially when they told us that the natives were very quiet and peaceably disposed with no desire to desert their homes. With the Indians from Acalán came two chief men from the ruler of that province, by name, Apaspalón, to say that he rejoiced greatly at my visit. Many days since he had had news of me from traders from Tabasco and Xicalango, and he was eager to meet me. He sent by their hands a little gold, which I received with as much show of delight as I could, thanking their master for the good will he showed in the service of your Majesty, and giving them a few small presents, after which I bade them return with the Spaniards whom they had accompanied, and they did so very contentedly.

They marvelled greatly at seeing the bridge we had built, and this had no slight effect on the peaceful intentions which they afterwards showed, for since their land lay among lakes and rivers they might well have thought of beating a retreat by means of them, but after seeing our handiwork they thought that nothing was impossible to us.

The same day, immediately after their departure, I set off again with all my men. We slept one night in the jungle, and on the morrow a little after noon approached the farms and plantations of Acalán. It was not long before we arrived at the prosperous town which is called Tizatepelt where we found all the natives in their houses very quiet and peaceful and great stores of food for man and beast, in such quantity indeed that it repaid us for our former want. We rested there six days, during which time a youth came to see me, of good disposition and well attended, who informed me that he was the son of the native ruler; he brought me a certain amount of gold and game, offering his kingdom and person in the service of your Majesty, and concluded by saying that his father was dead. I showed him that I was much grieved at the death of his father, though perceiving that he was lying, and gave him a collar of Flanders lace which I wore round my neck which he greatly prized. I told him that he was free to depart in peace, but he stayed a further two days with me of his own accord.

The native ruler of this town now told me that there was another town of his near at hand which could offer us better dwellings and greater store of provisions, since it was larger and had more inhabitants. He begged me to go there where I should be more comfortable. On my answering that it pleased me well he ordered the road to be opened and lodgings prepared for us. All this was duly performed and we took our way to the town which is five leagues off. We found the natives as before quiet and at home and a certain part of the town cleared for our use. This town, Teutiacá by name, is very fine, and has many magnificent temples, in two of which we lodged, throwing out the idols from their former abode; at this the people showed no great discontent for I had already spoken to them, giving them to understand the error in which they were, how that there was only one God, Creator of all things, and such other doctrines as could be briefly exposed to them, although later I did speak at greater length both to the ruler and to all his people.

I learnt from them that the larger of these two temples was dedicated to a goddess whom they held in great faith and veneration, sacrificing to her only virgin maidens of great beauty, for were they otherwise the goddess was greatly angered with them, for which reason they ever took special care to seek out such that the goddess might be satisfied, and even brought up from their earliest days those of likely appearance for this office. I likewise gave them my opinion as to what was seemly to be done in this matter with which they seemed fairly contented.

The native ruler of this town showed himself very friendly to me, entering into long conversations in which he gave me a long account of the Spaniards I was seeking and the road that I was to take. Finally he confided to me as a great secret, begging me to let no one know that he had warned me, that Apaspalón, the ruler of all that province, was alive, though he had sent to us that he was dead by the youth who was indeed his son, and was intending to turn me from my direct road in order that I should not visit his land and towns. He was warning me of this, so the chieftain confessed, because he wished me well, having received fair treatment from me. But he again begged me to keep the matter very secret for if it were known that he had warned me Apaspaóln would kill him and burn his kingdom. I thanked him much, repaying his loyalty with a few small gifts, and promised secrecy as he desired; I further promised in your Majesty's name to reward him amply in days to come.

I lost no time in summoning to my presence the youth who had come to visit me and told him that I marvelled greatly at himself and his father wishing to deceive me, knowing as he did how much I desired to see him, to do him honour and give him certain presents as recognition of those many kindnesses which I had received in his land and which I was eager to repay. I now knew for certain that his father was alive, and earnestly requested the youth to seek him and try and bring him to me for I was certain that he would gain much by it. In answer he confessed the truth saying that he had only denied it because under orders to do so, and offered to do all he could to bring his father to me, in which he thought he would be successful, since on learning that I was not come to do any harm but actually gave presents of my own substance, he was anxious to see me, although somewhat ashamed to appear before me after his first refusal. The youth accordingly set out and on the morrow both returned whereat I welcomed them with much pleasure. The chieftain excused himself for his refusal to meet me explaining that he

was afraid to do so until he knew my intentions, but
once known he was glad to do so; moreover it was
true that he had given orders to guide me by roads
which did not touch his towns, but now he begged
me to accompany him to the prosperous town where
he resided, since there were more facilities there for
providing me with all the necessities of life. Forthwith he had a broad road cut thither and on the morrow
we set out. I ordered a horse to be given him and he
rode on it very contentedly until we came to the town
which is called Izancanac, very large and with many
temples, standing on the bank of a great stream which
runs down to the estuary of the Xicalango and Tabasco.
Some of his people had left the city, the remainder
were in their houses. We obtained plentiful provisions there and the ruler dwelt with me in my
lodging although his own house was near by. He
continued to give me detailed information about the
Spaniards I was seeking and drew me a map on a
piece of cloth of the road that I had to take. He
also made me a present of a little gold and some
women without my asking anything of him, whereas
up to the present I have asked the native chieftains
of these parts whether they were not willing to give
me a certain amount of it. We had to pass the river
and the swamp which lay on the nearer side of it.
He had a bridge built, provided me with a great
number of canoes, as many as were necessary, and
gave me guides both for our journey and for messengers whom I wanted to send back to Mexico.
Having settled these matters I presented him with a
few trifles for which he had taken a liking and so
leaving him very contented and all the land very
quiet, I finally quitted the province on the first Sunday
in Lent of the year 1525, and the whole of that day
was spent in crossing the river, which was no small
matter. I gave this chieftain a note at his request

so that should other Spaniards come there they might know that I had passed that way, and so he remained my very good friend.

In this province an incident occurred which it is well your Majesty should know. A worthy citizen of Tenochtitlan, formerly called Mesicalcingo and now Cristóbal, came to me very secretly one night bearing a certain drawing on a paper after the fashion of their country, and gave me to understand that Guatimocin, ruler of Tenochtitlan when we captured it, and before that of Tezcuco, whom I held prisoner as a dangerous man, and afterwards brought him with me together with other native chiefs whom I thought likely to disturb the peace in Mexico, had held converse with Tetepanquencal, former ruler of Tacuba, and one Tacitecle, who had been with him in Mexico during the siege. Mesicalcingo had also been admitted to these conferences, in the course of which Guatimocin had declared that they were dispossessed of their lands and suffered under the yoke of the Spaniards, and it would be well to seek some remedy by which they might once again enjoy their ancient rights. After many such discussions it was decided that the surest remedy was to contrive the death of myself and all those who accompanied me, afterwards calling the people of these parts together and killing Cristóbal de Olid and all his company. This done they would send messengers to Tenochtitlan bidding them slay all Spaniards who had remained there, which they said would be no difficult matter since the Spaniards left there were all newly come to the land and knew nothing of war. Finally they would proclaim themselves throughout all the land so that in whatever township or village there were Spaniards they might be killed off; strong guards would be placed in the ports to see that no ship coming to these shores should ever leave them, and so no news go back to Castile. In this way they would be rulers as they had been before. They had already divided out the land amongst them and had allotted one province to Mesicalcingo.

I gave thanks to God that I had been warned of his treachery and as soon as dawn came arrested all the chieftains concerned, placing them in separate confinement. I then questioned them about the matter telling each one that the others had confessed, since they were unable to communicate one with another. On this they all admitted that Guatimocin and Tetepanquencal had been prime movers in the affair and that while it was true that they had listened to them yet they had not consented to the matter. Accordingly the two leaders were hanged and the others freed, their guilt apparently amounting to no more than that of listening, although that in itself was worthy of death. Nevertheless the judgment was left open so that if at any time they attempted any such treachery they might be severely punished. Yet I think they are unlikely to attempt it for they have never found out how I learnt of the plot and think that I must have done so by some magical means. They consequently believe that nothing can be hidden from me. For they have often seen me draw out a mariner's chart and compass in order to ascertain the way, particularly when we are near water, and believed, as they confessed to many of my men and even on occasion to myself, that I made use of these instruments to find out whether they were faithful to me, and have often desired me to look into the mirror and at the map, saying that I should see there that they were faithful, since there was nothing I did not know by means of that instrument: I gave them to understand that this was true.

FIFTH LETTER

This province of Acalán is indeed of great size, containing many people and towns, a large number of which were visited by the Spaniards of my company. It is likewise abounding in food of all kinds, especially in honey. Many traders and natives carry their merchandise to every part, and they are rich in slaves and such articles as are commonly sold in the country. The province is completely surrounded by streams, all of which run into the Bay or Harbour of Endings (*Términos*) as they call it; from here they carry on a great trade by means of canoes with those of Xicalango and Tabasco, and even it is thought, although not known entirely for certain, that they cross in their canoes to the other Southern Sea, so that this land of Yucatán would prove to be an island. I shall endeavour to discover the secret of this and will send your Majesty a true account of it. I could not find that there was any other chieftain in the province except this Apaspalón, whom I have already mentioned to your Majesty, and who is the biggest trader and owner of sea-going ships.

And the manner of his acquiring such wealth and trade I observed in the town of Nito, where as I shall describe to your Majesty I found certain Spaniards of the company of Gil González de Avila; for even there, there was one quarter of the town peopled by his agents, among whom was his own brother, who sold such goods of his as are most common in these parts, to wit, cocoa, cotton cloths, colours for dyeing, another sort of paint which they use to protect their bodies against the heat and the cold, candlewood for lighting, pine resin for burning before their idols, slaves, and strings of coloured shells, which they prize greatly for the adornment of their persons. At their feasts and merrymakings a certain amount of gold changes hands, but of poor quality containing an admixture of copper and other metals.

To Apaspalón and the other chief men of the provinces who came to see me I spoke juſt as I had done to all others whom I had met with in my march concerning their idols, and what they muſt do and believe to be saved, as also that which they were obliged to do in the service of your Majeſty. In both these matters they seemed well pleased, and burnt many of their idols in my presence, saying that thenceforward they would honour them no more and promising ever to obey whatever was commanded them in your Majeſty's name. I thus took my leave of them and set out as I have already described.

(*Four Spaniards had been sent on ahead with a couple of native guides to spy out the road, and the main body were ordered to carry each man provisions sufficient for a six days' march. The scouts returned saying that the road was good and that they had aſtually reached some outlying farms of the province, where they had seen a few natives without themselves being perceived. Further scouts were immediately poſted a league in advance of the vanguard opening up the road in order to capture any ſtray natives whom they might come across and so prevent the alarm being given. Two traders of Acalán were thus caught and consented to accompany the Spaniards as guides. The whole body slept that night in the jungle. The next day four Mazatcan Indians were discovered armed with bows and arrows, seemingly on the watch, of whom only one was captured owing to the denseness of the foreſt. The others accordingly waited until the Spaniards were paſt and then attacked their Indian followers but were soon beaten off. In order to avoid delay Cortés now pushed on with a small body hoping to reach the town before nightfall, but was held up by a bad swamp and had to wait till morning to bridge*

308

*it with boughs. The night was spent in a tiny
hut. Riding forward on the morrow they came to
the town three leagues on the further side of the
marsh. It was high and strongly fortified so that
they rode round it for some time seeking an entrance.
Finally, on forcing their way in they found it deserted
but well stocked with provisions. The fortifications
were more than usually elaborate and included the
natural ones of a lake and torrent flowing into it
and also, within, a deep ditch, a wooden breastwork, and lastly a circular stone wall some twelve
feet high. The neighbouring town of Tiac was
likewise taken and messengers sent forth to the
natives who began to come in, bringing gifts of food
and clothing. The chiefs, however, remained ob-
durate, and Cortés dismissing the Acalán traders
to their own homes proceeded on his way eastward.)*

Leaving the province of Mazatcan I followed the
road to Taica, sleeping in the open after marching
four leagues. The road ran through entirely deserted
country, traversing great mountain lands in one of
which there was a dreadful pass named by us the
Alabaster Pass, on account of the rocks and peaks
being all made of that material, very fine. On the
fifth day the outriders ahead came upon a huge lake,
seemingly an arm of the sea, and such I believe it is
on account of its size and depth, although its water
is sweet. They perceived a town on the island in
the middle of it which the guide assured them to be
the biggest in the whole province of Taica, but without
canoes it was impossible to cross over to it. On
this, the Spaniards who were riding ahead being
uncertain what to do sent back one of their number
to acquaint me with what was happening. I halted
all my troops and went forward on foot to examine
the shape and position of the lake. On coming up

with the advance guard I found that they had captured
one of the inhabitants of the town as he was coming
armed in a tiny canoe to spy out the road and see if
there were any strangers abroad: and although he was
not on his guard he would yet have escaped my men
had it not been for a dog which they had there, and
which got hold of him before he could throw himself
into the water. I questioned this Indian and he told
me that nothing was known of my coming. On my
asking whether there was any passage to the town
he replied no, but that nearby on the further side of
a small stream leading from the lake there were
certain farms and houses where, he thought, we could
procure some canoes, if we arrived there without
being perceived. I immediately gave orders that the
main body was to follow after me and went forward
with ten or a dozen bowmen on foot whither the
Indian guided us. We waded through a long stretch
of marsh and water, such as would have come up to
a horse's girth and sometimes higher, and finally
arrived at some farms, but what with the badness of
the road and the fact that for a great part of the time
we could make no effort to conceal ourselves, it was
impossible to remain unseen, and at the moment
when we arrived the people were already putting off
in canoes and making for open water.

I quickly pressed on along the bank for two-thirds
of a league through the farmland, but everywhere we
had been perceived and the natives were already
fleeing. It was now late, and though I still continued
the pursuit it was in vain.

I camped in the farms nearby assembling all my
men and allotting them sleeping quarters with all
the care I could, since the Mazatcan guide informed
me that this was a very numerous and warlike people.
He declared himself willing to go to the town on the
island something over two leagues distant, in the little

canoe in which the native had come. He would speak
to the chief, Canee by name, whom he knew very
well, and would tell him my intentions and the reason
of my coming to these lands which he himself knew
and had seen having come with me thus far; and he
believed that the chief would be reassured by this
and would give credence to what he said, for he was
very well known to him and had stayed many times
in his house. I forthwith handed over to him the
canoe and the Indian who had come in it thanking
him for his offer and promising him that if he succeeded in his mission he should be very amply rewarded. He accordingly went off and was back at
about midnight with two chief men from the town
who declared that they were sent by their lord to see
me and assure themselves as to what my messenger
had said that they might know what I desired. I
received them kindly making them certain trifling
presents and told them that I was come to these lands
at your Majesty's command to explore them and
convey to the rulers and peoples of it certain things
behoving to your royal Majesty's will and service.
I bade them tell their chief that putting aside all fear
he should come where I was, and that meanwhile for
greater security I was willing to give them a Spaniard
to go with them and remain as a hostage until their
chief should return. Upon this they went off, and
the guide and one of my men with them. Early on
the morrow the chief arrived with some thirty warriors
in five or six canoes and with him the Spaniard whom
I had sent as a hostage. He appeared very pleased
to come and for my part I received him very warmly.
It was the hour of mass when he arrived and I accordingly had it sung before him with great solemnity,
the players on the flageolets and the sackbuts whom
I had with me assisting. He listened to these with
great attention and regarded the ceremony with equal

wonder. Mass finished, the friars who accompanied us approached and made him a sermon by means of the interpreter, in such fashion that he was well able to understand the mysteries of our faith, for they explained with many reasons how that there was only one God, and discovered to him the error of his own religion. He plainly showed and said that he was well content and declared himself eager to destroy his idols straightway and believe in that God of Whom we told him, for he wished greatly to know in what way he must serve and honour Him. If I would visit his town, he said, I should see him burn the idols in my presence, and he desired me to leave there in his town such a cross as he was told I had left in all the other towns through which I had passed.

After this sermon I again had speech with him, telling him of the greatness of your Majesty, and how both he and all of us in the world were your Majesty's subjects and vassals and obliged to do him service in return for which your Majesty would grant great favours to those who so obeyed, such as I had already granted in your Majesty's name to all in these parts who had offered themselves in his service and placed themselves under the royal yoke, and so I promised to him also.

He told me in reply that until then he had recognized no one as his rightful lord nor had known anyone who should be so. It was true that some five or six years since certain Indians from Tabasco had told him of a captain who had passed that way with a company of our nation, and after beating them three times in battle, had told them that they must become vassals of a great ruler, and all else which I now declared to him; was the matter, he asked, all of a piece? I replied that the captain of whom the Tabasco Indians had informed him was none other than myself, which he might verify by speaking with the interpreter, Marina, who has ever accompanied me, for it was in Tabasco that I had been given her together with twenty other native women. She accordingly spoke with him and assured him of the truth of what I said, telling him how I had won Mexico and describing all the lands which I held subject under the imperial yoke of your Majesty. He showed himself delighted to hear this and declared himself very willing to become the vassal of your Majesty, saying that he should be happy to serve so great a lord as I described your Majesty to be. Upon this he ordered birds, honey, a little gold and a few strings of coloured shells which they greatly value to be brought and presented them to me. I also gave him certain trifles which I had with me with which he was very well pleased. He had dinner with me with great content and after dinner I told him that I was seeking certain Spaniards on the sea-coast, for they were of my company and I had sent them thither but had had no news of them for many days. I begged him to tell me anything that he knew of them. He replied that he had much information about them, for quite close to them were certain of his vassals who provided him with supplies of peanuts with which the land abounded, and from these and other traders who were constantly travelling backwards and forwards he often received news of them. He offered to give me a guide to where they were, but warned me that the road was very rough and lay over many steep and rocky mountain lands. It would be far less fatiguing if I were to travel by sea.

To this I bade him consider that for so large a company as that which followed me together with our baggage and horses it was impossible to provide sufficient ships and we were therefore forced to go by land. I begged him to show me a way to cross the lake, and he advised me to proceed up the shore some three leagues to a point where there was dry ground, when again proceeding my men could take the road opposite his town. Meanwhile he begged me very earnestly while the troops were making this detour to go with him in a canoe to visit his town and house where I should see him burn the idols and could have a cross made for him. Accordingly, in order to please him, though against the wishes of my men, I got into one of the canoes with about twenty men, mostly bowmen, and crossed to his town where we spent all the day in festival. At nightfall I took my leave of him, embarked again in a canoe with a guide whom he gave me and crossed to the other side to sleep on land, where I found already many of my men who had circled the lake, and so we passed that night together. I left in this town or rather on a farm a horse which had run a sharp stake into its leg and could not walk. The chief promised to take care of it for me, but I know not what he will make of it.

On the morrow, assembling my men I set off following the path pointed out by the guides. After about half a league we came to a stretch of flat pasture land which was succeeded by another rocky portion some league and a half in length which again changed to a very fine open plain. I here sent on a few horse and foot a very long way ahead to take prisoner any natives that they met with on the plain for I was informed by the guides that we should come up to a town before nightfall. In this place we found many fallow deer of which we killed eighteen on horseback with our lances. But what with the sun and the fact that the horses had not run for many days (since we had been travelling through nothing but mountainous country) two of them died and many more were in great danger of doing so.

Our hunting done, we pursued our way and soon

came up with some of the outriders who had stopped, with four Indian huntsmen whom they had caught, together with a dead lion and some iguanas, a kind of large lizard which are to be found also in the Islands. I enquired of these persons whether news of me had reached their town. They replied no, and pointed it out to me, which seemed to be not more than a league away on the side of a hill. I made all haste to arrive there thinking to find no hindrance in the way, but as I was about to enter the town and saw my men already making towards it, I suddenly perceived a very deep stream lying right in our way. Upon this I halted and shouted out to the natives. Two of them approached in a canoe bringing about a dozen chickens and game quite near to where I had stopped with the water up to the saddle-girths of my horse. They then stopped and would come no further, and although I stayed there a long time talking and attempting to reassure them they refused to approach any closer, and finally began to paddle back towards the town in their canoe. Upon this a Spaniard who was on horseback near me leapt off his horse into the water and swam towards them. Frightened, they abandoned the canoe and other foot soldiers who were able to swim came quickly up and captured them. By this time all the natives whom we had seen in the town had disappeared and I demanded of the captives where it was possible to cross, upon which they showed me a road leading to a place about a league up-stream where there was dry ground. We reached the town that night and slept in it having marched eight good leagues that day. The town is called Thecon and its ruler Amohan. I remained here four days getting together provisions sufficient for six, which was the time, so the guides told me, it would take to cross the desert. I was also hoping that the ruler of the town would come in, having sent a reassuring message to him by the hand of the Indians we had captured, but neither he nor they ventured to show themselves. Having gathered together all the stores that could be found there I again set out, travelling the first day through very good country, level and fertile, with no mountains and but few stones. After six leagues we came upon a great house standing at the foot of some hills and hard by a river with two or three smaller ones close to it, and surrounded by tilled land. The guides informed me that the house belonged to Amohan, ruler of Thecon, and was kept by him there as an inn, since great numbers of traders were accustomed to pass that way.

I stopped there the whole of the day following our arrival. It was a feast day and the delay gave the men who were going ahead time to open up the road. We had some excellent fishing in the river, catching a large number of shad without losing so much as a single one out of the nets. On the morrow we again set off along a bad road leading over hills and through wooded country for close on seventeen leagues when we came out on to the plains again bare save for a few pines. The plain lasted two leagues in which space we killed seven deer, which we ate in the valley of a delightfully fresh stream which we came upon at the further side of the plain. We now began to ascend a pass, short but so rough that the horses though led by the bridle could only climb it with difficulty. About half a league of downhill easy going succeeded this and then we began to climb another hill, measuring almost a league and a half up to its summit and an equal distance in descent, and all over such rough and stony ground that there was not a single horse which did not lose a shoe. I slept that night in a dried-up river bed and remained there almost till vespers of the next day waiting for the horses to be shod, yet although there were two blacksmiths and more than ten soldiers assisting them, they could not finish shoeing all through that day. I accordingly went forward some three leagues to pass the night leaving many of my men behind both to shoe the horses and to wait for the baggage which on account of the bad roads and the great rains had not been able to keep up with us.

I again set out on the morrow, the guides telling me that nearby there was a village called Asuncapín belonging to the ruler of Taica, and that we should reach it in good time to camp there for the night. After four or five leagues we arrived at the village and found no natives there. I remained in camp there two days to wait for the baggage to come up and to gather together provisions, after which we resumed our road passing through Taxuytel five leagues further on where we slept the night and found great abundance of peanuts but only a meagre quantity of maize and that green.

The guides and the head man of the village here informed me that we should have to pass a very high and rocky range entirely devoid of habitation before arriving at the next village, known as Tenciz, belonging to Canee, chief of Taica. We did not stay long here but set out the very next day, and after seven leagues of flat began to climb a pass which was in truth one of the marvels of the world—I mean the roughness and cragginess of the pass and surrounding hills, in such wise that one is powerless to describe it in words, nor would anyone hearing them be able to form any true idea, only your Majesty must know that we took no less than twelve days in getting through the pass which was eight leagues long. It was on the twelfth day that the last of my men passed through, and of the horses which accompanied them seventy-eight died either through falling down precipitous slopes or breaking their legs: all the rest were so crippled and broken that we thought that not a single one would be fit for use again, and indeed those that escaped were more than three months before they really recovered. During all the time that we were filing through the pass rain never ceased night or day. The rocks were such that no water remained on the surface for drinking and we thus suffered greatly from thirst. Most of the horses died on account of this, and had we not collected water in pots and vessels which were hung outside the rough huts we erected each night, and which owing to the tremendous rainfall provided some for ourselves and our horses, not a single man or horse would ever have escaped from those mountains.

On the road a nephew of mine fell and broke his leg in three or four places, which increased not only his burden but that of all, for to carry him across those mountains was no light matter. To put an end to our ills we found a league before Tenciz a great river so swollen and torrential with the rains that it was impossible to pass: but the Spaniards who were going on ahead had gone up-stream and found a way of passing, which is, I think, the most marvellous that has yet been heard or even thought of. The river winds at this point some two-thirds of a league out of its course by reason of two great mountain peaks which stand right in its way. Between these peaks there are ravines through which the river rushes in the most terrifying and impetuous manner, and of these there are so many that the river can only be crossed between the two peaks. Accordingly we cut down great trees and threw them across from one side to the other, and so passed over in no little peril, clutching hold of a rope of thin reeds which was also fastened from one side to the other: but anyone who had lost his balance in the slightest and had fallen would have met with certain death. There were over twenty of these ravines to be passed before the whole river was crossed, and the business took two days. The horses swam across lower down where the current was less swift, and many of them took three days after that to reach Tenciz, which was not, as I have said, over a league away, but they were so broken by crossing the mountains that they had to be practically carried, being unable to walk.

I arrived at this village of Tenciz on the Saturday before Easter. Many of my men who had horses arrived three days later, but the Spaniards composing the vanguard had arrived two days before, and finding natives in three or four of the dwellings had taken some twenty of them prisoner, for they were quite unprepared for my arrival. I enquired of these whether there were any provisions to be had, to which they replied that there were none either there nor anywhere in their land. This put us in yet greater need than in what we were already, for during the last eighteen days we had eaten nothing but the shoots and nuts of cocoanut palms, and but meagrely of these since we had not the force to cut them. The headman of the village told me, however, that a day's journey up the other bank of the river there was a large town in the province of Tahuycal and that there we should find great store of maize, cocoa and chickens. He offered to provide me a guide thither, and I immediately dispatched an officer with thirty foot and more than a thousand of our Indian allies, in which venture it pleased our Lord that they should find great abundance of maize, and the land itself deserted of people. We thus secured some provisions although on account of the distance only with much labour.

I sent forward at this time certain Spanish bowmen with a native guide to explore the road which we had to take towards Acuculin. They reached a village

some ten leagues further on and six from the chief
town of the province which goes by the same name
(its ruler being one Acahuilguín). Being unperceived, they captured seven men and a woman in
one house and returned with them, to report that the
road so far as they had followed it was somewhat
difficult but light in comparison with what we had
already passed. I questioned the Indian captives as
to the Christians whom I was seeking, in particular
one native of Acalán, who informed me that he was
a trader and had his warehouse in the town of Nito
where the Spaniards whom I sought were residing,
and where a large amount of trade was carried on
between merchants from all parts. The traders of
Acalán had their own especial quarters in this town
among whom was a brother of Apaspalón, the ruler
of Acalán. The Christians, he proceeded to relate,
had attacked them by night, taken the town and robbed
them of the merchandise stored in it, which was in
no small quantity. Since then, which was perhaps
as much as a year ago, all the former traders had made
their way to other provinces; he and certain other
merchants of Acalán had obtained permission from
Acahuilguín to settle in his territory, and had built
a little town in a place which he had assigned to them.
There they carried on their trade, diminished though
it was since the coming of the Spaniards, for the
easiest passage lay through Nito and they no longer
dared to take it. He offered, however, to guide me
to where they were, but warned me that we should
have to cross at no great distance a huge arm of the
sea, together with mountain ranges both many and
steep, some ten days' journey in all. I rejoiced
greatly at finding so excellent a guide and did him
much honour. The guides whom I had taken with
me from Mazatcán and Taica spoke with him, saying
how well they had been treated by me, and on what

friendly terms I was with Apaspalón, their lord. At this he appeared somewhat reassured, and so trusting to this I ordered him to be unbound together with those who were captured with him. Moreover, I so far placed my confidence in him as to send back the guides I had brought with me, giving them a few trifling presents for themselves and their rulers, and thanking them for their pains, with all which they departed very contented. I then immediately sent on four of the natives of Acuculín and two from Tenciz to speak with Acahuilguín and reassure him so that he should not attempt to flee. After them came those who were entrusted with the business of opening the road. I myself set out two days later owing to shortage of provisions, although we had need enough of rest, especially so far as the horses were concerned. However, leading them for the most part by the bridle we set out, and when dawn of the next day appeared it was to find that both the guide and the other natives of Acuculín had disappeared, at which God knows what grief I felt, especially in that I had sent the other guides back to their homes.

I continued my way, camping that night in the woods five leagues further on and traversing that day mountain passes of no small difficulty, in one of which indeed a horse broke down completely which up till then had been sound. The following day we marched six leagues and crossed two rivers, the first by a tree which had fallen across it from one side to the other, the men crossing by this means and the horses by swimming, two mares being drowned; the second we crossed in canoes, the horses again swimming, and we then camped at a little settlement formed of as many as fifteen newly-made huts. I learned that these had been built by the Acalán traders who had abandoned Nito, the town of which the Spanish settlers had taken possession. I remained there a whole day waiting for my men and the baggage to come up, and accordingly sent ahead two companies of horse and foot to the town of Acuculín. They wrote to me, saying that they had found the town deserted, save for two men in a great house belonging to the ruler, who, so they declared, had been ordered to remain there until my arrival in order to acquaint their lord of it, since he had already heard of my approach and would rejoice greatly to see me. He himself would come immediately on hearing that I had arrived; accordingly one of the two had gone off to inform their ruler and bring back certain provisions while the other had remained behind. They had found cocoa-nuts on the trees, but no maize: the pasturing for the horses, however, was fairly good. On arriving at the town I enquired whether the chieftain had arrived or his messenger returned, to which they replied no, and I accordingly questioned the one native remaining as to why he did not come. He did not know and was himself expecting his arrival, but it might be that he had waited to know that I had definitely arrived.

I waited two days and then spoke to him again; he still could give me no reason for the delay, but asked me to send some Spaniards with him, since he knew where their chieftain was and would tell him. He was straightway sent off with ten Spaniards and led them some five leagues through the jungle to some huts which they found deserted, but which according to the Spaniards certainly seemed to have been lately occupied. The same night their guide gave them the slip and they returned. I thus remained entirely without a guide, which in itself was enough to double our difficulties, and accordingly sent out bands both of Indians and Spaniards who patrolled the whole of the province for more than a week without so much as catching sight of a native, save for a few women who were little to our purpose, for they neither knew the road nor could they give any news of the chieftain or the people of the province. One of them told us that she knew of a town two days' journey thence, called Chianteca, where there were people who would give us news of the Spaniards whom we sought, since there were many merchants and persons there who held commerce in diverse parts. Accordingly I sent some of my men with this woman as guide, and although the town was two good days' march from where I was and the road uneven and deserted, yet the natives got wind of my coming and no one was captured.

We had now practically lost all hope in that we were without a guide, and were unable to use the compass on account of the mountain ranges encircling us which were the roughest and steepest ever seen, without so much as a road leading out of them in any direction other than that by which we had entered. At this moment, however, it pleased our Lord, that we should find in the jungle a boy of about fifteen years, who on being questioned replied that he would guide us to some farms in Teniha, another province which, I remembered, we had to pass through. These, he said, were two days off, and accordingly we set out, and in two days' time arrived at the farms where the advance guard captured an old man, who in turn guided us to the town of Teniha, another two days' march further on.

Here four more Indians were captured who straightway gave me very definite news of the Spaniards we sought, saying that they had seen them and that they were but two days' journey off in the town whose name I had already heard, Nito, which as being the centre of much merchandise was well known in those parts. Indeed, I had already had reports of it in the province of Acalán, as I mentioned to your Majesty, and now two women, natives of Nito, were actually brought before me. From these I received a more detailed report, for they informed me that they had been in Nito when it was captured by the Spaniards, who had attacked it by night and so taken prisoner both themselves and many more, following which they had served certain of the Spaniards as slaves, the names of whom they now recounted to me.

I cannot express to your Majesty the gladness which I and those of my company received from this news which the natives of Taniha gave us, to find ourselves so near the end of so arduous a journey. For even during the four days' march from Acuculín we met with innumerable difficulties. There were no roads and our way lay through rough and precipitous mountain paths from which several of the horses slipped and were killed. A cousin of mine, Juan de Ávalos, rolled with his horse down one steep slope, broke an arm, and, had it not been for the breastplate he was wearing which saved him from the stones, would have been dashed to pieces; as it was he was only rescued with great difficulty. We suffered many other trials too long to recount and especially that of hunger, for while we still had a few pigs left from those which we had brought with us from Mexico, yet for more than a week before arriving at Taniha we had not tasted bread, and had eaten only cocoanuts cooked with the meat, without salt, which had long run out, and a few kernels. And even on coming to these villages we found there nothing to eat, for being so near the Spaniards the natives had long ago deserted them through fear of being attacked, although from what I afterwards found out from the state of the Spaniards they were perfectly safe. Nevertheless the news that we were so near our destination made us forget all our sufferings of the past and enheartened us to bear those of the present which were no less acute, especially that of hunger, which was indeed worse for we even ran short of cocoa-nuts, which could be cut only with great difficulty from exceptionally large and lofty palms, the work of cutting a single one taking two men a whole day and the fruit being then consumed in half an hour.

The Indians who brought me the news told me that there were two days of bad road ahead and that then we should come upon a great river flowing between us and Nito which could only be crossed by canoes since it was too wide to swim. I immediately dispatched fifteen of my men on foot to go with the guides, examine the road and the river, and try without raising an alarm to capture one of the Spaniards in order to find out what company they were, whether of those whom I had sent with Cristóbal de Olid or Francisco de las Casas or of Gil González de Avila. They accordingly reached the river, took a canoe from some native traders and there remained hidden for two days, at the end of which time a canoe put off from the other bank of the river where the Spaniards were with four men in it fishing. These they captured without being perceived from the town, and returned with them to me. I learnt that the inhabitants of the town were of the company of Gil González de Avila, all weak and almost dying of hunger. On this I sent two of my servants back to the town in the canoe with a letter acquainting them of my arrival, telling them that I intended to cross the river, and begging them to come with all boats and canoes that they had to this end. I then set out with all my company for the river where we arrived after three days' journey. There I met a certain Diego Nieto who informed me that he was there to represent the chief justice. A boat and canoe were brought in which I and some ten or twelve others passed over to the town, though not without some considerable difficulty, for a wind caught us in the crossing which is very wide there (being near the mouth of the river), and we were all in grave danger of being drowned: however it pleased God to bring us to the harbour. On the morrow I procured other boats which were there and bound the canoes together two and two, in which manner the whole company, men and horses, passed over during the next five or six days.

The Spaniards whom I found there numbered some seventy men and twenty women, whom Captain Gil González de Avila had abandoned. They were in such a strait that it was the most sorrowful sight in the world to see them and the joy with which they greeted my arrival, for in truth if I had not come not one of them could possibly have escaped alive. For in addition to being few in numbers and without arms or horses, they were ill, wounded and half-dead with hunger, the provisions they brought from the Islands being all finished together with such as they had found in the village when they captured it from the natives. And once finished they had no means of securing more, for they were not in a condition to forage for provisions in the land and even if such had been brought from the Islands they were settled in a part which had no way open to the coast, or at any rate they had been totally unable to find one, and indeed such a road was only found with great difficulty afterwards. They had therefore never ventured more than half a league from the village in which they were settled. Seeing, then, the great necessity of these people, I determined to seek some means of providing for them until I could send them back to the Islands, whither they were preparing to go. For out of their whole company there were not eight fit to remain as settlers. I immediately sent out some of my men in the two ships which were there and in five or six smaller Indian boats to go in various directions. The first expedition I directed to the mouth of the river Yasa, ten leagues from this town and in the direction from which I had come, for I had been informed that there were villages there and plentiful supplies. A party penetrated some six leagues up this river where they came upon some large cultivated farms, but the natives perceiving their coming moved all stores into some large barns hard by and betook themselves with their wives, their children and their belongings into the mountains. Just as the Spaniards were approaching the barns, so it was reported to me, a tremendous storm of rain came on, upon which they took shelter in a large building, and thoughtlessly, being soaked to the skin, they laid aside their arms and even removed their armour and clothes, to dry them and warm themselves in front of fires which they had made there. Suddenly they were attacked by the natives and many taken unawares were wounded, in such wise that they were forced to re-embark and return to where I was, without more provisions than those which they had taken hastily as they departed. God knows how grieved I was not only to see them wounded and some dangerously so, but also on account of the encouragement this success would give the Indians, and finally at the small succour they brought us for the great need in which we were.

I immediately sent out another and larger expedition in the same boats with a different captain in command of both Spaniards and Mexicans who had come with me: and as the boats could not contain them all I ordered them to cross to the other side of the great river which runs near this village and then proceed along the coast, the brigs and native canoes keeping pace with them so as to assist them across the rivers and inlets which abound on this coast. They proceeded in this wise until they came to the mouth of the river where the first party of Spaniards had been

wounded, and so returned thence without bringing
any·provision nor having accomplished anything save
capturing four Indians who were putting to sea in a
canoe. I asked them how they came thus and they
replied that owing to the great rains the river was
flowing so furiously that they had been unable to get
more than a league up it, and thinking that it would
abate they waited at the mouth for more than a week
without food or fire, eating nothing but wild fruits,
from which diet some were in such plight that no
small care was necessary to preserve their lives. I
now found myself truly in dire straits, for were it not
for the few pigs remaining of those we had brought
with us, which were strictly rationed and eaten without
bread or salt, we should have been entirely cut off
from food. Through my interpreter I asked the
Indians captured in the canoe whether they knew of
any place where we could find provisions, promising
that if they guided me to such they should be set at
liberty and given many presents. One of them declared that he was a trader, the others being his slaves,
and that he had often voyaged with his ships in these
parts for merchandise: he knew, he said, of an estuary
leading to the great river which was used as a harbour
by all trading ships when on account of bad weather
they could not put out to sea. On the banks of that
river there were many large townships and the natives
were rich and well supplied with food. He offered to
guide our men to where they could load up with all
the provisions they might require. Since I was certain
he spoke the truth (for I had him bound on the end of a
chain so that if he spoke false he might receive the
penalty he deserved) I ordered the ships and boats
to be made ready and putting all the fit men of my
company on board I sent them off with the guide.
At the end of ten days they returned as they had set
out saying that the guide had led them into marshes

where neither the ships nor the native boats could make headway and they had been in no wise able to find any way out. I asked the guide why he had deceived me. He replied that he had not done so, but that the Spaniards with whom I sent him had been unwilling to go forward, although they had been very near to coming out at the point where the river enters the estuary, and indeed many even of the Spaniards confessed to having heard the noise of the sea quite distinctly, so that it could not be very far from where they were. I cannot express what dismay I felt at finding myself so helpless and almost without hope of help, and with the thought that not one of us could escape from where we were but must die of hunger. I was in this perplexity when our Lord God, Whose providence always watches over and succours us in these necessities (and has especially preserved and succoured me, unworthy as I am, when busy in the royal service of your Majesty), our Lord, I say, sent hither a ship bound from the Islands little thinking to find me here, and bearing as many as forty men in addition to its crew, thirteen horses, some seventy pigs, twelve measures of salted meat and thirty loads of bread such as they reckon in the Islands. We all gave hearty thanks to our Lord who had succoured us in such necessity and I bought forthwith all the stores and the ship itself which cost me in all 4,000 *pesos*. I had already set all hands to fitting out the caravel which the Spaniards at Nito had allowed to fall almost to pieces and to building a brig from the remains of several which had been wrecked there so that by the time this ship came the caravel was already finished. But I think we should have been unable to finish the brig if the ship from the Islands had not come, for in it was a man who though not a carpenter by profession proved to have no small talent for it. In the meantime searching the surrounding country we found a path leading over some extremely rugged mountains to the township known as Leguela some eighteen leagues away, in which place plentiful provisions were found: but the road was too long and rough to make it possible to convey them to us.

From certain Indians who were captured there in Leguela I learned news of Naco, a town settled by Francisco de las Casas, Gil González de Avila and Cristóbal de Olid, where the last-named met his death (as I have reported to your Majesty and will recount at length), in particular of the Spaniards actually there, and the exact position of the town. I forthwith had a road pierced to it and sent thither a captain with all the people and horses. There remained with me only my own servants, the sick and certain persons desirous of returning with me over the sea. I gave the captain orders to make for Naco and endeavour to pacify the natives of the province, for it had remained in a state of disturbance since the arrival of the former captains there: he was then immediately to send on ten or twelve horsemen and as many bowmen to the Bay of San Andrés, some twenty leagues further on. I myself would put out to sea with the ships, taking on board all those who were remaining with me, and would make for the bay and port of San Andrés, where (if I arrived before them) I would await the men whom he was to send, and if after, they should wait there for me to hear what was to be done.

This expedition having set off and the brig finished, I was about to embark with the rest when I found that while we had sufficient stores of meat we had none of bread, and it was in the highest degree inexpedient to put to sea under such conditions with so many sick. For should we be detained by bad weather so far from bettering our conditions we should be like to perish all of hunger. In this quandary the captain

330

of the survivors told me that when they had first come there with Gil González they numbered some two hundred men with a good brig and four smaller ships in all; in the brig and the ships' boats they had ventured up the great river where they had found two huge lakes both fresh and surrounded by many townships and buildings; they had gone as far as the end of the lakes, which was some thirteen leagues up the river; the river then narrowed and became so rapid that in six days they did not succeed in advancing more than four leagues; it remained, however, quite soundable, and they had not been able to discover the secret of it. He was persuaded that there were plentiful supplies of maize to be obtained there, but confessed that I had few men for the purpose since on their expedition there had been eighty Spaniards who had fallen upon one township and taken it by surprise: later, however, the natives had joined together and fought against them, finally forcing them to take to their ships, and had wounded not a few of them.

I, seeing the extreme case we were in and that it was more dangerous to put to sea without provisions than to go and seek them on land, put aside all other considerations and determined to ascend the river. For apart from the fact that we could do no other than seek provisions for those wretched men, it might be that our Lord God would be pleased to discover to us some secret which might redound to your Majesty's service. I accordingly set to count the men fit to accompany me and found about forty Spaniards, some far from nimble, but all capable of guarding the ships after I had landed. With these therefore and some fifty Mexicans I put to sea in the brig, two ships and four native boats, leaving in the town an official dispenser of my own charged with portioning out the food to the sick who remained there. In this fashion I proceeded up the river with no little difficulty on

331

account of the great rapidity of the current, and after two nights and a day reached the first of the two gulfs some three leagues from the mouth. This gulf must be about twelve leagues long and has not so much as a single village on its shores on account of their being exceedingly marshy. I spent the whole day sailing across this lake before coming to where the river narrowed again; I continued to ascend it and arrived at the second lake on the following morning. It was the most beautiful sight in the world to come upon this inland sea surrounded by exceptionally steep and rocky mountains and spreading some thirty leagues from side to side. I proceeded to skirt one shore until nearly nightfall when I came upon an inlet and some two-thirds of a league further on a village, where, it appeared, we had been perceived, for everything was deserted and abandoned. We found there a great quantity of green maize in the fields which we ate that night, and the next morning seeing that we could not provide ourselves there with what we sought we loaded ourselves up with the maize to eat on our journey and returned to the boats without either meeting or so much as seeing any natives. I then crossed to the other side of the lake, which crossing took some little time, for it was only accomplished with difficulty and the loss of one canoe, whose occupants, however, were saved by one of the larger boats with the exception of one Indian who was drowned. We drew near the shore at about nightfall and had to wait till the morning to land, when with the smaller boats and canoes we advanced up the small river, leaving the brig at its entrance. I here alighted upon a track and landed with thirty men and all the Indians, ordering the boats and canoes to return to the brig. I followed up the path and after about a quarter of a league came upon a village which had been apparently deserted for many days, for the houses were overgrown with grass, though there were good orchards containing bread-fruit and other trees. I explored the village to see whether there were any roads leading anywhere from it and found one very much overgrown which seemed as if it had not been used for a long time. Finding none other, however, I proceeded by it and covered that day five leagues over mountainous country, so rough that the greater part of it we traversed on our hands and knees. On the way we came upon a maize plantation where three women and a man, doubtless the owners of the plot, were captured in a little hut. These guided us to other such holdings where two more women were captured, who showed us the road leading to a large farm with as many as forty little huts in the middle of it apparently but newly made. Our arrival, it seemed, had been perceived, and all the people had fled into the hills, but as they fled hurriedly they had been unable to take all their goods and consequently left us certain of them, in particular, fowls, ducks, partridges and pheasants, which they kept in cages, but of dry maize or of salt we found none whatever. I camped there that night and we somewhat appeased our hunger with some green maize which we found and ate with the flesh of the birds. We had not been above two hours in the village when two of its Indian inhabitants approached, very unprepared to find such visitors in their houses, and were captured by the sentries I had posted. On being asked whether they knew of any township nearby they answered " Yes," and that they would guide us thither on the morrow, but that it would take almost the whole day to get there.

We set out accordingly next morning with the guide who led us by a road even worse than that of the day before, for in addition to being no whit less rough every two hundred yards or so we had to cross a river. All the rivers of this district flow down into the lake, the various streams joining to form these lakes and marshes; this also explains the great violence with which the river takes its course towards the sea, as I have already described to your Majesty. Proceeding on our way after this manner we journeyed seven leagues without coming to any township, crossing forty-five large rivers and numberless smaller streams. Three women were captured coming from the town whither we were bound and loaded with maize. They assured us that the guide was not deceiving us. Finally when the sun was well-nigh set we heard certain noises of people and on my asking the women what this signified, they replied that it was the sound of a certain festival which they were accustomed to hold that day. On this I hid my men in the mountains as silently and secretly as I could, and placed spies some almost on the outskirts of the town and others in the road with orders to capture any Indian who might pass. In this fashion I remained all that night with a most excellent supply of water but the most evil plague of mosquitoes, and indeed what with the mountainous ground, the road, and the darkness and roughness of the night, I was more than once tempted to leave our position and fall upon the town, yet at no time did I succeed in making out for certain the position of the road, although we were so near the village that we could almost hear the natives talking within it.

Thus I was forced to wait for dawn, at which time we came on them so early that we took them all sleeping. I had given orders that no one should enter a hut or raise a shout, but we were to surround the largest of them, especially that of the local chieftain and a large barn-like structure where, so the guides had informed us, all the warriors slept. Our good fortune was such that this building was indeed the very first we came upon, and as it was now growing light and things could be plainly distinguished, one of my company seeing so many men and arms took it into his head to call out for help seeing that we were few and the enemy as it seemed to him very numerous, although asleep. Accordingly he began to cry out at the top of his voice " Santiago, Santiago:" at which the Indians awoke and some succeeded in snatching up their arms and others not: and as the house in which they were had no walls of any kind (the roof being supported on stakes), they leapt out on whatever side they liked, since we were unable to surround it completely. But I can assure your Majesty that if the fellow had not cried out every single Indian would have been taken prisoner, which had been the most excellent piece of strategy that was ever seen in these parts, and might even have resulted in a general pacification; for I could then have freed them, acquainted them with the object of my visit, and thus reassured them, seeing we did them no harm but rather let them go free after having captured them, and thus much good fruit might have been reaped: instead the contrary occurred. We captured some fifteen men and as many as twenty women, and ten or a dozen others who refused to give themselves up were killed, among whom was the chief, although he was not known as such until our prisoners pointed him out.

We found as little provision that would be of service to us in this village as in the other: there was green maize, but we were not seeking for that. I remained two days here to rest my men and enquired from our Indian prisoners whether they knew of any township where we could obtain stores of dry maize. They answered yes and that its name was Chacujal, a very large and ancient town, well supplied with every kind of provisions. After resting two days, accordingly, I set out again guided by the Indians towards the town of which they spoke, and that day we covered six good leagues, the road still being bad and intersected by numerous rivers. We then came to certain very large farms which, said the guide, belonged to the town which we were seeking. We passed by them for quite two leagues keeping to the woods so as not to be perceived, and in this fashion eight natives were captured, either woodmen and other labourers or men who had come to hunt, and quite unsuspiciously fell in with us; but as I always had outriders posted they were all taken prisoner, not one escaping. The sun was about to set and the guides bade me halt as we were now near the town. I halted accordingly and remained in the wood until about the third hour of the night. I then set out and came upon a river which we crossed breast high and which ran so fiercely that there was no small danger in crossing it, but clinging hold one to another we passed it in safety. The guides now told me that the town was hard by. I accordingly halted all my men and went forward with two companies until we could see the first houses on the outskirts of the town. We could even hear the natives talking and it seemed to me that they were undisturbed and knew nothing of our presence. I returned to my men and gave orders that they were to rest, at the same time posting six sentries on either side of the road to watch the town: this done I returned to rest with my company. I had just laid myself down on some straw when one of the sentries came in to tell me that he could see a large number of armed men coming along the track, talking and as if alarmed at our arrival. I went out to see the oncoming natives as quickly as I could. Now as the road from our position to the town was but short they soon fell in with my sentries at whom (so soon as they perceived them) they shot a volley of arrows, and sent back news to the town. In this fashion they continued retiring and fighting until we came to the entrance of the town, and as it was now dark they

almost immediately disappeared in the side streets.
I would not allow the men to lay aside their arms,
seeing that it was night and that as we had been perceived they might well be preparing some kind of
ambush for us. Keeping my company together I came
out on to a great square where they had their mosques
and temples, and the sight of these buildings after the
form and manner of Culua inspired us with a greater
fear than any we had felt till then, for since passing
Acalán we had seen none of such a fashion. Many of
my company were for leaving the town immediately
and crossing to the other side of the river before the
natives should have found out how few we were and
cut off that line of retreat. And in truth the counsel
was not wholly bad for in everything that we had seen
of the town there was cause to fear. In this manner
we stayed some long time all gathered together in the
great square, hearing no sound or stir from the natives,
and it seemed to me that we ought in no wise to leave
the town after that fashion; for perchance the Indians
seeing that we remained would be the more frightened
whereas seeing us retire they would realize our weakness, and so we should be in worse danger. And
so it pleased God to order it, for after remaining a very
long space in the square I gathered my men together
in one of the large buildings surrounding it and sent
certain of them to spy out the town to see if they could
perceive anything or hear any disturbance. But so
far from meeting with any such they entered many
of the houses, for all of them were lit up, and found
there great store of provisions with which they returned
very cheerful and contented, and so we passed the rest
of the night there keeping the best guard we could.
As soon as day came we examined the whole town which
was very well laid out, the houses close together and
stoutly built, and found there much cotton both spun
and unspun and clothes such as they wear, in good

condition, together with abundance of dry maize, *cacao*, kidney beans, pepper and salt, and many fowls and pheasants in cages, also partridges and the ducks which they breed for eating purposes and which are tasty enough, together with all kind of provisions: in such quantity, indeed, that had we had ships there and been able to load them I should have accounted myself well provided for many days; but to profit by them we had to bear them twenty leagues upon our backs, and we were in such plight unless we should rest there for some days that it would have been as much as we could do to make our way back to the ship without any other burden.

One of the Indians of the town who had been taken prisoner on an outlying farm during our advance appeared to be a man of some rank from his dress,— he was out hunting when captured and was carrying a bow and arrows,—and also from his person and upright bearing. I spoke to him through the interpreter who was with me bidding him seek out the ruler and people of that town and tell them for my part that I came to do them no harm but rather to speak with them on matters which greatly concerned them. If the ruler or any chieftain would come to me he should learn the cause of my visit, and they might be very certain that if they would come and hold speech with me much good would follow them and if not, much harm. I accordingly dispatched him with a letter, for many had been pacified by my letters in these parts, although it was against the wish of many of my company, who declared that it was not wise to send him, since it would show the natives how few we were, and the town was strong and well peopled as plainly appeared from the buildings it contained; it might be (said they) that the enemy learning how few we were would join with the people from other towns and come and attack us. I saw plainly that they had reason for

speaking thus.   But my desire to find some means of
provisioning ourselves and the belief that if this tribe
came in peace they would provide a means of carrying
the provisions, made me put aside all that might befall;
for in truth the danger that we ran of dying of hunger
if we failed to take back provisions was no less than
that which threatened us from the attack of the Indians.
I persisted therefore in sending off the Indian and
it was agreed that he should return the next day since
he knew where the ruler and all the people were.
But on the morrow when he should have returned, two
Spaniards riding on the outskirts of the town to survey
the country discovered the letter which I had given
him fixed on a stake in the road, from which we concluded for certain that we should get no reply.   And
so it was, for during the eighteen days we remained
resting in that town and seeking some way of removing the provisions neither that Indian nor any other
appeared.   Thinking on this matter it seemed to me
that it would be good to follow the river on which
the town stood down to see whether it flowed into the
main river and so on into the great lakes where I left
the boats, and on asking the Indian captives they
replied, yes, although they did not understand us well,
nor we them, since they are of a different language to
those we have hitherto seen.   Using signs and the
few words that I understood of their language I requested two of them to go with ten Spaniards and guide
them to where their river joined the main one, on which
they said that it was very near and that they would
return the same day.   And so it pleased God that
journeying through two leagues of very fine orchards
containing bread-fruit and other fruits, they came upon
the main river, which (said the guides) was that which
flowed down into the gulfs where the ships had been
left, and was called in their language Apolochic.
    I asked them how many days it would take by canoe

to reach the great lakes; they replied, five: and I immediately dispatched two Spaniards with one of the Indians as guide in case they should miss their way: the guide promised to conduct them as far as the brig. I ordered them to bring the brig, smaller boats and canoes up to the mouth of the great river, and endeavour with one canoe and a boat to come up-stream to the point where the smaller river joined it. On their departure I ordered four rafts to be made of stakes and exceptionally large reeds. Each one carried forty measures of maize and ten men, together with abundance of other stores such as kidney beans and red pepper and cocoa, which each of the Spaniards threw in for himself. The making of this took eight days, and by the time they were made and loaded the Spaniards who had been sent for the brig returned. They told me that they had begun to ascend the river six days before, but had been unable to bring the brig to where we were; they had left it some five leagues down-stream with ten Spaniards to guard it, and even with the canoe they had failed, being by that time very fatigued with rowing; the canoe, however, was now hidden but a league away. As they ascended the river a few Indians had attacked and fought with them, and they believed they would unite to oppose our passage. I sent men immediately to bring the canoe up to where the rafts were, and having placed in it all the provisions we had gathered, I ordered such men to take their places as we needed to guide us with long poles and thus keep the vessels clear of trees, which were not a little dangerous in the middle of the river. I appointed a captain for those that remained, ordering them to follow the road which we had taken, and to wait for us where we had originally landed, if they should arrive first: I would do the same if I should arrive there before them and would there take them on board. I myself embarked in the canoe accompanying the rafts, with but two crossbowmen, having none others. Thus although the journey was dangerous on account of the tremendous current and the fierceness of the river, since I held it certain that the Indians would attempt to ſtop us, I was desirous of accompanying them so as to observe all precautions.

Accordingly commending myself to God I set off down the river and we went with such speed that in three hours we came to the place where the ship was and even were desirous of transferring some of the load into her in order to lighten the rafts, but the current was so ſtrong that they could not ſtop. I myself got on board the boat and gave orders that the canoe well-manned with rowers should always keep ahead of the rafts in order to discover whether there were any Indians in canoes and give warning of any dangerous places. I remained in the rear with the boat, waiting until all the rafts had passed in order to be able to render assiſtance down-ſtream, should such prove necessary, for to do so up-ſtream would be impossible.

Juſt before sunset one of the rafts ſtruck a ſtake below the surface of the water which somewhat upset it, but the fury of the water righted it although not before it had loſt half its cargo. We continued our journey thus for three hours into the night when suddenly I heard in front a great shout from Indians, but unwilling to leave the rafts behind I did not row forward to see what it was, and after a little time it ceased and was heard no more. Again I heard it and this time, as it seemed, clearer, and again it ceased, without my being able to discover its cause, for the canoe and three of the rafts were now well ahead and I remained behind with the slower raft. We were proceeding now somewhat less on our guard for it was some time since we had heard any shouting and I had left the watch I was keeping to lie down, for the night was very hot, when suddenly we were caught in a furious whirlpool at a bend in the river which cast us, both raft and boat, on shore despite all our efforts. It was from there as it appeared that the shouting had come which we had heard. For the Indians, knowing the river (having been brought up on its banks) had spied on us throughout our journey and were well aware that the current would inevitably throw us on shore there. There were therefore many of them waiting for us at that spot, and as the canoe and rafts in front had grounded there before us, they had wounded nearly all the rowers with their arrows, although knowing that we were behind they did not attack them quite so furiously as they did us. The occupants of the canoe, moreover, had been unable to turn back and warn us on account of the strength of the current. As we touched land they raised a tremendous clamour and poured such a flight of arrows and stones into us that not one of us but was wounded, myself in the head, for it was the only place where I was unarmed. It pleased God that there should be in that place a great cleft and the river flowed exceptionally deep by reason of which we were not taken prisoner, for several of the natives attempting to leap on to the rafts and boat to engage us found themselves in sore plight, it being so dark that they fell into the water and I think but a few escaped. We were so swiftly borne away from them by the current that in a very short space of time we could hardly hear their yells. So we continued almost the whole of the night having no other meeting with the natives save a few shouts from canoes which kept far off and others from the banks of the river. For it is inhabited on both sides with very fine plantations of cocoa and other trees. When dawn came we were about five leagues from the mouth of the river which flows into the lake where the brig was awaiting us, and about noon we reached the lake itself; so that in one whole day and night we had journeyed no less than twenty leagues down the river.

On beginning to unload the rafts and transfer their contents to the brig, however, we found that the greater part of the maize was wet; and seeing that unless it were dried all would be loſt and our labour vain (and knowing moreover that there was no other place where provisions might be sought), I gave inſtructions to set apart all the dry which I ordered to be placed in the brig, and the wet was caſt into the two boats and two canoes, which I dispatched to the town with all haſte that they could to dry their load, since there was no place on all the shore of the lake where it could be dried on account of the floods. They departed forthwith, and I ordered them further to return with the boats and canoes to assiſt in transporting the men, for which the brig and one canoe remaining did not suffice. On their departure I also set sail and came to the place where I was to meet the party coming by land. At the end of three days they arrived all in good health and spirits, with the exception of one Spaniard whom they said had eaten of certain shrubs growing by the way and had died almoſt at once. They brought an Indian with them, captured in the town where I left them, who had ventured carelessly into the open, and since he differed from the other natives both in speech and dress, I enquired of him by signs and by means of another captive who underſtood his language, who he was, on which he revealed that he was a native of Teculutlan : and on hearing the name of this town pronounced it seemed to me that I had heard it several times before. Since then I have consulted certain memoranda which I had by me, and discovered that in very truth I had heard it, and that from where I was across to the Southern Sea where Pedro de Albarado is, cannot be more than some seventy or eighty leagues. For I found from my memoranda that several Spaniards of Albarado's company had been in that town of Teculutlan, and this the Indian confirmed, and I rejoiced greatly to hear of the short distance which separated us.

My men were now all come up, and seeing that the ships did not return and we were exhausting the small remnant of our provisions which had remained dry, we all embarked in the brig though not without difficulty since it was too small to contain us, and intended to cross to the town where we had first landed and whose maize fields we had left soaked through with hail; but seeing that twenty-five days had now elapsed we quite thought to find much of it dry enough to be of use; we accordingly set sail and half-way across the lake sighted our boats returning so that we joined forces and proceeded together. Immediately on landing, the whole company, Spaniards, Indian allies and even the Indian prisoners made straight for the town, and found the maize fields in very good condition, a large quantity of it being dry and no one to hinder our taking it. Christians and Indians joined that day to make three roads, for the fields were close to the shore. In this way I loaded up the brig and boats and proceeded straight to Nito, leaving all my men carrying the maize; I then sent them back two of the boats and another from a vessel bound for New Spain which had foundered on the coast, and also four canoes, in which all the company returned bringing great quantities of maize. This success was worth all the labour it cost, for without it we must have perished of hunger without hope of succour.

I forthwith loaded up the ships with all our provisions and set sail [25] for the port of San Andrés with all the original settlers under Gil González who had remained with me. I anchored at a point some distance along the coast and put on shore all those who could walk together with a couple of horses, with

inſtruﬆions to make for San Andrés by land where
they were to meet or await the party from Naco, for
they had already passed along that road once, and there
was no slight danger in our proceeding with so many
on board for we were very low in the water. I sent
a boat to accompany them along the coaﬆ and assiﬆ
them across the rivers in their way. I myself arrived
at San Andrés to find that the party from Naco had
preceded me by two days. From them I learnt that
all the reﬆ were well and had abundance of maize,
pepper and native fruits, but neither meat nor salt,
which for two months now they had had to do entirely
without.

I remained at San Andrés twenty days seeking to
reﬆore order in the affairs of the settlers left at Naco
and trying to find a suitable place to settle a town close
to this port, for it is the beﬆ yet discovered on the
whole coaﬆ of Tierra-Firme, or I might say, from
Las Perlas to Florida.[26] It pleased God that I should
find what I sought in a very convenient and good
position: I immediately ordered fresh water springs
to be searched for, and in a very short space of time
at a diﬆance of one and two leagues respeﬆively from
the town, good samples of gold were found. On this
account and seeing that the harbour was so fair and
the surrounding country so prosperous and well
peopled it seemed to me that your Majeﬆy would be
well served by such a settlement, and I forthwith
sent to Naco where the remainder of the settlers were,
to enquire whether any of them were willing to remain
here as citizens: and as the land is fruitful, about fifty
decided to do so, including some (indeed they were
in the majority) of those who had come with me from
Mexico. Accordingly I founded a town there in your
Majeﬆy's name which, since we ﬆarted to clear the
ground for it on the Nativity of Our Lady, I called by
that name (*Natividad de Nueﬆra Señora*), and appointed

alcaldes and *regidores* ; I also left priests provided with church ornaments and all things necessary for the celebration of mass, and in addition officials of a mechanical kind, a blacksmith with an excellent forge, a carpenter, a shipwright, a barber and a tailor; twenty mounted men and several bowmen were included in this company, and they were left in addition a certain number of guns and some powder.

Immediately on arriving at San Andrés I had learnt from the Spaniards who had come from Naco that the natives both of that town and others nearby had rebelled and left their houses for the woods and hills, nor would they be reassured, though I had speech with a few of them, on account of the sufferings they had received at the hands of those who had accompanied Gil González and Cristóbal de Olid. I accordingly wrote to the captain in command at Naco bidding him do all in his power to capture certain of the natives by whatever means and send them to me that I might speak with them and reassure them. This he did, sending me certain of them whom he took in a sudden attack, whom I spoke to and reassured greatly, bidding them also have speech with the chiefs I had brought with me from Mexico, who informed them who I was and what I had done in their country, the good treatment that they had all received from me since they had become my friends, how they themselves, their property, wives and children were upheld in their rights, and how grievously those were treated who rebelled against the service of your Majesty, together with many other things which pacified them not a little. Yet (they told me) they still feared that what these people said was false, for the former captains who had visited them had promised them the same things and more, and had then broken their promise, carrying off the women to make bread and the men to carry loads, and they feared that I would do the

same: yet seeing how those from Mexico were treated
and after speaking with the interpreter whom I had
with me they became somewhat more reassured, upon
which I sent them to speak with the rulers and peoples
of the other towns. A very few days later the Spanish
captain wrote to me that several of the neighbouring
towns had already come in peaceably, particularly
the largest of them, which are Naco itself (where the
Spaniards are), Quimiotlan, Sula and Tholoma, the
smallest of which is two thousand houses, and exclusive
of a number of villages which each town holds subject.
The towns assured him that the whole land would now
soon be quiet, since they had sent messengers abroad
informing the natives of the fact that I was in the land
and of all that they had heard from the natives of Mexico.
They earnestly desired that I would visit that part,
for seeing me the natives would be much reassured:
the which I would have done very willingly had it
not been necessary for me to pass to another matter
which I shall now report to your Majesty.

On my first arrival at Nito, Invincible Cæsar,
where I found the settlers abandoned by Gil González,
I learnt from them that Francisco de las Casas whom
I had sent to bring back news of Cristóbal de Olid,
as I have already informed your Majesty, had left
certain Spaniards some seventy leagues along the coast
at the port of Honduras, as the pilots call it, where
they had definitely settled. On coming to San Andrés
and while busy there in matters concerning both the
town of *Nuestra Señora* and the affairs of Naco I sent
a ship that I bought there to visit the port of Honduras
and bring me news of the party there. It now returned
with the *procurator* and one *regidor* of the town on
board who begged me to visit and assist them for they
were in great need. The captain and the *alcalde*
appointed by Francisco de las Casas had decamped with
a ship and fifty men out of the 110 of their party and

had taken moreover arms, armour and all that they had from those who remained, so that they feared each day that the Indians would attack and kill them, or that they would die of hunger from being unable to go abroad and seek provisions. Accordingly, to remedy this matter I again embarked in my ships with all the sick except those who were now dead, and so bore them thither and then on to the Islands and to New Spain. I took also certain of my private servants and ordered twenty horsemen and ten bowmen to proceed by the road which I knew was a good one, although there were several rivers to be crossed. We were five days at sea on account of rough weather. Finally, casting anchor in the port of Honduras I leapt into a small boat with two Franciscan friars, who have ever accompanied me, and about ten of my own servants, and so made for the shore. Already all the people of the town were gathered together on the water-front awaiting me, and as I approached the shore, they trooped into the water, lifted me out of the boat and bore me to the land, showing great joy at my arrival, after which we went towards the town and the church that they had there. Having given thanks to God they begged me to be seated, being desirous of giving me an account of all that had passed, for they feared that I was displeased with them on account of some evil report made to me, and they desired me to know the truth before judging them by that. I did as they bid me, upon which a clerk stood forward and proceeded to give me the following account:

" Señor, you are already aware in what manner all or most of us present were sent by you from New Spain with Cristóbal de Olid, your Captain, to settle these parts in his Majesty's name, being ordered by you to obey the said Cristóbal de Olid in everything he should command us, as we should yourself, and so we set sail with him for Cuba to finish taking on board certain provisions and horses which we needed. There, on arriving at the port of Habana he exchanged letters with Diego Velázquez and his Majesty's officials residing in that island, who sent him a number of men, and after being very completely supplied with all that we needed by your servant Alonso de Contreras, we again set sail and continued our voyage. Omitting incidents that befell us on the way which would be long to tell, I will simply say that we arrived at this coast fourteen leagues east of the port of Caballos and landed. Cristóbal de Olid immediately took possession of it in the name of your Honour and there founded a town under the government of the *alcaldes* and *regidores* who came with him. He made certain decrees touching both the holding of property and the peopling of the town, all in your Honour's name and as your Captain and lieutenant, and then some few days later joined with certain followers of Diego Velázquez who accompanied him from Cuba, and thereupon issued certain edicts in which he showed himself plainly disobedient to your Honour. And although all or the most of us thought it ill done we dared not dispute it since he threatened us with the gallows. Accordingly so far from opposing him we consented to all he wished, including even certain followers and relatives of your Honour who dared do no otherwise. After this, knowing that certain of González de Avila's men were making for where he was (this he learnt from six messengers whom he captured), he took up a position close to a ford in a river which they would have to pass, in order to take them prisoner and so remained there some days on the watch for them. But as they did not come he left a captain on guard there and himself returned to the town where he set to fitting out two caravels, loading them with many guns and much powder in order to go and attack a town lying on the coast to the east which Gil González had founded. While he was preparing for his departure Francisco de las Casas arrived with two ships: and as soon as he knew who it was he ordered the guns in the ships to fire on him. Moreover, although las Casas hoisted the flag of peace and showed that he was come from your Honour, yet he ordered his men not to cease firing, and fired yet another ten or twelve shots at him, one of which passed clean through the ribs of the ship. Las Casas, perceiving now his evil intentions and seeing that his suspicions of him were but too well founded, ordered his men into the long boats, returned the fire of his enemy, and finally took the two ships that were lying in the port, with all the guns in them. The adventurers fled to the shore and Olid now began to attempt to treat with him, not intending to come to any agreement, but simply to delay him until the men whom he had left on the look-out for Gil González should return; he thought he would be able in this way to deceive las Casas. The latter, indeed, willingly carried out all that was suggested, and began treating with him without concluding anything until a severe storm broke out: and as there was no real harbour there but only the bare coast, las Casas' ship was driven on shore, some thirty men were drowned, and everything on board was lost. He and his men escaped with their lives, but were so rudely handled by the sea that they could not defend themselves and were all taken prisoner by Olid, being forced before they entered the town to swear upon the gospel that they would obey him as their Captain and would never turn against him. At this moment news arrived from his lieutenant saying that he had taken fifty-seven men commanded by an *alcalde mayor* of Gil González and had then released them, the two parties separating and going off in different directions. He was greatly angered at this and forthwith travelled inland to Naco where he had been before, taking with him Francisco de las Casas and some of the others whom he had captured, and leaving the rest in the port of Honduras in the charge of his lieutenant, who acted as *alcalde*.

" Many times las Casas asked him in the presence of all to allow him to go where your Honour was to give him an account of what had passed, and warned him that if he would not grant him this he had better guard him well and put no trust in him, but Olid would never give him such permission. A few days later he learnt that Gil González de Avila was at the port of Tholoma with a few men, and immediately sent a small party there who fell upon them by night and captured all, bringing them back as prisoners to Naco. There he kept both Captains for many days, refusing to free them although many times they begged him to do so, and made González's men swear that they would recognize him as Captain just as he had done to all those of las Casas. Time and again after the capture of Gil González, las Casas requested him either to free them or to guard them with especial care, for they were determined to kill him, but he would never consent. Finally since his tyranny was now well known to all, one night when the three of them were talking of certain matters in a room with many others present, las Casas seized him by the beard and stabbed him with a paper-knife, with which he was in the act of cutting his nails, for he had no other weapon, crying out at the same time: ' We have suffered this tyrant long enough.' Gil González and others of your Honour's servants immediately leapt forward, disarmed his bodyguard and inflicted other wounds upon him. The captain of the guard, the ensign and the lieutenant were taken prisoner in a moment, no man being killed, and Cristóbal de Olid in the uproar escaped into hiding. In two hours las Casas and González had restored order among the people, imprisoned the chief of their opponents and published a declaration to the effect that anyone who knew of Olid's whereabouts was to inform them under pain of death. It was not long before they found out his hiding-place and imprisoned him under a strong guard. The next morning he was tried and both Captains jointly sentenced him to death, the which sentence was carried out on his person and his head was struck off. From that time the people lived in great content and freedom.

" A proclamation was now made bidding all decide whether they would stay and settle in the land or accompany las Casas and Gil González elsewhere to that part in which your Honour was, upon which it was found that 110 were willing to settle and the remainder, among whom were 20 mounted men, decided to go on further: to this party all we belonged who are in this city. Francisco de las Casas then gave us all we needed, appointed a Captain, and ordered us to make for this coast and to settle there on your Honour's behalf and in his Majesty's name, appointing *alcaldes*, *regidores*, notary, and *procurator* of the town council and an *alguacil*, and ordering the town to be called Trujillo. He promised that he would get your Honour within a very short space of time to provide us with all things necessary to pacify the land and gave us two interpreters, an Indian girl and a Christian. So we set out and coming to the port of San Andrés, which is de Caballos, we found there a ship from the Islands. The port appeared to us ill suited for settling and we had heard of this one. Accordingly the Captain went on board with forty men and all the stores, leaving the rest of us (including all the horsemen) on land, and carrying but a single shirt to our backs in order that we might go more lightly and with less encumbrance should anything befall us on the way. The Captain gave over his powers to one of the *alcaldes*, who is even now still with us, and to whom he bade us owe obedience in his absence, for the other *alcalde* was accompanying him in the ship. In this manner we separated, intending to join one another again at this port. We had certain encounters with the natives on the road, in which two Spaniards and certain Indian carriers were killed. Finally we came near this port, worn out and our horses lacking shoes, yet light-hearted with the thought of finding the Captain before us with all our stores and arms, but on arriving we found nothing at all: and it was no slight blow to us to find ourselves lacking clothes, weapons and horse-shoes, all of which the Captain had gone off with in the ship, and so we remained in great perplexity not knowing what to do. At length we resolved to await help from your Honour which we held very certainly would come and forthwith founded our town, taking possession of the land on your Honour's behalf and in his Majesty's name, all being duly registered before the public notary in a decree which your Honour may see for himself.

"Five or six days later a ship was perceived at dawn anchored some two leagues out and on the constable rowing out to enquire who she might be, he informed us that her master was a certain Pedro Moreno, Bachelor,[27] of Hayti, who was come to these parts by order of the judges of that Island to settle certain matters as between Cristóbal de Olid and Gil González, and that he had great store of arms and provisions on board, all of which belonged to his Majesty.

"We were all very merry at this news and offered up many thanks to God believing that we were saved from our evil plight. Forthwith the *alcalde* with the *regidores* and a few citizens went out to request their help and acquaint them with our need. But as their rowing boat approached armed men were posted in the ship and not a single man was allowed to go on board. Finally after long discussion four or five were allowed to board without arms, who straightway informed them that we were settled there in his Majesty's name and of all the misfortunes that had befallen us, begging them that since what they carried belonged to his Majesty to furnish us with it, for not only would such be pleasing to his Majesty but we would bind ourselves to repay all that should be given us. The master replied that he had not come hither to bring us supplies and he would give us nothing of what he carried save in exchange for gold or native slaves.

"There were two merchants in the ship and a certain Gaspar Troche from the Island of San Juan,[28] who urged him to give us what we asked and offered themselves as security up to five or six thousand *castellanos* to be paid at any time he should agree upon; and he was well aware that they were solid for this amount and were willing to advance it because they believed it to be in his Majesty's interests, holding it also for very certain that your Honour would repay them as well as thank them, yet still Pedro Moreno refused to grant us anything whatsoever: he merely bade us depart in peace for he himself was eager to set sail. On this he forced us to leave the ship being abetted by one Juan Ruano who had been the principal mover in Cristóbal de Olid's treachery towards your Honour. This man took the *alcalde*, *regidores*, and some others of us aside and told us that if we would do what he counselled he would make Moreno give us everything we needed and would even so arrange matters with the judges in Hayti that we should not have to pay for what was given us; he himself would return to Hayti and see to it that the judges should furnish us with men, horses, provisions and all other necessities, with which Moreno would very swiftly return together with authority from the judges to be our Captain. As to what we had to do, he explained, before anything else was to replace the royal officials, the *alcalde, regidores, tesorero, contador* and *veedor*, who had been appointed in his Majesty's name, and request Moreno to appoint Juan Ruano as our Captain, seeing that we wished to owe allegiance to the judges in Hayti and not to your Honour. We were all to make this request and swear to obey the said Juan Ruano as our Captain, while if any decree or men arrived from your Honour we were not to obey them, and should even resist them with arms if any attempt to infringe our liberty were made. We replied that it was impossible; we had sworn otherwise and were settled there in the Emperor's name, owing allegiance to your Honour in his name as our Captain and Governor, and we would not go back on this. Juan Ruano again urged that we should decide on this course or be left to die; for should we decide otherwise Moreno would not give us so much as a jug of water, and we might be very sure that so soon as he should learn that we were unwilling he would set sail and leave us thus to our fate; it would be well therefore for us to consider the matter deeply. We accordingly gathered together and by the sheer force of necessity decided to do what he wished and so escape death either by starvation or at the hands of the Indians, for we were unarmed. We informed him of this decision, upon which he put back to the ship and returned with Moreno who landed with a large number of armed men. Juan Ruano himself drew up the petition in which we requested that he should be made our Captain, and all or most of us signed it: the royal officials all resigned their offices and the name of the town was changed to that of Ascension: in addition certain proclamations were made declaring that we were settled in the name of the judges and not in that of your Honour. Then and only then he gave us what we asked for. He ordered an attack on the natives and captured certain of them whom he chained and carried off as slaves; but he refused to pay the royal fifth to his Majesty and ordered that there should be no special offices of *tesorero*, *contador*, and *veedor* to look after the royal rights, but that Juan Ruano as Captain should take all this business upon himself without any other check or account being made.

" In this fashion he departed, leaving Juan Ruano as Captain with a proclamation which he should cause to be read if any of your Honour's men visited this town, and promising to return in a very short time with such power that no one would be able to resist him. But after his departure, seeing that what had been done was far from agreeable to the service of his Majesty and was likely to stir up yet greater scandals than those we had seen already, we took the aforesaid Juan Ruano and sent him back to the Islands, upon which the *alcaldes* and *regidores* began to exercise their office as before; and so we have been and are still loyal to your Honour whom we serve in the name of his Majesty: and we beg, señor, that you will forgive those things which were done with Cristóbal de Olid, for both in that matter and in this latter one we were forced to act as we did."

I replied that I forgave them in your Majesty's name for those things which were done with Cristóbal de Olid, and that in this recent matter they were not to blame since their need had forced them to act as they had done, but that henceforward they must avoid such disturbances and scandals by which great disservice was done your Majesty, and for all of which they would be punished if any such should occur in future. And that they might the more certainly believe that I had wiped the memory of these past things from my mind and would in the future help and favour them in your Majesty's name so long as they bore themselves as loyal vassals, I confirmed those in their offices (such as *alcaldes* and the like) whom Francisco de las Casas in my name and acting as my lieutenant had appointed. With this they were very satisfied and not a little relieved that their crimes would not be brought up against them.

Hearing that Moreno was likely to return very shortly with decrees from the judges in Hayti I was unwilling to leave the port and venture inland. I was informed, however, by the Spaniards of certain native towns some six or seven leagues away with whom, they said, they had had a few encounters when seeking food, but many were of the opinion that if an interpreter could be found to make himself understood by them, they might be pacified, for they had given evidence by signs of good intentions: not that they had received good treatment from the Spaniards but the reverse, for Moreno had attacked them, taken numbers of women and boys prisoner, whom he had then chained and carried off with him as slaves. God knows what grief I felt on hearing of this for I know well the great harm that would follow such an action: and accordingly in the ships that I sent to the Islands I dispatched a letter to the judges setting down at length all that Moreno had done in this town and with the latter a warrant bidding them in your Majesty's name to send the said Moreno hither as a prisoner and under strong guard, together with all those natives whom he had carried away from this land as slaves: for this he had done in very deed against all law, as they might see from the evidence which I sent them. I know not what they will do in this matter, and will inform your Majesty of their reply when it comes to hand.

357

(Cortés succeeded by means of a native interpreter in getting into touch with the natives, in particular with those inhabiting the two towns of Chapagua and Papayeca, some seven leagues away from Trujillo. Their respective populations were as much as 8,000 and 10,000. Ambassadors came in, saying that they had hitherto feared to approach, thinking they would be carried away as slaves, and on this Cortés reassured them, declaring his own object in visiting their country and promising them peace and liberty if they would become the vassals of his Catholic Majesty. He concluded by giving them small presents with which they were very pleased and desired them to found a town on a lofty hill nearby. To this they agreed and within a few days some fifteen or sixteen other towns and villages sent in messengers to offer themselves as subjects and to assist in the work of building.)

During this time I dispatched the three ships which I had and one which afterwards came here and which I bought, putting on board all those of the sick who had remained alive. The first I sent to the ports of New Spain with a long letter to your Majesty's officials, whom I had left to take my place and to all the town councils telling them of all that I had done and the need that there was for my remaining yet some time further in these parts. I urged them strongly to fulfil that which I had left in their charge and gave them my counsel on certain necessary matters. I ordered these ships to call at the Island of Cozumel, which was on their way, and take off a number of Spaniards (as I had heard over seventy in number) whom one Valenzuela, a mutineer who had seized a ship and looted the town founded there by Cristóbal de Olid, had abandoned there.

The second ship which I had bought in Cuba I sent

to the town of Trinidad in Cuba to load up with meat, horses and men, and return as quickly as possible. The third I sent to Jamaica with like orders. The caravel or brig which I had made I sent to Hayti bearing a servant of mine on board with letters to your Majesty and the judges who reside in the capital there. As it afterwards appeared, however, not one of these ships reached its proper port. That sent to Trinidad touched land at Guaniguanico and the men had to go fifty leagues overland to Habana for their cargo. On the return of this ship (which was the first) they brought me news that the ship sent to New Spain had taken off the people from Cozumel but had then run ashore on Cape San Antonio at the western extremity of Cuba. There they had lost all their cargo, the captain, a cousin of mine, one Juan de Avalos, was drowned together with two Franciscan friars who had accompanied me from Mexico, and some thirty other persons who were taken as crew. Those who got to land had wandered over the mountains not knowing where they went and had for the most part died of hunger: so that out of over eighty persons not more than fifteen remained alive, and these finally arrived at the port of Guaniguanico where my other ship lay anchored. A merchant of Habana happened to have an estate there and with produce from this which was very abundant the ship was loaded. There the travellers who had thus succeeded in remaining alive reposed themselves. God knows the grief I felt at this loss; for over and above losing a relative and servants, together with many breastplates, muskets, crossbows and other arms which were on board the ship I was yet more grieved at the non-arrival of my dispatches on account of what I shall shortly relate to your Majesty.

The two ships bound for Jamaica and Hayti fetched port in Trinidad and there met with the licentiate

Alonso de Zuazo whom I had left as Chief Justice and a member of the council in charge of the government of New Spain. They found also a ship in that port which the Judges in Hayti were on the point of dispatching to New Spain to acquaint them with the news of my death. Hearing that I was alive the ship's captain changed her course, for he carried thirty-two horses, some harness, and certain stores which he thought to sell at a better price where I was. This ship also bore a letter from Alonso de Zuazo saying that there had been great disturbances and scandals in New Spain among your Majesty's officials; they had given me out as dead, proclaimed two of themselves as governors, and had themselves sworn as such. They had imprisoned Zuazo and the other two officials, as also Rodrigo de Paz whom I left in charge of my house and estate, which they had then proceeded to loot. They had removed Justices appointed by me and replaced them by others of their own making, and many other things had they done which, since your Majesty may read them in the original letter which I am sending, I do not set out here.

Your Majesty may well imagine the grief that I felt at this news, particularly to learn of the way in which they repaid my services, robbing me of my house as a reward for my deeds in Mexico, which had been ill done even if I had been dead indeed; for though they may say or insinuate that I owed your Majesty over 70,000 *pesos* of gold, yet they knew full well that I owed no such sum, but rather that over 150,000 *pesos* are owing to me, the which I have spent and well-spent in the service of your Majesty. I forthwith considered how best to remedy this. On the one hand it seemed to me that I ought to set sail in that ship immediately and punish such insubordination; for already all men here think when they are put in charge of some expedition that unless they make a great show of insolence they will not be regarded as people of any importance:

thus there is another captain whom the governor Pedro Arias sent out to Nicaragua who has likewise renounced his allegiance, as I shall elsewhere recount fully to your Majesty. On the other hand it grieved me to the heart to leave this land in the unsettled state in which it was, for it meant its total loss, and I am very certain that it is going to contribute much to your Majesty and prove a second Mexico. For I have reports of great and rich provinces governed by great lords with regal pomp, and especially one, Eneitapalan, or as some say Xucutaco, which I have known of these last six years, have pursued throughout this my last journey from Mexico, and will be bound it cannot be more than eighteen days' march, or, say, fifty to seventy leagues from Trujillo where we now are.

And of this province there is such great news that one may well marvel at what is told of it, of which if only a third be true it must greatly surpass Mexico in riches and equal it in the size of its towns, the multitude of its peoples, and the gentleness of their manners.

Being in this perplexity I bethought me that nothing can be well done or directed unless by the hand of the Mover and Doer of all things, and accordingly ordered masses to be said and processions and sacrifices to be made beseeching God to guide me in that path most pleasing to Him. After this had been done for several days I came to the conclusion that putting aside all else I ought to go and settle the disturbances in New Spain. Accordingly I left some thirty-five horsemen and fifty foot in Trujillo, under the command of a cousin of mine, one Hernando de Saavedra, brother of that Juan de Avalos who was drowned. Then after giving him certain instructions as best I could and having spoken with some of the native rulers I took ship with my household servants, sending orders at the same time to the people at Naco to proceed along the road which Francisco de las Casas had taken running along the southern coast, and so join forces with Pedro de Albarado.[29] I likewise sent instructions to the town of the *Natividad de Nuestra Señora*. We embarked in fine weather, with the ship riding at the stern anchor, but no sooner were we on board than a dead calm succeeded so that we could not put to sea. Early next morning news reached me on board ship that there were murmurings among the people in the town and they feared disturbances as soon as I was gone. On account of this and the calm I landed again, made investigations and by punishing certain of the ringleaders restored complete quiet. I remained two days on shore: on the third a wind sprang up, I embarked again and we set sail. But two leagues from where we set out in doubling a point the main mast broke and we were forced to put back into port to mend it. The job took three days and I then again set sail with a fair wind which bore us on our journey for two nights and a day, during which time we covered some fifteen leagues or more, but then a tremendous gale from the north met us, which snapped the main mast off at its base and forced us to return with great difficulty to port, where once arrived we all gave hearty thanks to God, for we had thought ourselves lost. And I and all my men were now so wearied and battered by the sea that we had need take some repose, until the weather improved and the ship was put to rights. Meantime, accordingly, I landed with all my men, and seeing that having thrice put to sea in fair weather I had each time been compelled to return, I considered that God was unwilling that this new land should be so abandoned, and, what added force to my conviction, a few of the Indians who had peaceably surrendered had risen, upon which I again commended the matter to God and ordered processions and masses to be made. I then resolved to send the ship (in which I had already ventured) to New Spain, and by it a proclamation giving all my powers to my cousin, Francisco de las Casas, together with letters to the town councils and your Majesty's officials rebuking their evil deeds. I also sent certain Indian chiefs who had come with me that the Mexicans might know that I was not dead, as had been published there, and so peace and order would be restored and an end put to the treachery which had been begun. I accordingly arranged matters in this way, but there were many things left unprovided for (which I should have provided had I been aware of the loss of the first ship which I had sent, and which I reckoned as certainly having arrived there many days since) particularly in the matter of dispatching ships to the southern sea.

(*Cortés was still suffering from the effects of his voyage and accordingly sent a lieutenant on an expedition inland. Operations were conducted peaceably and a number of further tribes came in to offer their allegiance. A slight revolt among the natives was put down and one of their chiefs executed which had a great effect on the rest.*

Francisco Hernández, one of Pedro Arias de Avila's captains, had been sent by him to explore Nicaragua. A detached party of his men reached Trujillo and was warned by Cortés against following the example of Moreno and betraying their allegiance to their own commander.

Shortly afterwards natives arrived from the province of Huilacho seventy-five leagues away with the news that a body of Spaniards some sixty strong at the head of a large number of Indians from neighbouring provinces was destroying their land, robbing them of their property and enslaving their women and children. Almost at the same time a message arrived from Gonzalvo de Sandoval, whom Cortés had left as his lieutenant in those parts, to say that the marauders were men belonging to Francisco Hernández under the captaincy of one Gabriel de Rojas. Cortés wrote vigorously both to his lieutenant and to Hernández and the latter withdrew his men but continued to stir up bad feeling with the natives.)

" I myself," says Cortés, " was eager to go to Nicaragua, believing myself able to set the matter aright, by which your Majesty would be greatly served. While still making preparations, in particular cutting a path through the pass in the mountains which is somewhat rough going, the ship which I had sent to New Spain arrived back at Trujillo, with a cousin of mine on board, a friar, Diego Altamirano, of the order of Saint Francis. From him and from the letters which he bore I learnt of the many scandals and disturbances which had taken place among the officials of your Majesty whom I had left in charge, and the urgent need of my presence to put an end to them. Accordingly my visit to Nicaragua and return along the southern coast had to be put off, though I think that it would have redounded greatly to the service of your Majesty on account of the many great provinces which I should have passed through. Some of them have already been pacified, but I think that my visit would have strengthened them in your Majesty's allegiance, especially those of Utlatan and Guatemala, where Albarado has been governor, but which ever since they rebelled on account of harsh treatment have never really settled down again. Rather they do and have done great hurt to the Spaniards and their Indian neighbours, for the land is wild and well populated and the people fierce and warlike; they have invented many methods of attack and defence, making pits and other traps to upset the horses of which they have killed many.

For although Albarado has never ceased to make

war on them and is still doing so with over two hundred horse and five hundred foot, and with anything from five to ten thousand Indian allies, nevertheless he has not yet succeeded in bringing them under your Majesty's yoke. On the contrary they fortify themselves more strongly and receive reinforcements from other tribes. Yet I think that if it pleased God that I should go there, I could bring them either by love or by other means to a better course; for there were several provinces which rebelled against harsh treatment during my absence and over 120 horse and 300 foot together with many guns and native allies under the command of the *veedor* (who was acting as governor at that time) went against them and could do nothing: indeed they lost some ten or a dozen Spaniards and many natives, and things remained in the same unsettled state. Yet on my arrival no sooner had I sent them a message acquainting them of my presence than the chiefs of the province, which is called Coatlan, came to me without the least delay, and informed me of the cause of the rising, for which indeed there was cause enough. For one of the Spaniards who had been given a *repartimiento* of natives had burnt eight chieftains so that five died at the stake and the three others within a few days. They had asked for justice in this matter but it was denied them. I placated them as best I could and they are now at peace and serving your Majesty as loyally as before I went there, without any danger of war or any other disturbance.

And so I think might have occurred with the other tribes which were in this unsettled condition in the province of Coazacoalco, for on learning of my visit to their land, even without receiving any messenger from me, they would have quietened down.

I have already informed your Majesty of certain small islands lying off the port of Honduras, known as the Guanajos,[30] several of which are now entirely depopulated, the natives having been taken off in ships as slaves to the Islands; others have still a few natives left. I learnt at this time that new fleets were putting out from Cuba and Jamaica to complete the work of destruction and despoliation. To avert this I sent a caravel to seek the fleet in the vicinity of the islands and require them on the part of your Majesty not to land on the said islands nor do any hurt to the natives, for I was intent upon pacifying them and bringing them to the service of your Majesty. I had already had some intelligence with them by means of those who had come over to live on the mainland of Tierra-Firme. The caravel fell in with one of the ships of the fleet whose captain was a certain Rodrigo de Merlo at the island of Huitila, whereupon my captain compelled him and all the natives whom he had taken off from the island to accompany him to Trujillo where I was. I immediately had the natives taken back to their homes, but did not proceed against the captain himself since he showed me a licence for what he had done granted by the Governor of Cuba in virtue of the powers which he holds from the judges resident in Hayti. I accordingly dismissed him and his men, their only loss being that of the natives whom they had captured on the islands, and the captain and most of those who came in his company remained as settlers in the town, the land liking them well.

The rulers of the islands learning of the good turn I had done them and hearing from those on the mainland of the good treatment they received, came to thank me for my kindness and to offer themselves as subjects and vassals of your Majesty, asking that I should command them in what they might serve him. I ordered them in your Majesty's name for the present to set to work tilling fresh ground, for in truth they can serve in naught else. So they departed taking for each island a decree from me to show to any persons who should land there, whereby I assured them in your Majesty's name that they should not receive hurt. They begged me to let them have one Spaniard to be on each island, which request owing to the closeness of my departure I could not provide for, but I left orders to my lieutenant, Hernando de Saavedra, to provide for it.

I now went aboard the ship which had brought me the news from New Spain, and some twenty of my own followers with their horses came on board this ship and two others. The greater number of them were remaining as settlers in the towns, and others were awaiting me on the road thinking that I was to travel by land. These I sent for telling them of my departure and the cause of it and they were soon on their way.

Having given final instructions to the towns which I left peopled in your Majesty's name, with no little grief and sickness of heart at being unable to leave them as I had hoped to do and as was fitting, I set sail with those three ships on April 25th, and had such fine weather that in four days we were come within 150 leagues of the port of Vera Cruz; but then we met such a storm that we could make no headway. Thinking that it would wear itself out we battled against it for a day and a night, but it was so strong that it tore away the sails and rigging of the ships and I was forced to make for Cuba where after six days I cast anchor in the port of Habana. There I landed and rejoiced greatly with the citizens of that town, for there were many among them who had been my friends when I lived on that island. The ships had been .somewhat battered by the storm and it was consequently necessary to repair them, which business occupied us there ten days; however, to shorten my journey I bought a ship which I came across in that port and left behind the one in which I had so far sailed, as she was leaking badly.

The very morning following my arrival at Habana, a ship arrived from New Spain, as did one on the next day and also the day following. From them I learnt that the land was restored entirely to peace and order after the death of the *factor* and *veedor* (*i.e.*, Salazar and Chirinos), although they admitted that there had been certain disturbances, but those responsible for them had been punished. I was greatly cheered by this, for I had been grieved at going so far out of my way and was not a little anxious. I forthwith wrote to your Majesty although quite briefly, and set sail again on May 16th, taking with me some thirty natives of Mexico who were being privily carried off in those ships. After eight days I arrived off Vera Cruz, but could not enter the harbour owing to contrary weather. Accordingly a little before nightfall I put in two leagues further up the coast and by means of a brig which I found derelict and the ship's boat I landed that same night and made my way on foot to the little town of Medellín some four leagues distant without being perceived by a soul. I went straight to the church and gave thanks to our Lord. The morrow was Sunday and the citizens were as rejoiced to see me as I to see them. That night I dispatched messengers both to the capital and all other towns informing them of my return and ordering certain matters which might further the service of your Majesty and the good of the land. I remained at Medellín for eleven days recovering from the toil of the journey, during which time many of the natives, both rulers and common people round about, came to visit me and express their delight at my return. Thence I set out for the capital and was fifteen days on the road, during the whole course of which I was met by vast numbers of the natives, many of whom had come over eighty leagues to see me, for they had posted relays of messengers to pass on the news of my coming which they were eagerly awaiting: so that in a very short time great numbers were gathered together from various and distant regions, and all wept on seeing me, describing the pains they had suffered in my absence and the harsh treatment that they had received with such burning and piteous words that they broke the hearts of all that heard them. It would be difficult to give your Majesty an account of all the things they told me, but there are some that I could find worthy of noting down, which nevertheless I refrain from doing, since they are not becoming *ex ore propio*.

On my arrival in the capital its inhabitants, both Spaniards and natives, and others from all the country round joined together and welcomed me with as much joy and merrymaking as if I had been their father.

Your Majesty's treasurer and *contador* came out to meet me with many horse and foot in parade order, displaying the same goodwill as did all the citizens. I went straight to the house and monastery of Saint Francis to render thanks to God for having brought me out of so many great dangers and hardships, into such a state of peace and rest, beholding the land which had been in such turmoil restored to such quietness and order. There I remained six days with the friars giving an account of my sins to God. When I had been there four days a messenger arrived from Medellín and told me that certain ships had cast anchor there, bearing, so they said, an examining judge (*pesquisidor*) of some kind by your Majesty's orders, which was all that he had been able to learn. I myself thought that your Majesty must have heard of the disturbances and rebellions into which your Majesty's officials to whom I entrusted the government had plunged the land and was desirous of settling the matter, at which God knows how much I rejoiced, since I was very anxious not to have to be the judge of this question. For since I was insulted and despoiled by those tyrants, it seemed to me that anything that I should do in the matter would be set down by evil-minded men to personal resentment, than which there is nothing I hate more, although in truth no actions of mine could exceed in severity what they had richly deserved by their crimes. Accordingly I dispatched in haste a messenger to the port to know the truth of the matter, and sent word to the lieutenant and justices of Medellín that no matter with what powers the judge arrived, since he came by command of your Majesty, he was to be well received and waited on and lodged in a house which I possess in the town, where I ordered that both he and all his followers should be served in every way, although, as it afterwards appeared, he was unwilling to accept this service.

The following day, that of Saint John, another messenger arrived in the midst of certain bull-fights, tournaments and the like, bringing me a letter from the judge and from your Sacred Majesty, by which I learnt who he was, and that your Catholic Majesty was pleased to order me to give an account of the government of this land during such time as your Majesty has been pleased to entrust me with it: at which, in truth, I rejoiced greatly, both for the kindness your Sacred Majesty did me in wishing to be informed of my services and faults as also for the benevolence with which your Majesty acquainted me of his royal desire and intent to grant me favours; for both of which things I kiss the feet of your Sacred Majesty a hundred thousand times, and pray God that He may deign so far to favour me that I may repay in some slight measure this immeasurable kindness and that your Majesty may know of my desire to serve you; for such recognition alone will be no slight reward for me.

In his letter Luis Ponce de Leon wrote that he was on the point of setting out for the capital; and since there are two main roads and I knew not from his letter which he proposed to take, I dispatched my servants along both of them to meet him and do him service and point out the lie of the land to him. But such was the haste with which Luis Ponce travelled that although I dispatched these men with all speed they met him but twenty leagues from the city. And although as they said, he showed himself much pleased at meeting with my men, yet was he unwilling to receive the least service from them. Thus, while it grieved me that he did not receive it, for, as I was told, by reason of his haste he was in need of it, yet I had also occasion to rejoice, in such as he appeared by this an upright man who desired to perform his office with all rectitude, and since he was coming to examine my dealings, was unwilling to give any ground for suspicion.

That night he arrived within two leagues of the town before retiring to sleep, and I ordered preparations to be made to receive him in the morning, but he sent asking me not to come out to him in the morning because he wished to remain where he was until dinner. He desired me to send him a priest to say mass, the which I did; but fearing his real intention, which was to avoid an official reception, I kept on my guard; yet even then he was so early that in spite of all my hurry he had already entered the town when I met him, and so we went together to the Monastery of San Francisco where we heard mass. This done, I requested him to present his papers of authority, if he were willing, since all the city council were gathered there with me, including your Majesty's treasurer and *contador*; but he was unwilling to do this, saying that he would put it off until another day. Accordingly on the morrow we all met together in the morning in the principal church of the town, the council, the aforementioned royal officials, and myself. He then presented his papers which were duly received by us, kissed, and placed on our heads as the decrees of our natural king and lord, and obeyed and carried out to the letter, according as your Majesty commanded us; at the same time the wands of justice were handed over to him. All other provisions were duly observed as your Majesty commanded in greater detail, all this taking place before the public notary. My *residencia*[31] was then publicly proclaimed in the city square, and for seventeen days I was busy with it, during which time not a single plaint was brought against me. Meanwhile, however, Luis Ponce fell ill and all those that had come with him, of which illness it pleased God that he should die, together with more than twenty others among whom were two friars of the order of Santo Domingo who accompanied him. Even today there are still many persons sick and in danger of death, so that it seems almost a kind of plague that they brought with them. It even attacked some of the citizens, two dying of it, and still there are many in the city who have not yet recovered.

As soon as Luis Ponce had passed from this life and been buried with such honour and pomp as befits a person sent by your Majesty, the council of the capital and the procurators of all the towns who were assembled here, begged and requested me on behalf of your Catholic Majesty to take upon myself again the burden of government and the administrating of justice, as I had up to that time according to your Majesty's royal command and authority. Many were the reasons they gave, many the inconveniences which, they said, would follow should I refuse to accept it, all of which your Majesty may see (as he asked to do) in the copy of them which I am sending. I excused myself from the office, as will also appear in the separate document, and since then they have made further requests of the like tenor and urged still more violent inconveniences that may follow if I do not accept. So far I have resisted all such proposals in spite of the fact that I have perceived certain inconveniences in my doing so, but I am desirous that your Majesty should be entirely convinced of my fealty and wholehearted desire to serve him, holding that as my principal object, since if your Majesty should have any other opinion of me, I should desire no goods or rewards in this world but rather to quit it altogether.

To this end I have put aside everything, nay, more, I have done everything I could to support Marcos de Aguilar in that office, who was the chief justice of the late Luis Ponce and accompanied him here; I have more than once asked and required him to proceed with the accounts of my governorship and complete them; but he has been unwilling to do so saying that he has no power to conclude such a matter, which grieved me not a little, since I desire above all things and not without cause that your Majesty should be truly informed of my services and faults; for I hold it certain (and not without reason) that knowing them your Majesty will grant me great and extensive favours, considering not how little my slight capacity may be capable of receiving but how much your Majesty is obliged to bestow on one who has served him as well and faithfully as I have done. I therefore beg your Majesty with all the earnestness of which I am capable not to allow this matter to remain in doubt, but to see that what is good and evil in my services to your Majesty be published openly and with all frankness. It is a matter in which honour is concerned, to gain which I have suffered great toils and exposed my person to a thousand dangers: may God not grant, nor your Majesty permit nor consent that the tongues of envious, evil and angry men should succeed in despoiling me of it. I neither wish nor beg your Majesty in reward of my services to grant me any other boon than this, without which God grant I may cease to live.

In my judgment, moſt catholic Prince, while I have had since firſt I concerned myself with this business, many, various and powerful rivals and enemies, yet their envy and malice have been unable to effeć anything which my notorious loyalty and services have not overborne; so that despairing of all other measures they have at laſt hit on two by which, it would seem, they have obscured the eyes of your Majeſty by some manner of cloud or falsehood, and so moved him from that godly and catholic intent which your Majeſty has ever displayed to requite and pay me for my services. One of those measures is to accuse me before your Majeſty of the crime of high treason (*crimine lesæ majeſtatis*), declaring that I have refused obedience to royal decrees and hold this land not in the might of your name but in a tyrannical and abominable manner, to which end they give base and diabolical reasons which are nothing more than false and idle conjećtures. Whereas, were they to regard my works themselves like unbiassed judges they would have to give a very different opinion. For up to this present there has not been, nor shall there be while I live, a single letter or other decree of your Majeſty addressed to me or brought to my notice which has not been and shall not be in the future duly obeyed and complied with by me down to the smalleſt detail. But of late the malice of those who have made such accusations has been more clearly and openly revealed, for were their accusations true I should never have journeyed six hundred leagues away from this city through an uninhabited land and by dangerous roads nor left the land in the charge of your Majeſty's officials, whom one might have thought the persons moſt likely to display the greateſt zeal in your Majeſty's service, although their aćtions were far from corresponding to the truſt I reposed in them.

The second accusation is that I have possessed myself

of all or nearly all the inhabitants of this land who serve me and by whom (they say) I have gathered together great store of silver and gold which I keep treasured up. They add that I have spent more than 70,000 gold *pesos* of your Majesty's revenue over and above what was necessary; also that I have not sent all the gold due to your Majesty's revenue, but have kept back some portion of it by certain subtle ways and means, whose working is beyond my power to fathom. But doubtless since they have heard the rumour they will have given some colour of truth to it, though for my part I confess that if any such malversation had taken place it would need no very minute observation to discover the fraud. As to their accusation that I possess a large part of the land, I admit that it is true and that no small quantity of gold has been had from it. But I maintain that such gold as has been obtained has not been sufficient to prevent my remaining a poor man and in debt to the tune of over 500,000 *pesos* of gold without so much as a *castellano* with which to pay it.[32] For if much has been received much more has been spent, and that not in buying lordships or other sources of income for myself but in extending your Majesty's dominions and property in these parts, conquering and winning over at the cost of such gold (as also at the cost of exposing my person to numberless toils, risks and perils) many kingdoms and lordships for your Majesty: which conquests cannot be hidden or glossed over by the serpent tongues of these evil men. For if my books be examined there will be found more than 30,000 *pesos* of my own fortune spent on these conquests; and it was only when what I had was spent that I used the 70,000 *pesos* of your Majesty, and even then not spending them myself nor taking possession of them but handing them over to others to defray expenses of conquest: that they were profitably used is abun-

dantly clear from the results. As to their accusation
that I have not sent your Majesty's revenues, it is
manifestly false, since during this short time that I have
been in this land, I believe, and it is the truth, that
more treasure has been sent from here to your Majesty
than from the Islands and the mainland during the
whole of the thirty odd years since they were discovered and settled, be it noted, at great expense to
your Majesty's ancestors, the Catholic Kings. There
has been no expense here; and not only has that portion
belonging to your Majesty's revenue been duly sent but
also some portion of what belonged to myself and those
who helped me, excepting those sums which we spent
in the royal service. For with my very first letter
to your Majesty by the hands of Alonso Hernández
Portocarrero and Francisco de Montejo I sent not
merely the fifth due to your Majesty but all that we
had so far obtained, which seemed to me right as being
the firstfruits of the conquest. Then during Muteczuma's lifetime all the gold that was obtained in the
capital was melted down and a fifth sent to your
Majesty, which amounted to over 30,000 *castellanos*;
and although the jewels would also normally have
been divided up, each man receiving his share, yet
both they and I gladly decided not to distribute them
but to send them all to your Majesty, to the value of
over 500,000 *pesos*. Both the gold and the jewels,
I admit, were lost, being taken from us by the enemy
when we were forced to leave the city as a result of the
rising provoked by Narváez's visit to this land; and
thus, while it were perhaps a reward for my sins, it
was not due to any negligence of mine. Moreover
when the capital was afterwards recaptured and reduced
to your Majesty's royal service I again settled that
after a fifth of the melted gold had been set aside for
your Majesty all the jewels should be sent with it,
which were of no less value than those we formerly

possessed, and to this all my companions agreed. Accordingly I dispatched them with great haste and caution together with 30,000 *pesos* in golden ingots under the charge of Julian Alderete, then your Majesty's treasurer, but the French captured them. Yet again this was not my fault but the fault of those who failed to supply the convoy for them as far as the Azores, as they ought to have done for so valued a cargo.

Again when I left the capital for Honduras, 70,000 *pesos* were dispatched to your Majesty in the charge of Diego de Ocampo and Francisco de Montejo, and the only reason that more was not sent was that in my opinion, as also in that of your Majesty's officials, even to send so much was exceeding and contravening the provisions laid down by your Majesty for the shipping of gold from these parts; yet we were so bold as to send this sum on account of the need which we knew your Majesty had of it. And in this ship I also sent your Majesty by the hand of Diego de Loto, my servant, all that I had, retaining not so much as a *peso* for myself; my offering took the form of a silver cannon which, including the metal, casting and other expenses, cost me over 35,000 golden *pesos*. I likewise sent certain ornaments of gold and precious stones, not for their intrinsic value, though that was not inconsiderable for me, but because the French had captured those I had originally sent, and I was grieved that your Majesty should not have seen them, but now seeing a sample of them your Majesty might consider what the total amount had been like. Thus, since I have ever been eager to serve your Majesty loyally with what I had, I know not what reason there can be for thinking that I should retain anything that belongs to your Majesty. In addition the officials have informed me that in my absence they did not fail to dispatch a certain quantity of gold at every opportunity that they had.

(Finally, says Cortés, out of the 200 *separate estates from which he draws revenue in Mexico he is willing as a proof of his entire loyalty to hand over* 180 *to the Emperor, retaining only* 20 *for himself : he begs that all suspicion may be removed from his Majesty's mind and that he will grant him the opportunity of serving him at Court ; by which, he said,* " I think your Majesty will profit greatly, since as one who is first in information I shall be able to advise your Majesty of what I actually provided for and what is expedient to be done in your Majesty's service, so that he will run no risk of being misled by false reports." *Too often, Cortés adds, both on the Islands and on the mainland the annual revenue is diminished instead of increased solely on account of bad government and because those who advise the Emperor are zealous for their own particular interests, not the service of his Majesty. He has already done much in extending the royal dominions, conquering many provinces and noble towns and cities, stamping out idolatry and bringing many to the bosom of the Catholic faith, so much so indeed that in a short time one may expect to see arise in this new land a church, in which more than any other in the world God may be worshipped and glorified. If, however, concludes Cortés, the Emperor cannot grant him this favour of returning to Spain, he begs at least that he will grant him suitable provision in Mexico for himself and his heirs that he may not find himself forced on arriving in Spain to beg for bread. He adds a brief outline of his plans for further exploration.*

There are three ships at Zacatula prepared to examine the Southern Sea for spice islands and find if possible the long-sought strait communicating with the Atlantic. Another expedition is being sent by land and sea to settle the Tabasco river. Three captains are also being dispatched to the province of the warlike Zaputecans to subdue them; for not only have they been disturbing their peaceful neighbours but within their territory are the richest mines in all New Spain. Another expedition is going north to the las Palmas river in the direction of Florida. Between the province of Mechuacan and the sea to the north are the Chichimecas, a savage tribe; a small army is being sent against them. The captain has orders " if he find any aptitude or capacity in them to live as the other native inhabitants, accept the Catholic faith, and acknowledge the service they owe to his Majesty, he is to pacify them and bring them under his Majesty's yoke, establishing a settlement there in whatever part seem to him best; but if he find no such signs, but rather that they are unwilling to be obedient, he is to make war on them and take them as slaves, that there may be no useless tribes in the land nor such as do not recognize and serve his Majesty, and by enslaving these tribes, who are indeed almost savages, his Majesty will be served and the Spaniards profited not a little, for they can dig gold from the mines, and it may be that merely by coming into contact with us some of them will become civilized." *Finally, the captain who had been dispatched some two months before Cortés left the capital for Honduras to the town of Coliman, over a hundred leagues away on the Southern Sea, had just returned, having proceeded a hundred and thirty leagues further down the coast as ordered. He brought news of many tribes, some peaceful, some warlike, great cities, and a river so large that it might well be the strait for which they were seeking. Cortés accordingly sent him back with fresh troops and munitions to explore further. He then proceeds:)*

379

The captains of all these expeditions are prepared to depart almost all at once. May it please God to guide them, for though I lose your Majesty's favour I cannot cease from serving him, for it is impossible but that in time your Majesty will come to recognize my services; and even though this time never come, yet I am satisfied in doing my duty and in the knowledge that I hold myself in debt to no man while my services and loyalty are well known to all with whom I deal. I desire no other estate to bequeath to my sons than this.

Invincible Cæsar, our Lord God preserve the life and expand the kingdom of your Sacred Majesty for many days to come, as your Majesty desires.

From this city of Tenochtitlan, the 3rd of September 1526.

HERNAN CORTÉS.

NOTES

[1] *Page* 1. *Yucatán:* The earliest Spanish discoverers (Gomara recounts) enquired the name of the land, upon which the natives answered them (not knowing the language) " Yucatán " (*i.e.*, " I do not understand ").

[2] *Page* 3. The office of *alcalde* (from the Arabic *al-cadi*, the judge) corresponded in many ways to that of an English mayor. He was president of the municipal council, and was responsible for the carrying out of its decisions. The good order, cleanliness and health of the district were his concern. To this end the local police and all other municipal officers were under his supervision. The *alcalde* also acted as a magistrate,—the local justice of the peace,—and within his jurisdiction had power of life or death.

[3] *Page* 14. The *peso*, as its name implies, was originally a measure of weight. The *peso de oro*, or *castellano*, was one-hundredth part of a pound of gold. The *peso* of silver, however, seems to have been equivalent to an ounce, silver being weighed in *marcos* and *onzas* or *pesos* : 8 *onzas* or *pesos* equalled one mark.

The value of the *peso* or *castellano* is almost impossible to ascertain. Prescott has given it as $11.67; Folsom, as $2.75. It will be appreciated that such conjectures in terms of modern currency are valueless.

[4] *Page* 17. The *regidores* (or *corregidores*, the second is now the term habitually used in Spain) were municipal officials, having various duties. One of the most important was the collection of taxes. They could also, if need be, act as magistrates.

[5] *Page* 22. *Potuyuca* was a special form of maize, ground up, moistened and then roasted.

[6] *Page* 29. This first treasure-ship arrived safely in Spain. The articles were received by the Indies House (the *Casa de Contratación*) in Seville and forwarded to the Emperor, whereupon they were handed over to the charge of Luis Veret (*guarda-joyas de Sus Majestades*).

The treasure included the following :

Firstly : a large wheel of solid gold with a monster's face upon it, worked all over with ornament in bas relief and weighing 3,800 *pesos* of gold.

Item : two collars of gold and precious stones. One of them is eight rows thick with 232 red stones in the eight rings, and 163 green,

381

and from the outer edge hang 27 golden bells, in the midst of which are four faces cut from huge gems set in gold.

Item : a pair of leather slippers in colour much like the skin of pine-martens, the soles white and sewn with threads of gold.

Item : in another square box a huge head of an alligator in gold. . . . Also two large eyes of beaten metal and blue stones to put in the head of the alligator.

Item : eighteen shields ornamented with precious stones with coloured feathers hanging from them.

Also : two books such as the Indians use.

Also : half a dozen fans in feathers of various colours for keeping off flies.

In addition : a huge silver wheel ; also bracelets and beaten silver ornaments.

[7] *Page* 37. *Castellano.* See note 3 on *peso.*

[8] *Page* 42. "*there were but few . . .*" Cortés has just said that the Indians numbered from four to five thousand. Here, as elsewhere, he uses numbers rather indiscriminately. It seems probable that in skirmishes with his enemies he habitually overestimated their forces,—at any rate in his reports of the engagements.

[9] *Page* 47. *Pedro Carbonero* (Peter the charcoal burner) : a personage belonging to popular speech and proverb, as one who was always getting into awkward situations. I have not been able to find any *refrán* still in use in which Pedro Carbonero appears. *Pierre Charbonnier,* a similar character, was also known in France at this period.

[10] *Page* 53. *De monte . . . sale quien el monte quema (i.e.,* Out of the wood comes he who shall burn it up) : which warns one (says our Spanish lexicographer) that the bad luck we meet with often proceeds from causes very near at home.

[11] *Page* 57. "*a native Indian girl . . .*" So Cortés briefly dismisses her. She had been handed over to him as a slave in Tabasco on his first arrival in Yucatán. But she was of altogether superior birth and intelligence. Her parents had died early, and she had been sold into captivity. Cortés was not slow to mark her powers. She accompanied him as an interpreter in all his travels, and bore him several children. Her Indian name had been *Malinal*; as a Christian she was baptized *Marina.* This was corrupted to *Malinche,* and it was as Captain *Malinche* that the natives were wont to salute Cortés.

[12] *Page* 60. *Panicap :* probably a drink made from maize, water and sugar. The reading "*pan y cacao*" (*i.e.,* bread and the cocoanut) has been suggested : unnecessarily, I think.

[13] *Page* 61. This was *Popocatepetl.* The name means in Mexican smoking mountain, and it is about 16,000 feet high. Close to it stands *Ixtaccihuatl*—white woman ; the two mountains were venerated as man and wife.

[14] *Page* 86. "*seventy leagues in circumference.*" Cortés's esti-

NOTES

mation of distances is naturally somewhat rough and ready. The Spanish " legua " may be taken for practical purposes to be rather more than 3 English miles and less than 4.

[15] *Page* 88. *Maguey* is the Mexican aloe. Its juice is extracted to make the fermented liquor known as *pulgue*.

[16] *Page* 154. *Alguacil mayor* might well be translated into English High Constable. But there is a danger in using official terms which can never be exact equivalents, and so the Spanish has been retained (similarly, *alcalde*, *regidor*, and so on). The *alguacil* (from Arabic *al-uazir*, the lieutenant) was also the actual officer of the law, the constable or sheriff, as opposed to the *alcalde*, the judge.

[17] *Page* 180. *Don Fernando* (such was his Christian name) was one of several brothers who had wielded supreme power in Tezcuco, not always without fraternal strife. Guanacacín, the last ruler, had fled to the capital; and Cortés took the opportunity of installing a governor, who, though young, had given evidence of warlike qualities and was known to be friendly to the Spaniards.

[18] *Page* 232. *Father Pedro de Urrea* (Cortés adds) was a *comisario de la cruzada*, a crusade commissioner. He was empowered by the Pope to issue " Crusade " indulgences to those engaged in converting the infidel.

[19] *Page* 233. " *the procurators* . . ." The word is used in its most restricted sense—that of " attorneys," or " representatives." Cortés habitually uses the word " *procurador* " for any man charged with doing business " on behalf " of others. Thus the local councillor in Cuba chosen to visit the Governor and render an account of the municipality is a *procurador*. So also are Montejo and Portocarrero, sent by Cortés himself from New Spain to bear letters to the Emperor.

[20] *Page* 245. The *Bishop of Burgos* had been made President of the Royal Council of the Indies. He was touchy and vindictive, and had been bitterly hostile to the Columbuses, father and son. He died on March 14th, 1524.

[21] *Page* 245. " *a hundred letters*. . . ." The recipients' names were even left blank (Cortés adds) in order that Juan Bono might exercise his own discretion after arriving in New Spain.

[22] *Page* 278. The treasure-ship was indeed captured by a French corsair just off the Azores. It carried many marvels, gold and silver work, clothes and skins, also three tigers. One of the tigers escaped on board ship, killed two persons, and finished by plunging into the sea. Juan de Ribera, Cortés's secretary, was on board, charged with carrying 4,000 ducats to his parents.

[23] *Page* 287. *Veedor*, *factor*, *contador*, and *tesorero* (treasurer).

The *veedor* was an overseer, or inspector. He was an imperial official appointed either to a town or district to see that laws were carried out, particularly in regard to the farming and agricultural industries.

The *factor* was also an imperial official, whose special duty was to see that the revenue due to the Crown was properly paid over; often he would have to estimate the value of treasure in terms of Castilian currency.

The *contador* exercised a general supervision over all goods, bullion, treasure, etc., either entering or leaving New Spain. He would therefore normally be stationed at the capital or one of the great ports on the northern coast.

The *tesorero* (as his name implies) was the official responsible to the Emperor for the receipt of all monies due to him. The business of collecting such monies was, of course, shared with the local *veedors* and *factors*.

[24] *Page* 293. *Yucas*: a Central American plant growing some nine feet high and commonly known as Adam's Needle. It has thick, fleshy leaves at the top, white globular flowers, and a large root from which the natives make a kind of flour.

[25] *Page* 344. "*and set sail . . .*" Cortés added "on the —— day of the month of ——," but omitted to insert either the date or the month. Presumably it was early in 1526.

[26] *Page* 345. *Tierra-firme*. This comprised the Isthmus of Panama and the neighbouring States of Veragia, Darien and Biruguete. I have elsewhere translated it (where no particular emphasis is intended) as "the mainland."

Las Perlas . . . The Pearl Islands are in the Gulf of Panama.

[27] *Page* 353. *Pedro Moreno, Bachelor*. One can only assume that his title of "*bachiller*" had been gained when he was a youth at some University in Spain; but whether in arts, law or what, must be left to conjecture.

[28] *Page* 354. "*The Island of San Juan . . .*" This is the modern Porto Rico.

[29] *Page* 362. Bernal Diaz del Castillo was a member of this party, and the route they took is shown in map facing p. 300.

[30] *Page* 365. *The Guanajos*: lit. "the turkeys." They are now known as the Bay Islands.

[31] *Page* 372. *Residencia*. The public examination of a local Governor was known by this term, and was so proclaimed that all who had any plaint against him might present it before the imperial officials. The *residencia* included not only an examination into the acts of government of the individual concerned, but a very full inspection of accounts, particularly as they affected the Emperor's revenue.

[32] *Page* 375. "*in debt to the tune of over 500,000 pesos of gold without so much as a castellano with which to pay it.*" There seems to be a distinction drawn between the *peso* and the *castellano*, but it is, I think, only an apparent one (*i.e.*, the meaning is, "He does not possess a single *peso* out of the 500,000").

There can be little doubt that the terms, when applied to gold, were interchangeable.

INDEX

AGUILAR, GERÓNIMO DE, interpreter, 7, 9
Aguilar, Marcos de, 373
Albarado, Pedro de, xxxi-xxxii; commands first company in Tacuba, 167; a setback while besieging the capital, 189-91; sent south to subjugate Tatutepec and Tecoantepec, 236; ordered ahead to resist Garay's landing, 254-8; sent on expedition to Guatemala, 267-8; governor there, 364
Albórnoz, Rodrigo de (*contador*), xlvi, 369
Alderete, Julián, 377
Algiers, xvii
Altamirano, Diego, 364
Apaspalón, 300, 303, 320
Ascension Bay, 2, 288
Avalos, Juan de, cousin of Cortés, 359
Avila, Alonso de, 278, 281
Avila, Gil González de, 307, 325, 326, 346, 349, 350-3
Avila, Juan de, 261
Avila, Pedro Arias de, local governor, 288, 361, 363
Ayllón, Lucás Vázquez de, 101

Barrientos, Hernando de, 164
Becquar, Duque de, xv

Cacamazín, 80-1
Canee, 311, 317
Castelleja de la Cuesta, xix
Castromocho, 257
Cempoal: first visited, 32; headquarters of Narváez, 102

Cermeño, Diego, 33
Cerda, Antonio de la, 261
Chalco Indians, 147, 153, 187
Charles V, Emperor, xvi-xvii
Chichimecatecle, 149-50, 202
Chirinos, Per Almíndez (*veedor*), xlvi, 287, 289, 368
Cholula, xxxvi, xl; massacre in, 56-8
Ciguacoacin, 226
Colón, Don Bartolomé, xxvi
Colón, Don Diego, Admiral, xxvi, 247, 254
Contreras, Alonso de, 349
Córdoba, Francisco Hernández de, xiii, 1-2
Córdoba, Gonsalvo de (the Great Captain), ix, xxxiii
Corral, Cristóbal, 155
Cortés, Hernando: his life, ix-xix; the man, xix-xxv; sets out for Yucatán, 3; founds Vera Cruz, 18-20; breaks up ships, 34; his march to the capital, 32-69; marches against Narváez, 101; re-enters capital, 109; besieged there, and forced to retreat, 109-124; arrives safely in Tlascala, 125; sets out on reconquest, 138; makes a circuit of the lakes before attacking the capital, 154-165; the brigs' first victory, Cortés encamps on the causeway, 171-3; besieges the capital, 174; dangerous setback, in which he nearly loses his life, 195-9; unsuccessful attempts at peace, 208, 219;

INDEX

the capital surrenders, 228; he settles at Cuyoacan, 229; goes north to the Pánuco, 247-255; royal provisions arrive forbidding Garay's interference, 254; Pánuco rebels and is again subjugated with great severity, 262-6; he builds four ships on the southern coast, 269-70; leaves Mexico for Honduras, 287; builds the great bridge, 297; arrives at Nito, 326; voyages up the great gulf, 331; founds a town on the northern coast, 345; proceeds to San Andrés, 346; returns to New Spain via Habana, 368; receives Luis Ponce de León, 372; deals with accusations made against him to the King, 373-9

Cortés, Martin (father), ix

Cortés, Martin (son), xxiv

Cozumel, Island of, xxxi, 2, 4-8, 358

Cristóbal, 305

Cuernabaca, xvi, 158, 201

Diaz del Castillo, Bernal, xiii, xix, xxi, xxix-xxxiii

Dircio, Pedro, 155

Dovalle, Gonzalo, 255-6

Escudero, Juan, 33

Estrada, Alonso de (treasurer), xlvi, 287, 289

Fernando, Don, ruler of Tezcuco, 180

Figueroa, 101

Fonseca, Don Juan de, Bishop of Burgos, 245, 254, 274

Garay, Francisco de: first encounter with Cortés, 34-6; men of his party killed by natives, 247; reported to be about to land at Pánuco, 247; actually lands, with hostile intentions, 253-6; but then acknowledges royal warrant, 258; he comes to Cortés in Mexico, 260-1; arranges a marriage between the families, 261; and dies, 263

Gomara, Francisco López de, xix, xx, xxix

Grijalba, Juan de, xiii, 2, 257-8, 261

Grijalba, River, 2, 9

Guanacacín, ruler of Tezcuco, 142-3

Guatimucín: succeeds Mutecczuma, 131; refuses to appear before Cortés, 222, 223; captured, fleeing in a canoe, 227; still kept a prisoner, 271; hanged for treason in Honduras, 305-6

Gulf of California, xvi

Guzman, Cristóbal de, 198

Hayti, ix, 231

Hernández, Francisco, captain, 363, 364

Huitzilopocthli, 220

Hurtado, Diego de, cousin of Cortés, 267

Istrisuchil, 180

Iztapalapa: first visited, 67; description, 67; narrow escape at, 146; taken in the reconquest, 145-146

Jamaica, 34

Jeronymite Fathers, 2

Las Casas, Bartolomé de, xiii, xxiv, xxxiv-xxxvii, xlv.

INDEX

Las Casas, Francisco de, 288, 347, 350-353, 357, 363
León, Juan Ponce de, 207, 275
León, Juan Velázquez de, 100, 103
León, Luis Ponce de, xv, 370-2
López, Vincente, 257

Magiscatzín, 51, 125, 136
Malinalco, expeditions against, 201, 203-4
Malinche, xlvii (and see note to Marina on p. 382)
Marina, a native Indian girl, 57, 313
Martin de San Juan, 257
Medellín (*Spain*), ix
Medellín (*New Spain*), founded, 231
Medina, Juan de, 261
Mendoza, Alonso de, 135, 261
Merlo, Rodrigo de, 366
Monjaraz, Andrés de, 155
Montejo, Francisco de, 20, 31, 376
Moreno, Pedro, 353-6, 357
Muteczuma: first heard of by Cortés, 32 ; requests Cortés to advance no further on the capital, 66 ; greets Cortés, 69 ; imprisoned, 75-6 ; estate and personal service, 96-7 ; death, 112

Narváez, Pánfilo de, xxvii-xxix, 100-107
Nieto, Diego, 325
Nombre de Dios Pass, 38

Ocampo, Diego de (alcalde mayor), 255-9, 377
Olid, Cristóbal de, xxxii; commands second company in Cuyoacan, 167 ; sent on expedition to Honduras, 267 ; reported treachery in league

with Velázquez, 280 ; his conduct in Honduras as reported by the colonists, 348 *et seq.* ; his death, 352
Oñate, Cristóbal de, xxxi
Orduña, Francisco de, 256
Otumba, Battle of, xx
Ovando, Nicolás de, ix, x

Palos, xv, xxx
Paz, Rodrigo de, xlvi, 290, 360
Peñate, Alonzo, 33
Popocatepetl, 21, 61
Portocarrero, Alonso Fernández, 20, 31, 376

Qualpopoca, 72-3, 74, 76
Quejo, Juan Bono de, 245
Quiñones, Antonio de, 278, 281

Rangel, Rodrigo, 269
Recalde, Juan López de, 274
repartimiento, xi, xxiii, xxiv, 365
requerimiento, xxxvi, 11, 43
Rojas, Gabriel de, 364
Ruano, Juan, 354-6

Sáavedra, Hernando de, 361, 367
Salazar y Peralmírez, Gonzalo de (*factor*), xlvi, 280, 287, 289, 368
Sandoval, Gonzalvo de, xv, xxviii, xxx-xxxi; ordered to arrest Narváez, 105 ; sent on expedition to Chalco, 147 ; brings back the brigs, 148-150 ; again sent to help the Chalco Indians, 153 ; commands third company in attack on the capital, 167 ; takes Iztapalapa, 170 ; joins Cortés on the causeway via Cuyoacan, 175 ; wounded slightly, 175 ; conducts successful expedition against Temascalcingo, 203-5 ; sent north to quell tribes, and

387

INDEX

founds town of Medellín, 231 ; in charge of expedition in Honduras, 363

Santisteban del Puerto founded, 251

Segura de la Frontera founded, 130

Sicutengal, 45, 48, 125

Soto, Diego de, 234, 278

Suchimilco captured, 159-162

Tabarda, 261

Tapia, Andrés de, xxiii, xxvi, 201

Tapia, Cristóbal de: arrives at Vera Cruz, 231 ; persuaded to re-embark, 234 ; after-effects of his visit, 243, 245

Tenochtitlan : first sighted, 62 ; Cortés enters, 69 ; description, 86-94 ; final surrender, 228 ; its rebuilding, 271-3

Tetepanquencal, 305-6

Tezcuco, 80, 142

Tianquiz, Indian market, 194

Tlascala : fighting in, 41-47, peace made with, 48 ; return to, 125

Troche, Gaspar, 354

Ulloa, Lorenzo de, 261

Ungría, Gonzalo de, 33

Urrea, Father Pedro Melgarejo de, 232

Valdenebro, Diego de, 234

Valenzuela, 358

Vallejo, Pedro de, 256

Velázquez, Diego, xi-xiv, xxv-xxvii ; finances first expedition to Yucatán, 1-3 ; colonists beseech the Emperor that no power be given him in New Spain on account of his misdeeds in Haiti, 26-7; sends Narváez to New Spain, 100 ; his partisans devise treason against Cortés in New Spain, 237-9; reported to be about to land at Pánuco, 247 ; persuades Olid to betray Cortés, 280

Vera Cruz, Rica Villa de, founded, 18

Verdugo, Francisco, 155

Villafaña, Antonio de, 238

Villafuerte, Juan Rodríguez de, 155

Ximénez, Cardinal, 2

Xuárez, Juan, xi-xii

Xúñiga, Doña de, xv

Yucatán, 1, 9

Yuste, Juan, 149

Zuazo, Alonso de, 287, 290, 360